CAMBRIDGE GREEK AND LATIN CLASSICS

GENERAL EDITORS

P. E. EASTERLING
Regius Professor Emeritus of Greek, University of Cambridge

PHILIP HARDIE
Corpus Christi Professor of Latin, University of Oxford

RICHARD HUNTER
Regius Professor of Greek, University of Cambridge

Kennedy Professor o̶

GREEK AND LATIN LETTERS

AN ANTHOLOGY, WITH TRANSLATION

EDITED BY

MICHAEL TRAPP

Reader in Greek in the Department of Classics,
King's College London

CAMBRIDGE
UNIVERSITY PRESS

PUBLISHED BY THE PRESS SYNDICATE OF THE UNIVERSITY OF CAMBRIDGE
The Pitt Building, Trumpington Street, Cambridge CB2 1RP, United Kingdom

CAMBRIDGE UNIVERSITY PRESS
The Edinburgh Building, Cambridge CB2 2RU, UK
40 West 20th Street, New York, NY 10011–4211, USA
477 Williamstown Road, Port Melbourne, VIC 3207, Australia
Ruiz de Alarcón 13, 28014 Madrid, Spain
Dock House, The Waterfront, Cape Town 8001, South Africa

http://www.cambridge.org

First published 2003

Printed in the United Kingdom at the University Press, Cambridge

Typefaces Baskerville 10/12 pt and New Hellenic   *System* LATEX 2$_\varepsilon$ [TB]

A catalogue record for this book is available from the British Library

ISBN 0 521 49597 0 hardback
ISBN 0 521 49943 7 paperback

CONTENTS

PREFACE

It is a pleasure to acknowledge the many debts incurred in the compilation of this anthology. The original idea came from Pat Easterling, and she and her co-editor, Professor Kenney, have been characteristically generous with advice, encouragement and corrections throughout. A spell at the Fondation Hardt, funded by the Fonds Nationale Suisse de la Recherche Scientifique and the British Academy, allowed serious work on the project to begin in constructive and congenial surroundings, and a Research Fellowship from the Leverhulme Trust, awarded principally for another project, has eased the completion of the final stages. Audiences in Cambridge, Newcastle, St Andrews, Dublin and London have listened patiently and done their best to inject some sophistication into what they have heard. Help and advice of many kinds have come from individual friends and colleagues: my thanks go in particular to Carlotta Dionisotti, Richard Hunter, Roland Mayer, Dominic Montserrat, Charlotte Roueché, Jane Rowlandson, Cathy Schneider, Michael Sharp and J. B. Trapp; also (for opportune consultations) to Hilary O'Shea of Oxford University Press and Pauline Hire of Cambridge University Press. Pauline Hire's successor as Classics Editor, Michael Sharp, must take a second bow for the efficient kindness with which he has supervised the final stages of the preparation of the typescript, and the production of the book. Linda Woodward's copy-editing was a model of tact and efficiency.

For its Greek and Latin texts, this anthology relies heavily on the editorial work of other and better scholars. In addition to my general obligation to all the editors involved, I am formally indebted to the copyright holders for permission to reprint the following: letters **9** and **53–4** from M. van den Hout, ed., *M. Cornelli Frontonis Epistulae*, Leipzig, 1988, © K. G. Saur, Munich/Leipzig; **20** and **61** from *Select Papyri ii*, Loeb Classical Library 282, ed. A. S. Hunt and C. C. Edgar, Cambridge, Mass.: Harvard University Press, 1934, and *Alciphron, Aelian, Philostratus*, LCL 383, ed. A. R. Benner and F. H. Fobes, Cambridge, Mass.: Harvard University Press, 1949, reprinted by permission of the publishers and the trustees of the Loeb Classical Library (the Loeb Classical Library ® is a registered trademark of the President and Fellows of Harvard College); **5** from *Papyri and Ostraka from Karanis* (Michigan Papyri viii), ed. H. C. Youtie and J. G. Winter, Ann

Arbor, 1951, © University of Michigan Press. The texts of **3**, **4** and **35** are reprinted by courtesy of the Egypt Exploration Society; **65** of the Trustees of the Chester Beatty Library, Dublin; **49** of Vita e Pensiero, Milan; **56** of the Università degli Studi di Milano, Dipartimento di Scienze dell'Antichità; **14** of Acta Universitatis Gotoborgensis; **22** of the British Museum Press; **41** and **48** of the Société d'édition 'Les Belles Lettres'; and **64** of the Society for the Promotion of Roman Studies and Dr Joyce Reynolds.

Anyone with an interest in ancient letters is bound to be disappointed to find favourite items missing in what follows. Anyone with specialist knowledge of the authors and collections exploited will probably be able to think of better instances of the various kinds of letter than those actually chosen. Some omissions are due to the decision to avoid lengthy items, in favour of quantity and variety, and the inclusion of a facing translation; most are due to editorial ignorance. I hope none the less that this collection will be felt to have some kind of rationale and coherence, and will to some degree supplement and support the lively scholarship that is now increasingly being directed towards the writing and reading of ancient letters.

M. B. T.

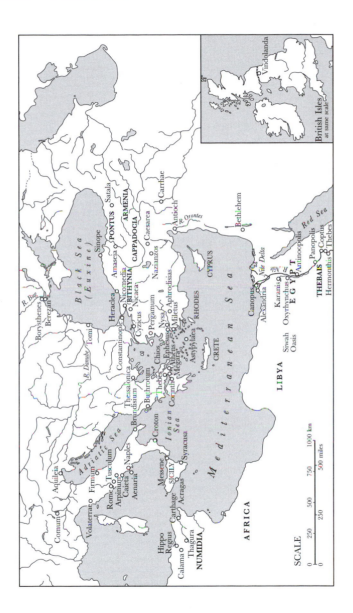

INTRODUCTION

1 WHAT IS A LETTER?

[handwritten annotations: "Sealed", "(strict)"]

What is a letter? As long as this question is treated as a request for an explanation, rather than for a watertight definition, it seems easy enough to answer it usefully, for ancient and more recent letters alike, by appealing to a combination of contextual and formal characteristics. A letter is a written message from one person (or set of people) to another, requiring to be set down in a tangible medium, which itself is to be physically conveyed from sender(s) to recipient(s). Formally, it is a piece of writing that is overtly addressed from sender(s) to recipient(s), by the use at beginning and end of one of a limited set of conventional formulae of salutation (or some allusive variation on them) which specify both parties to the transaction.[1] One might also add, by way of further explanation, that the need for a letter as a medium of communication normally arises because the two parties are physically distant (separated) from each other, and so unable to communicate by unmediated voice or gesture; and that a letter is normally expected to be of relatively limited length.[2] All the pieces anthologized in this collection (except for **73** and **75–6**) can be categorized as letters because they either have these characteristics, or somehow play at having them.[3] But behind this family unity there lies a very considerable diversity.[4]

The examples collected – forty-one in Greek, thirty-six in Latin, and one bilingual piece (**49**) – span something over nine hundred years in time. They originated in parts of the Greco-Roman world as widely separate as the Black Sea, Egypt, the North of England and Asia Minor, as well as in the cultural heartlands of the Italian peninsula and mainland Greece, and are available for us to read thanks to a number of different processes of creation and transmission. In thirteen cases, the text of the letter in question has

---

[1] For further discussion of epistolary formulae, see 34–8 below.

[2] See also 23 and 44 below.

[3] The question where the boundary is to be set between 'letters' and other pieces of writing that are in various ways comparable without qualifying as members of the family is not a trivial one, but lies beyond the scope of this introduction. Much depends on one's reasons for raising the question 'is this a letter?' in the first place, and one's keenness to press issues of genre and definition.

[4] Two classic surveys of the range of epistolary writing are those of Sykutris (1931) and Schneider (1954).

1

been preserved in its original form, inked or scratched on to the papyrus, lead or wood to which it was originally committed;[5] in three further cases (**62–4**), although the original physical missive is lost, what we have is an inscribed copy, made soon after the first sending, in which the message has been transferred to the more durable (and more public) medium of stone. These survive essentially as individual items, even though a good many such pieces were already collected together in some way in antiquity, into private or public archives. And they survive in spite of the absence of any original intention to bring them to the attention of anyone like us (a general 'readership', potentially far removed in time), even though the inscribed letters at least were thus being in some sense 'published'. With all the remaining items – the vast majority, that is to say, sixty-one out of seventy-eight – there is no such contact with the original missive as physical object. But (as if in compensation) a positive intent to make them available to a general readership has played a part. They survive in book form, as works of literature transmitted in the normal way for ancient writings, handed on down a family tree of manuscript copies from antiquity to the Middle Ages and Renaissance. And they survive not as individual items, but built into more substantial compositions, either letter-collections assigned to a single author or set of authors, or works of other kinds (speeches, histories, novels) that have reason to quote letters somewhere along the way.

Other distinctions too can be made, at least in order to give a first sense of the range of material collected together here. Besides being in two different languages, being composed at widely differing points in space and time, and being transmitted by different means, these letters are also the product of differing social and educational backgrounds, from the worlds of the modest (though modestly well-educated) provincials who wrote the items on papyrus, wood and lead, to highly cultivated and socially eminent correspondents of the stamp of a Cicero, a Pliny, a Basil or a Libanius; and they are, correspondingly, of many differing degrees of conceptual and stylistic sophistication, from the naïve to the exquisite. The balance of functional and aesthetic considerations – getting the message across and securing the required response to it, as against getting it across in a manner

---

[5] **1–5**, **15**, **21–2**, **26**, **35**, **46**, **56**, **61**. Of the other two papyrus items, one (**65**) is an official copy, not the original message, and the other (**49**) is a model letter. One letter (**1**) seems never to have been opened and read by its intended recipient.

that will itself give pleasure and excite admiration – differs accordingly from letter to letter.

Moreover, in what might at first seem the most fundamental distinction of all, these letters differ also in degree of closeness to actuality: some of them are 'real' and others 'fictitious'. That is to say, we seem to be able to distinguish (*a*) letters composed for sending by historical individuals (whether or not they are known from other sources besides), but never subsequently released in an edited collection (e.g. the items in this collection preserved on lead, wood and papyrus); (*b*) letters composed for sending by historical individuals, but subsequently also released in an edited collection for a broader readership, with perhaps some 'improvement' of the contents (e.g. the letters of Cicero, 'The Elder' ('John'), Pliny, Fronto, Julian, Libanius, Basil, Gregory, Jerome and Augustine; cf. also that of Catiline); (*c*) letters by and to historical individuals, but never physically sent as individual items in letter mode, because intended from the start more for a broader readership than for the specified addressee (e.g. – probably – the letters of Seneca, Horace and Ovid in this collection; cf. also the dedicatory epistles of Martial and Pollux); (*d*) letters purporting to be by (and sometimes to) historical individuals, but in fact the work of a later literary impersonator, again writing exclusively for a reading public ('pseudepigrapha', e.g. the letters of Chion, Aeschines (?), Diogenes, Crates and Phalaris); and (*e*) letters by and to invented characters, whether invented by the epistolographer, or inherited by him from earlier literature (e.g. the letters of Phoenicium (Plautus), 'Polyaenus' and 'Circe' (Petronius), Gemellus, Salaconis and Glycera (Alciphron) and the Exile (Philostratus)).

The letters in this anthology – and the category of 'the letter' in general – thus seem to span several significant divides, between reality and fiction, and between active engagement in the real world and passive aesthetic enjoyment. Letters are implicated in both life and literature, they can be both real and invented; indeed, they can be both 'real' and 'pretend' letters, either really sent, or never intended for sending, but meant from the start to be part of a literary work for a different kind of readership. Yet, as with all systems for pigeon-holing letters, these categories – and in particular, the underlying antithesis between 'proper' letters and letters that are somehow not so proper – should not be pressed too hard. There are indeed distinctions to be drawn in what can be called the degree of fictionalizing involved in the various letters in this collection; and these distinctions identify widely recognized types of letter in general. But how

useful a firm categorization constructed along these lines really is, is open
to question. Too blunt a contrast between 'real' and 'fictional' ignores the
fact that no letter is a simple, direct transcript of 'reality', a wholly transparent window, any more than any other piece of writing can be. Consciously
or unconsciously, letter-writers select what they are going to say and what
they are not going to say, and choose how they are going to slant what
they do say, and thus construct a personalized version of the reality they
are referring to. Similarly, in writing, letter-writers construct and project a
persona which may bear all kinds of relationship (including a very slender
one) to their character as perceived by others than their correspondent of
the moment.[6]

This is not to say that all letters are in fact fictitious; rather that all
letter-writing is liable to involve processes sometimes hastily taken as distinctive marks of fiction.[7] More generally, the drawing of any such lines
unhelpfully distracts attention from what letters have in common: how any
piece of writing that is recognizable as a letter (whether in a standard or
a non-standard version, whether united with or divorced from physical
sending) shares features not only of form but also of content and topic
with other members of the class, and how alertness to these shared features
helps us to appreciate each individual item. Drawing lines of this kind also
detracts from an awareness of what we – any compiler and any reader of
a collection of letters such as this one – are thus doing with letters: how
the vantage-point of the subsequent reader, initially a stranger to the epistolary transaction (real or imagined), but now eavesdropping on others'
conversation, can efface perceived differences between one category of letter and another, transforming an originally functional communication into
a source of aesthetic (or other) pleasure.

More straightforward, at first glance, is another form of categorization, based on the observation that letters – into whichever of the groups
sketched above they may fall – perform a wide range of specific functions. In
the first place, one can distinguish 'public' from 'private' correspondence:
both private individuals, seeking responses and effects in the context of
everyday social interaction (or indeed in more fraught or unusual circumstances), and holders of public positions, seeking effects and responses in
the formal business of villages, towns, provinces, kingdoms – and religious

[6] On the question of character-portrayal in letters see below, 32 and 39.
[7] Cf. Rosenmeyer (2001) 9–12.

communities – have recourse to letters to do so. And, secondly, on each of these (not always wholly separate) levels, the specific effects and responses aimed at are themselves hugely diverse. As one recent study puts it, 'letters are as varied in function as are the possibilities of social [and, he might have added, political] intercourse';[8] or, as another explains, more discursively, a letter can be used to 'order or request provisions, elicit a virtue or promote a habit of behavior, initiate a relationship with another person or group, maintain . . . end . . . [or] restore a relationship with a person or group, praise someone, cause someone to be sorry, give orders . . . , give a report of events, cause a group to share a common hope, elicit capacities for social bonding, threaten someone, console someone, mediate between individuals or groups . . . , give advice, request advice, express thanks, give honor.'[9] This diversity, too, seems to provide grounds for classification, in terms of both context and content of communication. But the promise is a slippery one, for the diversity is if anything too great to yield a tidy set of categories, and further problems are created by the stubborn refusal of actual letters to confine themselves neatly to just one communicative function apiece, and the difficulty of drawing a watertight distinction between public and private communication.[10] Certainly no exhaustive classification into kinds on this basis can be made (not that some ancient theorists didn't try: see pp. 44–5 below, and no. **76**). At best, only a limited number of stable and (sometimes) fairly single-minded forms can be distinguished along these lines, in cases where a particular individual function does seem to exercise a monopolizing effect, and generates a distinct set of formulae: notably the letter of recommendation, the letter of condolence or consolation, and (perhaps) the invitation.[11]

The letter, then, is clearly a diverse form of writing, and that diversity is reflected in the contents of this anthology. But mapping the diversity, and fixing labels on its various constituents, is interestingly problematic. These issues will remain in the air as we turn to further details of the writers and letters anthologized and the form in which they are working, and will be faced (and ducked) again in conclusion.

[8] Stirewalt (1993) 1.

[9] Stowers (1986) 15–16; some of the items betray the author's particular concern with Christian epistolography (cf. 17–21 below).

[10] See headnotes to sections AIV and B on 236 and 295–6 below.

[11] See headnotes to sections AIV, AVI and AIII on 236, 267 and 228 below.

2 THE LETTER-WRITERS, THEIR WORKS AND CONTEXTS

(a) The letters from papyrus, wood, lead and stone

The earliest physically surviving letters in Greek are three pieces scratched on to thin sheets of **lead**: the 'Berezan letter' (**1** in this anthology), *SIG*[3] 1259, from Athens (**2** in this anthology), and *SIG*[3] 1260, from Olbia.[12] The first dates from around the year 500 B.C., the other two from some time in the fourth century. How close the first takes us to the very beginnings of letter-writing as a practice in the Greek-speaking world is an intriguing question that is hard to answer confidently, though internal and external evidence suggests that it gets us quite close. Literacy of any kind was not widespread in the archaic period,[13] and the first historical correspondence referred to in our sources, that of Amasis and Polycrates,[14] dates from around 530–525. Moreover, the Berezan letter itself (see commentary) seems to show, on the one hand, a lack of familiarity with what are later to emerge as standard conventions of letter-writing, and on the other a sense that sending a message by this particular means is a measure for emergencies only.

Other evidence suggests that both the habit of writing in general, and the specific practice of letter-writing as a mode of communication, remained restricted down to the closing decades of the fifth century, but had become much more widespread and part of normal experience by the middle of the fourth.[15] The two fourth-century letters on lead seem to bear this out, in their use of the medium for much more mundane transactions, and their use of what begin to look like familiar epistolary formulae (see commentary on **2**). Lead was of course not the only, or indeed the most common material used for letter-writing in this period and subsequently. Potsherds (*ostraka* – a

[12] For the Berezan letter, see Chadwick (1974); for the other two, Crönert (1910).

[13] Harris (1989) 45–64.

[14] Hdt. 3.40–3. References to letters in mythological time (Phaedra's suicide-note in *Hippolytus*, Iphigenia's and Agamemnon's letters in *IT* and *IA* – for which see Rosenmeyer (2001) 61–97) tell us about the experience and assumptions of the author's own period. The interesting case in this connection is the celebrated folded tablet, scratched with 'many life-destroying things', sent with Bellerophon by Proetus in the story told by Glaucus in *Iliad* 6.166–70. The reference must be earlier than, say, 600 B.C., but does it betray familiarity with letter-writing as a contemporary activity, or rather a vague (and suspicious) awareness of it as something done only in the distant past, or in far off places?

[15] Harris (1989) 65–115; Stirewalt (1993) 6–15.

particularly cheap option, cf. Diog. Laert. 7.174), waxed or whitened wooden tablets and (initially, mainly for the well-to-do) papyrus were all used as much and more.[16] The use of lead is unlikely to have stemmed from the unavailability of other materials when needed (can potsherds ever have been unavailable?), but to have been a positive choice. A message on lead is tough, and has a good chance of avoiding obliterating damage in transit, even if roughly treated;[17] and it can be folded in such a way as to make tampering and unauthorized reading difficult. Moreover, thanks to its malleability, the same piece of lead can be used many times over.[18]

It is with the third century B.C. that the epistolary habit seems really to have established itself in Greek culture. And it is from this time on that survivals start to become numerous, thanks to finds of **papyrus** material, above all from Ptolemaic, and then Roman Egypt, dating from the 260s all the way to the end of antiquity. Up to a thousand papyrus letters now survive, spanning private, business and official correspondence, and publication continues at a steady rate.[19] They have been found both as separate items, and in the remains of organized archives (*P.Beatty Panop.* 1, from which item **65** below is taken, is one such), all excavated from heaps of waste paper abandoned to the encroaching desert in late antiquity.[20] The great majority are in Greek – the language of the overclass which assumed the running of Egypt after the conquests of Alexander and the foundation of the kingdom of the Ptolemies, and retained much of its power and status up until the Arab conquest in the seventh century A.D.; but there is also a good number in Latin, the language of the country's political masters following Octavian's victory at Actium in 31 B.C. and its incorporation as a province of the Roman Empire, and above all the language of their army.[21]

[16] Harris (1989) 94–5; White (1986) 213–14; Rosenmeyer (2001) 22–3.

[17] Complaints about damage to letters written on less durable papyrus can be found in *P.Col.Zen.* II 68, *PSI* IV 403, and Cic. *ad Q. Fr.* 2.10.4 (reporting Caesar).

[18] It is also worth noting that lead was the favoured material for two other kinds of message, to non-human recipients: questions to an oracle (as for instance at Dodona, cf. Parke (1967) 100–14, 259–73) and curses (see Gager (1992) 3–41). Whether this reflected (or created) any sense that such messages were like letters is an intriguing but open question.

[19] To give just one indicative figure, the nine volumes of the Oxyrhynchus series published between 1992 and 2001 (59–67) contained 49 new letters, 11 official and 38 private or business.

[20] See Turner (1980) 17–53; White (1986) 4–8.

[21] For the political and social background, see Bowman (1990), Lewis (1983), Rowlandson (1998), Alston (1995), Bagnall (1993), Haas (1997).

They are published – made available again to readers after centuries of oblivion – in a whole range of papyrological series, as well as in selective anthologies and commentaries based on those primary editions.[22]

Besides the simple thrill such letters give of direct contact with the ancient world and its people, at the level of everyday life and business, the physical survival of what was actually written and sent by the original letter-writers gives special access to questions about ancient letter making and sending.[23] We can see how writing-paper was made and prepared, how it was folded, secured and sealed for sending, and how addressed on the outside. We discover what written instructions could be added to help the messenger deliver to the right location.[24] We encounter measures taken to ensure that letters once arrived will be read out and if necessary translated to recipients who cannot read, or even speak Greek.[25] And we can make at least some headway with the question of who did the writing: the presence of particularly skilful hands, and of changes of hand between the main body of the letter and the final salutation, suggest just how often the bulk of the work, or all of it, was done by secretaries (for the affluent) and (for the less well-off) professional letter-writers.

Coming as they did from correspondents unknown to grand history, and from everyday milieux similarly ignored in the more formal record, papyrus letters (along with other documents on papyrus) opened up whole new chapters of ancient social history when they started to be excavated

[22] See the source information given for items **3–5**, **15**, **21**, **26**, **35**, **46**, **49**, **56**, **61** and **65**; there is a full list of papyrological publications and their nomenclature in Turner (1980) 154–79. Anthologies and commentaries include Milligan (1910), Witkowski (1911), Hunt and Edgar (1932–4), White (1986) and Chapa (1998). Latin papyrus letters can be found collected in *CPL* (nos. 246ff.) and Cugusi (1992).

[23] Cf. Parsons (1980) 3–6; White (1986) 213–17. Pictures of papyrus letters can be found in (e.g.) Turner (1980), Turner (1971), White (1986), and the relevant volumes of the *Oxyrhynchus Papyri*, but the best and most informative images readily available are now to be found on papyrological websites (in a nice convergence of ancient and modern IT): http://www.csad.ox.ac.uk, http://odyssey.lib.duke.edu:8o/papyrus, and http://www.lib.umich.edu/pap/welcome.html all make good starting-points. In this anthology, the dimensions of all papyrus items are given, as a reminder of their status as physical survivals.

[24] The most elaborate instructions are on *P.Oxy.* 2719; see also (e.g.) *P.Oxy.* 1678.28, 1773.40, *P.Mich.* VIII 490.24, and for something similar on lead, item **2** in this anthology.

[25] *P.Haun.* 14–15 + *P.Mich.* 679, discussed by Bülow-Jacobsen and McCarren (1985) = Rowlandson (1998) no. 246; the non-Greek speakers in question are women.

in bulk in the 1890s.[26] It is an intriguing aspect of twentieth-century scholarly history that much of the impetus to the study of this material, above all the letters, has come from historians of Early Christianity, seeking insight both into the humble social circumstances of the first Christians, and into the language and forms of early Christian writing (in which the letter played such an important role[27]). This particular interest has had its advantages (in the sheer volume of scholarly time and energy it has caused to be devoted to letters), and also its disadvantages, as scholars have forced the material in pursuit of their own very specialized ends. To give one of the most famous examples, Deissmann's general classification of letters as belonging either to the category *Brief* (real, unelaborated letters, such as are preserved on papyrus) or the category of *Epistel* (worked-up, sophisticated, 'literary' letters, such as come down to us in manuscript tradition) was aimed specifically at supporting a particular interpretation of the letters of St Paul (as the simple, sincere communications of a man of the people with the people), and thus also of the truest form of the Christian heritage.[28]

Letters on **wood** are represented in this anthology by one of the thousand and more tablets discovered since 1973 at the fort of Vindolanda (Chesterholm) on Hadrian's Wall (of which over 170 of the fully published items – nos. 21–48 and 210–353 – are letters). Postcard-sized or smaller, and between one and five mm thick, these miraculously preserved documents, dating from the twenty-five or thirty years after around A.D. 92, are part of the paperwork of a Roman frontier garrison and its associated civilians: military reports, orders and applications; accounts and lists; and the correspondence of the officers of the garrison and their wives.[29] The same sort of fascinating everyday detail is preserved as in the Egyptian papyri: worries about the beer supply,[30] lists of items of clothing sent from one correspondent to another,[31] contemptuous references to the local population.[32]

[26] Cf. the works cited in n. 21 above.

[27] Cf. 17–21 below, and Stowers (1986) 17–26.

[28] Deissmann (1927), discussed by Rosenmeyer (2001) 5–8.

[29] The tablets are published in Bowman and Thomas (1983), (1994) and (1996), all with photos. Briefer and less technical accounts, but with attention to the military, material, social and cultural background, in Bowman (1983) and (1994), also illustrated.

[30] Inv. no. 93.1544, Bowman and Thomas (1996) 323–6.

[31] Tab. 38.   [32] Tab. 164 (*Brittunculi*).

Much official correspondence – letters of rulers and administrators to and from peers, colleagues, subordinates and subjects – of course survives either on papyrus or wood, or with the published letter-collections of individuals (e.g. Pliny, Trajan, Julian). Some, however, survives because preserved in the form of inscriptions in **stone**, made because the content of the letters concerned was felt to be of particular importance to the public life of the city where the inscription was set up – a letter from a king or emperor, for example, granting certain privileges or amending a piece of legislation, or one honouring a leading citizen.[33] The examples in this anthology are drawn from two published collections with commentaries: C. B. Welles's of 1934, containing seventy-five letters from Hellenistic monarchs, dating from between 311 B.C. and A.D. 21; and Joyce Reynolds's of 1982, containing sixty-seven inscribed documents from the theatre of the city of Aphrodisias in Asia Minor, from the second century B.C. to the third century A.D. in date, of which twenty-two or -three are letters.[34]

Collectively, all these kinds of primary, unreprocessed correspondence on lead, papyrus, wood and stone, are of huge value to the historian, affording a ground-level view of aspects of ancient life not always covered by other surviving documentation (such as the great narrative works of the Greek and Roman historians). Among other things, they preserve a notable quantity of writing by women, which is otherwise notoriously hard to come by in the ancient world.[35] They are also immensely important as documents for the history of the development of the Greek and Latin languages, telling us about both levels of literacy in general in different periods, and more specifically about the habits of spelling, pronunciation and grammar of their more or less extensively educated writers.[36] In connection with epistolography, they have further fascinations. They allow us to see by comparison both what is specific to educated, 'literary' letter-writing as it survives in the published collections, and what is characteristic of letter-writing across

[33] See Welles (1934) xxxvii–xli; Woodhead (1981) 35–47; Thomas (1992) 162–8. An early but eccentric set of instances is the messages carved on stone that Themistocles left for the Ionians at selected points on the shoreline near Artemisium (Hdt. 8.22). The most recent treatment of royal letters, with reflections on how they should be read and used as historical evidence, is Ma (1999) 179–242, with 284–372.

[34] Plates I, III, and XVIII–XXII in Reynolds (1982) all show inscribed letters.

[35] Items **22** and **46** in this volume; contrast item **71**, a 'woman's' letter in fact composed (and read out) by a man. See also Rowlandson (1998), nos. 45, 77, 92–9, 115, 172–3, 180, 205–6, 220, 225, 228, 231, 259, Cribiore (2001).

[36] For the Greek material, see Horrocks (1997) 65–70, 114–27; for Latin, Bowman and Thomas (1983) 72–4, Bowman (1994) 82–99, Adams (1977).

the board.[37] And they offer in a particularly intense form the pleasures and puzzles of eavesdropping that come with the reading of any letter intended for another's eyes, as we listen in to fragments of ancient conversations, filling in the gaps in our contextual knowledge as best we may, drawn in and at the same time tantalized by the incomplete hints and allusions that correspondents in the know can safely limit themselves to.

Note on conventions of transcription
The following conventions are used in the presentation of material tran-scribed from lead, wood, papyrus and stone:

- [α] letters removed by physical damage, but restorable
- [..] letters removed by physical damage, but not restorable
- (α) expansion of abbreviations/contractions by the scribe/writer
- ⟨α⟩ letters missed out by the scribe/writer and added by the editor
- ạ letters not decipherable with complete confidence
- [[α]] letters written but crossed out by the scribe/writer
- ˋαˊ letters added above the line
- † word/passage of which the editor cannot make sense

In these transcriptions word-division, punctuation and (in Greek) accents and breathings are all editorial additions, to help the modern reader; they are not to be seen in the documents themselves. The original spelling has however been preserved, both for its interest as evidence for contemporary pronunciation and for the educational level of the writer, and to retain as much of the flavour of the original as possible.[38] For fuller details of the standard papyrological and epigraphic conventions (as used in, e.g., the Oxyrhynchus volumes and Welles and Reynolds), see Turner (1980) 187–8 and 203, and Woodhead (1981) 6–11.

---

[37] It is striking, for instance, how much more functional papyrus letters are than even the least 'retouched' of the letter-collections surviving in a manuscript tradi-tion. They focus very closely on the business of reporting recent events and issuing commands and requests, with very little space or energy left over for more general reflection or even friendly gossip. This may betray a class difference in familiarity and ease with letters as a medium of communication.

[38] An early experiment in trying to preserve eccentric spellings in the translations too was very sensibly vetoed by the series editors; for a sample of what such transla-tions might look like, see Westermann (1919), and compare the letter of 1896 given as no. 245 in Kermode and Kermode (1995), 423 (inherited from E. M. Forster's *Commonplace Book*).

(b) Edited collections – from utility to literature and monument

Both senders and recipients have motives for keeping copies of their own and their correspondents' letters, either sporadically or in regular archives (single sheets of letter-papyrus, for instance, could be gummed together to make one or more large book-rolls of correspondence).[39] And both they, and outsiders to the original transactions, have motives for 'publishing' the resulting collections (i.e. under the conditions of ancient 'publishing', making a fair copy of the letter-set available to others for further copies to be taken[40]): to safeguard reputations and help in the building of personal monuments, to document a key period of history or set of events, to preserve the valuable lessons and/or the fine writing contained. Personal archives must go back a long way, but just when in antiquity a collection of letters was first published as a work for circulation in its own right is unclear. All the sets attributed to early correspondents are under more or less certain suspicion of being later fabrications. Those of the sixth-century figures Solon, Thales, Phalaris, Anacharsis, Heraclitus and the Pythagoreans, and the fifth- and fourth-century figures Themistocles, Artaxerxes, Hippocrates, Euripides, Socrates and the Socratics, Xenophon, Diogenes, Crates, Aeschines, Chion and Dion, are undoubtedly pseudepigraphic;[41] the status of Plato's and Demosthenes' letters has been fiercely debated, but they may well belong in the same category.[42]

On the available evidence, the earliest letters we can be sure were kept and circulated in something like this way seem to have been those of the philosopher Epicurus (341–270 B.C.). Although only three now survive in full, because quoted in the biography of Epicurus by Diogenes Laertius (*Lives* 10.34–135), fragments preserved in other ways show how many once circulated, chiefly but not exclusively among the Epicurean community.[43]

[39] See e.g. Cic. *Att.* 16.5 (= 410 SB).5.

[40] On ancient 'publishing', see Easterling and Knox (1985) 14 and 17–22, Kenney and Clausen (1982) 19–22.

[41] See below, 27–8.

[42] On pseudepigraphic letters, see below, 27–31. On the question of Plato's letters, see Morrow (1935) 11–22, Gulley (1972); on Demosthenes, Goldstein (1968) 3–34, 64–94.

[43] See Frr. 40–133 in Arrighetti's edition. The collection attested as being made by the second-century (B.C.) Epicurean Philonides (*P. Herc.* 1044, fr. 14) is unlikely to have been the very first; Plutarch, *Non posse* 1101 b testifies both to Epicurean circulation, and his own reading of the *Letters*. The continuing availability of the letters, and the possibility of re-presenting them in media other than manuscript, are best illustrated

Letters of Aristotle were apparently united into a collected edition with a preface by one Artemon not later than the second century B.C.[44] In Latin, we hear of collections by the Elder Cato (234–149 B.C.) and Cornelia, mother of the Gracchi (second century B.C.).[45]

The earliest collections now surviving, and perhaps the most influential both in antiquity and subsequently, are those of **M. Tullius Cicero** (106–43 B.C.).[46] 914 letters now survive (about ninety of them by other hands), 426 in the sixteen books of the *Ad Atticum* (covering the years 68–44 B.C.[47]), 435 in the sixteen of the *Ad familiares* (62–43), twenty-seven in the three *Ad Quintum fratrem* (59–54) and twenty-six *Ad Brutum* (all from 43 B.C.). At least twice as many were known in antiquity, including sets to Pompey, Caesar, Octavian, M. Cicero Jnr, and Q. Axius (cf. on **54** and **75** in this anthology). Collectively, these letters give an unparallelled insight into Cicero's career and attitudes, as well as into the social world and informal language of the Roman élite of the late Republic.

Cicero himself contemplated publication, from the archive kept by his secretary Tiro, supplemented from that also kept by Atticus,[48] but did not live long enough to see the project through. The actual publication of the *Ad fam.*, the *Ad Quintum* and the *Ad Brutum* seems to have happened during the reign of Augustus, probably thanks to Tiro, that of the *Ad Atticum* not until the Neronian period.[49] Evidence that would allow us to assess the extent of any editorial processing the letters underwent is thin,[50] though the arrangement of the *Ad fam.*, partly by correspondent and partly by type of letter,[51] suggests

by the inscription set up in the second century A.D. by Diogenes of Oenoanda, which quotes Epicurus' letter to his mother (frr. 52–3 Chilton = 125–6 Smith): cf. Chilton (1971) 108–13, Smith (1992) 312–16, 555–8.

[44] Demetrius, *Eloc.* 223; David on Aristotle, *Cat.* 24a28.

[45] C.f. e.g. Cic. *Off.* 1.37, *Brut.* 211; Cugusi (1970–9) 1 65–70 (LXVI) and 110–13 (CXXIV).

[46] Major commentaries: Shackleton Bailey (1965–70), (1977) and (1980a); his text and translation also in the most recent Loebs. Selective commentaries with useful introductions: Shackleton Bailey (1980b), Stockton (1969), Willcock (1995). Criticism: Hutchinson (1998), Griffin (1995). Life and times: Shackleton Bailey (1971), Rawson (1983), Scullard (1982).

[47] Though all but eleven date from 61 and after.

[48] *Att.* 16.5 (= 410 SB).5, *Ad fam.* 16.17 (= 126 SB).1; cf. Nepos. *Att.* 16.2–4.

[49] Shackleton Bailey (1965) 59–76, (1977) 23–4; cf. Hutchinson (1998) 4.

[50] Though at least one editorial deletion has been detected, at *Att.* 13.9 (= 317 SB).1.

[51] Book 13 consists of letters of introduction, 14 of letters to Cic.'s wife, 16 of letters to or about Tiro.

a desire to facilitate several different kinds of reading. However that may be, Cicero's letters rapidly became established as classics of epistolography,[52] read both for their information content (about the man himself and the times he lived through), and for their admired style. As a recent study has re-emphasized, this latter way of reading surely answers to at least some of Cicero's own expectations. Although the letters certainly contributed to building his political and social monument (e.g. in demonstrating the extent and weight of his friendships and alliances), they were also carefully contrived structures of words, consciously working at many different levels of formality, depending on the nature of the communication and the identity of the correspondent.[53] However much the letter may be thought of as an unofficial kind of writing, Cicero was never truly off duty, as stylist or as self-presenter.

The letter-collection of the **Younger Pliny, C. Plinius Caecilius Secundus** (A.D. *c.* 61 –*c.* 112), comprises some 370 letters in ten books, nine of Pliny's own letters to family, friends and social contacts, and one of letters to and from the Emperor Trajan, written when he was imperial special legate in Bithynia-with-Pontus in 110.[54] Before his final appointment, Pliny – landowner, lawyer, administrator and man of letters – had been consul in 100 and Chairman of the Rome drainage-board (*curator aluei Tiberis*) in 104–7. Books 1 to 9, containing 247 letters, were published during Pliny's own lifetime, perhaps from A.D. 104/5 onwards, apparently at fairly regular intervals.[55] The contents are by and large noticeably more polished stylistically than the 123 letters (73 by Pliny himself) in Book 10, which may not have been published until after his death.[56] In contrast to Cicero's, the bulk of Pliny's letters were thus seen into general circulation in book form by the writer himself. It is therefore hardly surprising that they give the impression of a collection carefully calculated to show off their author in all the identities he prided himself on, as administrator, friend, husband, patron and benefactor of individuals and communities,

[52] Sen. *Ep.* 21.4 (cf. e.g. 97.3ff., 118.1–2), Quintilian 10.1.107, Pliny 9.2 (= **52** in this anthology), Fronto *Ad Ant. Imp.* 3.7–8 van den Hout (**54**).

[53] Hutchinson (1998) 1–24. One particularly strong indication of careful composition Hutchinson points to is the prevalence of rhythmical cadences (*clausulae*) in the majority of the *Ad fam.*

[54] Commentaries: complete, Sherwin-White (1966); selective, Sherwin-White (1969a), Williams (1990). Exegesis and criticism: Sherwin-White (1969b), Radice (1975), Shelton (1990), Rudd (1992).

[55] Sherwin-White (1966) 54–6.   [56] Williams (1990) 2–4.

and man of learning and literary cultivation.[57] It is similarly likely, though not directly provable, that many of them were edited and improved for publication. A bonus of the collection is that it also preserves for us, in Trajan's contribution to Book 10, examples of one species of imperial correspondence, to set alongside those known from other sources.[58]

Yet another kind of collection is represented by the correspondence of **M. Cornelius Fronto** (A.D. *c.* 90/5–*c.* 167), who like Pliny was a distinguished orator and advocate, and holder of a consulship (as suffect consul in July–August 143).[59] Unlike Pliny, he added to his public distinction the honour of serving as tutor in Latin rhetoric to the future emperor Marcus Aurelius, from 139 to 145 (when Marcus became co-regent with his adoptive father, Antoninus Pius). Something over 220 letters and fragments of letters survive, from what was originally a still larger collection, now preserved on a single damaged palimpsest manuscript: five books (135 letters) to and from Marcus while still Caesar, four books (23) from the period after his accession, two books (140) to and from Pius' other adopted son, Lucius Verus, one book (10) to Antoninus, and two books (40) *Ad amicos*, plus some other rhetorical treatises in epistolary form. The letters to and from Aurelius reflect both the personal and the pedagogical aspects of their relationship, and are correspondingly varied in style and tone; some do and some do not embody their author's own stylistic doctrines for formal prose, which emphasized above all the fastidious choice of vocabulary, drawing on the full resources of classic Latin literature. External evidence suggests that the letters were not edited and circulated by Fronto himself, nor immediately after his death; they are not quoted at all in surviving literature until the early fourth century;[60] thereafter, citations

---

[57] Radicke (1997), Ludolph (1997). More even than Cicero's collected letters, Pliny's thus seem to offer themselves to the reader as a kind of (auto)biography, particularly in that ancient sense of 'biography' (Plutarch, *Life of Alexander* 1.2) that emphasizes revelation and analysis of character over simple narrative; see also 30–1 below, on Chion of Heraclea.

[58] See **66** in this anthology, along with **24**, **57** and **67** (Julian), **53–4** (M. Aurelius from Fronto's correspondence), and **64** (inscribed letter of Octavian). On the topic of imperial correspondence, see Millar (1977) 213–28.

[59] Commentary, van den Hout (1999), keyed to his Teubner text of 1988; the only full English translation, by C. R. Haines in the Loeb edition (1919–20), is unreliable. Works and stylistic ideas: Kennedy (1972) 592–602, (1989) 293–6. Historical and cultural background: Champlin (1980) and Holford-Strevens (1988) 93–9.

[60] Nazarius, *Paneg.lat.* 4.24 (A.D. 321) = Test. 20 van den Hout.

by the grammarian Charisius and the poet and epistolographer Sidonius Apollinaris testify to their belated popularity. As with Pliny's, the inclusion in the collection of a good number of letters from another, imperial hand gives it an added value.[61]

Julian, **Flavius Claudius Julianus** (A.D. 331–63, acceded 361), is celebrated as the Emperor who briefly suspended the official approval of Christianity accorded by Constantine († 337) and attempted to restore the primacy of the traditional pagan cults.[62] The surviving manuscripts of his epistolary output present us with a number of different collections, adding up to just over 200 items, embracing (*a*) imperial edicts or rescripts (written adjudications on points of legislation), (*b*) letters to priests, in Julian's capacity as Pontifex Maximus, and (*c*) private correspondence, mainly written after his elevation to the rank of Caesar in 355.[63] This combination seems to go back to several alternative ancient editions, presumably made after Julian's death on campaign, one of the letters to friends and fellow *literati*, answering to an interest in Julian as stylist and upholder of Hellenic literary culture, and one in which private correspondence was mixed with his more official letters and legislation, answering to an interest in his importance in the history of the Church and the rise of Christianity.[64] From the letters, the reader learns not only of Julian's efforts to revive old cults and foster proper values in those entrusted with their care, but also of his own literary learning and devotion to the classics of Greek literature and thought. Given what we know of the literary culture of the times (see below on Libanius), it is not unlikely that Julian envisaged eventual publication, even if he did not live long enough to see to it himself.

A close ally of Julian's in the defence of Hellenism[65] was the orator and teacher **Libanius** (314–*c*. 393/4), who having held the Imperial Chair of

---

[61] Cf. n. 58 above.

[62] Full set of letters and rescripts, Bidez and Cumont (1922); letters minus rescripts, with translation, Wright (1922); something in between, with French translation, Bidez (1960). Historical and cultural background: Browning (1975), Bowersock (1978), Athanassiadi (1992).

[63] Not all are genuine: 28 of the 207 in Bidez and Cumont (1922), 10 of the 83 in Wright's (1922) Loeb, are listed as suspect or spurious.

[64] Libanius in *Ep.* 1264 Förster (A.D. 364) speaks as if Julian's letters have not yet been published, but a complete collection seems to have been known to Zosimus (*Hist.* 3.2.4) in the second half of the fifth century, and is also quoted from by the historians Socrates and Sozomenus. See Bidez and Cumont (1922) v–xxi, Wright (1923) xxvii–xxx.

[65] See his laments for Julian in *Orr.* 17 and 18.

rhetoric at Constantinople from 349 to 354, taught for the last forty years of his long life in his home city of Antioch.[66] His huge surviving literary output (64 orations, 51 declamations, and a set of model progymnasmata) includes also over 1,500 letters.[67] The collection as we now have it in the fullest medieval manuscripts seems to derive from an edition put together by an editor after Libanius' death, to commemorate a great man of letters and the troubled times he had lived through, and to make his letters available as models to future generations of letter-writers and readers. But the core of this edition (Letters 19–607) seems to stem from an earlier six-book version, covering the years 355 to 361, drawn from Libanius' own files of letters sent, and very probably put together by Libanius himself, in part as an advertisement for his teaching.[68] The bulk of the collection (1,250 items) dates from between 355 and 365, with a further 270 from the years 388–93. It comprises correspondence with friends, pupils and their parents, and the great and the good of the social, political and religious life of the times, and is full of the concerns of a literary and pedagogic star, who enjoyed considerable moral authority among his peer group and his pupils, and was for a time the confidant of the Emperor. Stylistically, these letters are very self-conscious, which is hardly surprising in the light of the fact (*Epp.* 476–7) that Libanius was in the habit of summoning his friends to read aloud and discuss letters received, and must have taken it that the same would be done with his own.[69] The reputation that he enjoyed already in his own lifetime as a master epistolographer[70] was consolidated after his death; a supposed correspondence with Basil helped to cancel out the taint of association with Julian and so save him for Christian appreciation.[71]

Perhaps even more than for the members of the Greco-Roman pagan élite, and its administrators and rulers, the letter was a highly significant form for Christians, being a major tool for the propagation of doctrine,

---

[66] Full text: Förster (1921–2). Selection with introduction and translation, Norman (1992). Background and place in the history of rhetoric: Kennedy (1983) 150–63.

[67] 1,544 genuine and nine spurious items in Förster's edition, plus a supposed exchange with St Basil running to twenty-six letters.

[68] The year 361, the last in this hypothesized edition, sees Libanius at the height of his powers and fame in Antioch, and on the verge of his endorsement as a spokesman for Julian's programme of pagan revival. See Norman (1992) 35–43.

[69] For another, earlier instance of letters as material for public performance, see Dio Chrysostom *Or.* 44.

[70] *Or.* 13.52, *Ep.* 716.3.

[71] Eunapius, *VS* 496, John Rhakendytes, *Synopsis rhetorikes* 14 (*Rhetores graeci*, ed. Walz, iii 55–9, cited by Mullett (1997) 42–3).

the maintenance of group solidarity in the face of worldly temptations and persecution, and the administration of the structures and processes of the young Church.[72] It has been calculated that over 9,000 Christian letters survive from the ancient world; of the twenty-seven books of the New Testament, no fewer than twenty-one are letters (not counting the letters enclosed within a larger narrative structure in Acts and Revelation).[73] The earliest are those of Paul, which date from between *c.* A.D. 45 and 65 and show the apostle addressing moral and doctrinal teaching both to individuals and to the Church communities he himself had founded or fostered in his travels round the Mediterranean world. These were then followed by the letters of James, Peter, Jude, and **John**, performing by and large the same functions.[74] The collection of all this material into the authoritative compendium now known as the New Testament was a complex process, in which the final canon only gradually took shape.[75] But though the individual stages are obscure, the overall motivation for the preservation of the letters is clear: to be the bearers of what had won through as orthodox teaching, and at the same time, to give the young Church a gallery of role-models and figures of authority to support its sole founder, and a body of writings to match that of the Old Testament patriarchs and prophets.

Thereafter, letters continued to be major tools for Christian teachers and administrators, and continued to be gathered into collections to perpetuate the memory of great individuals and preserve their learned teaching for the edification of posterity. Just as the early letters mirror the characteristic social status of the first Christians – generally unsophisticated, and lacking any high rhetorical or literary culture – so the later ones (from the third and fourth centuries A.D. onwards) reflect the new religion's progress up the social scale, into the world of the cultivated élite, and show a literary polish comparable with the best products of a Julian or a Libanius. The collections mined in this anthology are those of **St Basil**, **St Gregory of Nazianzus**, **St Jerome** and **St Augustine**, three at least of whom were figures of great influence in the history and development of the Church.

---

[72] Stowers (1986) 15.   [73] Stowers (1986), Doty (1973).

[74] This role of helping to hold together a geographically scattered community, united by its shared values, is an interesting common element between early Christian letters and those of Epicurus (above, 12).

[75] See Chadwick (1967) 41–5.

Basileios (*c.* 330–79), St Basil, Basil the Great, the founder of Eastern monasticism, was born in Caesarea in Cappadocia, and educated in Constantinople and Athens.[76] Like Libanius, he won early renown as a teacher, holding the Chair of rhetoric at Caesarea from 356 to 358, before abandoning a worldly career. Baptized in 358, he established a monastic community at Neocaesarea, for which he composed the Rule which was to be so influential on Eastern monasticism in general, and through St Benedict on Western monasticism too. He was called back to the active business of the Church in 365, to assist the struggles of orthodox Christianity against what came to be branded the heresy of Arianism (*ODC*[3] s.v.), becoming Bishop of Caesarea in 370 and dying in office nine years later. The 365 surviving letters are divided in the standard edition into (*a*) letters written before Basil became Bishop, from the years 357–70 (1–46); (*b*) his letters as Bishop, from 370–8 (47–291); and (*c*) doubtful and spurious items (292–365). The majority of them show Basil in his public capacity, sorting out administrative details and good doctrine and morals for his flock, and for those who had otherwise called on his assistance as patron or political ally; some are more personal (e.g. 1, to the (pagan) philosopher Eustathius), but improving aims are never far away. The first collection we hear of going into circulation was made, probably only after Basil's death, by his contemporary and fellow-countryman, Gregory of Nazianzus (*Epp.* 51–4, esp. 53). It may be that the larger collections from which the surviving medieval manuscripts descend took this as their nucleus.[77] By Byzantine times, Basil had become established as a classic of Christian epistolography.[78]

Gregory of Nazianzus (*c.* 330–90), another Cappadocian,[79] was like Basil (and indeed, under his influence) torn between the monastic life and active participation in the affairs of the church.[80] Educated in Athens, he at first chose monastic retreat, but was made Bishop of Sasima (Cappadocia) in

[76] Text and translation: Deferrari (1926–34), Courtonne (1957–66). Life, times and controversies, Deferrari, xv–xl, Chadwick (1967) 148–51, 178–83.

[77] Bessières (1923) 146–51.

[78] He is listed along with Libanius in Rhakendytes's *Synopsis*, cited in n. 71 above; cf. also the forged correspondence with Libanius mentioned above, which besides co-opting Libanius for Christian appreciation and imitation, also implies a flattering view of Basil's own literary quality.

[79] He, Basil and Basil's brother Gregory of Nyssa are sometimes referred to as the 'Cappadocian Fathers'.

[80] Text: Gallay (1964–7) and (1969). Criticism: Guignet (1911). Background and thought: Ruether (1969).

372. Summoned to Constantinople to assist in the restoration of orthodoxy to a substantially Arian city, he came close to being elected Bishop there in 381, but withdrew in the face of determined opposition from hostile factions. Returning to Nazianzus in the hopes of retiring into semi-monastic retreat on his family's estates, he eventually achieved this ambition in 383, but not before he had been manoeuvered into serving a further two years in charge of the local Church. 249 letters now survive, dating from between 359 and the late 380s, not all by Gregory himself; twenty are to his close friend and ally, Basil. The first attested collection was Gregory's own work, in answer to a request from his great nephew Nicobulus – the same, in fact, as also contained the selection of Basil's letters mentioned above. What the relationship is between this and the direct ancestors of the medieval manuscript collection is unclear.

Of approximately the same generation, but in the Latin-speaking West, was the ascetic, scholar and teacher **St Jerome, Eusebius Hieronymus** (345–420), bracketed with Augustine, Gregory the Great and Ambrose as one of the four original 'Doctors of the Church' and compiler of the so-called 'Vulgate' Latin Bible.[81] Born in Stridon in Dalmatia (near Aquileia), Jerome studied in Rome, then lived a life of ascetic retreat in both Italy and the deserts of the East, before being ordained presbyter in Antioch in 379. The remaining forty years of his life were divided between Rome (382–5), where he presided over an ascetic circle largely composed of women, and began his definitive revision of the existing Latin translations of the Psalms and the New Testament, and Bethlehem, where he founded and administered a monastery, a convent and a church, and added a revised Latin Old Testament to his earlier work. Of the 144 items in his surviving correspondence, thirty-one are by other hands (including ten of Augustine's); his own range in length from a few lines to thousands of words. They can be roughly categorized as eleven on points of dogma, twenty-four exegetic, thirty on moral issues, eleven funeral orations (obituaries), thirty-one polemical, and a few private letters to friends. We know from Jerome himself (*De uiris illustribus* 135) that he kept copies of his own correspondence, in some kind of organized archive, in his personal library. They were thus theoretically available for copying and diffusion, but it is not known when the possibility was first realized;

---

[81] Text: Hilberg (1996), Labourt (1949–63). Full English translation, Fremantle (1983). Selections, with translation, Wright (1933); see also Scourfield (1993). Life and thought, Kelly (1975).

at any rate, they were generally known to a reading public by the sixth century.[82]

Jerome's correspondent and fellow Doctor of the Church, **St Augustine, Aurelius Augustinus** (354–430), Bishop of Hippo Regius in N. Africa, had as great an influence on Christian theology and moral teaching as Jerome did on the propagation of the Scriptures.[83] Educated in Carthage, Augustine was baptized in 387, after a youthful fascination with Manichaeism and a first career (compare Basil and Libanius) as a teacher of rhetoric in Rome and Milan. He returned to Africa in 388, to spend the rest of his career there. As bishop, he was heavily involved in the struggle to assert the authority of orthodox Christianity against a number of rival sects ('heresies') and their theologies: Manichaeism, Donatism and Pelagianism (see *ODC*[3] s.vv., and compare the involvement of Basil and Gregory with Arianism). He wrote many polemical works on doctrine, but is now best remembered for his *City of God*, an analysis of the contrast between Christian and worldly values, inspired by the Sack of Rome, and *Confessions*, a foundational text in the history of autobiography. Nearly 300 letters of Augustine's survive, 270 in the main manuscript tradition, plus another twenty-nine only rediscovered in the twentieth century and published in 1981. They show Augustine in contact and discussion with other leading Christian intellectuals and administrators, or sorting out the pastoral and other problems of his and his colleagues' North African sees. It is not known when and by whom the collection that underlies the main manuscript tradition was first assembled.

(c) 'Edited collections' – extensions of epistolary form

All the collections of letters discussed in the preceding section give every appearance of deriving from 'real' correspondence, that is from letters really sent, as letters,[84] at determinate points in time to and from the individuals whose names they bear – however much they may subsequently have been edited and improved for release *en bloc* to a general reading public. With

---

[82] Cassiodorus, *De institutione diuinarum litterarum* (*Patrologia Latina* LXX 1135).

[83] Text: Goldbacher (1895–1923) and Divjak (1981), Translation: Cunningham (1872–5), Parsons (1951–6) and Eno (1989). Selection with translation: Baxter (1930). Life and times: Brown (1967).

[84] I.e. within the conventional institution of letter-writing and -sending, so as to be recognized on receipt as letters, rather than as (say) presents, or exercises for correction.

some other collections, there is room for a strong suspicion, or a downright conviction, that the items 'collected' were never sent in that manner, and that we have to do instead with a kind of co-option or extension of the letter and letter-collection form, and an element of fiction.[85] Two different versions of such a co-option of the letter-collection are represented in this anthology: the verse epistles of **Horace** (**23**, **29**, **32**) and **Ovid** (**10**, **45**), and the moral epistles of **Seneca** to Lucilius (**33**, **34**, **74**). Related to these, though on the level of the single piece rather than the collection, is the use of the form to make a kind of literary preface, the dedicatory epistle, represented here by **Martial** (**58**) and **Julius Pollux** (**59**).

All these texts date from the first two centuries A.D. By this time, letter form had already a long history of exploitation in Greco-Roman writing (quite apart from the firm establishment of the practice of turning letters from private, utilitarian items into a kind of literature, attested by the collections already surveyed). The use of the letter as a vehicle for what were in effect short treatises offering advice or instruction, addressed to a specified individual but intended from the start for a broader readership too, had been flirted with by Isocrates,[86] and decisively endorsed by Epicurus,[87] already in the fourth century B.C. Pseudepigraphic collections – sets of letters supposed to have been assembled from the work of great figures of the past, but in fact composed all together by a later impersonator – had begun to circulate at some time in the Hellenistic period.[88] And sporadic experiments in verse transposition of the letter form go back at least to Lucilius in the second century B.C. and Catullus in the first.[89] With all such

[85] The element of fiction is however quite tightly limited, covering only the actual mechanics of the delivery of this material to its readers, not the identity of sender or recipient, or the world referred to in the letters. It can also be observed that the gap in kind is not a large one between a collection of 'pretend' letters and one made up of what were once 'real' letters but now no longer are, because re-created in altered guise by the very process of collection and re-release to a general readership.

[86] *Orr.* 1–2, to Demonicus and Nicocles, not *quite* epistolary because lacking the conventional opening and closure, and spoken of as friendly gifts (*Dem.* 2, ἀπέσταλκά σοι τόνδε τὸν λόγον δῶρον) rather than as letters; but letters too were conceptualized as friendly gifts (Dem. *Eloc.* (**73** in this anthology) 224, 231), so the gap is not large.

[87] The *Epistles* to Herodotus, Menoeceus and Pythocles; cf. above 12 with n. 43, and below 26. Epicurus' use of the letter form is to be seen in the context of his deep preoccupation with philosophical communication and his ongoing search for varied and effective means of putting his message across to the greatest possible diversity of audiences: see Clay (1983) 54–81 and 169–85.

[88] See below, 27–31.

[89] Lucilius, *Sat.* 5, described and quoted in Gellius, *NA* 18.8; Catullus 35, 13 (?), 65 and 68A.

works, the question arises of what – in the absence of actual sending – identifies them specifically as letters, rather than as some other more or less closely related form of writing.

It is perhaps to **Horace, Q. Horatius Flaccus** (65–8 B.C.) that the credit belongs for first conceiving of the publication not of individual verse letters but of a whole bookful, as he did with Book I of his *Epistles* in 20 or 19 B.C.[90] The twenty short hexameter poems of this collection (between thirteen and 112 lines in length) are all cast as personal messages to friends, except for the last, which takes the form of an address to the book itself. They contain advice, exhortation and reflection on (broadly) moral philosophical themes, including (implicitly and explicitly) the proprieties and obligations of friendship. In a move characteristic of both philosophical preaching in general, and specifically Roman traditions of moral thinking,[91] Horace often uses discussion and display of his own attitudes as a means of advising and instructing. This particular combination of philosophical theme, letter form and verse is warranted partly by the tradition of philosophical epistolography stemming from Epicurus, partly by the formal similarity between letters and various kinds of personal (especially elegiac) poetry.[92]

What identifies the resulting products as letters is in the first instance the overall book-title. Restricted length, an individual addressee, a preoccupation with friendship, and the warm individual relationship between author and addressee, are all appropriate to the letter,[93] but not exclusively characteristic of it. Overtly epistolary formulae[94] are not consistently present; for instance, the standard salutations at start and finish are not directly quoted, or even always alluded to. Instead, Horace establishes the epistolarity of his 'letters' by including the occasional allusive paraphrase of such salutations (e.g. 10.49–50), and the occasional mention of the business of sending and receiving the pieces as written messages (e.g. 3.30, 5.30 = **23** in this anthology), and by mimicking from time to time the characteristic layout and miscellaneous content of real correspondence (e.g. 12.25–9 = **32** in this anthology).[95] The overall effect, that is to say, is achieved by applying discontinuous patches of epistolary colouring, rather than by the consistent adherence to any set pattern. Horace's remaining epistolary output – the

---

[90] Commentary with introduction, Mayer (1994); further discussion and criticism, Dilke (1973), Allen et al. (1978), Kilpatrick (1986).

[91] Mayer (1994) 4.

[92] Restricted length and a sustained paraenetic address to a specified individual.

[93] On letters and friendship, see below, 40–2.

[94] See below, 34–8.   [95] See Allen et al. (1978).

two long items of *Epistles* II (270 and 216 lines) and the *Epistle to the Pisones* (the *Ars Poetica*, 476 lines)[96] – has rather less of this colour (though such epistolary commonplaces as the apology for being a bad correspondent can occur, as at *Ep.* II 2.20–5). In contrast to *Epistles* I, these are instances of the use of letter form to clothe short treatises, in this case on the nature of poetry.

The contribution to verse epistolography made in the next generation of Latin poets by **Ovid, P. Ovidius Naso** (43 B.C. – *c.* A.D. 18) began with *Heroides*, a book now containing twenty-one elegiac poems of between 115 and 378 lines in length, purporting to be missives from distressed mythological heroines to their beloveds, accompanied in three cases by a reply from the other party.[97] Here the precedent of both real and pseudepigraphic letter-collections in prose combines with those of the earlier verse experiments of Horace and (closer still) Propertius (*Elegies* 4.3); the use of mythological themes in elementary school exercises and in declamation is also part of their background.[98] One version at least of the original collection was published at the latest before 2 B.C., with perhaps a revised edition a few years later. Following his banishment by order of Augustus to Tomi on the shores of the Black Sea in A.D. 8, Ovid returned to verse epistolary form sporadically in the *Tristia* (fifty elegies arranged in five books), and at the length of a whole work in the *Epistulae ex Ponto* (forty-six in four books).[99] In these later works, Ovid moves from one great epistolary topic and motivator of letter-writing (love) to another (separation and distance, in his case, that of the exile, cut off from all that he once felt made life worth living). Although directed to many different addressees, the two collections share a single underlying agenda: to mobilize opinion at Rome on Ovid's behalf, and bring pressure to bear on the *princeps* to mitigate his sentence. Ovid's technique for establishing the epistolary credentials of his verse letters is broadly comparable to Horace's: he begins (and less often ends) with allusive paraphrases of standard epistolary salutations, and in between he reproduces sporadically other epistolary elements – enquiries

[96] Commentary, Rudd (1989).

[97] Selective commentaries, Knox (1995) and Kenney (1996). A good number of these twenty-one, in particular *Ep.* 15, Sappho to Phaon, are under suspicion of not being by Ovid: Knox, 5–8 and 12–14, but contrast Kenney, 20–6.

[98] On classroom exercises, declamation, and the use of topics and characters from myth, see Bonner (1977) 250–327, Kennedy (1972) 312–27.

[99] Commentary and translation (*Tristia*): Luck (1967–77), Melville and Kenney (1992). Criticism: Dickinson (1973), Evans (1983).

and news about health, complaints about non-arrival of letters and (though here he goes rather beyond Horatian precedent) references to the epistolary transaction itself, the writing, sending, transportation, receipt and reading of the message. According to the density of these devices in any given case, the resulting product has a more or less strongly epistolary character.[100]

The 124[101] *Epistulae Morales* of **L. Annaeus Seneca** (*c.*1 B.C–A.D. 65) represent a rather different exploitation of the letter form (though in broad terms sharing their preoccupation with moral philosophy and moral instruction with Horace's *Epistles*).[102] Written (probably) in the years 63 and 64, between Seneca's retirement from public life (he had been tutor to the future emperor Nero, suffect consul in 56, and an imperial advisor) and his enforced suicide in 65 (Tac. *Ann.* 15.60–4),[103] and addressed to his younger friend Lucilius Iunior (*PIR*² L 388), they constitute a kind of course in (Stoic) moral philosophy. Casting himself not as a perfected sage, but as a *proficiens* (one 'making progress' towards wisdom and virtue), Seneca seeks to draw Lucilius on too by a combination of exhortation, reflection, doctrinal instruction and appeal to his own personal example.[104] As the collection unfolds, it dramatizes not only Seneca's effort, and skill in delivering well-phrased, well-constructed and well-targeted instruction, but also his success: Lucilius is seen to be responding, and making at least some of the progress envisaged.[105] The degree of fictionalizing in this set of letters has been hotly debated.[106] It is generally agreed (even by those who wish to see a real correspondence underlying) that Seneca from the start had publication to a general readership in mind, as for his other philosophical writings, rather than communication with Lucilius alone. But the careful shape of the whole collection, the existence

[100] See commentary on **10** in this collection, *Tristia* 5.13, with Davisson (1985). Besides 5.13, the overtly epistolary items in *Tristia* are 3.3, 5.2, and 5.7, but others too (e.g. 1.5, 1.7, 3.6, 3.7 and 5.6) have some epistolary colouring.

[101] Divided into twenty books, perhaps by Seneca himself. What now survives is not the whole original work: Gellius (*NA* 12.2) knew of at least twenty-two books.

[102] Commentary (selective): Summers (1910), Costa (1988); among translations, the version of Barker (1932) is particularly good. Criticism and exegesis: Russell (1974), Griffin (1974) and (1992), Coleman (1974), Hadot (1969) and (1986).

[103] Brief account of the life, Griffin (1974); longer treatment of life and thought, Griffin (1992).

[104] See Hadot (1986), drawing on and partly summarizing Hadot (1969).

[105] Russell (1974) 75–6, pointing to *Epp.* 2.1, 4.1, 19.1, 20.1, 31.1.

[106] Russell (1974) 72–9, Griffin (1992) 416–19.

of a 'plot' within it (Lucilius' progress), and certain difficulties with the chronology make it seem reasonable to go further, and doubt whether large stretches of this correspondence, even the whole of it, were ever sent at all. Seneca may indeed have exchanged letters on moral philosophy with Lucilius, and acted as his mentor, but the *Epistles* as we have them and read them are, in Griffin's phrase, more like 'dialogues with an epistolary veneer'.

Seneca's two great models in this venture were the correspondences of Epicurus[107] and Cicero.[108] Epicurus' letters are frequently quoted with approval (e.g. 7.11, 9.1 and 8, 21.3–4, 22.5, 79.15, 92.25) and the parallel between his correspondence and the *Epistulae* explicitly drawn in 21.5. Cicero's correspondence, specifically the letters to Atticus, is held up, along with Epicurus', as proof of the power of letters to confer undying fame (on the recipient) in 21.3–4, but contrasted with Seneca's own in terms of content and values in 118.1–4. In formal terms, the epistolarity of his compositions lies in their use of standard formulae of salutation at beginning and end, and incorporated references to various aspects of the epistolary transaction (receipt of letters from Lucilius, discussion of the ideal frequency of exchange, and so on), combined with their restricted length and a carefully contrived looseness in transition between topics.

The dedicatory epistle, finally, represented in this anthology by pieces by **Martial** (**58**) and **Julius Pollux** (**59**), constitutes yet another kind of extension of the letter form, to make an introduction to a non-epistolary work. The usefulness of the letter in this role – corresponding to a rhetorical or poetic proemium – seems to stem from its combination of direct personal address with limited length and well-marked closure. In a way more obviously self-contained than if the proemium has the same literary form as the body of what is to follow (rhetorical prose, or a particular verse metre), a dedicatory epistle effectively presents its work to the dedicatee, and highlights that act of dedication for a more general readership, without allowing the presence of the addressee, and the author's expressions of goodwill, to leak out into the main text. Thus (for instance) Pollux' *Lexicon* can be placed under the protection of Commodus' patronage, and Commodus given unambiguously to understand that he 'owns' it, without the Emperor's name or person having to become entangled in the minutiae of lexicography.

[107] See above, 12 and 22, with nn. 43 and 87.   [108] Above, 13–14.

(d) 'Edited collections' – pseudepigrapha

Alongside those already discussed, there also survive from antiquity sets of letters attributed to a whole series of historical or supposedly historical figures dating from between the sixth century B.C. and the second century A.D. The full list of the texts printed in Rudolf Hercher's monumental *Epistolographi graeci* of 1873 embraces the letters of Aeschines, Anacharsis, Apollonius of Tyana, Aristotle, Artaxerxes, Brutus, Chion of Heraclea, Crates, Demosthenes, Dio, Diogenes, Euripides, Heraclitus, Hippocrates, Isocrates, Periander, Phalaris, Plato, Pythagoras and the Pythagoreans, Socrates and the Socratics, Solon, Thales, Themistocles and Xenophon.[109] Written in Greek (including those of Brutus), these works present themselves as the outcome of the same process as was undergone by (e.g.) the letters of a Cicero or a Julian, that is to say the assembling and re-release to a wider reading public of an originally 'real', functional correspondence. The status of some (especially those of Plato and Demosthenes) is disputed, but since the celebrated work of Richard Bentley at the end of the seventeenth century[110] it has been generally (and rightly) accepted that the vast majority are not what they claim to be, but instead the work of later authors impersonating these great figures of the past (hence 'pseudepigraphic', involving a false or lying attribution).

In date, the earliest may belong to the fourth century B.C., those with the best chance of going back that far being the ones attributed to Anacharsis and (even if not containing any genuine items) Isocrates, Demosthenes and Plato.[111] Some others – those of Diogenes, Socrates and Hippocrates – may date from the first century B.C.[112] Most of the collections, in any case,

---

[109] The complete set of texts, with Latin translation, only in Hercher (1873); text and translation of Anacharsis, Crates, Diogenes, Heraclitus and Socrates and the Socratics, with brief introductions, in Malherbe (1977); selections from Anacharsis, Diogenes, Crates, Socrates and the Socratics, Euripides, Themistocles, Hippocrates and Chion in Costa (2001); text and translation of Apollonius, with commentary, in Penella (1979); text and translation of Hippocrates in Smith (1990); text, German tr. and discussion of Euripides in Gösswein (1975); text, German tr. and comm. of Pythagorean letters in Städele (1980). For Socrates and the Socratics, see also Sykutris (1933); for Hippocrates, Rütten (1992); and for Themistocles, Doenges (1981). General discussion, Rosenmeyer (2001) 193–252.

[110] Bentley (1697) and (1699); see Hinz (2001) 295–392.

[111] Sykutris (1931) 210, Malherbe (1977) 6; Kindstrand (1981) 50, citing Reuters (1963) 3–5.

[112] Sykutris (1931) 210 and (1933) 106–22, Malherbe (1977) 17, Smith (1990).

seem to have grown over time, as later writers augmented the efforts of their predecessors, and so cannot be assigned unequivocally to any one date; an extreme instance is the letters of Phalaris, which seem to stretch in date of composition from the second century A.D. into the Byzantine period.[113] The motives for their composition seem also to have been mixed: interests in producing model letters for different types of correspondence,[114] in filling in parts of the historical record left blank by more mainstream texts, in imparting improving moral teaching in an attractive guise, and in the simple entertainment value of the supposed private exchanges of the great figures of the past, all played their part, alone or in varying combinations in the different collections. In connection with the last of these motives, an important aspect of the background to the production of such letters, already mentioned *à propos* Ovid's *Heroides*, must have been the popularity in both education and adult leisure of historical declamation, the practice of inventing speeches in character for historical personages at this or that well-known moment from their careers.[115]

The collections chosen for attention in this anthology are five: those of Phalaris (**11**, **12**, **25**, **38**, **51**, **60**, **70**), Socrates and the Socratics (**13**), Diogenes (**36**), Crates (**37**) and Chion of Heraclea (**14**). The *Epistles* of **Phalaris,** 148 in number,[116] stand out both for the size of the collection, and for the fact that it was they that Bentley put at the centre of his demonstration of the true origins of this whole class of writing. As has already been pointed out, they are very various in date, and this diversity is matched by the variety of the apparent aims of their anonymous composers. Some are clearly model letters, others are more concerned to develop implied narratives of episodes from their supposed author's career (such as his dealings with the poet Stesichorus and his family, which is material for *Epp.* 54, 88, 78 (= **60**), 79, 92–3, 103, 108–9, 114, 121, 145, 147 and others); there is no unified 'plot' or chronological sequence linking them all together. Most of them in one way or another play with the ambiguous record of their author, who was tyrant of Acragas at some now unspecifiable period in the sixth century B.C. For, from at least the early fifth century onwards,[117] Phalaris came to be held up as a model of tyrannical

---

[113] Russell (1988) 96–7.   [114] See below, 38 and 44–6.

[115] In addition to the works cited in n. 98 above, see also Russell (1983) 106–28, Bowie (1970/74) 4–10 = 168–74, Costa (2001) xi–xiii.

[116] Russell (1988), Rosenmeyer (2001) 224–31, Hinz (2001).

[117] Pindar, *Pyth.* 95–8.

cruelty, epitomized in his use of the notorious hollow bronze bull, made by the craftsman Perillus/Perilaus, to roast his victims alive. But, in a way that seems to take its cue from perceived parallels with other archaic tyrants (Periander, for example, or Pittacus), who were known not only as wielders of arbitrary power, but also as sages, Phalaris also appears (or at least is made to pose) as a man of stern, self-conscious virtue, determined to rise above the misunderstanding and slanders of his contemporaries. Uncertainty over which of these Phalarises is being presented to us at any given moment in the collection (an uncertainty perhaps deliberately sought by at least some of its true authors) gives an intriguing edge to a reading of it.

In the letters of **Socrates and the Socratics**, the first seven by Socrates himself, and the remaining twenty-eight by his pupils and successors,[118] we seem to see a combination of historical, moral–philosophical and literary interest: a desire both to re-run the story of Socrates from the viewpoint(s) of those most intimately involved, and to restate the ethical truths they stood for (including the well-known differences in interpretation of the Socratic legacy that surfaced between Antisthenes and Aristippus). Although there is no strong narrative line linking the successive letters together, a rough chronological sequence can be detected: *Epp.* 1–13 contain exchanges between Socrates and pupils, and between one pupil and another, while the Master himself is still alive; 14–17 (17 is item **13** in this anthology) report and react to the death;[119] and 18–27 move on to aspects of the aftermath – the subsequent travels of the pupils, the beginnings of their careers as Socratic authors, and measures to take care of Socrates' widow, Xanthippe.

The letters of **Diogenes** and **Crates**, fifty-one and thirty-six in number respectively, combine their element of simple interest in the lives and doings of two notably colourful characters with a rather more marked concern for improving moral lessons.[120] Diogenes was the founder, and Crates one of the first adherents, of the values and lifestyle known as Cynicism, a

[118] The main sequence in fact ends with *Ep.* 27, after which come miscellaneous items by rather later 'Socratics', and at least one item (35) that does not belong at all. Sykutris (1933: 106–22) suggests that, though the Socrates letters may go back to the first century B.C., those of his pupils were not composed until the third century A.D. See also Costa (2001) xvii and 80–3.

[119] In 14, in particular, there is a strong sense of improving on the classic accounts: in this version we get not only the death, borrowed from Plato's *Phaedo*, but also the subsequent burial of Socrates, on which Plato is silent.

[120] Costa (2001) xvii and 72–9.

development of Socratic ethics that emphasized the unimportance of material comforts to the pursuit of moral virtue, and the positive desirability of an austere, ascetic style of living. Thus we find Diogenes (*Ep.* 6 = **36**) telling the famous story of how he realized he could live a still simpler life by throwing away his drinking-cup and using his hands instead, and Crates (*Ep.* 30 = **37**) briskly declining the gift of a warm cloak from his wife Hipparchia. The history of Cynicism, and of Cynic writing and teaching, is a complicated area;[121] it is seldom clear, for any given period, how many practising Cynics there were, as opposed to writers and teachers with a sympathetic interest in Cynic ideas, and a readiness to cite them with some degree of approval. The authors of these letters were probably *not* practising Cynics, but rather individuals interested in using such colourful characters as a good way of putting across non-materialist values in a striking way. But the degree of didacticism must not be exaggerated: they are open to a reading that enjoys the window they open on the world of Diogenes and his followers without necessarily feeling obliged to accept their values wholesale;[122] and even when instruction does seem to be the aim, it is tame compared to the teaching style attested elsewhere for the notoriously acerbic, shocking Diogenes.[123]

The seventeen letters of **Chion of Heraclea** are another case again, belonging to that small subset of pseudepigraphic letter-collections that critics have wanted to style 'epistolary novels' (or, more modestly 'novellas').[124] Whereas most collections – like those of Phalaris, Socrates, Diogenes and Crates – have no strong narrative line running through the individual constituents, in a minority of cases a linking plot can be seen. The letters of Themistocles, and *Epp.* 10 to 17 within the set attributed to Hippocrates, are smaller-scale instances; but Chion's letters show the phenomenon in its most developed form.[125] Purporting to be by a pupil of Plato, a historical individual of the fourth century B.C.,[126] and sent over a period of more than

[121] Dudley (1937); Branham and Goulet-Cazé (1996).

[122] Cf. Rosenmeyer (2001) 221–4.

[123] For a summary of Diogenes' usual image, see Moles (2000) 417–23.

[124] Holzberg (1994), cf. Doenges (1981), Smith (1990), Rosenmeyer (2001) 196–204, 217–21. Costa (2001) xix argues that considerations of chronology prevent us reading Chion's letters as a 'novel', but this is to confuse historical accuracy with narrative coherence: it is the latter, which they have, not the former, which they indeed lack, that matters.

[125] Text and commentary: Düring (1951), Costa (2001) xviii–xix and 108–23 (*Epp.* 3, 13, 14, 16); criticism: Holzberg (1996), Rosenmeyer (2001) 234–54.

[126] He is known also from Diodorus (16.6) and Memnon's history of Heraclea (*FGrH* 336, quoted by Photius, *Bibl.* 224).

five years, they combine to tell the story of how the young aristocrat Chion left home, travelled via Byzantium to Athens, met and was won over to philosophy by Xenophon and Plato, studied at length in the Academy, and then returned at freedom's call to rid Heraclea of the tyrant Clearchus. The penultimate letter (all but one of the preceding fifteen have been to Chion's father) is a lying message of reassurance to Clearchus, seeking to persuade him of Chion's innocuousness, and the very last (**14** in this anthology) is Chion's farewell to his mentor Plato, written on the eve of the assassination attempt, in full consciousness that it is likely to be his last. This is an adventure-story, a moving tale of heroism and self-sacrifice, perhaps also a kind of biography (in that it tells the story of one individual's coming of age and discovery of his true identity and vocation[127]). At the same time, it also embodies a view of philosophy, and the duty of the philosopher to engage with the world of public affairs. Given the likely time of composition (the first century A.D.), it is an intriguing thought that the endorsement of tyrannicide may also have had a contemporary resonance, with the well-known phenomenon of philosophical opposition to the Emperor.[128]

(e) 'Edited collections' – invention

It remains to consider the category of fully fictitious letters, those in which not only is the occasion of the supposed sending of the message invented, but the correspondents too. This category is represented in this anthology by the letters of 'Polyaenus' and 'Circe' from Petronius' *Satyrica* (**17**),[129] Phoenicium from Plautus' *Pseudolus* (**71**), Gemellus, Salaconis and Glycera from Alciphron's *Rustic letters* and *Letters of the courtesans* (**18**, **19**), and the anonymous exile from the *Erotic epistles* of Philostratus (**20**). Those of Petronius and Plautus are discussed briefly below on pp. 33–4, as they are also examples of letters embedded in a larger, non-epistolary literary structure. Alciphron's and Philostratus' by contrast (like those of Aelian and Aristaenetus, not included in this anthology)[130] are taken from themed sets of correspondence, purporting like the pseudepigraphic collections

---

[127] Cf. Trapp (forthcoming).   [128] MacMullen (1966) 46–94.

[129] In which there is in fact a still further layer of fiction, in that the names attached to both correspondents, within the world of Petronius' story, are themselves pseudonyms.

[130] For Aelian (2nd–3rd cent.), see Costa (2001) xv and 4–9, Rosenmeyer (2001) 308–21; and for Aristaenetus (5th cent.), Arnott (1973) and (1982) and Costa (2001) xvi and 60–7.

discussed above to be collected editions of originally separate, functional messages.

The manuscripts of **Alciphron** credit him with 123 letters, divisible into four categories according to the professions of their supposed senders – fishermen, farmers, parasites and courtesans.[131] Their date of composition is uncertain, but somewhere in the late second century or early third century A.D. seems right, as they share many features of style and content with such authors of that period as Longus, Lucian and Philostratus. For this is highly literary, stylistically self-conscious writing, drawing more on the fishermen, farmers, parasites and courtesans of classic Greek literature (above all in pastoral poetry, mime and New Comedy) than on those of 'real life'; it belongs fairly and squarely (like some of the pseudepigrapha discussed above) with other manifestations of the cultural and literary movement known as the 'Second Sophistic'.[132] Aelian writes in a carefully 'Atticizing' style, modelling himself on the prose classics of the fifth and fourth centuries B.C.[133] Each set of letters constitutes a series of vignettes of rural or urban low-life, rather than a connected narrative; although there are answering pairs of letters, and a few longer sequences, no overall plot links all the items in any of the four categories. The reader is offered instead the pleasures of reconstructing a whole series of different situations, half-illuminated by each of the separate letters or letter-pairs. Equally important is the evocation of character (again to be seen against the background of rhetorical education, in which *ethopoeia*, 'construction of character', was an important exercise);[134] it only added to the fun that there was such a gap between the low social status of the characters created, and the exquisite diction with which Aelian made them write.

The *Erotic Epistles* of **Philostratus**[135] belong broadly to the same period and category as Alciphron's. They are written in the same erudite, allusive style, for a readership steeped in the classics of Greek literature, and alert to their evocations of classic precedents. Like Alciphron's, they offer a series

[131] Text and translation with introduction, Benner and Fobes (1949) 3–339; selective text, tr. and comm. (21 letters), Costa (2001) xvi and 10–49. Study: Rosenmeyer (2001) 255–307.

[132] Bowie (1970/74); Anderson (1993); Swain (1996) 17–131; Costa (2001) xi–xvi.

[133] On Atticism, see Swain (1996) 17–64, Horrocks (1997) 71–86.

[134] Cf. n. 98 above.

[135] Text and translation with introduction, Benner and Fobes (1949) 387–545; selective text, tr. and comm. (8 letters), Costa (2001) xvi and 50–9. Study: Rosenmeyer (2001) 322–38.

of independent vignettes, challenging the reader to reconstruct the situation hinted at by each, rather than telling a connected story. But unlike Alciphron's they are anonymous, with neither the sender nor (usually) the intended recipient given a name; the point seems to be to throw the emphasis all the more strongly on the situations and relationships evoked (exile, rejection and so on) in themselves, perhaps also to mimic the experience of stumbling by chance on letters by correspondents of whom one knows nothing. Because literary history knows not one but four Philostratuses of the right period, the attribution of these letters is not entirely certain;[136] general opinion, however, favours the Philostratus who was also responsible for the *Lives of the Sophists* and the *Life of Apollonius of Tyana*.

(*f*) *Embedded letters*

Letters belong in Greek and Roman literature not only in their own right, but also as elements in other literary structures. The writing, sending, receiving, reading, forging, concealing and exploitation of letters feature as events in both historical and fictitious narrative, as well as in drama, and this often leads to the quotation of whole messages in histories, novels and plays.[137] Letters and the writing of letters may also feature in legal and political argumentation, and so form part of oratorical texts too. The exchange of **'Polyaenus'** and **'Circe'** (**17**) from Petronius' *Satyrica* is included in this anthology to represent letter-writing in the novel; a rich topic that can be pursued to great effect also through the works of Chariton (*Chaereas and Callirhoe*), Achilles Tatius (*Leucippe and Clitophon*) and Heliodorus (*Ethiopian Story*).[138] Besides functioning like speeches, to introduce voices other than the narrator's own, letters in novels can play a part in many further narrative manoeuvres, for instance of foreshadowing, irony, suspense, deceit and misdirection. They may also serve to stimulate reflection on the problems characters within the works have more generally in communicating and in securing the knowledge they need in order to overcome their troubles. This particular Petronian example helps forward both the *Satyrica*'s preoccupation with transgressive and not wholly successful sex, and its narrative play with situations and episodes from Homer's *Odyssey*. **Catiline**'s letter from

[136] Rosenmeyer (2001) 322; Anderson (1986) 291–6.

[137] Rosenmeyer (2001) 39–192.

[138] For letters in the Greek novel, with special reference to Chariton, Achilles Tatius and Heliodorus, Rosenmeyer (2001) 133–68.

Sallust's *Catiline* (**50**) shows one possible use of letters in historical texts, serving to illuminate the character and motivation of one of the major participants in the story, and to convey something of the historian's judgement upon him.[139] The other two instances, **Phoenicium** in Plautus' *Pseudolus* (**71**) and **Timarchides** in Cicero's *Second Verrine* (**72**) likewise illustrate the use of quoted letters in two further kinds of writing, drama[140] and legal oratory. But here there is a further element, as in both cases we see the letter in question being not only quoted, but also analysed and discussed in the process. Letter-reading as well as letter-writing can help build a scene or an argument.

3 LETTER-WRITING, LETTER-READING

The writing and reading of letters, as the preceding survey has made clear, bulked large in the ancient world, not only as a medium of communication, but also as a means of creating and sustaining personal, social or political relationships, and as a valued form of cultivated entertainment. Letters and the ability to write them were highly prized, at both a utilitarian and an aesthetic level: literate individuals of all ranks in society devoted time and pains to their correspondence, and preserved the results, whether as a purely private archive, or with a view to eventual publication; and the composition of stylish and/or contentful 'fictitious' letters was felt both as a stimulating challenge to a writer's abilities and as a source of educated pleasure to the knowledgeable reader. A number of general issues in the writing and reading of letters in antiquity now call for further attention.

(a) *Epistolary formulae*

As noted at the beginning of this Introduction, letters are most quickly and easily recognized as letters by certain features of their form. The most obviously formulaic element is the presence of an opening and closing salutation. In Greek, the standard, basic opening formula is ὁ δεῖνα τῶι δεῖνι χαίρειν (sc. λέγει), 'X (bids) joy to Y', but many additions and variations are possible:[141] sender and addressee can be named in the reverse order (τῶι δεῖνι ὁ δεῖνα – this seems to happen particularly in official letters, and

---

[139] For letters in the Greek historians, Rosenmeyer (2001) 45–60.
[140] For letters in tragedy, Rosenmeyer (2001) 61–97.
[141] See Exler 23–73; White (1986) 198–202; Cugusi (1989) 385.

later in letters between Christians); the relationship to the recipient can be specified (τῶι πατρί, τῶι ἀδελφῶι, etc.) or he can be styled φιλτάτωι or τιμιωτάτωι; χαίρειν can become πολλά or πλεῖστα χαίρειν. Sometimes χαίρειν is replaced by an alternative verb, though this seems always to be done to make a special point: εὐψυχεῖν or εὖ πράττειν in letters of condolence (where joy is out of place),[142] εὖ πράττειν or ὑγιαίνειν in letters to and from philosophers, demonstrating their superior moral seriousness.[143] The curter and cooler τῶι δεῖνι παρὰ τοῦ δεῖνος or ὁ δεῖνα τῶι δεῖνι (the latter mainly in business and official correspondence) are also found.[144] Latin shows a parallel, but more restricted set of variants on a basic 'X bids well-being to Y':[145] *aliquis alicui salutem dicit* (abbreviated to *s.d.*, *salutem*, or *s.*), expandable to *s(alutem) p(lurimam)*; *alicui aliquis s.d.* (first in Martial 8 *praef.* and frequent in Fronto); *alicui ab aliquo salutem* (from the mid-second century onwards). The simplest concluding formula in Greek is the bare imperative ἔρρωσο ('be strong/healthy'), but this too is commonly expanded to ἔρρωσθαί σε/ὑμᾶς εὔχομαι, with the possible further addition of vocatives (e.g. φίλτατε, κυρία μου ἀδελφή) and/or πολλοῖς χρόνοις ('for a long time', qualifying ἔρρωσθαι). εὐτύχει and διευτύχει ('be fortunate' and 'go on and on being fortunate') are sometimes found in more formal correspondence.[146] Latin too wishes healthy strength in conclusion, with *uale* or *cura ut ualeas*;[147] a very occasional variant is *(h)aue*.[148]

Also to some degree (though not so highly, or so obligatorily) formulaic is what comes immediately within these opening and closing formulae, just after the initial or just before the final salutation. Just after the opening is often the place to make a fuller wish for the correspondent's health, and to comment on one's own. In Greek the standard clichés are: πρὸ μὲν πάντων ὑγιαίνειν σε εὔχομαι and εἰ ἔρρωσαι εὖ ἂν ἔχοι· ὑγιαίνομεν δὲ καὶ αὐτοί.[149]

---

[142] See Koskenniemi (1956) 161–2, and cf. **46** in this anthology.

[143] See Lucian, *Pro lapsu* (64) 3–6, citing Plato, Epicurus and the Pythagoreans, and cf. **56** (but not **35**) in this anthology.

[144] Alexander the Great is said to have dropped χαίρειν from his letters to all but the most respected correspondents after his rise to eminence (Plutarch, *Phocion* 17.6). In edited collections the occurrence of an abbreviated salutation (sometimes just the bare τῶι δεῖνι) is usually a sign of editorial (or pseudepigraphic) activity, rather than a purposeful manipulation of the formula.

[145] Cugusi (1989) 385–6.   [146] Exler 74–7; White (1986) 198–202.

[147] Cugusi (1989) 386–8.   [148] E.g. **22** and **50** in this anthology.

[149] Exler 103–10. For more elaborate discussions of the correspondent's health, see **8–10**, **17** and **53**.

Latin has *ante omnia opto te bene ualere (cum tuis omnibus)* and *si uales bene est, ego quidem ualeo (s. u. b. e. e. q. u.)*.[150] Just before the final salutation is the place to reiterate one's personal concern for the recipient, pass on the greetings of others, and ask for one's own to be passed on to them: ἐπιμέλου δὲ καὶ σαυτοῦ ὅπως ὑγιαίνεις, ἀσπάζεται ὑμᾶς ὁ δεῖνα, ἀσπάζου τὸν δεῖνα;[151] *saluta aliquem / salutem dic alicui*.[152]

In the cases considered so far, both position and wording are more or less formulaic, with particular words and phrases (e.g. *salus*, ἀσπάζομαι, πρὸ μὲν πάντων, *ante omnia*) achieving the status of epistolary clichés. Yet further topics or thoughts gravitate to positions near the beginnings or ends of letters without such uniformity in the vocabulary used to express them.[153] Near the beginning is often felt as an appropriate place to talk about the process of correspondence itself, acknowledging receipt of a previous letter and recording one's feelings on doing so; asking for a letter (or more letters) when one has not been forthcoming, or not enough; explaining the speed and scale (or lack of it) of the response now being made. By the same token, this is the place to acknowledge receipt of other items sent with the correspondence, and give one's reactions to news.[154] Near the end is the place to pass a(nother) comment on the length of one's own letter, sweep up small miscellaneous items of news-in-brief and instructions, and look forward to the meeting for which the present epistolary contact is only an inferior substitute.[155]

One further formal feature of letters can usefully be considered here: the phenomenon of the so-called 'epistolary tenses'.[156] It is intrinsic to the business of communication by letter that there is a clearly felt gap in time between writing and reading:[157] what is present to the writer at time of writing will be past to the reader at time of reading. This fact is sometimes (though not always) acknowledged in the tenses chosen by letter-writers, who may use an imperfect or an aorist (more rarely a perfect or pluperfect) where we would automatically choose a present tense: aorist or

[150] Cugusi (1989) 386.   [151] Exler 113–16.   [152] Cugusi (1989) 388.

[153] These are the main subject of Koskenniemi (1956); see also White (1986) 204–13.

[154] Koskenniemi (1956) 64–87, cf. 186–9. In this anthology, see e.g. **5, 6, 7, 15, 16, 33, 35, 39, 41, 43, 47, 48, 52, 55**.

[155] E.g. in this anthology **3, 6, 7, 9, 10, 32, 39, 41, 48**.

[156] Koskenniemi (1956) 189–200; WS §1942. In this anthology, see **8, 13, 14, 56**.

[157] Such a gap exists for almost all writing and reading; the point is that it is felt with special clarity (and often commented on explicitly) in the case of letters.

perfect for an instantaneous present action ('I send you' – *misi*, ἀπέσταλκα), imperfect for a continued present action or state ('I am upset' – *dolebam*), and so on. This tendency to adopt the viewpoint of the recipient rather than the writer's own is one of the subtler ways in which the letter's status as a particularly personal, directed piece of writing comes out.

Historically, these conventions of letter-writing – for conventions they are, even though many of them are still in force with us, and so risk seeming 'natural' – did not emerge all at once. A glance at the first and earliest item in this anthology, the Berezan letter, illustrates the point. Although securely a letter – it is a short written text made for physical transmission between two parties, specifying both of them in its opening words – it uses none of what are later to become the standard formulae, but instead gives the air of improvising in the absence of any established norms, from the experience of sending messages by word of mouth. The same impression emerges from the works of the fifth-century historians: the letters quoted by Herodotus and Thucydides read like spoken messages or miniature speeches, and likewise use none of the later standard formulae.[158] It is with Xenophon, in *Cyrop.* 4.5.27–33, a supposed letter of Cyrus to Cyaxares, that the opening and closing formulae of salutation first appear in the surviving literary record; they do so, however, with a matter-of-factness that suggests Xenophon feels himself to be following convention rather than forging it, which in turn suggests that these formulae at least had achieved general acceptance well before the middle of the fourth century B.C.[159]

It is a plausible assumption that this general acceptance, and the subsequent stability of epistolary formulae over time, owed something to

---

[158] Hdt. 1.124, 3.40, 7.128, 8.22; Thuc. 1.128, 1.137, 7.8–15. In another way, however, Thucydides is closer to the later situation than Herodotus. Though both can use the verb ἐπιστέλλειν to denote sending instructions by letter (Hdt. 3.40.1; Thuc. 8.38.4), only Thuc. calls the message itself ἐπιστολή/-αί (e.g. 1.128–9, 132–3); Herodotus uses words denoting the material or format of the letter-medium (βυβλίον, 1.123, 3.40, 3.127–8, 6.4, 8.128; δελτίον, 7.239) or refers to γράμματα (5.14, 8.22). Cf. Stirewalt (1993) 67–87.

[159] This impression is supported by the fourth-century letter on lead by Mnesiergus (**2** in this collection), which all but employs the later standard opening (though lacking a formulaic conclusion). A story current in antiquity, known from Lucian *Pro lapsu* (64) 3 and the Atticist *Lexicon* of Moeris (s.v. χαίρειν, p. 213 Bekker), credited the politician Cleon with the first use of epistolary χαίρειν, in a dispatch to the Athenians announcing the victory at Sphacteria, but this seems to be based solely on a debatable interpretation of a passage from a fifth-century comedy.

elementary instruction in schools.[160] There is no direct evidence from the fifth, fourth or third centuries – the crucial period for their establishment – but later papyrus material which seems to come from a scholastic environment (e.g. item **49** in this anthology, a set of model letters in Greek and Latin from the fourth or fifth century A.D.), and the practical slant of many surviving works of epistolary theory (see below) pretty well guarantee that the proprieties of letter-writing featured to *some* extent in the curricula of *grammatistes* and *grammatikos* in the centuries A.D. Given that the need to be able to write acceptable letters, both for the socially lowly to deal with their superiors and rulers, and for the élite to maintain its social and political networks, was not new with the arrival of the Roman Empire, it is highly likely that the same educational provision was also made rather earlier.

(b) *Epistolary topics and themes*

As consideration of the formulae and clichés of letter-writing has begun to make clear, there are also certain themes and topics that seem to have a special tendency to crop up in letters – naïvely and straightforwardly in the correspondence of naïve and straightforward letter-writers, more elaborately, calculatedly and reflectively in the work of more sophisticated and reflective writers, whether composing 'real', utilitarian, or 'fictitious' correspondence. For the reflective writer and (perhaps even more) for the reflective reader, these come to be felt as particularly epistolary topics, helping to reinforce the epistolarity of the text containing them, as initially established by the presence of some of the verbal and structural formulae already discussed.[161]

Three broad areas of concern in particular stand out as distinctively epistolary, all fairly obviously related to the place of letters and letter-writing in common practical experience. The first centres on an awareness of the gap already referred to between the two parties to an epistolary exchange, the physical (or, occasionally, emotional) separation that made the composing of a letter necessary in the first place. This gap may be felt/characterized spatially, chronologically (in terms of the time it is anticipated the letter will take to bridge it), emotionally, or a mixture of any or all of these; and it may be felt/characterized more or less painfully, as anything from an

---

[160] White (1986) 189–91.

[161] These epistolary themes are the main subject of Thraede (1970); see also Koskenniemi (1956) 35–47, 172–80, and Altman (1982) 184–90.

opportunity (for fine writing, the demonstration of affection, and enjoyable reading), to a minor inconvenience, to a major personal misfortune (as in the case of a wretched exile and/or a pining lover). Correspondents are regularly found expressing their wish to narrow or abolish the gap, and do so in memory (recalling past meetings with the addressee) and in anticipation (looking forward, confidently or wistfully as the case may be, to a future one).[162] Less often, but occasionally, they express their gratitude for it.[163]

Going closely with awareness of a gap is a second set of concerns, about the adequacy or otherwise of a letter to close it. Letters are regularly conceived of, by writers and readers (critics) alike, as fragments of a conversation (dialogue) between the correspondents.[164] As such, they stand in for living speech, and for the living presence of the speakers, each representing its writer to its recipient in his or her inevitable absence. It counts as a special, arresting moment when a letter-writer presents or reads his or her own letter in person to the addressee.[165] But the effectiveness of letters in this role can be differently assessed, according to mood and circumstance: a letter can be welcomed and praised as a true image of the person who sends it, faithfully expressing his character, and bringing him vividly before the mind's eye; or it can be disparaged (in disappointment or mock modesty) as an unsatisfying stopgap, sadly incapable of working that same effect. According to the vantage-point of the moment, letters can thus be seen either as a bridge, linking the two parties, or as an unwelcome reminder that they are after all inescapably divided.[166] An extra twist is provided by letters of recommendation or introduction,[167] in which a standard element is the request from the sender (who is not present at the time the letter is

[162] For letters that in one way or another play on the idea of separation, see items **1**, **7**, **10**, **12**, **13**, **15**, **16**, **20**, **44**, **45**, **47** in this anthology. A special case in this connection is constituted by invitations (items **21–5**), which most actively of all seek to close the gap by directly summoning the addressee to the sender's presence.

[163] A nice example is Cic. *Ad fam.* 5.12 (= 22 SB).1: writing to L. Lucceius in March 55 B.C., to enquire about the possibility that L. might write a history of his consulship, C. confesses that it is easier to make such an enquiry by letter, as letters cannot blush (*epistula enim non erubescit*). Letters of rejection, or other bad news, are apt to arouse the same kind of feelings in their senders.

[164] E.g. **10**.27–30, **73**.223–4 and **76**.2 below.

[165] Rosenmeyer (2001) 186–7.

[166] For some letters in this anthology that make play of this range of thoughts, see **10**, **16**, **39**, **48** and **71**.

[167] Items **26–30** in this anthology.

read) to the recipient to treat the subject of the recommendation (who often is) as if himself. Such letters thus aim to make present not one person but two, to somewhat different ends. In 'fictitious' and pseudepigraphic epistolography, skill in the representation of character is a major criterion of success;[168] and epistolary theory, both following and reinforcing this trend in thinking about letters, likewise treats representation of character as a central consideration.[169]

Not often expressed in letters themselves, but available to any reader when this question of the representation of the person is in play, is the suspicion that a letter can misrepresent or misconstruct a personality as well as reflecting it faithfully. Both when recommending another, and when representing himself, a letter-writer is always putting on an act for the correspondent of the moment, and the contact of that act can bear all kinds of different relationships to the ways the correspondent (or his subject) is perceived by himself and others at other times. In this anthology, one might compare and contrast the ways Cicero presents himself to Atticus and to Julius Caesar (**6–7**, **28**), or Pliny to his wife, his friends and his Emperor (**16**, **30**, **66**); and one might also (as already suggested above) reflect on the way the ghost-written letters of Phalaris seem to toy with conflicting perceptions of the tyrant's real character,[170] or the placing of Catiline's letter in Sallust's history (**50**) prompts the reader to see its writer in a different light to that he seems to be trying to bathe in himself.

A third area of concern is the connection between letters and friendship. Letters have an important role to play in creating and sustaining friendships, whether between private individuals, or in contexts in which friendship has some larger public or organizational importance. Moreover, they have friendliness built into their standard, defining formulae at beginning and end. For, as we have seen, correspondents are compelled by convention to begin by wishing each other joy, courage, or well-being, and to end by wishing each other health and strength. In the light of this, a letter with hostile contents risks appearing an abuse of the medium. It is therefore not surprising that the letter is often conceptualized, and spoken of by practising letter-writers, as an essentially friendly form,[171] whether in its basic, utilitarian manifestations, or in such extensions as its use for moral

---

[168] See above, 24, 28 and 32 (on Ovid, pseudepigrapha and Aelian).
[169] See below, 44.
[170] See especially the headnotes to items **12**, **25**, **38** and **70**.
[171] See Demetrius, *Eloc* (**73**) 225, 231; Koskenniemi (1956) 35–7.

advice and exhortation.[172] Yet, as with the thought that letters exist to bridge gaps, so here too there is a darker obverse to this way of thinking about them. Everyone knows that the moods, tones and purposes of letter-writing are as varied as the moods, tones and purposes of social interaction in general, and that social interaction embraces hatred, malice and deceit as well as more benevolent feelings. And this in turn engenders a worry that any individual letter may itself be a hostile gesture or a possible source of harm only masquerading as a friendly communication. It perhaps follows from the standard motives of the compilers of letter-collections, which are normally laudatory and commemorative, that such worries do not surface much in the 'real' correspondence of historical figures. They are slightly more prominent in pseudepigrapha and fictitious collections: the letters of Phalaris can be cited again in this connection, as well as those of Chion of Heraclea, one of which (16) is an exercise in deliberate deceit. It is, however, in the treatment of letters in narrative and drama that such worries are most openly indulged and explored. It is often remarked that the first letter to be mentioned in Greek poetry, Proetus' to the King of Lycia in *Iliad* 6. 166–70, bears a deviously malicious message, urging the recipient to do away with the bearer. Thereafter, tragedy, history and the novel are full of instances of epistolary deceit and harm.[173]

   The connection of letters with friendship and the question of the representation of personality together indicate a very important general point about letters, with consequences for both writers and readers. More obviously than many other kinds of writing, letters exist in order to establish and conduct relationships, between senders and recipients. In this role they are constantly liable to become involved in games of etiquette and power, especially (but not only) when passing between correspondents of relatively high social status. Calculatingly or unconsciously, writers attempt to control style and presentation in the light of their sense of their own and their correspondents' status, and the particular relationship they are attempting to cultivate.[174] Readers, reading either a single message or (better still) a pair or series, are drawn to form their own conclusions about the true nature, honesty, realism, attractiveness, and success of the writers' strategies (and may also learn something about ancient manners

---

[172] Items **32–43** in this anthology.

[173] Rosenmeyer (2001) 39–192; cf. also Steiner (1994).

[174] Compare the recommendations of Julius Victor in item **75**.

and social conventions in the process). Perhaps the most obviously striking cases are those where there is (or is felt to be) a large discrepancy
in status between the parties to the exchange, when a humble petitioner
writes to one of the mighty, or a ruler to his subjects (or potential subjects).
Something of what is liable to happen in such cases can be seen in the letters collected in Section **B** below, where formal relationships of authority
are much in evidence.[175] But the implicit etiquette of messages between
Emperors and their tutors (**9**, **53–4**), or of a Bishop to male and female
correspondents (**40–1**, **55**), or a Senator to his wife, his friends and allies
and his Emperor (**16**, **30**, **52**, **66**), can be equally rewarding to ponder.[176]

In conclusion, it is worth pointing out that the question of epistolary
topics and themes can also be approached from quite another angle, as
the question of what ancient letter-writers choose *not* to write about in this
format. Ancient epistolary theorists sometimes explicitly define the letter in
part by what it cannot appropriately deal with: for instance, the exposition
of systematic, technical material, ruled out by Demetrius on the authority
of Aristotle.[177] Equally, it can be a rewarding question to ask of any individual letter-collection what topics that particular author seems concerned
to avoid or obscure.

(c) Epistolary theory in antiquity

A number of factors combine to make it wholly unsurprising that besides letters themselves, there survives also from antiquity a fair volume of
writing *about* letters. Practical need for instruction in the basic forms and
conventions, already mentioned, was one strand, but as with rhetorical instruction in antiquity more generally, there was also an aesthetic and social
component,[178] with which the ability to read and judge letters knowledge-
ably, as well as the ability to write them acceptably, came into the frame.
Social acceptability, at whatever level, depended in part for anyone on the
ability to compose a recognizable letter; for the educated élite, accustomed
in general to judging and being judged on verbal ability, it mattered to be

[175] See also the headnote to Section **B** below, 296.
[176] On the importance of considerations of social etiquette in Horace's *Epistles*,
see Mayer (1994) 7.
[177] See below, 43–4, 319.
[178] On the social and political aspect of élite literary (rhetorical) education, see
Swain (1996) 33–42.

able to write *elegantly* (and to recognize and appreciate elegant writing by others), and to follow the rules at a much higher level of sophistication. The fact that the letter was recognized as a particularly personal form – thus exposing the individual more nakedly to judgement than some others – can only have intensified performance anxiety, and thus the desire for guidance, still further.

Thus it is that the substantial surviving works of ancient epistolary theory reflect, in differing proportions, both the viewpoint of the letter-writer, keen to produce a good and proper letter, and that of the reader, keen to be able to judge what is good letter-writing by others (whether in their own personal correspondence, or in the reading of letters as literature). Both the earliest and the most reflective of these major discussions is chapters 223 to 235 of the work *De elocutione*, '*On style*', by **Demetrius**. Otherwise unknown, though later wrongly identified with Aristotle's pupil Demetrius of Phalerum, Demetrius and his work cannot be securely dated; scholarly consensus, for the moment at least, favours the mid-second century B.C.[179] If that date is right, Demetrius may stand quite close to the beginning of the tradition of analytical writing about letters. The Artemon to whom he refers as a predecessor, who seems to have edited Aristotle's letters and made at least some theoretical/critical observations in the process, is clearly earlier, but may not have written on anything like the same scale.[180] It may in part be because of Artemon's precedent, and the absence of any other comparable critical writing at this date, that Demetrius concentrates so heavily on the letters of Aristotle (though he also mentions Plato and Thucydides).

Although he casts his observations as prescriptions for good letter-writing, Demetrius' interest (in keeping with the overall thrust of his whole treatise) is at least as much in how a reader/critic can discriminate between good and bad performance in this domain. He lays particular stress (again, in keeping with the overall preoccupations of his treatise) on the requirement to maintain a suitable informality, and to avoid stylistic elaboration more appropriate to other kinds of writing; in particular, while acknowledging that letter and dialogue have something in common, he insists that there are some distinguishing marks that must be respected (223–6). Informality in its turn is connected with the status of the letter as a friendly medium (225, 229, 231) and a demand for clarity (226). Demetrius also highlights

[179] Innes (1995) 312–21; Kennedy (1972) 285–90 and (1989) 196–8. Full translation in Innes (1995), Russell and Winterbottom (1972) 171–215.

[180] Cf. **73**.223, with comm. ad loc.

the effectiveness of letters as conveyers of character (227), the desirability of brevity (228) and the need to avoid 'unepistolary' topics (230: he thus attempts to define letters in terms of characteristic content as well as style).

The other two treatises covered in this anthology are both rather later, dating from the fourth and fifth centuries A.D. They are also both more obviously slanted towards the practicalities of letter-writing, closer to the handbook than the theoretical essay. **C. Iulius Victor**'s discussion (**75**) comes, like Demetrius', as a kind of excursus or appendix to a larger work of more general rhetorical theory, following on from a similar discussion of conversational style (*De sermonibus* – compare Demetrius' connection of letters with dialogue).[181] Like Demetrius, he insists on the need for informality and the avoidance of high-style sentence-structure, and on the desirability of clarity (though, unlike Demetrius, he observes that deliberate obscurity, and even writing in code, can sometimes have its uses). Whereas Demetrius had distinguished between letters to private individuals and letters to rulers (on the basis again of Aristotle's correspondence?), Victor distinguishes official (*negotiales*) and private (*familiares*), each with its own proper variant of epistolary style. And unlike Demetrius, he pays attention to other features of an epistolary exchange: the fact that one cannot, as in face-to-face conversation, respond to requests for clarification, and that you cannot know what the circumstances and mood of your correspondent will be when your letter arrives and is read. He deals also with the etiquette of corresponding with those of different social status, the proper degree of elaboration in salutations, and proper caution in composing letters of recommendation.

Both Victor and Demetrius show only a moderate interest in the question of subdividing letters into different kinds. By contrast, this is central to a third text, the work *On Letter Form* (**76**), which survives in two versions, one attributed to **Libanius** and one to Proclus. After an opening declaration about the importance (sc. to one's status as an educated and cultivated individual) of cultivating a good epistolary style (1), and a definition of the letter form in general (privileging the ideas of separation, conversation, and practical ends) (2), the treatise settles to its main business, the distinction, definition and exemplification of forty-one allegedly separable kinds

---

[181] Text, Giomini and Celentano (1980); text and translation, Malherbe (1988) 62–5.

of letter, defined partly by content and purpose and partly by tone (3–45, 52–92). Though this exercise in minute taxonomy might seem to us to reflect above all the interests of the critic or editor, it is presented as advice for the practising letter-writer, and the evidence of both late-antique letter-collections and later handbooks suggest that this is to be taken seriously; indeed, it may be that 'Libanius'' categories have something important to teach us about the social attitudes of his class and time.

In between the definitions and examples of the different letter-types comes a discussion of epistolary style in general (46–51), making much the same points as Demetrius and Victor, though with some differences of emphasis. Particularly notable, and a sign of the changes in literary culture that had taken place in the Greek-speaking world between Demetrius and this treatise, is the way concern for careful style is now identified above all with Atticism, the imitation of the vocabulary and sentence-structure of the authors of the fifth and fourth centuries B.C.[182] Thus Demetrius' call for a careful but not over-elaborated style in letters is translated into the demand that they should atticize moderately, but avoid hyper-atticism.

Besides Demetrius, Victor and Proclus/Libanius, there is one other substantial discussion of letter-writing which, though not included in this anthology, needs brief mention. The Τύποι Ἐπιστολικοί, *Epistolary types*, of pseudo-Demetrius,[183] like the work of Proclus/Libanius, concentrates on the business of discriminating and illustrating different kinds of letter, listing twenty-one to Proclus/Libanius' forty-one. Addressed to one Heraclitus, this treatise presents itself as an educational aid, intended to improve what the author claims to be the low standards of epistolography prevailing in public life. All the author's effort goes into identifying and exemplifying the twenty-one kinds, and there is no general discussion of epistolary style. The date of the treatise is unknown; anything from 200 B.C. to A.D. 300 has been suggested, with a strong possibility that we are dealing with a text that has gone through several editions at different times.

It is perhaps remarkable, given the volume of rhetorical writing that survives from antiquity, how relatively few these discussions of epistolography are. In spite of what was said above about the teaching of letter-writing in school, it rather looks as if theoretical discussion of the topic (as opposed to basic practical instruction) was not an entirely inevitable part of mainstream

[182] On Atticism, see Horrocks (1997) 79–86, Swain (1996) 17–64.
[183] Text, Weichert (1910); text and translation, Malherbe (1988) 30–41.

education, just as the letter never quite made the grade as a major subject for ancient critical attention. This state of affairs may be contrasted with the integration of letter-writing into mainstream educational theory and training in the medieval period, as the major component of the *ars dictaminis/ars dictandi*.[184] However, it is not only to set treatises that one can look in antiquity for theoretical discussion of letter-writing. This went on also in the process of letter-writing itself. The letter is in any case a notably reflexive form – letter-writers find it easy enough to comment on the process while in the midst of it at the best of times. This may often issue only in descriptions for the correspondent's benefit of where the letter-writing is going on, or comments on the length (or otherwise) of the letter being written; but equally, in the hands of more reflective correspondents, it may issue in more elaborate discussion of the proprieties of letter-writing, that is to say in a species of epistolary theorizing. One example only is given in this anthology, item **74**, which finds Seneca explaining how the proper informality of the letter makes it also a highly suitable vehicle for moral instruction, but many others could be cited: *Ep.* 51 of Gregory of Nazianzus, for instance, or Cicero, *Fam.* 2.4 (= 48 SB).1, to mention only two particularly celebrated cases.[185] Such discussions in part repeat what their authors knew from more formal treatments, but constitute also a modest contribution to theorizing in their own right.

4 THE ORGANIZATION OF THIS ANTHOLOGY

As the preceding discussion has tried to show, there is no one uniquely right way to sort letters; categorizations are relative to the purposes and desires of the categorizers, and there are many possible desires and purposes with which letters can interestingly be approached. Accordingly, the labels and categories adopted in this anthology betray just one set of interests among many, and steer the reader towards ways of reading the contents that will, with luck, prove rewarding, but claim no other kind of authority. One grounding assumption was formulated above in §1: that attention to the shared features of the broad class 'letter' – across prose and verse, high and low style, real and invented correspondents and episodes of correspondence – makes for interesting and rewarding reading, both of the class and

[184] Murphy (1974) 194–268.
[185] Malherbe (1988) 58–61 (Gregory), 20–1 (Cicero, with further Ciceronian examples on 22–7).

of its individual constituents. Placing and reading a papyrus recommendation ('real', and strictly utilitarian) next to a Ciceronian example ('real', but
republished for aesthetic and commemorative effect), next to a Horatian
Epistle (a verse transposition of the form) gives an opportunity to understand better the frame of reference within which each of them works, and
to reflect more effectively on the whole institution that they jointly spring
from. There is thus, in the major headings, no sorting by degrees of 'reality' or 'fictionalization' (though the reader may of course cut across this by
jumping between what look like equivalently 'fictitious' items). Instead, the
major categorization is partly by function (information (news), invitation,
recommendation, instruction, consolation, self-defence), partly by theme
(erotic relations, literary concerns; cf. also the sub-themes of exile in the
'news' letters, and simple living in the letters of instruction), and partly
by context of communication, with a special section for correspondents
writing in some formal, official capacity on an item of public business. If
there seems to be a lack of theoretical rigour here, that is intentional, or at
least accepted. The aim is to illustrate, short of exhaustiveness, the range
of transactions letters can be implicated in, and what themes and motifs
come and go according to specific contexts and purposes (or pervade the
kind of writing as a whole), and thus to illuminate both the diversity and
the coherence of the kind 'letter'. Ideally, this will mean that the anthology
can serve either as a self-standing reader in 'the letter', or as a source of
comparison-pieces to accompany a reading of one of the letter-writers most
often studied on their own (above all Cicero, Horace, Ovid, Seneca and
Pliny).

A PRIVATE LETTERS (1–60)

1 ACHILLODOROS (OLBIA/BEREZAN, *c*. 500 B.C.)

(*SEG* 26.845.3; cf. Chadwick [1973])

Ὤ Πρωταγόρη, ὁ πατήρ τοι ἐπιστέλλε. ἀδικε͂ται ὑπὸ Ματάσυος,
δο͂λο͂ται γάρ μιγ καὶ το͂ φορτηγεσίο͂ ἀπεστέρεσεν. ἐλθὼμ παρ'
Ἀναξαγόρην ἀπήγησαι, φησὶ γὰρ αὐτὸν Ἀναξαγόρεω δο͂λον
ἔναι μυθεόμενος· τἄμ' Ἀναγόρης ἔχε͂, καὶ δο͂λο͂ς καὶ δο͂λας κοἰκίας. ὁ
δὲ ἀναβῶι τε καὶ οὔ φησιν ἔναι οὐδὲν ἑωυτῶι τε καὶ Ματασιν καί
φησιν ἔναι ἐλεόθερος καὶ οὐδὲν ἔναι ἑωυτι καὶ Ματατασυ. ἒ δὲ τί
αὐτῶι κἀναξαγόρηι αὐτοὶ οἴδασιν κατὰ σφᾶς αὐτός. ταῦτ' Ἀνα-
ξαγόρηι λέγε͂ν καὶ τῆ γυναικί. ἕτερα δέ τοι ἐπιστέλλε͂. τὴμ μητέρα
καὶ το͂ς ἀδεφεὺς † ιεσσιν † ἐν Ἀρβινάτηισιν ἄγε͂ν ἐς τὴμ πόλιν,
αὐτὸς † δεε͏ονεορος † ἐλθὼμ παρά † μινθυωρα † καταβήσεται.

Ἀχιλλοδώρο͂ τὸ μολίβδιον παρὰ τὸμ παῖδα κἀναξαγόρην.

2 MNESIERGOS (4TH CENTURY B.C.)

(*SIG*³ III 1259)

Μνησίεργος ἐπέστειλε τοῖς οἴκοι χαίρε͂ν καὶ ὑγιαίνε͂ν· καὶ αὐτὸς
οὕτως ἔφασ[κ]ε [ἔχε͂ν]. στέγασμα, εἴ τι βόλεστε, ἀποπέμπσαι ἢ
ὢας ἢ διφθέρας ὡς εὐτελεστας καὶ μὴ σισυρωτὰς καὶ κατύματα:
τυχὸν ἀποδώσω.

φέρε͂ν ἰς τὸν κέραμον τὸν χυτρικόν, ἀποδο͂ναι δὲ Ναυσίαι ἢ Θρασυκλῆι ἢ θυιῶι.

3 APOLLONIOS (EGYPT, 3RD CENTURY A.D.)

(*P.Oxy.* 2783)

Ἀπολλώνιος Ἀρτεμᾶ τῶ ἀδελφῶι χαίρειν· πρὸ μὲν παντὸς εὔχομε πᾶσι τοῖς θεοῖς τὰ ἐν βίω σοι κάλλιστα ὑπαρχθῆναι· καὶ
νῦν τῶι ἀδελφῶι σου ἔδωκα (δραχμὰς) φ' καὶ τῶ Πτολεμαίω ἤδη
μετεβαλόμην ἀπὸ μέρους, καθὼς ἠθέλησεν· θαυμάζω δὲ ὅτι εἰς μὲν

1 ACHILLODOROS

Protagoras, your father sends you these instructions. He is being wronged by Matasys, because he is trying to enslave him and has deprived him of his cargo-vessel. Go to Anaxagoras and tell him, because he insists that he is the slave of Anaxagoras, claiming 'Anagoras has my property, male and female slaves and houses.' But he complains loudly and denies that he and Matasys have any business with each other, and insists that he is a free man, and Matatasys and he have no business with each other. But if he and Anaxagoras have some business with each other, they know it between themselves. Tell this to Anaxagoras and his wife. He has further instructions for you: take your mother and your brothers [? who are ?] among the Arbinatae to the city, while [?] himself will come to [?] and go down [?].

Achillodoros' piece of lead, to his son and Anaxagoras.

2 MNESIERGOS

Mnesiergos bids greetings and good health to the people at home; he says that he too is like that. Dispatch a covering, if you please, sheepskins or goatskins, the cheapest possible and not shaped into cloaks, and shoe-soles; I will make a return when I get the chance.

Take to the earthenware pottery and give to Nausias or Thrasycles or his son.

3 APOLLONIOS

Apollonios to his brother Artemas, greetings. Before all else, I pray to all the gods that things in your life may be of the finest. Just now I gave 500 drachmas to your brother, and I have already remitted a part payment to Ptolemaeos, just as he wanted. But I am surprised

ἔλαιον τὸ τοσοῦτο ἀργύριον ἐχώρησαι· ἐξ δὶς ἔβαλας· ἐνθάδε
γὰρ τὸ Ἀμμωνιακὸν (δραχμῶν) σκ, τὸ δὲ Ἀὐασιτικὸν (δραχμῶν)
σ· ὅθεν ἡ εἰς ἄλλην χρίαν λαμμβάνις δυναμένην ἡμᾶς ὠφελῆσαι,
καλῶς ποιεῖς· ἔγραψας δέ μοι ὡς ἐμοῦ σε κατακόπτοντος ἄποντα,
καὶ τοῦτο δὲ χείρω τῶν πρώτων· εἰ γὰρ ἀπαρτὶ ἐπίστασαί
μου τὴν γνώμην, οὐκ ὀφίλις ἄνθρωπος κρίνεσθαι· καὶ ἄλλοτέ
σοι ἔγραψα ὅτι οὖτ' ἐγὼ τὸν κάμηλον Ἑρμία κατέσχον οὔτε
ἄλλου τινός· εἰ δὲ ταῦτα θέλις με γράφιν, γράφω σοι· τάχα γὰρ
οὐκ ἀναγινώσκις ἃ σοι γράφω· ὅσα δὲ ἔπαθαν ἐνθάδε χάριν
τῶν καμήλων τῆς Κόπτου ὅ τε Ἀμμωνᾶς καὶ ὁ αὐτοματάρις
Ἀνθρωπᾶς καὶ οἱ ἄλλοι πάντες δύνασαι ἀκοῦσαι ἀπὸ τοῦ
ἀδελφοῦ σου· οἱ δὲ τάμροι σου οἱ κατάρατοι στρηνιῶσι καὶ
πολλὰ ὑπὲρ αὐτῶν προῆλθα χάριν σοῦ ἐὰ[ν...........]
βουλὴν ἔχω, ἐρῶ σοι· ἵνα μὴ δοκῶ πολλὰ γράφιν, ἐρρῶσθαί
σεχομαι.

Margin: τὸν τύφλον ὁ ἀδελφός σου ἀνήκασαί μαι πωλῆσαι.

Reverse: Ἀρτεμᾶ π(αρὰ) Ἀπολλωνίου.

4 KOPRES (ALEXANDRIA, EARLY 4TH
CENTURY A.D.)

(*P. Oxy.* 2601)

Κοπρῆς Σαραπιάδι ἀδελφῇ πλεῖστα χαίρειν· πρὸ μὲν πάντων
εὔχομε ὑμᾶς ὁλοκληρῖν παρὰ τῶ κυρί(ω) θ[(ε)ῶ.] γινώσκιν σε θέλω
ὅτι τῆ ια΄ εἰσήλθαμεν καὶ ἐγνώσθη ἡμῖν ὅτι οἱ προσερχόμενοι
ἀναγκάζονται θύειν καὶ ἀποσυστατικὸν ἐποίησα τῶ ἀδελφῶ
μου καὶ μέχρι τούτου οὐδὲν ἐπράξαμεν ἐκατηχήσαμεν δὲ ῥήτορα
τῆ ι. ἵνα τῆ ιδ΄ εἰσαχθῇ τὸ πρᾶγμα περὶ τῶν ἀρούρω(ν). εἴ τι
δὲ ἐὰν πράξωμεν γράφω σοι· οὐδὲν δέ σοι ἔπεμψα ἐπειδὴ εὗρον
αὐτὸν Θεόδωρον ἐξερχόμενον· ἀποστέλλω σοι δὲ αὐτὰ διὰ ἄλλου
ταχέως· γράφε δὲ ἡμῖν περὶ τῆς ὁλοκληρίας ὑμῶν πάντων καὶ πῶς
ἔσχεν Μαξιμῖνα καὶ Ἀσενά· καὶ εἰ δυνατόν ἐστιν ἐρχέσθω μετὰ
τῆς μητρός σου ἵνα θεραπευθῇ τὸ λευκωμάτιον· ἐγὼ γὰρ εἶδον

that so much money went on olive oil. You really threw two sixes! Because here Ammoniac (Siwa) oil sells at 220 drachmas and Oasis oil at 200 drachmas. So if you can buy for some other purpose that can actually do us some good, you'll be doing well. You wrote to me claiming that I am cutting you down in your absence, and worse than before too. Yes, because if you only this moment understand what's in my mind, you do not deserve to be counted as a human being. I have already written to you on another occasion that I did not detain Hermias' camel or anyone else's. If this is what you want me to write, I'll write it to you; because perhaps you don't read what I write to you. What Ammonas and Anthropas the toy-maker and all the others went through on account of the Coptos camels, you can hear from your brother. Your blasted bulls are running wild and I have appeared in court several times because of them, thanks to you. If . . . I have, I shall tell you. So that you won't think I'm writing too long a letter, I'll bid you keep well.

Margin: (P.S.) Your brother forced me to sell the blind one.

Reverse: To Artemas from Apollonios.

4 KOPRES

Kopres to his sister Sarapias, very many greetings. Before all else, I pray for your good health before the Lor(d) G(o)d. I want you to know that we arrived on the 11th and it became known to us that people presenting themselves in court are being made to sacrifice and I made a power-of-attorney in favour of my brother and so far we have accomplished nothing, but we instructed an advocate on the 12th (?), so that the case about the land could be brought in on the 14th. If in the event that we accomplish anything, I'll write to you. I've sent you nothing since I found Theodoros himself setting out. I'll send them to you by another hand soon. Write to us about the health of all of you and how Maximina has been and Asena. And if it's possible let him (her?) come with your mother so that his (her?) leukoma can be cured, because I've seen others cured myself.

ἄλλους θεραπευθέντας· ἐρρῶσθαί σε εὔχομε· ἀσπάζομαι πάντας τοὺς ἡμῶν κατ᾽ ὄνομα.

Last three lines in margin and on reverse: in margin from καὶ Ἀσενά; on reverse from ἵνα θεραπευθῆ.

Reverse: ἀπ(όδος) τῇ ἀδελφῇ π(αρὰ) Κοπρῆτος Ϙθ.

5 CLAUDIUS TERENTIANUS (ALEXANDRIA,
EARLY 2ND CENTURY A.D.)

(*P. Mich.* viii 468 (inv. 5390) = *CPL* 251)

Claudius Terentianus Claud[i]o Tiberi[ano pat]ri suo ed domino plur[i]mam sal[utem]. ante omnia opto te bene [u]alere, que m[ihi ma]xime uota [su]nt. scia[s me, p]ater, a[ccepisse] res quas mi misisti per … ium Th … uetranum et per Nemesianum … et palliolum, et ago tibi gratias quod me dign[um] habuisti et sequrum fecisti. misi t[i]bi, pater, per Martialem imboluclum concosu[tu]m in quo habes amicla par unu amictoria p[ar] unu sabana par unu saccos par unu gla[b]alum ligni. emeram aute illuc con culcitram et pulbin[o] et me iacentem in liburna sublata mi s[unt]. et abes in inboluclum amictorium singlare, hunc tibi mater mea misit. et accipias caueam gallinaria in qua ha[bes] sunthe[seis] uitriae et phialas quinarias p[ar u]nu et calices paria sex et chartas sch[ola]res duas et in charta atramentum et calamos q[u]i[nq]ue et panes Alexandrinos uiginti. rogo te, [p]a[t]er, ud contentus sis ista. modo si non iacu[i]sse speraba me pluriam tibi missiturum ed itarum spero si uixero. rogo te, pater, si tibi uidebitur ut mittas mihi inde caligas cori subtalare⟨s⟩ ed udones par. caligae autem nucl[e]atae nugae sunt, bis me im mensem calcio. et rogo ut mi mittas dalabram. ea q[u]am mi missisti optionem illan mi ab[s]tulisse, sed gratias illi ag[o …] … e. alta mi praestat. ed praeterea oro [et rogo] te, p[ater, ut] contin[uo mih]i [resc]rib[as de] salutem t[ua]m te ha[b]ere bo[na] re accept[am. s]ollicitus sum autem de uic[e] in do nese mihi rescribas. et si deus uolueret spero me frugaliter [u]iciturum et in cohortem [tra]nsferri.

I pray that you are well; my best wishes to all our friends by name.

Reverse: Del(iver) to my sister, f(rom) Kopr(es) 99.

5 CLAUDIUS TERENTIANUS

Claudius Terentianus to his father and lord Claudius Tiberianus, warmest greetings. Before all else I pray that you are well, which is my greatest wish. Let me tell you, father, that the things you sent me with the veteran . . . ius Th . . . and with Nemesianus . . . and the short mantle, have arrived safely; thank you for thinking me worth the trouble and setting my mind at rest. With Martialis, father, I'm sending you a tarpaulin sewn together in which you have one pair of cloaks, one pair of scarves, one pair of linen cloths, one pair of sacks, and a wooden bedstead. I bought it together with a small mattress and a pillow, and while I was lying ill on the ship they were stolen from me. In the tarpaulin you also have a one-ply scarf; my mother sends you this. Please find also a chicken coop, in which you have some sets of glassware, one pair of quinarius bowls, six pairs of cups and two rolls of exercise-paper, and inside the paper ink and five pens and twenty Alexandrian loaves. I ask you, father, to be content with this. If only I had not been lying ill, I hoped as I would send you more, and again I hope I shall if I live. I ask you, father, if you agree, to send me from there some low-sided boots and a pair of felt socks. Pitted boots [= boots with buttons?] are rubbish; I need new footwear twice a month. And I ask you to send me a pick. The lieutenant took the one that you sent me, but I am grateful to him for providing me . . . And besides I ask you please, father, to write back to me straight away about your health, that you have been well. I worry that there may be trouble at home unless you write back to me. And god willing I hope as I'll live soberly and get my transfer into a battalion.

hic a[ut]em sene aer[e ni]hil fit neque epistulae commandaticiae
nihil ualunt nesi si qui sibi aiutaueret. rogo, pater, ud continuo mihi
rescribas. ed [sci]as Carpum hic errasse, ed inu[e]ntus est Dios in le-
gione, et a[cce]pisse me pro illo (denarios) VI. sal[u]tat te mater mea
ed pater ed fratres mei, et scias domo perb[e]ne omnia recte esse.
sal[u]ta Aprodisia et Isituchen. sal[ut]a Arium centurionem con
suis ed Saturninum scriba con suis et Capitonem centurione con
[s]u[i]s et Cassium optionem con suis [et T]urranium optionem
con suis [et Sal]lustium con [s]uis et Terentium gubernatorem
[e]t Frontone con suis et Sempronium Hitalicum et Puplicium et
Seuerinu et Mar[c]ellu collega tuum et Lucium. saluta Serenum
scriba c[o]n suis. saluta omnes contubernales nostrous. uale
mihi.

Margin: bene ualere te opto multis annis felicissime im perpetuo.
ual(e).

Reverse: [Claudius]   Terentianus   Claudio   Tib[eriano.] . . .
Terentianus. [tr]ad[e] C[l]a[ud]io T[iberian]o p[at]ri a Claudio
Terentiano filio.

6 M. TULLIUS CICERO (TUSCULUM,
MAY/JUNE 67 B.C.)

(Ad Atticum I .10 = 6 SB)

Cicero Attico sal. **1** cum essem in Tusculano (erit hoc tibi pro illo tuo
'cum essem in Ceramico'), uerum tamen cum ibi essem, Roma puer
a sorore tua missus epistulam mihi abs te adlatum dedit nuntiauitque
eo ipso die post meridiem iturum eum qui ad te proficisceretur. eo
factum est ut epistulae tuae rescriberem aliquid, breuitate temporis
tam pauca cogerer scribere. **2** primum tibi de nostro amico placando
aut etiam plane restituendo polliceor. quod ego etsi mea sponte ante
faciebam, eo nunc tamen et agam studiosius et contendam ab illo
uehementius quod tantam ex epistula uoluntatem eius rei tuam
perspicere uideor. hoc te intellegere uolo, pergrauiter illum esse

But nothing will get done here without money and letters of recommendation are useless unless a man looks after himself as well.
I ask you, father, to write back to me straight away. Let me tell
you that Carpus has come here in his wanderings and Dios has
turned up in the army, and I have received six denarii on his behalf. My mother and father and brothers send you greetings, and
you should know that everything is going thoroughly well and good
at home. Best wishes to Aphrodisia and Isityche. Best wishes to
centurion Arius and his family, and Saturninus the scribe and his,
and Centurion Capito and his, and lieutenant Cassius and his, and
lieutenant Tyrannius and his, and Sallustius and his, and Terentius
the pilot, and Fronto and his family, and Sempronius Italicus, and
Publicius, and Severinus, and your colleague Marcellus, and Lucius.
Best wishes to Serenus the clerk and his family. Best wishes to all
our friends. Keep well.

Margin: I pray for your good health for many years to come with
every happiness for ever. Farewell.

Reverse: Claudius Terentianus to Claudius Tiberianus. Deliver to
my father Claudius Tiberianus from his son Claudius Terentianus.

6 M. TULLIUS CICERO

Cicero to Atticus, good health. **1** I was in my place at Tusculum –
take that in return for your 'I was in the Ceramicus' – as I was
saying, I was there when a slave sent by your sister from Rome
brought me a letter which had been delivered from you, and told
me that someone who was going to join you would be leaving this
very afternoon. That's how it came about that I should be writing
a reply of some sort to you, but should be forced by lack of time
to write so briefly. **2** First, I give you my word about placating our
friend or even bringing him round altogether. Even though I was
already working on this of my own accord, I shall now get on with
it all the more enthusiastically and will put all the more pressure on
him because I think I see from your letter how strongly you wish

offensum; sed quia nullam uideo grauem subesse causam, magno opere confido illum fore in officio et in nostra potestate. **3** signa nostra et Hermeraclas, ut scribis, cum commodissime poteris, uelim imponas, et si quid aliud οἰκεῖον eius loci quem non ignoras reperies, et maxime quae tibi palaestrae gymnasique uidebuntur esse. etenim ibi sedens haec ad te scribebam, ut me locus ipse admoneret. praeterea typos tibi mando quos in tectorio atrioli possim includere et putealia sigillata duo. **4** bibliothecam tuam caue cuiquam despondeas, quamuis acrem amatorem inueneris; nam ego omnis meas uindemiolas eo reseruo, ut illud subsidium senectuti parem. **5** de fratre, confido ita esse ut semper uolui et elaboraui. multa signa sunt eius rei, non minimum quod soror praegnans est. **6** de comitiis meis, et tibi me permisisse memini et ego iam pridem hoc communibus amicis qui te exspectant praedico, te non modo non arcessi a me sed prohiberi, quod intellegam multo magis interesse tua te agere quod agendum esset hoc tempore quam mea te adesse comitiis. proinde eo animo te uelim esse quasi mei negoti causa in ista loca missus esses. me autem eum offendes erga te et audies quasi mihi si quae parta erunt non modo te praesente sed per te parta sint. Tulliola tibi diem dat, sponsorem non appellat.

7 M. TULLIUS CICERO (BRUNDISIUM, 29 APRIL 58 B.C.)

(*Ad Atticum* 3.7 = 52 SB)

Cicero Attico sal. **1** Brundisium ueni a.d. XIIII Kal. Mai. eo die pueri tui mihi a te litteras reddiderunt, et alii pueri post diem tertium eius diei alias litteras attulerunt. quod me rogas et hortaris ut apud te in Epiro sim, uoluntas tua mihi ualde grata est et minime noua. esset consilium mihi quidem optatum si liceret ibi omne tempus consumere; odi enim celebritatem, fugio homines,

this matter to be settled. One thing I do want you to realize is that he is very seriously offended; but since I can't see any serious reason at the bottom of it, I am fully confident that he will do as he ought and do as I tell him. **3** As for my statues and Heracles herms, yes please, do as you suggest and ship them whenever you conveniently can, along with anything else you may find that is *convenable* you know where, especially what you think right for an exercise yard and lecture theatre. In fact I am sitting there now as I write this to you, so that the place itself reminds me. Besides, I commission you to get me some low-reliefs that I can set into the plasterwork in the small entrance hall, and two carved well-panels. **4** Mind you don't engage your library to anyone, however ardent a suitor you may find. I am saving up every little scrap I can glean so as to be able to buy it as a prop for my old age. **5** As for my brother, I am sure things are as I have always wanted and worked for. There are many tell-tale signs, not least that your sister is expecting. **6** As for my election, I remember that I left the decision to you, and I have for ages been telling friends we have in common who expect you back that, far from summoning you, I positively forbade you to come because I realize that it is much more important for you to be doing what has to be done at this time than it is for me to have you here for the election. So I should like you to feel as though you had been sent over there on business of mine. My own feelings towards you, as you will find for yourself, and hear from others, are as if any gains I may make will be made not only in your presence but also by your doing. Little Tullia is bringing you to court, but without calling on your guarantor.

7 M. TULLIUS CICERO

Cicero to Atticus, good health. **1** I reached Brundisium on 17 April. Your slaves gave me a letter from you that day, and others brought me another two days after that. I am very touched but not in the least surprised by your kindness in inviting me so pressingly to stay at your place in Epirus. It's a plan that would appeal to me very much if I could spend all the time there – I hate crowds and shun

lucem aspicere uix possum, esset mihi ista solitudo, praesertim tam familiari in loco, non amara. sed itineris causa ut deuerterer, primum est deuium, deinde ab Autronio et ceteris quadridui, deinde sine te. nam castellum munitum habitanti mihi prodesset, transeunti non est necessarium. quod si auderem, Athenas peterem. sane ita cadebat ut uellem. nunc et nostri hostes ibi sunt et te non habemus et ueremur ne interpretentur illud quoque oppidum ab Italia non satis abesse, nec scribis quam ad diem te exspectemus. **2** quod me ad uitam uocas, unum efficis ut a me manus abstineam, alterum non potes ut me non nostri consili uitaeque paeniteat. quid enim est quod me retineat, praesertim si spes ea non est quae nos proficiscentis prosequebatur? non faciam ut enumerem miserias omnes in quas incidi per summam iniuriam et scelus non tam inimicorum meorum sed inuidorum, ne et meum maerorem exagitem et te in eundem luctum uocem; hoc adfirmo, neminem umquam tanta calamitate esse adfectum, nemini mortem magis optandam fuisse. cuius oppetendae tempus honestissimum praetermissum est; reliqua tempora sunt non iam ad medicinam sed ad finem doloris. **3** de re publica uideo te colligere omnia quae putes aliquam spem mihi posse adferre mutandarum rerum; quae quamquam exigua sunt, tamen, quoniam placet, exspectemus. tu nihilominus, si properaris, nos consequere. nam aut accedemus in Epirum aut tarde per Candauiam ibimus. dubitationem autem de Epiro non inconstantia nostra adferebat sed quod de fratre, ubi eum uisuri essemus, nesciebamus; quem quidem ego nec quo modo uisurus nec ut dimissurus sim scio. id est maximum et miserrimum mearum omnium miseriarum. ego et saepius ad te et plura scriberem nisi mihi dolor meus cum omnis partis mentis tum maxime huius generis facultatem ademisset. uidere te cupio. cura ut ualeas. d. prid. Kal. Mai. Brundisio proficiscens.

human company, I can hardly bear to see the light of day, so the solitude, especially in such a friendly place, would not be hard for me to take. But as for stopping off there en route, for a start it is out of my way, then it's only four days' journey from Autronius and the others, and on top of that you wouldn't be there. A fortified place would be useful to me as somewhere to live, but I don't need it just to pass through. If I dared, I should head for Athens. Certainly things were shaping up at one stage to make me want that. But as it is, there are enemies of mine there, I don't have you, and I am afraid that they may stipulate that even Athens isn't far enough from Italy, and you don't say in your letter when I am to expect you. **2** Your exhortation to me to live is effective to the extent that you prevent me doing violence to myself, but you cannot also prevent me regretting my decision and the fact that I am still alive. What is there to hold me back, especially if I no longer have the hope that accompanied me when I set off? I shan't go on to enumerate all the tribulations I have incurred through the excessive maleficence and villainy not so much of people who hate me as of those who envy me, since I don't want either to revive my own grief or to invite you into the same state of mourning. What I do claim is that no one ever suffered such a crushing blow, or had stronger reason to pray for death. The most honourable time to meet it has been let slip; the time that remains can no longer cure my pain but only put an end to it. **3** I see you are collecting every scrap of political news that you think can bring me some hope of a change for the better; they don't add up to much, but since this is what you want, let us wait and see. If you hurry, you can catch me up even so, because I will either go on to Epirus or travel slowly through Candavia. My hesitation about Epirus is not down to fickleness on my part but because of uncertainty about where I am to meet my brother, though I really don't know how I can bring myself to see him or say good-bye to him. This is the greatest and most miserable of all my miseries. I would write to you more often and at greater length if my grief had not robbed me of all my mental powers, and especially of this sort of ability. I long to see you. Take care of yourself. Dispatched 29 April, on departure from Brundisium.

8 M. TULLIUS CICERO (CAIETA PORT,
8 JUNE 49 B.C.)

(Ad familiares 14.7 = 155 SB)

Tullius Terentiae suae s.p. **1** omnis molestias et sollicitudines
quibus et te miserrimam habui, id quod mihi molestissimum
est, et Tulliolam, quae nobis nostra uita dulcior est, deposui et
eieci. quid causae autem fuerit postridie intellexi quam a uobis discessi. χολὴν ἄκρατον noctu eieci. statim ita sum leuatus
ut mihi deus aliquis medicinam fecisse uideatur. cui quidem tu
deo, quem ad modum soles, pie et caste satis facies. **2** nauem
spero nos ualde bonam habere. in eam simul atque conscendi,
haec scripsi. deinde conscribam ad nostros familiares multas epistulas, quibus te et Tulliolam nostram diligentissime commend-
abo. cohortarer uos quo animo fortiores essetis nisi uos fortiores
cognossem quam quemquam uirum. et tamen eius modi spero
negotia esse ut et uos istic commodissime sperem esse et me aliquando cum similibus nostri rem publicam defensuros. **3** tu primum ualetudinem tuam uelim cures; deinde, si tibi uidebitur, uillis
iis utere quae longissime aberunt a militibus. fundo Arpinati bene
poteris uti cum familia urbana si annona carior fuerit. Cicero bellissimus tibi salutem plurimam dicit. etiam atque etiam uale. D. VII
Id. Iun.

9 M. CORNELIUS FRONTO (A.D. 154/6)

(Ad M. Caesarem 5.55)

Domino meo. **1** cholera usque adeo adflictus sum ut uocem
amitterem, singultirem, suspirio tum angerer, postremo uenae
deficerent, sine ullo pulsu uenarum animo male fieret; denique con-
clamatus sum a nostris; neque sensi aliquamdiu: ne balneo quidem
aut frigida aut cibo recreandi me ac fouendi medicis tempus aut
occasio data, nisi post uesperam micularum minimum cum uino
destillatum gluttiui. ita focilatus totus sum. postea per continuum

8 M. TULLIUS CICERO

Tullius to his dear Terentia, best health. **1** All the troubles and worries with which I have kept you in a state of utter wretchedness too – for which I am heartily sorry – and dear Tullia as well, whom I love more than my own life, I have now got rid of and discharged. I realized the cause the day after I left you: it was undiluted bile, and I brought it up during the night. The relief was so immediate that I thought some god or another had treated me; please give that god his due with a pure and pious offering, as you always do. **2** I am confident that we have a really good ship. I am writing this just after boarding her; I'll go on to write a number of letters to my friends, and will commend you and dear Tullia to their care with the utmost warmth. I would exhort you both to be braver if I didn't know very well that you are braver than any man. At the same time I trust that everything is turning out so that you will be perfectly comfortable where you are and that I will at last be fighting for the commonwealth in the company of like-minded allies. **3** As for you, I should like you please above all to look after yourself; but also, if you agree, you will make use of the villas that are furthest away from army units. You could very well occupy the farm at Arpinum with the town household if the price of food goes up. Handsome young Cicero sends you warmest greetings. Once again, keep well. 8 June.

9 M. CORNELIUS FRONTO

To my Lord. **1** I have suffered such a bilious attack that I lost my voice and began to gasp, then had to struggle painfully for breath, and finally my blood-vessels failed, and as the pulse left them I became unconscious. In short, my people gave me up for lost, and it was some little time before I regained consciousness. The doctors couldn't find a suitable moment for reviving me or treating me even with a warm bath or cold water or food, except that after nightfall I managed to swallow the tiniest of crumbs moistened with wine, and in this way was completely revived. But for three whole days

triduum uocem non recuperaui. sed nunc deis iuuantibus commodissime ualeo, facilius ambulo, clarius clamito: denique, si dei
iuuabunt, cras uehiculo uectari destino. si facile silicem toler-
auero, quantum pote ad te curram. tum uixero quom te uidero.
a.d. VII Kal. Romae proficiscar, sei dei iuuabunt. **2** uale, domine
dulcissime, desiderantissime, causa optima uitae meae. dominam
saluta.

10 P. OVIDIUS NASO (TOMI, A.D. ? 11/12)

(*Tristia* 5.13)

Hanc tuus e Getico mittit tibi Naso salutem
    litore, si quisquam, quo caret ipse, potest.
aeger enim traxi contagia corpore mentis,
    libera tormento pars mihi ne qua uacet,
perque dies multos lateris cruciatibus uror,   5
    saeua quod immodico frigore laesit hiems.
si tamen ipse uales, aliqua nos parte ualemus:
    quippe mea est umeris fulta ruina tuis.
quid, mihi cum dederis ingentia pignora, cumque
    per numeros omnes hoc tueare caput,   10
quod tua me raro solatur epistola, peccas,
    remque piam praestas, sed mihi uerba negas?
hoc, precor, emenda: quod si correxeris unum,
    nullus in egregio corpore naeuus erit.
pluribus accusem, fieri nisi possit, ut ad me   15
    littera non ueniat, missa sit illa tamen.
di faciant, ut sit temeraria nostra querela,
    teque putem falso non meminisse mei.
quod precor, esse liquet: neque enim mutabile robur
    credere me fas est pectoris esse tui.   20
cana prius gelido desint absinthia Ponto,
    et careat dulci Trinacris Hybla thymo,
inmemorem quam te quisquam conuincat amici:
    non ita sunt fati stamina nigra mei.

afterwards I did not recover my voice. Now however, by the gods'
assistance, I am in perfect health and comfort, I can walk more
easily, I can talk more clearly; so, if the gods assist me, I intend
tomorrow to take a drive in a carriage. If I can bear the hard paving
without strain, I will hasten to you as fast as I can. Only when I see
you will I be fully restored to life. If the gods assist me I will set out
from Rome on the 25th. **2** Keep well, dearest Lord, whom I desire
above all to see, my best reason for living. Greet my Lady for me.

10 P. OVIDIUS NASO

Naso your friend sends you best wishes for your good health in this
letter from the shores of the Getae – if anyone can send what he
himself lacks. I am sick: so as to make sure that no part of me is free
and untormented, my mental anguish has infected my body too.
For many days now I have been racked by a burning pain in my
lungs; savage winter with its extreme cold has done me this harm.
But if you yourself are well, then I also to some degree am well,
as your broad shoulders have supported me in my ruin. You have
given me overwhelming proof of your affection, and have watched
over this head of mine through every turn of events. Why then are
you found wanting in this, that a letter from you only rarely arrives
to console me? Why show yourself a loyal friend in deed, yet deny
me friendly words? Set this right, I beg you; and if you make just
the one correction, there will not be a single blemish on the whole
distinguished frame. I would make the accusation at greater length,
were it not for the possibility that your letter never reached me,
even though it was sent. May the gods grant that my complaint is a
hasty one, and that I am in error in thinking that you have forgotten
me. What I pray for is manifestly so: it would be sacrilege for me
to think your stalwart heart inconstant. Cold Pontus would lose
its hoary wormwood, and Sicilian Hybla its sweet thyme, before
anyone could convict you of forgetfulness of a friend. The threads
of my fate are not so black as that. For your part, though, so as

tu tamen, ut possis falsae quoque pellere culpae   25
   crimina, quod non es, ne uideare, caue.
utque solebamus consumere longa loquendo
   tempora, sermoni deficiente die,
sic ferat ac referat tacitas nunc littera uoces,
   et peragant linguae charta manusque uices.   30
quod fore ne nimium uidear diffidere, sitque
   uersibus hoc paucis admonuisse satis,
accipe quo semper finitur epistula uerbo,
   (aque meis distent ut tua fata!) 'uale'.

11 PHALARIS

(*Epistles* 49)

Ἐπιστράτωι. ὡς πρὸς εὐτυχῆ τινὰ ἔοικας γράφειν, ἐγὼ δέ σοι ἃ οἶδα περὶ ἐμαυτοῦ συνελὼν ἐν βράχει δηλώσω. εἰ τοῦτ' ἔστιν εὐτυχεῖν, τὸ γεννηθέντα μὲν ὀρφανίας πειραθῆναι, νεάζοντα δὲ κατὰ περίστασιν ἐκπεσεῖν τῆς πατρίδος, ἀπολέσαι δὲ τὰ πλεῖστα τῆς οὐσίας, φθαρῆναι δὲ εἰς βάρβαρα ἔθνη, φεύγειν δὲ ἐξ ἀπάσης γῆς ἀδικούμενον, ἐπιβουλεύεσθαι δὲ μὴ μόνον ὑπ ' ἐχθρῶν, ἀλλὰ καὶ τῶν εὐεργετουμένων, τυραννήσαντα δὲ ἀπεύχεσθαι καὶ τὸν ἐν τυραννίδι βίον, εὐτυχοῦμεν.

12 PHALARIS

(*Epistles* 69)

Ἐρυθείαι. **1** εἰ μὲν εὐλαβουμένη τὸν ἐν τυραννίδι βίον οὐ τολμᾶις εἰς Ἀκράγαντα πέμψαι Παυρόλαν, συγγνώμην ἔχω σοι καὶ ὡς γυναικὶ καὶ ὡς μητρὶ δεδοικυίαι περὶ ἀγαπητοῦ παιδός· εἰ δὲ ὡς μόνη καὶ οὐ μετ' ἐμοῦ γεγεννηκυῖα μόνη καὶ ἔχειν δικαιοῖς αὐτόν, ἀγνωμόνως κρίνεις τὰ περὶ γονέων. κατὰ μὲν γὰρ τὸν ἀποτομώτατον λόγον πατρὸς ἂν εἴη παῖς μᾶλλον ἢ μητρός, κατὰ δὲ τὸν εὐγνωμονέστατον ἑκατέρων ἴσως. εἰ δὲ τὸ μετα-δοῦναί ποτε καὶ τῶι γεγεννηκότι τοῦ υἱοῦ σεαυτῆς ἐλάττωσιν ἡγῆι, τί δοκεῖς τὸν μηδὲ μέρους ἀξιούμενον; κοινωνικώτερον δὴ

to be able to refute accusations of wrongdoing, false though they
be, beware of seeming to be what you are not. Just as once we
used to consume long hours in talk, and day gave out before our
conversation was over, so now let the written word carry our silent
voices to and fro, and let hand and paper play the tongue's role.
Lest you think I have too little confidence that this will happen, and
so that it will suffice to have admonished you in a short poem, pray
accept the word that always terminates a letter – how I wish that
your fortunes may be different to mine! – 'keep well.'

11 PHALARIS

To Epistratos. You seem to be under the impression that you are
writing to a fortunate man; I will summarize and explain to you
concisely what I know about myself. If good fortune means tasting
the lot of an orphan at birth, being driven into exile from one's
homeland by hostile circumstance in youth, losing the greater part
of one's wealth, journeying wretchedly to uncouth foreign peoples,
being driven from every land by injustice, being plotted against not
only by enemies but also by those to whom one has done good,
winning tyrannical power and yet praying to be relieved even of the
tyrant's life, then indeed I am a fortunate man.

12 PHALARIS

To Erytheia. **1** If it is through wariness of the tyrant's life that you
shrink from sending Paurolas to Acragas, then I forgive you both
as a wife and as a mother who fears for her beloved son. But if you
are laying claim to sole custody on the grounds that you alone gave
him birth without my assistance, then your view of parenthood is ill-
judged. On the most summary account, a child is its father's rather
than its mother's, but on the most discerning, it belongs equally to
both. If you think it a personal defeat ever to share your son with
his father, what do you think are the feelings of the one not granted

ποιοῦσα πέμψον αὐτὸν ὡς ἐμέ, οὐ διὰ μακρᾶς ἥξοντα πρὸς σέ,
ἀλλὰ θᾶττον καὶ μεθ' ὅσων δεῖ Φαλάριδος καὶ Ἐρυθείας παῖδα,
ἵνα, εἰ καὶ μὴ μετ' ἐμοῦ, μετ' ἀλλήλων γοῦν ἐν ἀφθονίᾳ πλούτου βιοτεύητε. **2** εἰς τίνας γὰρ ἄν τις ἀναγκαιοτέρους εὔξαιτο
περιουσιάζειν, γυναικὸς καὶ παιδὸς οὐκ ἐπιμεληθείς; ἐγὼ δὲ περὶ
ὑμᾶς ἐσπουδακώς, ὡς εἰκὸς ἄνδρα καὶ πατέρα, βούλομαι τῶν
παρ' ἐμοὶ χρημάτων μοῖραν οὐκ ὀλίγην ἐν ὑμῖν τοῖς φιλτάτοις
ἐναπερείσασθαι καὶ τοῦτο σὺν τάχει πρᾶξαι, καὶ διὰ τἆλλα μέν,
οὐχ ἥκιστα δὲ καὶ διὰ τὸ ἐπιὸν γῆρας καὶ διὰ τὴν πρόσφατον συμ-
βεβηκυῖάν μοι χαλεπὴν νόσον. ὑπομιμνήσκει γάρ με τελευταίαν
ἡγεῖσθαι τοῦ ζῆν ἀνθρώπῳ προθεσμίαν τὴν ἐνεστῶσαν ἡμέραν.
τῆς δὲ παρουσίας τῆς Κρήτηθεν εἰς Ἀκράγαντα καὶ τῆς ἐνθάδε
πάλιν ἀφόδου τὸ πιστὸν αὐτῶι πρὸς ἀσφάλειαν ἡ τοῦ πατρὸς
εὔνοια παρέξεται μᾶλλον ἢ ὁ τῆς μητρὸς φόβος.

13 AESCHINES (?) (399/8 B.C.)

(Epistulae Socraticorum 17)

εἰδὼς ὅπως εἶχες πρὸς Σωκράτην ζῶντα καὶ πρὸς ἡμᾶς τοὺς ἐκείνου φίλους, καὶ ὅτι κατὰ τὸ εἰκὸς ἐθαύμασάς τε καὶ ἐσχετλίασας
εἰ ὁ πρὸς σέ τε καὶ τὸν Κεῖον Πρόδικον καὶ Πρωταγόραν τὸν
Ἀβδηρίτην διαμαχόμενος περὶ ἀρετῆς, ἧι ἂν γένοιτο καὶ ὅπως ἂν
γένοιτο καὶ ὅτι χρὴ ταύτης πάντας ἐφίεσθαι, οὗτος ὡς πονηρό-
τατος καὶ ἀμαθέστατος τοῦ καλοῦ καὶ τοῦ δικαίου πρός τε θεοὺς
καὶ πρὸς ἀνθρώπους τοῖς ἕνδεκα δόξαν ἀνῃρέθη, ἔγραψά σοι
πυθόμενος ὅτι οἴκοι εἴης ἐν Χίωι, περὶ τῶν ἔπειτα, ἵνα ἡσθείης.
Ἀθηναῖοι γὰρ ἤδη ποτὲ ἀφυπνώσαντες Ἄνυτόν τε καὶ Μέλητον ὡς ἀνοσιουργοὺς προκαλεσάμενοι ἀπέκτειναν ὅτι αἴτιοι
τῆι πόλει ἐγένοντο τοσούτου κακοῦ. προφάσεις δὲ αὗται κατ'
αὐτοῖν εὑρέθησαν· κατηφεῖς μὲν γὰρ Ἀθηναῖοι περιήιεσαν μετὰ
τὸν θάνατον αὐτοῦ παρὰ πάντων εὐθυνόμενοι τῶν γενομένων,
ὅτι ἄρα οὐκ ἐχρῆν οὐκ ἀδικοῦντα αὐτὸν κατηγορηθῆναι, μὴ
ὅτι ἀποκτιννύναι. τί γὰρ εἰ τὸν πλάτανον ἢ τὸν κύνα ὤμ-
νυε; τί δὲ εἰ ἀνηρώτα ἰδίαι καὶ κοινῆι πάντας ἀνθρώπους, ὅτι
οὐδὲν εἰδεῖεν οὔτε δίκαιον οὔτε καλόν; εἶτα δὲ οἱ νέοι πάντες εἰς

even a part-share? Behave in a more partnerly way and send him to me; he will not return to you only after a long interval, but quickly and with all that a child of Phalaris and Erytheia should have, so that at least with each other, even if not with me, you may live in unstinted wealth. **2** What closer relations could a man hope to prosper so as to aid, if he were to neglect his wife and son? Since I have your best interests at heart, as is only reasonable for a husband and father, I wish to settle no small share of my property on you, my nearest and dearest, and to do so with all speed, for a number of reasons but not least because of the approach of old age and the painful disease that I have recently contracted. It reminds me that the remotest term guaranteed for a man's life is the day he is now living. It is his father's love rather than his mother's fear that will assure his safety on his journey from Crete to Acragas and on his return from here.

13 ANONYMOUS SOCRATIC (AESCHINES?)

Knowing your feelings for Socrates while he was alive and for us, his friends, and knowing that in all probability you were astounded and outraged that the man who debated fiercely with you and Prodikos of Keos and Protagoras of Abdera about the place of virtue and the means of cultivating it and the necessity for all to pursue it, that this man should on the decision of the Commissioners be put to death as one guilty of the greatest villainy and the greatest moral deficiency, both towards gods and towards men, I write to you on learning that you are at home on Chios to gladden your heart with an account of what happened next. The Athenians rapidly woke up, put Anytos and Meletos on trial for impiety, and executed them for bringing such misfortune on the city. These were the grounds that emerged for their condemnation. After Socrates' death the Athenians went round with downcast eyes, admonished by every event that they should not after all even have put an innocent man on trial, let alone had him executed. What if he did swear by the plane-tree and the dog? What if he did question everyone, in public and in private, and demonstrate that they had no knowledge of justice and

ἀκρασίαν καὶ ἀκοσμίαν ἐτρέποντο ἐν τῆι πόλει. ἀεὶ γὰρ τοῦ
τον καθοσονοῦν ἠισχύνοντο. ἐκίνησε δὲ αὐτοὺς μάλιστα καὶ τὸ
τοῦ νεανίσκου τοῦ Λακεδαιμονίου πάθος. ἧκε γάρ τις κατ' ἔρωτα
Σωκράτους συγγενέσθαι αὐτῶι, μὴ προειδὼς Σωκράτην, ἀλλ'
ἀκούων περὶ αὐτοῦ. ὡς δὲ ἡδομένωι αὐτῶι τῆς ἀφίξεως ὄντι ἤδη
περὶ τὰς πύλας τοῦ ἄστεος προσηγγέλθη ὅτι Σωκράτης, πρὸς ὃν
ἐληλύθοι, τεθνήκοι, ἐς μὲν τὴν πύλην οὐκέτι εἰσῆλθε, διαπυθόμενος
δὲ ὅπου εἴη ὁ τάφος, προσελθὼν διελέγετο τῆι στήληι καὶ ἐδάκρυε,
καὶ ἐπειδὴ νὺξ κατέλαβεν αὐτόν, κοιμηθεὶς ἐπὶ τοῦ τάφου, ὄρθρου
πολλοῦ φιλήσας τὴν ἐπικειμένην αὐτῶι κόνιν, πολλὰ δὲ περιασ
πασάμενος πάσηι φιλότητι ὤιχετο ἀπιὼν Μεγαράδε. ἤισθοντο
οὖν καὶ τοῦτο Ἀθηναῖοι καὶ ὅτι μέλλοιεν Λακεδαιμονίοις διαβάλ
λεσθαι ἐπὶ τοῖς δεινοτάτοις, εἰ ἐκείνων μὲν οἱ υἱεῖς τοὺς παρ' αὐτοῖς
σοφοὺς δι' ἔρωτος ποιοῦνται, αὐτοὶ δὲ ἀποκτιννύασι, καὶ οἱ μὲν
τοσοῦτον διάστημα ἀφικνοῦνται ἰδεῖν Σωκράτην, οἱ δὲ οὐχ ὑπομέ
νουσι παρ' αὐτοῖς ἔχοντες αὐτὸν φυλάξαι. χαλεπηνάμενοι οὖν
μόνον οὐ διέφαγον τὼ πονηρὼ ἄνδρε ἐκείνω, ὥστε τὴν μὲν πόλιν
ἀπολελογῆσθαι ὅτι αὐτὴ τούτων οὐδὲν δρᾶι, τοὺς δ' αἰτίους
τεθνάναι. ἐκριφέντες οὖν οἷόν τε κοινὸν ἄγος τῶν Ἑλλήνων, μᾶλ
λον δὲ πάντων ἀνθρώπων, ὤνησαν μὲν ἡμᾶς, ὤνησαν δὲ καὶ τοὺς
ἄλλους ταῦτα παθόντες. πάλιν οὖν συνελευσόμεθα Ἀθήναζε οἱ
ἀναξίως ἀνασεσοβημένοι ὡς τὸ πρόσθεν.

14 CHION OF HERACLEA (HERACLEA, SPRING 353/2 B.C.)

(Epistles 17)

Χίων Πλάτωνι χαίρειν. 1 δυσὶν ἡμέραις τῶν Διονυσίων ἔμπροσθεν
τοὺς πιστοτάτους μοι τῶν θεραπόντων, Πυλάδην καὶ Φιλόκαλον,
ἐξέπεμψα ὡς σέ· μέλλω γὰρ τοῖς Διονυσίοις ἐπιτίθεσθαι τῶι τυράν
νωι, πολιτευσάμενος ἐκ πολλοῦ ἀνύποπτος αὐτῶι γενέσθαι.

goodness? Then, secondly, the entire juvenile population of the city began to succumb to immorality and disorder, whereas previously respect for Socrates had restrained them to the extent that they could be restrained. Furthermore, the Athenians were particularly stung by the fate of the young man from Sparta. This man came to Athens out of a desire to study with Socrates, though he had no prior acquaintance with him and knew of him only by report. He had already reached the city gates and was overjoyed at having arrived, when he was informed that Socrates, whom he had come to meet, was dead. Abandoning his intention of entering the gate, he enquired where Socrates was buried, and going there addressed the grave-stone with tears in his eyes, and when night overtook him, he lay down to sleep on the grave, and as dawn filled the sky he kissed the dirt that covered him, and with a long and most loving embrace he left and went on his way to Megara. The people of Athens became aware of this and realized that it would cause the severest of trouble between them and the Spartans, if the younger generation of Sparta were to conceive a passion for the sages of Athens, while they themselves had them put to death, and while the young of Sparta could make such a long journey to see Socrates, they themselves could not bear to keep him safe when they had him among them. In their distress, therefore, they all but devoured that pair of villains, so that now the city of Athens has cleared itself of all direct guilt in the matter, and those truly guilty have been put to death. Cast out then like a source of shared pollution to all Greeks, or rather to the whole of humanity, they have done good service not only to us but also to others in suffering this fate. So we who were previously so undeservingly expelled from the city will now return to Athens.

14 CHION OF HERACLEA

Chion to Plato, greetings. **1** Two days before the Dionysia, I send you the most trusted of my servants, Pylades and Philokalos. Having this long time since schemed to allay his suspicions, I plan to assassinate the tyrant at the Dionysia. On this day there is a procession in

πέμπεται δ᾽ ἐν ταύτηι τῆι ἡμέραι πομπὴ τῶι Διονύσωι, καὶ
δοκεῖ ὀλιγωρότερον ἕξειν δι᾽ αὐτὴν τὰ τῶν δορυφόρων· εἰ δὲ
μή γε, κἂν διὰ πυρὸς ἐλθεῖν δέηι, οὐκ ὀκνήσομεν, οὐδὲ καταισ-
χυνοῦμεν οὔτε ἑαυτοὺς οὔτε τὴν σὴν φιλοσοφίαν. καὶ τὰ τῶν
συνωμοτῶν δέ ἐστιν ἡμῖν ὀχυρά, πίστει δὲ ἢ πλήθει ὀχυρωτέρα.
2 οἶδα μὲν οὖν ὡς ἀναιρεθήσομαι, τελειώσας δὲ μόνον τὴν τυραννοκτονίαν τοῦτο παθεῖν εὔχομαι. μετὰ παιᾶνος γὰρ ἂν καὶ
νικητηρίων ἀπολίποιμι τὸν βίον, εἰ καταλύσας τὴν τυραννίδα ἐξ
ἀνθρώπων ἀπελεύσομαι. σημαίνει γάρ μοι καὶ ἱερὰ καὶ οἰωνίσ-
ματα καὶ πᾶσα ἁπλῶς μαντεία θάνατον κατορθώσαντι τὴν
πρᾶξιν. ἐθεασάμην δὲ καὶ αὐτὸς ἐναργεστέραν ἢ κατ᾽ ὄνειρον
ὄψιν. ἔδοξε γάρ μοι γυνή, θεῖόν τι χρῆμα κάλλους καὶ μεγέθους,
ἀναδεῖν με κοτίνωι καὶ ταινίαις καὶ μετὰ μικρὸν ἀποδεῖξαί τι
μνῆμα περικαλλὲς καὶ εἰπεῖν, "ἐπειδὴ κέκμηκας, ὦ Χίων, ἴθι εἰς
τουτὶ τὸ μνῆμα ἀναπαυσόμενος." ἐκ τούτου δὴ τοῦ ὀνείρατος
εὔελπίς εἰμι καλοῦ θανάτου τυχεῖν· νομίζω γὰρ μηδὲν κίβδηλον
εἶναι ψυχῆς μάντευμα, ἐπεὶ καὶ σὺ οὕτως ἐγίνωσκες. 3 εἰ δὲ καὶ
ἀληθεύσειεν ἡ μαντεία, μακαριώτατον ἐμαυτὸν ἡγοῦμαι γενήσ-
εσθαι ἢ εἰ βίος μοι μετὰ τὴν τυραννοκτονίαν εἰς γῆρας ἐδίδοτο·
καλὸν γάρ μοι μεγάλα διαπραξαμένωι πρότερον ἐξ ἀνθρώπων
ἀπαλλάττεσθαι ἢ χρόνου τι συναπολαῦσαι, καὶ ἃ ἂν δράσωμεν,
πολὺ νομισθήσεται μείζονα ὧν πεισόμεθα, καὶ αὐτοὶ τιμιώτεροι
ἐσόμεθα τοῖς εὖ παθοῦσιν, εἰ τῶι ἰδίωι θανάτωι τὴν ἐλευθερίαν
αὐτοῖς ὠνησόμεθα. μείζων γὰρ ὠφέλεια τοῖς εὐεργετηθεῖσιν εἶναι
φαίνεται, ἧς ὁ δράσας οὐ μεταλαμβάνει. οὕτως μὲν δὴ προθύμως
ἔχομεν πρὸς τὴν μαντείαν τοῦ θανάτου. σὺ δὲ χαῖρέ τε, ὦ Πλάτων,
καὶ εὐδαιμονοίης εἰς τέλειον γῆρας. προσαγορεύσω δέ σε ὕστατα,
ὡς πείθομαι.

15 SERENOS (2 ND CENTURY A.D.)

(P. Oxy. 528)

Σερῆνος Εἰσίδωρα [τῆι ἀδελ]φῆι καὶ κυρία πλαῖστ[α χαίρειν].
πρὸ μὲν παντὸς εὔχομ[αί σε ὑγιαί]νει καὶ καθ᾽ ἑκάστης [ἡμέρα]ς

honour of Dionysus, and I believe that his bodyguard will be more carelessly deployed for this reason. But even if this is not so, and even if I have to walk though fire, I will not flinch and I will not disgrace myself or your philosophy. I have confidence in my fellow conspirators, a confidence grounded more in their loyalty than in their numbers. **2** I am well aware that I shall lose my life, but if I can only bring off the assassination successfully, then I positively pray for that fate. If I could only have destroyed the tyrant's power when I depart from the world of men, then I would take my leave with a hymn of praise and a victor's crown. All portents and auguries – in a word, all forms of prophecy – indicate that I will succeed in my venture and die. I myself had a vision more compellingly vivid than any dream. I seemed to see a woman, a miracle of beauty and stature, crowning me with an olive-wreath and ribbons, and then after a brief interval showing me a marvellously beautiful tomb and saying to me, 'You are weary, Chion; come then to this tomb and take your rest.' As a result of this dream, I have high hopes of dying a noble death, as I am convinced that the soul never prophesies falsely, since you too are of this opinion. **3** And if the prediction were to prove true, then I think that I will be a most fortunate man, more so than if I were granted a life lasting into old age after the tyrannicide. I reckon it a fine thing that on completion of a great deed I should depart from the world of men before any benefit should accrue to me with the passage of time; whatever I manage to achieve will be considered far greater than anything I may suffer, and I myself will stand higher in honour than those I have benefited, if my gift of freedom to them is bought at the cost of my own life. Beneficiaries feel that they have been done a greater service if the agent himself does not share in it. Such is my eager confidence in the face of the prophecy of death. Keep well, Plato, and may you enjoy good fortune to a ripe old age. I am convinced that this is the last time I will address you.

15 SERENOS

Serenos to Isidora his sister and lady warmest greetings. Before all else I pray for your health and every day and evening I make

κα[ὶ] ὄψας τὸ προσκύνημά σου πυῶ παρὰ τῆ σε φιλούση Θοήρι. γινόσκειν σε θέλω ἀφ' ὡς ἐκξήλθες ἀπ' ἐμοῦ πένθος ἡγούμην νυκτὸς κλέων ἡμέρας δὲ πενθῶ. ιβ Φαῶφι ἀφ' ὅτε ἐλουσάμην μετ' ἐσοῦ οὐκ ἐλουσάμην οὐκ ἤλιμε μέχρει ιβ Ἀθύρ, καὶ ἔπεμσάς μυ ἐπιστολὰς δυναμένου λίθον σαλεῦσε, οὕτως ὁ λόγυ σοῦ καικίνηκάν με. αὐτὴν τῆ ὅρα ἀντέγραψά συ καὶ ἔδωκα τῆ ιβ μετὰ τῶν σῶν ἐπιστολῶν ἐσσφραγισμένα. χωρεὶς δὲ τῶν σῶν λόγων κὲ γραμάτων ὁ Κόλοβος δὲ πόρνην με πεπύηκεν, ἔλεγε δὲ ὅτι ἔπεμσέ μυ φάσειν ἡ γυνή σου ὅτι αὐτὸς πέπρακεν τὸ ἀλυσίδιον καὶ αὐτὸς κατέστακέ με ε[ἰ]ς τὸ πλὺν· τούτους τοὺς λόγους λέγεις ἥνα μηκέτι [[φ]] πιστευθῶ μου τὴν ἐνβόλ[ην]; ἐδοῦ ποσάρκεις ἔπεμσα ἐπὶ σέ. ἔρχη [εἴτε] οὐκ ἔρχη δήλοσόν μυ.[ἔρρωσο].

Verso: ἀπόδος Εἰσιδόρα π(αρὰ) Σερήνου.

16 C. PLINIUS SECUNDUS (ROME, A.D. ? 106)

(*Epistles* 6.7)

C. Plinius Calpurniae suae s(alutem). scribis te absentia mea non mediocriter adfici unumque habere solacium, quod pro me libellos meos teneas, saepe etiam in uestigio meo colloces. gratum est quod nos requiris, gratum quod his fomentis adquiescis; inuicem ego epistulas tuas lectito atque identidem in manus quasi nouas sumo. sed eo magis ad desiderium tui accendor: nam cuius litterae tantum habent suauitatis, huius sermonibus quantum dulcedinis inest! tu tamen quam frequentissime scribe, licet hoc me ita delectet ut torqueat. uale.

17 'CIRCE' TO 'POLYAENUS' (ENCOLPIUS) – 'POLYAENUS' TO 'CIRCE'

(Petronius, *Satyricon* 129.4–9, 30.1–6)

4 Circe Polyaeno salutem. si libidinosa essem, quererer decepta; nunc etiam languori tuo gratias ago. in umbra uoluptatis diutius lusi. **5** quid tamen agas, quaero, et an tuis pedibus perueneris

supplication for you before Thoeris who loves you. I want you to know that ever since you left me I have been in mourning weeping at night and mourning during the day. Since I bathed with you on 12 Phaophi I have not bathed or anointed myself up till 12 Hathyr, and you sent me letters that could move a stone, that's how much your words have moved me. Right that instant I wrote back to you and sent it off sealed up along with your letters. Contrary to what you say and write, 'But Kolobos has made me a prostitute,' *he* said 'Your wife sent me a message saying that "he sold the necklace himself and he put me into the boat himself".' Are you saying this so as to see to it that I'm not trusted any more over my loading? Look how many times I've sent for you. Let me know, are you coming or not. Keep well.

Verso: Deliver to Isidora from Serenos.

16 C. PLINIUS SECUNDUS

Caius Plinius to his dear Calpurnia, good health. You write that you are feeling my absence very much and that your only consolation when you don't have me is to hold my books and frequently even place them in my imprint beside you. I am happy to know that you miss me and happy too that you can ease the pain with this sort of medication. I for my part read and reread your letters and return to them again and again as if they had just arrived. But this only fans the flames of my longing for you: if there is such pleasure in reading what you write, think what joy it is to talk with you! Do write as often as you can, even though it will torture me as much as it delights me. Farewell.

17 'CIRCE' AND 'POLYAENUS'

4 Circe to Polyaenus, good health. If I were highly sexed, I'd complain that you'd let me down; but as it is, I'm even grateful to you for your limpness. I don't often enjoy the preludes to ecstasy at such length. **5** But what I want to know is how you are, and whether you

domum; negant enim medici sine neruis homines ambulare posse.
6 narrabo tibi, adulescens, paralysin caue. numquam ego aegrum
tam magno periculo uidi: medius iam peristi. **7** quod si idem fri-
gus genua manusque temptauerit tuas, licet ad tubicines mittas.
8 quid ergo est? etiam si grauem iniuriam accepi, homini tamen
misero non inuideo medicinam. si uis sanus esse, Gitonem rel-
ega. recipies, inquam, neruos tuos, si triduo sine fratre dormieris.
9 nam quod ad me attinet, non timeo ne quis inueniatur cui
minus placeam. nec speculum mihi nec fama mentitur. uale, si
potes.

1 Polyaenos Circae salutem. fateor me, domina, saepe peccasse;
nam et homo sum et adhuc iuuenis. numquam tamen ante hunc
diem usque ad mortem deliqui. **2** habes confitentem reum: quicquid iusseris, merui. proditionem feci, hominem occidi, templum
uiolaui: in haec facinora quaere supplicium. **3** siue occidere placet,
⟨cum⟩ ferro meo uenio, siue uerberibus contenta es, curro nudus
ad dominam. **4** illud unum memento, non me sed instrumenta peccasse. paratus miles arma non habui. quis hoc turbauerit nescio.
5 forsitan animus antecessit corporis moram, forsitan dum omnia concupisco, uoluptatem tempore consumpsi. non inuenio quod
feci. **6** paralysin tamen cauere iubes: tamquam ea maior fieri possit
quae abstulit mihi per quod etiam te habere potui. summa tamen
excusationis meae hac est: placebo tibi, si me culpam emendare
permiseris.

18 GEMELLOS TO SALAKONIS – SALAKONIS TO GEMELLOS

(Alciphron, *Epistles* 2.24–5)

Γέμελλος Σαλακωνίδι. **1** τί ταῦτα, ὦ Σαλακωνίς, ὑπερηφανεῖς
τάλαινα; οὐκ ἐγώ σε εἰς τοὐργαστηρίον καθημένην παρὰ τὸν ἀκ-
εστὴν τὸν ἑτερόποδα ἀνειλόμην, καὶ ταῦτα λάθραι τῆς μητρός,
καὶ καθάπερ τινὰ ἐπίκληρον ἐγγυητὴν ἀγαγόμενος ἔχω; **2** σὺ

made it home on your own two feet. Doctors say that men whose sinews won't stiffen can't walk. **6** I warn you, young man, watch out that you don't succumb to total paralysis! I've never seen anyone so dangerously ill: your mid-part's dead already. **7** If the same chill gets to your knees and hands, you can send for the funeral band! **8** So what are you to do? Even though I've been mortally offended, I still don't begrudge an unfortunate his treatment. If you want to get well, banish Giton. I mean that your sinews will return to their old stiffness if you can sleep without your brother for three days. **9** As for me, I have no worries about not finding admirers. My mirror and my reputation don't lie. Keep well, if you're up to it!

1 Polyaenus to Circe, good health. Mistress, I confess that I've often gone astray: I'm only human and I'm still young. But I've never before this day gone as far as a capital offence. **2** I plead guilty: whatever sentence you impose, I've deserved it. I'm a traitor, a murderer, a desecrator: you decide what punishment fits these crimes. **3** If you decide to kill me, I'll bring my weapon; if it's enough for you to have me whipped, I'll come running naked to my mistress. **4** Just remember this though: it wasn't I who was at fault, it was my equipment. I was ready to fight, but I was unarmed. I really don't know who has caused this upset. **5** Perhaps my mind went racing on while my body lagged behind; perhaps I frittered away our pleasure by dithering because I wanted everything at once. I just don't understand what I've done. **6** Yet you warn me to beware of total paralysis – as if there could be any worse paralysis than the kind that robbed me of my means of enjoying you of all women. My apology adds up to this: allow me to expiate my guilt, and I'll give you every satisfaction.

18 GEMELLOS AND SALAKONIS

Gemellos to Salakonis. **1** What's this stuck-up behaviour, Salakonis you bitch? Didn't I rescue you when you were sitting in the sweat-shop with the lame tailor, and without mother finding out about it, and haven't I brought you here and kept you like an heiress

δὲ φρυάττηι, παιδισκάριον εὐτελές; καὶ κιχλίζουσα καὶ μωκωμένη με διατελεῖς. οὐ παύσηι, τάλαινα, τῆς ἀγερωχίας; ἐγώ σοι τὸν ἐραστὴν δείξω δεσπότην καὶ κάχρυς ἐπὶ τῶν ἀγρῶν φρύγειν ἀναγκάσω, καὶ τότε εἴσηι παθοῦσα οἷ κακῶν σαυτὴν ἐνέσεισας.

Σαλακῶνις Γεμέλλωι. 1 πάντα ὑπομένειν οἷά τέ εἰμι πλὴν τοῦ σοὶ συγκαθεύδειν, δεσπότα. καὶ τὴν νύκτα οὐκ ἔφυγον οὐδὲ ὑπὸ τοῖς θάμνοις ἐκρυπτόμην, ὡς ἐδόκεις, ἀλλὰ τὴν κάρδοπον ὑπεισελθοῦσα ἐκείμην ἀμφιθεμένη τὸ κοῖλον τοῦ σκεύους εἰς κάλυμμα. 2 ἐπειδὴ δὲ κέκρικα βρόχωι τὸν βίον ἐκλιπεῖν, ἄκουε λεγούσης ἀναφανδόν, πάντα γάρ μου περιαιρεῖ φόβον ἡ πρὸς τὸ τελευτᾶν ὁρμή· ἐγώ σε, ὦ Γέμελλε, στυγῶ, τοῦτο μὲν βδελυττομένη τὸ δάσος τοῦ σώματος καὶ ὥσπερ τι κίναδος ἐκτρεπομένη, 3 τοῦτο δὲ τὴν δυσχέρειαν τοῦ στόματος ἐκ τοῦ μυχαιτάτου τῆς φάρυγγος τὴν δυσοσμίαν ἐκπέμποντος. κακὸς κακῶς ἀπόλοιο τοιοῦτος ὤν. βάδιζε παρά τινα λῆμωσαν ἄγροικον γραῦν ἐπὶ ἑνὶ γομφίωι σαλεύουσαν, ἀληλιμμένην τῶι ἐκ τῆς πίττης ἐλαίωι.

19 GLYKERA TO BAKCHIS

(Alciphron, *Epistles* 4.2)

Γλυκέρα Βακχίδι. 1 ὁ Μένανδρος ἡμῶν ἐπὶ τὴν τῶν Ἰσθμίων θέαν εἰς τὴν Κόρινθον ἐλθεῖν βεβούληται· ἐμοὶ μὲν οὐ κατὰ νοῦν. οἶδα γὰρ οἷόν ἐστιν ἐραστοῦ τοιούτου καὶ βραχὺν ἐστερῆσθαι χρόνον· ἀποτρέπειν δ᾽ οὐκ ἐνῆν μὴ πολλάκις ἀποδημεῖν εἰωθότος. 2 οὐδ᾽ ὅπως αὐτὸν παρεγγυήσω μέλλοντα ἐπιδημήσειν ἔχω, οὐδ᾽ ὅπως μή. βούλομαι μὲν αὐτὸν σπουδασθῆναι ὑπὸ σοῦ, κἀμοί τινα φέρειν φιλοτιμίαν τοῦτο λογίζομαι· οἶδα γὰρ τὴν οὖσαν ἡμῖν ἑταιρίαν πρὸς ἀλλήλας· 3 δέδοικα δέ, ὦ φιλτάτη, οὐ σὲ τοσοῦτον (χρηστοτέρωι γὰρ ἤθει κέχρησαι τοῦ βίου) ὅσον αὐτὸν ἐκεῖνον. ἐρωτικὸς γάρ ἐστι δαιμονίως, καὶ Βακχίδος οὐδ᾽ ἂν τῶν σκυθρωποτάτων τις ἀπόσχοιτο. 4 τὸ μὲν γὰρ δοκεῖν αὐτὸν οὐκ ἔλαττον

engaged to be married? **2** But you get all proud and difficult, you cheap little tart, and never stop giggling and making fun of me. Stop this stand-offishness, you bitch! I'll show you that your lover is also your master – I'll make you roast barley out on the farm. Then you'll realize first-hand, when it's too late to do anything about it, what a nasty jam you've got yourself into.

Salakonis to Gemellos. **1** I can put up with anything apart from sleeping with you, master. I didn't run away during the night and I didn't hide in the bushes, as you thought; I crept under the kneading-trough and lay there with the curve of it round me as a covering. **2** I've decided to end my life by hanging myself, so you can listen to me speak my mind – my keenness to die strips away all my fear. Gemellos, I hate you. For one thing, your hairy body revolts me, you're a repulsive monster; **3** for another, there's your disgusting mouth, with its bad breath fetched up from the furthest depths of your throat. You're so horrible I hope you come to a horrid end. Go and pester some bleary-eyed hag of a yokel, tethered to life by a single molar, who uses pitch-oil as her moisturizer.

19 GLYKERA

Glykera to Bakchis. **1** My Menander is set on going to Corinth to see the Isthmian games. I don't approve, because I know what it's like to be without a lover like him even for a short time, but I couldn't dissuade him given that he isn't in the habit of leaving home often. **2** I can't see how I can entrust him to your care now that he's going to visit your part of the world, and I can't see how I can refuse to either. On the one hand, I want him to be made a fuss of by you, and I reckon that this reflects some credit on me, because I'm well aware of the professional connection that exists between us. **3** But on the other hand, I am afraid, not so much of you my dear – you're a better person than your line of work would suggest – as of him. He is extraordinarily amorous, and not even the sullenest moralizer could resist Bakchis. **4** As for the impression getting around that he planned

τοῦ σοὶ ἐντυχεῖν ἢ τῶν Ἰσθμίων ἕνεκεν τὴν ἀποδημίαν πεποιῆσθαι,
οὐ πάνυ πείθομαι. ἴσως αἰτιάσηι με τῆς ὑποψίας. συγγίνωσκε δὲ
ταῖς ἑταιρικαῖς, ὦ φιλτάτη, ζηλοτυπίαις. ἐγὼ δ᾽ οὐ παρὰ μικρὸν
ἂν ἡγοίμην Μενάνδρου διαμαρτεῖν ἐραστοῦ. 5 ἄλλως τε κἄν μοι
κνισμός τις ἦι πρὸς αὐτὸν ἢ διαφορὰ γένηται, δεήσει με ἐπὶ τῆς
σκηνῆς ὑπὸ Χρέμητός τινος ἢ Φειδύλου πικρῶς λοιδορεῖσθαι. ἐὰν
δ᾽ ἐπανέλθηι μοι οἷος ὤιχετο, πολλὴν εἴσομαί σοι χάριν. ἔρρωσο.

20 ANON

(Philostratus, *Epist. Erot.* 39)

μηδὲ γράφειν φυγάδα ἀνέξηι; μηδ᾽ ἐπίνευε φιλοῦσιν οὐκοῦν οὐδὲ
ἀναπνεῖν, οὐδὲ κλάειν, οὐδὲ ἄλλα ὅσα ἡ φύσις. μή με διώξηις
τῶν θυρῶν, ὡς τῆς πατρίδος ἡ τύχη, μηδὲ ὀνειδίσηις πρᾶγμα
αὐτόματον οὗ τὸ λάμπρον ἐν τῶι ἀλόγωι τῆς δυνάμεως. ἔφευγε
καὶ Ἀριστείδης, ἀλλ᾽ ἐπανήρχετο· καὶ Ξενοφῶν, ἀλλ᾽ οὐ δικαίως·
ἔφευγε καὶ Θεμιστόκλης, ἀλλ᾽ ἐτιμᾶτο καὶ παρὰ βαρβάροις· καὶ
Ἀλκιβιάδης, ἀλλὰ παρετείχιζε καὶ τὰς Ἀθήνας· καὶ Δημοσθένης,
ἀλλ᾽ ὁ φθόνος αἴτιος. φεύγει καὶ θάλαττα, ὅταν ὑφ᾽ ἡλίωι ἐλαύν-
ηι· καὶ ἥλιος, ὅταν νὺξ καταλαμβάνηι. φεύγει καὶ μετόπωρον
χειμῶνος προσελθόντος, καὶ χειμὼν ἄπεισιν ἔαρος διώκοντος, καὶ
συνελόντι εἰπεῖν αἱ τῶν ὑστέρων καιρῶν ἐπιδημίαι τῶν προτέρων
εἰσὶ καιρῶν φυγαί. ἐδέξαντο καὶ Ἀθηναῖοι Δήμητραν φεύγουσαν
καὶ Διόνυσον μετοικοῦντα καὶ τοὺς Ἡρακλέους παῖδας ἀλωμένους,
ὅταν καὶ τὸν Ἐλέου ἐστήσαντο βωμόν, ὡς τρισκαιδεκάτου θεοῦ,
οὐκ οἴνου σπένδοντες αὐτῶι καὶ γάλακτος ἀλλὰ δακρύων καὶ τῆς
πρὸς τοὺς ἱκετεύοντας αἰδοῦς. ἀνάστησον καὶ σὺ τὸν βωμόν, καὶ
κακῶς πράττοντα ἄνθρωπον ἐλέησον, μὴ δὶς γένωμαι φυγὰς καὶ
τῆς πατρίδος στερηθεὶς καὶ τοῦ πρὸς σὲ ἔρωτος σφαλείς· ἐὰν γὰρ
ἐλεήσηις, κατελήλυθα.

the trip as much to meet you as because of the Isthmian games, I'm not altogether sure I believe it. Perhaps you will blame me for being suspicious. Darling, forgive my professional jealousy. I'd reckon it would make a great difference to me to lose Menander as my lover. **5** Besides, if there's any friction between me and him or we have a quarrel, I'll have to put up with the pain of being insulted on stage by a Chremes or a Pheidylos. But if he comes back to me the same as he went away, I shall be very grateful to you. Keep well.

20 THE EXILE

Won't you allow an exile even to write to you? Then don't allow lovers even to sigh either, or weep, or do anything else that comes naturally. Don't chase me away from your doors as Fortune has chased me from my homeland, don't hold me to blame for a chance event that impresses only for the capriciousness of the power that inflicted it. Aristides too was an exile, but he returned; and Xenophon, but he didn't deserve to be; Themistocles too was an exile, but he was honoured by foreign peoples also; and Alcibiades, but he blockaded Athens itself; and Demosthenes, but that was the work of malice. The sea too goes into exile when driven away by the sun; and the sun when night overtakes it. Autumn too goes into exile when winter comes on, and winter retreats before spring's onset; in short, the arrival of new seasons brings the exile of their predecessors. The Athenians welcomed Demeter when she too was in exile and Dionysus when he was changing homes and the children of Heracles on their wanderings, and it was then that they set up an altar of Compassion, as to a thirteenth god, and poured libations in its honour not of wine and milk but of tears and of respect for its suppliants. I urge you to raise this altar yourself and take pity on one in distress, lest I should be twice exiled, by being both banished from my homeland and cheated of my love for you. If you take pity on me, I am back home.

21 PETOSIRIS (EGYPT, 3 RD – 4 TH CENTURY A.D.)

(*P.Oxy.* 112)

χαίροις, κυρία μου Σερηνία, [...] π(αρὰ) Πετοσείριος. πᾶν ποίησον, κυρία, ἐξελθεῖ[ν τῇ] κ΄ τοῖς γενεθλείοις τοῦ θεο[ῦ καὶ] δήλωσόν μοι ἡ πλοίῳ ἐξέρχ[ει] ἢ ὄνῳ, ἵνα πεμφθῇ σοι, ἀλ᾽ ὅρα [μὴ] ἀμελήσῃς, κυρία, ἐρρῶσθ[αί σε] εὔχομαι [πο]λλοῖς [χρόνοις].

22 CLAUDIA SEUERA (VINDOLANDA,
AUGUST – SEPTEMBER, A.D. 97–102/3)

(Vindolanda tablet II 291, inv. no. 85.057)

Cl(audia) Seuerá Lepidinae [suae sa]l[u]tem. III Idus Septembr[e]s soror ad diem᾽ sollemnem natalem meum rogó libenter faciás ut uenias ad nos, iucundiorem mihi [diem] interventú tuo facturá si [u]e[nie]s. Cerial[em t]uum salutá. Aelius meus e[um] et filiolus salutant. sperabo te soror. uale soror anima mea, ita ualeam karissima, et haue.

Back: Sulpiciae Lepidinae Cerialis a S[e]uera.

23 Q. HORATIUS FLACCUS (ROME,
20–2 SEPTEMBER, 23–19 B.C.)

(*Epistles* 1.5)

si potes Archiacis conuiua recumbere lectis
nec modica cenare times holus omne patella,
supremo te sole domi, Torquate, manebo.
uina bibes iterum Tauro diffusa palustres
inter Minturnas Sinuessanumque Petrinum.   5
si melius quid habes, arcesse, uel imperium fer.
iamdudum splendet focus et tibi munda supellex:
mitte leuis spes et certamina diuitiarum
et Moschi causam: cras nato Caesare festus

21 PETOSIRIS

Greetings, my dear Serenia . . . from Petosiris. Make every effort, my dear, to come up for the god's birthday celebrations on the 20th, and tell me whether you are coming by boat or by donkey, so that it can be sent for you. Please make sure you don't forget, my dear. I pray for your lasting health.

22 CLAUDIA SEVERA

Claudia Severa to her dear Lepidina, greetings. Sister, I invite you warmly to make sure you come to us for my birthday celebrations on 11 September – you will make it a happier day for me by your presence, if you do come. Give my greetings to your Cerealis; my Aelius and my little son send him theirs. I'll expect you impatiently, sister. Good health, sister, my dearest soul, as I hope to be healthy myself, and greetings.

Back: To Sulpicia Lepidina, wife of Cerealis, from Severa.

23 Q. HORATIUS FLACCUS

If you can bear to lie on an Archias couch as a guest at my table, and aren't afraid to dine on vegetables alone, served on a simple dish, then I shall look forward to seeing you at my house at sunset, Torquatus. To drink, there'll be wine racked off between marshy Minturnae and Sinuessan Petrinum during Taurus' second consulship; if you have anything better, have it sent for, or else follow my orders. Hearth and furniture have been neat and shiny in honour of your arrival for some time now. Set trifling hopes and the race for profit and Moschus' case to one side: Caesar's birthday holiday

dat ueniam somnumque dies; impune licebit   10
aestiuam sermone benigno tendere noctem.
quo mihi fortunam, si non conceditur uti?
parcus ob heredis curam nimiumque seuerus
adsideat insano; potare et spargere flores
incipiam patiarque uel inconsultus haberi.   15
quid non ebrietas dissignat? operta recludit,
spes iubet esse ratas, ad proelia trudit inertem,
sollicitis animis onus eximit, addocet artes.
fecundi calices quem non fecere disertum,
contracta quem non in paupertate solutum?   20
haec ego procurare et idoneus imperor et non
inuitus, ne turpe toral, ne sordida mappa
corruget nares, ne non et cantharus et lanx
ostendat tibi te, ne fidos inter amicos
sit qui dicta foras eliminet, ut coeat par   25
iungaturque pari: Butram tibi Septiciumque
et nisi cena prior potiorque puella Sabinum
detinet adsumam; locus est et pluribus umbris;
sed nimis arta premunt olidae conuiuia caprae.
tu quotus esse uelis rescribe et rebus omissis   30
atria seruantem postico falle clientem.

24 FLAUIUS CLAUDIUS IULIANUS
(CONSTANTINOPLE, DECEMBER 361 / ANTIOCH, DECEMBER 362)

(*Epistles* 54 Wright = 41 Bidez = 8 Weis)

Εὐστοχίωι. Ἡσιόδωι μὲν δοκεῖ τῶι σοφῶι καλεῖν ἐπὶ τὰς ἑορτὰς
τοὺς γείτονας ὡς συνησθησομένους, ἐπειδὴ καὶ συναλγοῦσι καὶ
συναγωνιῶσιν, ὅταν τις ἀπροσδόκητος ἐμπέσηι ταραχή. ἐγὼ δέ
φημι τοὺς φίλους δεῖν καλεῖν, οὐχὶ τοὺς γείτονας· τὸ αἴτιον δέ,
ὅτι γείτονα μὲν ἔνεστιν ἐχθρὸν ἔχειν, φίλον δὲ ἐχθρὸν οὐ μᾶλλον ἢ τὸ λευκὸν μέλαν εἶναι καὶ τὸ θερμὸν ψυχρόν. ὅτι δὲ ἡμῖν
οὐ νῦν μόνον, ἀλλὰ καὶ πάλαι φίλος εἶ καὶ διετέλεσας εὐνοϊκῶς

tomorrow gives us permission to sleep in; we can stretch the summer night with friendly talk and not suffer for it. What good is money to me, if I'm not allowed to use it? Anyone who lets concern for his heir push him into exaggerated parsimony and austerity is next door to a lunatic; I shall start drinking deeply and scattering flowers and I won't even mind if people think that I've lost my judgement. What is there that inebriation can't bring off? It reveals secrets, commands hopes to be fulfilled, urges the coward into battle, takes the load off worried minds, teaches unsuspected skills. Have brimming glasses ever failed to make a man eloquent? Have they ever failed to free the sufferer from the pinch of poverty? My own self-appointed task – willingly undertaken, I'm just the man for it – is to ensure that no soiled coverlet or dirty napkin wrinkles your nose, that bowl and platter don't fail to present you with your own reflection, that there is no one among the group of faithful friends who will broadcast our conversation to outsiders, that the company and the pairings at table are well matched. I will secure you Butra and Septicius and – unless a prior invitation or a girl whose company he prefers prevents – Sabinus; there is also room for more than one of your own nominees – but when parties are too crowded the rich smell of goat becomes oppressive. Give me your learned opinion by return about how many fellow-guests you would like, drop your business, and if there's a client lying in wait in your front hall, give him the slip by the back door.

24 FLAVIUS CLAUDIUS JULIANUS

To Eustochios. Wise Hesiod's view is that we ought to invite our neighbours to our feasts to celebrate along with us, since they also share our grief and anguish when some unforeseen disturbance befalls us. But I say that it is our friends whom we ought to invite, not our neighbours. My reason is that it is possible to have a neighbour who is your enemy, but you cannot have a friend who is your enemy any more than white can be black or hot cold. Even if there were no other proof to hand that you are not only now my friend, but have been so for many a year, and have maintained your benevolent

ἔχων, εἰ καὶ μηδὲν ὑπῆρχεν ἄλλο τεκμήριον, ἀλλὰ τό γε ἡμᾶς
οὕτω διατεθεῖσθαι καὶ διακεῖσθαι περὶ σὲ μέγα ἂν εἴη τούτου
σημεῖον. ἧκε τοίνυν μεθέξων τῆς ὑπατείας αὐτός. ἄξει δέ σε ὁ
δημόσιος δρόμος ὀχήματι χρώμενον ἑνὶ καὶ παρίππωι. εἰ δὲ χρή
τι καὶ ἐπεύξασθαι, τὴν Ἐνοδίαν εὐμενῆ σοι καὶ τὸν Ἐνόδιον
παρακεκλήκαμεν.

25 PHALARIS

(Epistles 39)

Πολυστράτωι. καὶ τοῖς ἄλλοις ἅπασιν φίλοις ἐπέσταλκα διὰ
ταχέων ἐλθεῖν εἰς Ἀκράγαντα, καὶ σοῦ δέομαι παραγενέσθαι
πρὸ Ὀλυμπίων. βούλομαι γὰρ τῶν μάλιστα εὐνουστάτων σύλ-
λογον ἀγαγὼν τὴν πρέπουσαν ἐπιμέλειαν ὥσπερ ἄλλοτε καὶ
νῦν ποιήσασθαι καὶ περὶ πραγμάτων ἐπισφαλῶν καὶ μεγάλων
γνώμην λαβεῖν, ἀτόπου μὲν ἢ δυσκόλου μεταδώσων οὐδενός
(ἀρκέσω γὰρ ἐγὼ τοῖς ἐμαυτοῦ), πεισθησόμενος δὲ οἷς ἂν εἴποιτε,
ἵνα μενούσης μὲν τῆς ἀρχῆς ἐν οἷς ἐστὶ πολλάκις ὑμᾶς δεξιώσωμαι,
πιπτούσης δὲ ταύτης, ἂν δόκηι τῶι δαίμονι, τὴν ὑστάτην λαβόν-
τες προσαγόρευσιν μνήμονες εὐσεβεῖς ὧν ἐφιλοτιμήθημεν εἰς ὑμᾶς
γένησθε. ἥκετε οὖν ἀνυπερθέτως τῆι προτέραι προθυμίαι κε-
χρημένοι πρὸς Φάλαριν, ὃν μάλιστα ὑμεῖς γινώσκετε.

26 AURELIUS ARCHELAUS (EGYPT,
2 ND CENTURY A.D.)

(P. Oxy. 32+ = 249 *CPL* = 267 *CLA)*

I[u]lio Domitio tribuno mil(itum) leg(ionis) ab Aurelio Archelao
benef(iciario) suo salutem. iam tibi et pristine commendaueram
Theonem amicum meum et mod[o qu]oque peto domine ut eum
ant oculos habeas tanquam me. est enim tales omo ut ametur a te.
reliquit enim su[o]s [e]t rem suam et actum et me secutus est et per
omnia me secu[r]um fecit et ideo peto a te ut habeat intr[o]itum
at te et omnia tibi referere potest de actu[m] nostrum. quitquit
mi[hi d]ixit [i]l[lu]t et fact[...] ... amaui h[o]min[e]m [... ...]

feelings towards me, even so the fact that my own feelings for you have been and are still of this kind would be strong evidence. Come then, so as to participate in the consular celebrations in person. The state post will bring you, and you may have one carriage and an extra horse. If a prayer is required on top, I have called on Hekate of the Crossroads and Hermes of the Ways to be gracious to you.

25 PHALARIS

To Polystratos. I have written to all my other friends to come quickly to Acragas, so I beg you too to be there before the festival of Olympian Zeus. I wish to convene a meeting of my most devoted friends, so as to exercise the proper care now as always and to take counsel over a dangerous and serious situation. I do not mean to involve you in anything untoward or unpleasant (I shall have strength enough to deal with my own affairs), but to accept whatever advice you may have to give, so that if my empire remains I may often welcome you as my guests, but if it falls, if such be god's will, you may have one last chance of addressing me, and so preserve a reverent memory of my generosity towards you. So come without delay, with all your old zeal on behalf of the Phalaris whose character you above all know well.

26 AURELIUS ARCHELAUS

To Julius Domitius, legionary tribune, from Aurelius Archelaus, his aide, greetings. I have already on a previous occasion recommended my friend Theon to you, and now too, sir, I beg you to hold your eyes on him as if he were me, for he is just the sort of man you like. He left his family and his property and business and followed me, and in every way has kept me free from worry, and so I beg you to grant him access to you, and he can report you everything about our business. Whatever he told me ... indeed done ... I came to like the man ... sir ... intermediary ... for me to

domin[e... ...] illum ut [...] upse [...inter]cessoris u[t il]lum co[mmendarem]. estote felicissi[mi domine mul]tis annis cum [tuis omnibus] ben[e agentes]. hanc epistulam ant oculos habeto domine puta[t]o me tecum loqui. uale

Back: IOVLIO DOMITIO TRIBVNO MILITVM LEG(IONIS) ab Aurelio Archelao (beneficiario).

27 M. TULLIUS CICERO (LATE 46/45 B.C.)

(Ad familiares 13.5 = 319 SB)

Cicero s.d. Q. Valerio leg. pro pr. **1** non moleste fero eam necessitudinem quae mihi tecum est notam esse quam plurimis, neque tamen ob eam causam (quod tu optime existimare potes) te impedi⟨i⟩ quo minus susceptum negotium pro tua fide et diligentia ex uoluntate Caesaris, qui tibi rem magnam difficilemque commisit, gerere possis. nam cum multi a me petant multa, quod de tua erga me uoluntate non dubitent, non committo ut ambitione mea conturbem officium tuum. **2** C. Curtio ab ineunte aetate familiarissime sum usus. eius et Sullani temporis iniustissima calamitate dolui et, cum iis qui similem iniuriam acceperant amissis omnibus fortunis reditus tamen in patriam uoluntate omnium concedi uideretur, adiutor incolumitatis fui. is habet in Volaterrano possessionem, cum in eam tamquam e naufragio reliquias contulisset. hoc autem tempore eum Caesar in senatum legit; quem ordinem ille ista possessione amissa tueri uix potest. grauissimum autem est, cum superior factus sit ordine, inferiorem esse fortuna, minimeque conuenit ex eo agro qui Caesaris iussu diuidatur eum moueri qui Caesaris beneficio senator sit. **3** sed mihi minus libet multa de aequitate rei scribere ne causa potius apud te ualuisse uideatur quam gratia. quam ob rem te in maiorem modum rogo ut C. Curti rem meam putes esse; quicquid mea causa faceres,

recommend him. Allow me, sir, to wish you and your whole family every happiness and success for many years to come. Hold your eyes on this letter, sir, imagine that I am talking to you in person. Farewell.

Back: TO JULIUS DOMITIUS, LEGIONARY TRIBUNE from his aide Aurelius Archelaus.

27 M. TULLIUS CICERO

Cicero to Quintus Valerius, propraetorial legate, greetings. **1** It does not displease me that the friendship I enjoy with you should be known to as wide a circle as possible, but (as you are in an excellent position to judge) I have not made that a reason for hindering you in discharging the duty you have undertaken, with your characteristic loyalty and conscientiousness, and to the satisfaction of Caesar, who has entrusted you with a task as weighty as it is arduous. Although I receive many requests from many quarters, from people confident of your goodwill towards me, I have restrained myself from embarrassing you in the execution of your duty with solicitations of mine. **2** I have been on the closest of terms with Gaius Curtius since early youth. I was deeply upset by the wholly undeserved catastrophe he suffered in the days of Sulla, and when it seemed that there was a consensus in favour of allowing the victims of similar wrong to return home, in spite of the loss of all their fortunes, I assisted in his rehabilitation. He has an estate in the region of Volaterrae, in which he consolidated what remained to him after the shipwreck of his fortunes. More recently Caesar has co-opted him into the Senate, a station which he can hardly maintain if he loses that estate. It is very hard on him, when he has been raised to superior rank, to fall short in means, and it is outrageously inconsistent for a man who has been made a Senator by Caesar's good gift to be expelled from a district which is being shared out on Caesar's orders. **3** But I have no desire to dwell on the justice of his cause, lest it be thought that I have prevailed on you in virtue of the merits of the case rather than my own personal influence. Therefore let me particularly request you to regard Gaius Curtius' affair as my own; do for him whatever

ut, id C. Curti causa cum feceris, existimes quod ille per me
habuerit id me habere abs te. hoc te uehementer etiam atque etiam
rogo.

28 M. TULLIUS CICERO (ROME, 45 B.C.)

(*Ad familiares* 13.15 = 317 SB)

Cicero Caesari imp. s. **1** Precilium tibi commendo unice, tui neces-
sari, mei familiarissimi, uiri optimi, filium. quem cum adulescentem
ipsum propter eius modestiam, humanitatem, animum et amorem
erga me singularem mirifice diligo tum patrem eius re doctus intellexi et didici mihi fuisse semper amicissimum. em hic ille est de
illis maxime qui irridere atque obiugare me solitus est quod me non
tecum, praesertim cum abs te honorificentissime inuitarer, coniun-
gerem,

ἀλλ' ἐμὸν οὔ ποτε θυμὸν ἐνὶ στήθεσσιν ἔπειθεν.

audiebam enim nostros proceres clamitantes

ἄλκιμος ἔσσ' ἵνα τίς σε καὶ ὀψιγόνων ἐῢ εἴπῃι.

ὣς φάτο, τὸν δ ' ἄχεος νεφέλη ἐκάλυψε μέλαινα.

2 sed tamen idem me consolatur etiam. hominem <enim> perustum etiamnum gloria uolunt incendere atque ita loquuntur:

μὴ μὰν ἀσπουδί γε καὶ ἀκλειῶς ἀπολοίμην,

ἀλλὰ μέγα ῥέξας τι καὶ ἐσσομένοισι πύθεσθαι.

sed me minus iam mouet, ut uides. itaque ab Homeri magniloquentia confero me ad uera praecepta Εὐριπίδου:

μισῶ σοφιστήν, ὅστις οὐχ αὑτῶι σοφός.

quem uersum senex Precilius laudat egregie et ait posse eundem et

ἅμα πρόσσω καὶ ὀπίσσω uidere et tamen nihilo minus

αἰὲν ἀριστεύειν καὶ ὑπείροχον ἔμμεναι ἄλλων.

3 sed ut redeam ad id unde coepi, uehementer mihi gratum feceris
si hunc adulescentem humanitate tua,

you would do for my sake, and when it is done, take it that what he has gained by my influence is a gift from you to me. This I most earnestly and emphatically beg you.

28 M. TULLIUS CICERO

Cicero to Caesar, Imperator, greetings. **1** I recommend Precilius to you with unusual warmth. His father, a very worthy gentleman, is a relative of yours and a very close friend of mine. Just as I have an extraordinary regard for the young man himself, on the strength of his modesty, humane feelings, courage, and notably affectionate disposition towards me, so also experience has taught me to understand that his father has always borne me the greatest goodwill. Let me tell you, he is the one man above all others who used once to jeer at me and reproach me for not joining forces with you, especially when I was being invited by you in the most flattering terms,

but he never persuaded the heart in my breast.

Because I heard our leading lights clamouring

be valiant, so that men in future generations too may speak well of you.
So he spoke, and a black cloud of grief enfolded the other man.

2 Yet the same man now consoles me too. Badly burned though I am, they still want to kindle the fires of my ambition with words like these:

no, may I not die without a struggle and without glory,
but with some great deed for future generations too to come to know of.

But, as you can see, I don't respond so readily these days. So in flight from Homer's grand talk I take refuge in the sound precepts of Euripides:

I hate the pundit who is not wise to his own benefit.

This is a line that Precilius senior praises to the skies, saying that it is possible to look 'forward and backward at the same time', and still none the less

always to be best and to be superior to all others.

3 But to return to my starting-point, I would be deeply grateful if you were to take this young man under your wing, with the

quae est singularis, comprehenderis et ad id quod ipsorum Precil-
iorum causa te uelle arbitror addideris cumulum commendationis
meae. genere nouo sum litterarum ad te usus ut intellegeres non
uulgarem esse commendationem.

29 Q. HORATIUS FLACCUS

(*Epistles* 1.9)

Septimius, Claudi, nimirum intelligit unus,
quanti me facias; nam cum rogat et prece cogit
scilicet ut tibi se laudare et tradere coner
dignum mente domoque legentis honesta Neronis,
munere cum fungi propioris censet amici,   5
quid possim uidet ac nouit me ualdius ipso.
multa quidem dixi, cur excusatus abirem,
sed timui, mea ne finxisse minora putarer,
dissimulator opis propriae, mihi commodus uni.
sic ego maioris fugiens opprobria culpae   10
frontis ad urbanae descendi praemia. quodsi
depositum laudas ob amici iussa pudorem,
scribe tui gregis hunc et fortem crede bonumque.

30 C. PLINIUS SECUNDUS

(*Epistles* 4.4.)

C. Plinius Sosio Senecione suo s(alutem). **1** Varisidium Nepotem ua-
lidissime diligo, uirum industrium rectum disertum, quod apud me
uel potentissimum est. idem C. Caluisium, contubernalem meum
amicum tuum, arta propinquitate complectitur; est enim filius soro-
ris. **2** nunc rogo semestri tribunatu splendidiorem et sibi et auunculo
suo facias. obligabis me, obligabis Caluisium nostrum, obligabis ipsum, non minus idoneum debitorem quam nos putas. **3** multa

kindness that is your distinguishing characteristic, and accept my recommendation as the finishing touch, in addition to the goodwill I believe you already bear the Precilii themselves. I have written you an unconventional sort of letter to impress upon you that this is no everyday recommendation.

29 Q. HORATIUS FLACCUS

Claudius, Septimius apparently has a uniquely clear understanding of how highly you value me. Because he supposes me to have the status of quite a close friend, he begs me, and actually forces me with his entreaties into trying to sing his praises to you, and recommending him as someone worthy of the character and household of a Nero, devoted to the honourable path. In so doing, he sees and realizes what I am capable of more firmly than I do myself. Of course, I gave all sorts of reasons for being absolved from this duty and getting away with impunity, but I was afraid of being thought to belittle the extent of my influence, to be concealing my true resources, to be one who obliges only himself. So, in an effort to avoid being reproached for a worse offence, I have stooped to the self-assurance that townsmen take to be their privilege. If you approve of my laying aside my modesty on a friend's orders, then enrol this man as one of your set and be assured of his bravery and worth.

30 C. PLINIUS SECUNDUS

Gaius Plinius to his friend Sosius Senecio, greetings. **1** Varisidius Nepos is a man of industry, honour and eloquence (perhaps the strongest point in anyone's favour in my mind), and I have the most intense affection for him. He is also closely related to my associate and your friend Gaius Calvisius, being his sister's son. **2** May I now request that both for his sake and for his uncle's you dignify him still further by making him a six-month tribune. You will thus put me, our friend Calvisius, and the young man himself in your debt, and he is no less solvent a debtor than you hold me to be. **3** You have

beneficia in multos contulisti: ausim contendere nullum te melius,
aeque bene unum aut alterum collocasse. uale.

31 BASILEIOS (CAESAREA, A.D. 373)

(*Epistles* 147)

Ἀβουργίωι. μῦθον ἐνόμιζον τέως τὰ τοῦ Ὁμήρου, ὅτε ἐπήιειν
αὐτοῦ τὸ ἕτερον μέρος τῆς ποιήσεως, ἐν ὧι τὰ τοῦ Ὀδυσσέως
πάθη μεταδιδάσκει. ἀλλ᾽ ἐκεῖνα τὰ μυθικὰ τέως καὶ ἄπιστα πάνυ
ἡμᾶς πιθανὰ νομίζειν ἐδίδαξεν ἡ περὶ τὸν πάντα ἄριστον Μάξιμον περιπέτεια. καὶ γὰρ καὶ οὗτος ἄρχων ἐγένετο ἔθνους οὐ
φαυλοτάτου, ὥσπερ ἐκεῖνος ὁ στρατηγὸς τῶν Κεφαλλήνων. καὶ
πολλὰ χρήματα ἄγων ἐκεῖνος γυμνὸς ἐπανῆλθε καὶ τοῦτον οὕτως
ἡ συμφορὰ διέθηκεν, ὡς κινδυνεῦσαι ἐν ἀλλοτρίοις ῥάκεσιν ὀφθῆναι τοῖς οἰκείοις. καὶ ταῦτα πέπονθε Λαιστρυγόνας τάχα που
ἐφ᾽ ἑαυτὸν παροξύνας, καὶ Σκύλληι περιπεσὼν ἐν γυναικείαι μορ-
φῆι κυνείαν ἐχούσηι ἀπανθρωπίαν καὶ ἀγριότητα. ἐπεὶ οὖν μόλις
αὐτῶι ὑπῆρξε τὸν ἄφυκτον τοῦτον διανήξασθαι κλύδωνα, σὲ δι᾽
ἡμῶν ἱκετεύει, ἀξιῶν αἰδεσθῆναι τὴν κοινὴν φύσιν καὶ ἐπὶ ταῖς
παρ᾽ ἀξίαν αὐτοῦ συμφοραῖς ἀλγήσαντα, μὴ σιωπῆι κρύψαι τὰ
κατ᾽ αὐτόν, ἀλλὰ διαγγεῖλαι τοῖς ἐν δυνάμει, ὥστε μάλιστα μὲν
γενέσθαι τινὰ αὐτῶι βοήθειαν πρὸς τὴν σκευωρηθεῖσαν ἐπήρειαν·
εἰ δὲ μή, δημοσιευθῆναι γοῦν τὴν προαίρεσιν τοῦ εἰς αὐτὸν ἐμπαροινήσαντος. ἀρκοῦσα γὰρ τῶι ἠδικημένωι παραμυθία ἡ τῶν
ἐπιβουλευσάντων αὐτῶι τῆς πονηρίας φανέρωσις.

32 Q. HORATIUS FLACCUS (ROME, 19 B.C.)

(*Epistles* 1.12)

Fructibus Agrippae Siculis quos colligis, Icci,
si recte frueris, non est ut copia maior
ab Ioue donari possit tibi. tolle querelas;
pauper enim non est, cui rerum suppetit usus.

conferred many favours on many people, but I'd make so bold as to claim that you have never lodged one better, and only one or two equally well. Farewell.

31 BASILEIOS

To Abourgios. Once, when I read the second half of Homer's œuvre, in which he informs us of the tribulations of Odysseus, I used to think of his stories as wholly mythical. But the reverse of fortune suffered by the wholly excellent Maximus has taught me to find entirely credible what once was implausible myth. Maximus too was ruler of no mean people, just like the famous general of the Cephallenians. Odysseus went out with great riches and came back naked; Maximus too was so reduced by misfortune that he risked appearing before the eyes of his nearest and dearest in borrowed rags. What is more, this happened to him because he had roused the anger of a species of Laestrygonians against him, and had encountered a Scylla who concealed a canine inhumanity and savagery in woman's form. Since, therefore, he has just with difficulty managed to swim to safety from this cruelly stormy sea, he makes his supplication to you through me, begging you to respect the humanity you both share and, in sympathy for his undeserved misfortunes, not to suppress his story and say nothing about it, but to report it to the authorities, so that – ideally – he may receive some assistance in dealing with the outrage contrived against him, or at least, failing that, the true character of his persecutor may be made public. For the victim of wrongdoing, it is consolation enough if the villainy of those who have plotted against him is brought clearly to light.

32 Q. HORATIUS FLACCUS

Iccius, if you make right use, as you're entitled to, of the produce of Agrippa's Sicilian estates, which you collect, it is impossible for Jupiter to grant you any greater riches. Away with your complaints: the man who has the use of an estate available to him isn't a pauper.

si uentri bene, si lateri est pedibusque tuis, nil   5
diuitiae poterunt regales addere maius.
si forte in medio positorum abstemius herbis
uiuis et urtica, sic uiues protinus, ut te
confestim liquidus Fortunae riuus inauret,
uel quia naturam mutare pecunia nescit,   10
uel quia cuncta putas una uirtute minora.
    Miramur, si Democriti pecus edit agellos
cultaque, dum peregre est animus sine corpore uelox,
cum tu inter scabiem tantam et contagia lucri
nil paruum sapias et adhuc sublimia cures: 15
quae mare compescant causae, quid temperet annum,
stellae sponte sua iussaene uagentur et errent,
quid premat obscurum lunae, quid proferat orbem,
quid uelit et possit rerum concordia discors,
Empedocles an Stertinium deliret acumen?   20
    Verum seu pisces seu porrum et caepe trucidas,
utere Pompeio Grospho et, siquid petet, ultro
defer: nil Grosphus nisi uerum orabit et aequum.
uilis amicorum est annona, bonis ubi quid deest.
    Ne tamen ignores quo sit Romana loco res: 25
Cantaber Agrippae, Claudi uirtute Neronis
Armenius cecidit; ius imperiumque Prahates
Caesaris accepit genibus minor; aurea fruges
Italiae pleno defudit Copia cornu.

33 L. ANNAEUS SENECA

(*Epistles* 38)

Seneca Lucilio suo salutem. **1** merito exigis ut hoc inter nos epistularum commercium frequentemus. plurimum proficit sermo, quia
minutatim inrepit animo: disputationes preparatae et effusae audi-
ente populo plus habent strepitus, minus familiaritatis. philosophia
bonum consilium est: consilium nemo clare dat. aliquando uten-
dum est illis, ut ita dicam, contionibus, ubi qui dubitat inpellendus

If your stomach, chest and feet are in good shape, a king's fortune can add nothing more. But if by any chance you happen to be the sort to be sparing with what is available to all, and live on nettles or other green vegetables, you'll continue to pursue that style of life without interruption, even though Fortune's flowing river may suddenly shower you with gold, either because money can't change a man's character, or because you think that Virtue alone counts for more than anything else. Should we be surprised if Democritus' flocks ate up his fields and crops while his mind, released from his body, sped abroad, when you, in the midst of such furious, contagious itching for profit still possess the weightiest knowledge, and set your mind on higher matters: what causes hold the sea in check, what regulates the year, whether the planets wander and stray at their own whim or under orders, what thrusts the moon's globe into darkness and what brings it forth, the meaning and function of the discordant harmony of Nature, whether it is Empedocles or clever Stertinius who is out of his mind? But whether it is fish or only leek and onion that you murder, be a friend to Pompeius Grosphus and, if he asks for anything, grant it to him readily: Grosphus will ask for nothing but what is true and fair. The retail price of friends is low, when it is good men who need something. To keep you abreast of the current state of the Nation: the Spaniards have gone down to the valour of Agrippa and the Armenians to Claudius Nero's; Phraates on bended knee has accepted Caesar's power and sway; golden Plenty has showered crops on Italy from her brimming horn.

33 L. ANNAEUS SENECA

Seneca to his dear Lucilius, greetings. **1** You are right to demand that we should make this exchange of letters of ours more frequent. Informal conversation does the greatest good because it slips into the mind gradually; lectures prepared in advance and spouted in front of a mass audience are noisier but less intimate. Philosophy is good advice, and no one gives advice at the top of their voice. One does sometimes have to make use of harangues like that, if I may

est; ubi uero non hoc agendum est, ut uelit discere, sed ut discat, ad haec submissiora uerba ueniendum est. facilius intrant et haerent; nec enim multis opus est sed efficacibus. **2** seminis modo spargenda sunt, quod quamuis est exiguum, cum occupauit idoneum locum uires suas explicat et ex minimo in maximos auctus diffunditur. idem facit ratio; non late patet, si aspicias; in opere crescit. pauca sunt quae dicuntur, sed si illa animus bene excepit, conualescunt et exsurgunt. eadem est, inquam, praeceptorum condicio quae seminum: multum efficiunt, et angusta sunt. tantum, ut dixi, idonea mens rapiat illa et in se trahat; multa inuicem et ipsa generabit et plus reddet quam acceperit. uale.

34 L. ANNAEUS SENECA

(*Epistles* 61)

Seneca Lucilio suo salutem. **1** desinamus quod uoluimus uelle. ego certe id ago ne senex eadem uelim quae puer uolui. in hoc unum eunt dies, in hoc noctes, hoc opus meum est, haec cogitatio, inponere ueteribus malis finem. id ago ut mihi instar totius uitae dies sit; nec mehercules tamquam ultimum rapio, sed sic illum aspicio tamquam esse uel ultimus possit. **2** hoc animo tibi hanc epistulam scribo, tamquam me cum maxime scribentem mors euocatura sit; paratus exire sum, et ideo fruar uita quia quam diu futurum hoc sit non nimis pendeo. ante senectutem curaui ut bene uiuerem, in senectute ut bene moriar; bene autem mori est libenter mori. **3** da operam ne quid umquam inuitus facias: quidquid necesse futurum est repugnanti, id uolenti necessitas non est. ita dico: qui imperia libens excipit partem acerbissimam seruitutis effugit, facere quod nolit; non qui iussus aliquid facit miser est, sed qui inuitus facit.

so call them, in cases where a doubter has to be spurred on; but where the aim is to get someone actually to learn, rather than to want to learn, one needs to resort to more softly spoken words like these. They sink in and lodge more easily, because what is required is effective words, not a mass of them. **2** They should be scattered like seed. Small though it may be, when a seed lands on the right soil, it releases its strength and expands from the tiniest starting-point into the most far-ranging growth. So it is with reason too: it doesn't spread broadly, to external appearance, but it grows as it works. What is said is little enough, but if a mind takes it in well, it gathers strength and swells up. Yes, teaching has the same quality as seed: both achieve great results, and yet are themselves tiny. Only, as I say, let the right mind receive it and assimilate it; in its turn it too will engender much and give back more than it has received. Farewell.

34 L. ANNAEUS SENECA

Seneca to his dear Lucilius, greetings. **1** Let us cease from wanting what we once wanted. I at least am concerned to avoid wanting in old age what I wanted as a boy. My days and my nights are given over to this one objective, this is my task, this is what I brood on, to put an end to my chronic faults. My aim is to make each single day seem to me like the whole of my life. I don't (God forbid!) snatch at it as if it were my last, but none the less I look on it as if it might even be. **2** This is the state of mind in which I write this letter to you, as if death were about to call me away during the very act of writing. I am ready to depart, and I shall enjoy life precisely because I am not so very anxious to know how long this enjoyment will last. Before I grew old I took thought for living well; now that I am old, I am taking thought for dying well; and dying well means dying gladly. **3** Take care never to do anything unwillingly: whatever is bound to be a necessity if you struggle against it is not a necessity if you accept it willingly. Yes, I insist: he who takes orders willingly escapes the harshest form of servitude, doing what he doesn't want to; it isn't

itaque sic animum componamus ut quidquid res exiget, id uelimus, et in primis ut finem nostri sine tristitia cogitemus. **4** ante ad mortem quam ad uitam praeparandi sumus. satis instructa uita est, sed nos in instrumenta eius auidi sumus; deesse aliquid nobis uidetur et semper uidebitur: ut satis uixerimus, nec anni nec dies faciunt sed animus. uixi, Lucili carissime, quantum satis erat; mortem plenus expecto. uale.

35 AQUILA (c. 3 rd /4 th century a.d.)

(P. Oxy. 3069)

Ἀκύλας Σαραπίωνι χαίρειν. κομισάμενός σου τὰ γράμματα πάνυ ἥσθην· ἢ μάλιστα ὁ ἡμέτερος Καλλίνεικος ἐμαρτύρει περὶ τῆς διαίτης σου ἧς ποιῇ καὶ ἐν τοιούτοις ὢν πράγμασι[[ν]] μάλιστα μὴ ἀφιστάμενος τῆς ἀσκήσεως· ἄξιον οὖν ἐστιν ἐπαινεῖν ἑαυτούς, οὐχ ὅτι ποιοῦμεν ταῦτα ἀλλὰ ὅτι μὴ ἐξαγόμεθα ὑφ' ἑαυτ[ῶν]· ἀνδραγάθε[ι] οὖν καὶ τὰ λοιπὰ ἐπιτέλεσον ὡς ἀνὴ[ρ ἀ]γαθός, καὶ μ[ή σ]ε ταρασσέ[τ]ω ἢ πλοῦτος ἢ ὥρα ἢ ἄλλο τ[ι τ]ῶν τοιού[[ν]]των, ὡς οὐδὲν ὄφ[ελ]ός ἐστιν ἀρετῆς μὴ παρούσης, ἀλλὰ φροῦδα καὶ οὐδενὸς ἄξια. θεῶν σωζόντων προσδέχομαί σε ἐν τῇ Ἀντινόου. τὸ σκυλάκιον πέμψον Σωτηρίδι, ἐπεὶ αὐτὴ νῦν ἐν ἀγρῷ διατρείβει. ἔρρωσσο σὺν τοῖς σοῖς. ἔρρωσσο.

Back: Σαραπίωνι φιλοσόφωι παρὰ Ἀκύλου φίλου.

36 DIOGENES

(Epistles of Diogenes 6)

Κράτητι. **1** χωρισθέντος σου εἰς Θήβας ἀνέβαινον ἐκ Πειραιῶς ὑπὸ μέσην ἡμέραν, καὶ διὰ τοῦτο λαμβάνει με δίψος καρτερόν. ὥρμησα οὖν ἐπὶ τὴν Πάνοπος κρήνην. καὶ ἕως ἐγὼ τὸ ποτήριον ἐκ τῆς πήρας ἐξῇρουν, ἧκέ τις θέων θεράπων τῶν τὴν χώραν ἐργαζομένων καὶ συνάψας κοίλας τὰς χεῖρας ἤρύετο ἀπὸ τῆς κρήνης

the man who does something under orders who is wretched, but the
man who acts against his will. Therefore let us so compose ourselves
that we will whatever the situation dictates, and above all that we
contemplate our own demise without sadness. **4** We ought to be
prepared for death sooner than we are for life. Life is well enough
provided for, but we are too greedy for the means to sustain it. We
think we are lacking something, and always will: it isn't years and
days that will make a long enough life, but state of mind. My dearest
Lucilius, I have lived as long as sufficed me; I await my death replete.
Farewell.

35 AQUILA

Aquila to Sarapion, greetings. I was overjoyed to receive your letter.
Our friend Kallinikos testified in the strongest possible terms to the
style of life you practise, making a special point of not abandoning
your austerities, even when you are in the midst of such troubles.
Yes, we can fairly praise ourselves, not for doing these things, but
for not being diverted from them by ourselves. So be brave and
complete the job like a man, and do not let yourself be distracted by
wealth or beauty or anything else of the kind, because they are of
no use in the absence of Virtue, but vanish and are worthless. With
the gods' protection, I will expect to see you in Antinoopolis. Send
the puppy to Soteris, as she is now staying by herself in the country.
Good health to you and your family. Good health.

Back: To Sarapion the philosopher from his friend Aquila.

36 DIOGENES

To Krates. **1** After you had left for Thebes, I was on my way up from
the Piraeus in the middle of the day, and because of this was seized
by a parching thirst. So I hurried to the spring of Panops. As I was
taking the drinking-cup out of my knapsack, some slave or other,
one of the workers on the land, came running up and, cupping

καὶ οὕτως ἔπινε, καὶ ἐγώ, δόξαν μοι ποτηρίου σοφώτερον εἶναι, οὐκ ἠιδέσθην διδασκάλωι αὐτῶι τῶν καλῶν χρήσασθαι. 2 ἀπορρίψας οὖν τὸ ποτήριον ὃ εἶχον, καὶ σοὶ εὑρών τινας ἐπὶ Θηβῶν ἀνερχομένους τὸ σοφὸν τοῦτο ἐπέσταλκα οὐδὲν βουλόμενος τῶν καλῶν δίχα σοῦ ἐπίστασθαι. ἀλλὰ καὶ σὺ διὰ τοῦτο πειρῶ εἰς τὴν ἀγορὰν ἐμβάλλειν, ἵνα πολλοὶ διατρίβουσιν ἄνθρωποι. ἔσται γὰρ ἡμῖν οὕτω καὶ ἄλλα σοφὰ παρὰ τῶν κατὰ μέρος εὑρεῖν· πολλὴ γὰρ ἡ φύσις, ἣν ἐκβαλλομένην ὑπὸ τῆς δόξης ἐκ τοῦ βίου ἐπὶ σωτηρίαι ἀνθρώπων κατάγομεν ἡμεῖς.

37 KRATES

(Epistles of Krates 30)

Ἱππαρχίαι. ἔπεμψά σοι τὴν ἐξωμίδα, ἣν ὑφηναμένη μοι ἔπεμψας, ὅτι ἀπαγορεύεται τοῖς καρτερίαι χρωμένοις τοιαῦτα ἀμπέχεσθαι, καὶ ἵνα σε τούτου τοῦ ἔργου ἀποπαύσαιμι, εἰς ὃ πολλῆι σπουδῆι ἐξῆλυθες, ἵνα τις δόξηις φίλανδρος τοῖς πολλοῖς εἶναι. ἐγὼ δὲ εἰ μὲν διὰ ταῦτα σε ἠγόμην, εὖ γε ποιεῖς καὶ [αὐτὴ] διὰ τούτων ἐπιδεικνυμένη μοι· εἰ δὲ διὰ φιλοσοφίαν, ἧς καὶ αὐτὴ ὠρέχθης, τὰ τοιαῦτα σπουδάσματα ἔα χαίρειν, πειρῶ δὲ εἰς τὰ κρείττω τῶν ἀνθρώπων τὸν βίον ὠφελεῖν. ταῦτα γὰρ ἔμαθες καὶ παρ' ἐμοὶ καὶ παρὰ Διογένει.

38 PHALARIS

(Epistles 37)

Γοργίαι. 1 τὰ μὲν ἄλλα τῆς ἐπιστολῆς σου πάντα καλῶς ἡγοῦμαι γεγράφθαι, τὴν δὲ παράκλησιν τὴν ἐπὶ τοῖς μέλλουσι περιττεύειν νυνὶ μάλιστα λογίζομαι. ἐγὼ γὰρ οὔτε τελευτὴν οὔτε τελευτῆς εἶδος φεύγω σωφρονεῖν ὑπολαμβανόμενος· εἱμαρμένη γὰρ οὐχ ὑπ' ἀνθρώπων νομοθετοῦται. καθόλου δὲ τὸν ἐξετάζοντα περὶ τῶν ἐσομένων καλῶν ἢ κακῶν λίαν εὐήθη νομίζω, εἴ τις ἢ προγνῶναι

his hands, drew some water from the spring and drank. And I, thinking that this was cleverer than using a cup, wasn't ashamed to take him as my teacher in virtuous behaviour. **2** So I threw away the cup I used to have, and since I've found some travellers coming up in the direction of Thebes, I've written to you about this clever discovery, since I don't want to know anything about Virtue without your knowing it too. For this reason you too should try venturing into the public spaces, where many people spend their time. In this way we will be able to learn yet other clever things from individual encounters. Nature is mighty; so as vulgar opinion attempts to expel Her from ordinary life, it is our function to bring Her back, for the salvation of mankind.

37 KRATES

To Hipparchia. I am returning you the cloak which you wove and sent me, because we practitioners of endurance are forbidden to wear this kind of clothing; also in order to get you to desist from this activity, to which you have set yourself so very energetically in the hopes of winning a reputation with the general public for loving your husband. If I had married you for this, then well done for giving me this demonstration along with all the rest; but if it was for philosophy (to which you too aspired) that I married you, then say goodbye to such pursuits, and try to benefit human existence in ways that really matter. That is the lesson you have learned both from me and from Diogenes.

38 PHALARIS

To Gorgias. **1** Everything else in your letter I think is well said, but your exhortation concerning future events I judge superfluous, especially now. I flee neither death nor any appearance of death, and believe myself to show good sense in this; for Fate is not subject to human legislation. As a matter of principle I think that the man who enters into calculation about future good and ill is an utter

τὸ μέλλον δύνασθαι πέπεισται ἢ προγνοὺς φυλάξασθαι. εἰ δέ
τις τὸ μὲν προγνῶναι δυνατὸν ἡγεῖται, τὸ δὲ φυλάξασθαι ἀδύ-
νατον, τοῦ χάριν ἐσπούδακεν εἰδέναι τὸ γενησόμενον, ὅπερ καὶ
ἀγνοῦντος καὶ γιγνώσκοντος ἔσται; 2 οὐ μὴν ἀλλ' εἰ σὺν τῶι
γνῶναι καὶ τὸ φυλάξασθαι τούπιον ἀνυστὸν εἶναι φήσει τις, οἷός
τε ἔσται καὶ διατάξαι καὶ μεταθεῖναι ἄλλον ἀντὶ τοῦ προγν-
ωσθέντος χείρονος ἐπιεικέστερον τρόπον, ὧι τελευτῆσαι δύναιτ'
ἄν; ἐγὼ μὲν οὐκ οἶμαι· θεοῦ γὰρ ἔργον τὸ τοιοῦτον, οὐκ ἀνθρώπου. ἐνθυμηθεὶς δέ τις τοὺς λεγομένους ἀπὸ τοῦ Διός, Αἰακὸν
καὶ Μίνω καὶ Ῥαδάμανθυν, καὶ τοὺς ἄλλους ἡμιθέους οὔτε ἀθανάτους γενομένους οὔτε ἄλλως ἀποθανόντας ἢ κατὰ τὴν ἰδίαν ἑκάστου εἱμαρμένην, ἢ περὶ μοίρας ἢ θανάτου δυσανασχετῶν ἢ φοβού-
μενος ἐμπεδόφρων εἶναι σοι δοκεῖ; μάλιστα μὲν οὖν πειρῶ καὶ σὺ
τοιαύτην διάνοιαν ἐν τοῖς ἰδίοις περὶ τῶν ἀφανῶν ἔχειν, ὡς μηδὲν
περὶ αὐτῶν φροντίζειν, ἐπεί τοι περὶ ἡμῶν ὡς μηδὲν μεριμνώντων
ἐπίστασο.

39 THE ELDER (EPHESUS (?), A.D. 90–100 (?))

(John *Epistle* 2)

1 ὁ πρεσβύτερος ἐκλεκτῆι κυρίαι καὶ τοῖς τέκνοις αὐτῆς, οὓς ἐγὼ
ἀγαπῶ ἐν ἀληθείαι, καὶ οὐκ ἐγὼ μόνος ἀλλὰ καὶ πάντες οἱ ἐγν-
ωκότες τὴν ἀλήθειαν, 2 διὰ τὴν ἀλήθειαν τὴν μένουσαν ἐν ἡμῖν
καὶ μεθ' ἡμῶν ἔσται εἰς τὸν αἰῶνα. 3 ἔσται μεθ' ἡμῶν χάρις ἔλεος
εἰρήνη παρὰ θεοῦ πατρὸς καὶ παρὰ Ἰησοῦ Χριστοῦ τοῦ υἱοῦ τοῦ
πατρὸς ἐν ἀληθείαι καὶ ἀγάπηι.

4 ἐχάρην λίαν ὅτι εὕρηκα ἐκ τῶν τέκνων σου περιπατοῦντας
ἐν ἀληθείαι, καθὼς ἐντολὴν ἐλάβομεν παρὰ τοῦ πατρός. 5 καὶ νῦν
ἐρωτῶ σε, κυρία, οὐχ ὡς ἐντολὴν καινὴν γράφων σοι ἀλλὰ ἣν
εἴχομεν ἀπ' ἀρχῆς, ἵνα ἀγαπῶμεν ἀλλήλους. 6 καὶ αὕτη ἐστὶν ἡ
ἀγάπη, ἵνα περιπατῶμεν κατὰ τὰς ἐντολὰς αὐτοῦ· αὕτη ἡ ἐν-
τολή ἐστιν, καθὼς ἠκούσατε ἀπ' ἀρχῆς, ἵνα ἐν αὐτῆι περιπατῆτε.
7 ὅτι πολλοὶ πλάνοι ἐξῆλθον εἰς τὸν κόσμον, οἱ μὴ ὁμολογοῦντες
Ἰησοῦν Χριστὸν ἐρχόμενον ἐν σαρκί· οὗτός ἐστιν ὁ πλάνος καὶ ὁ ἀντίχριστος. 8 βλέπετε ἑαυτούς, ἵνα μὴ ἀπολέσητε ἃ εἰργασάμεθα,

fool, if indeed there is anyone who is actually convinced that he can foretell the future or guard against it once he has done so. On the other hand, if someone thinks that forecasting is possible, but guarding against the future is impossible, why is he so keen to know what is going to happen, when it will happen whether he knows it or not? **2** Even if someone is going to maintain that both knowing and guarding against what is to come is possible, will he really be able to arrange and substitute some other better manner in which to die in place of the worse one that has been foreseen? I for one do not think so: such a feat belongs to God not man. If someone reflects that the so-called sons of Zeus, Aeacus and Minos and Rhadamanthys, and the other demi-gods, were neither immortal nor died in any other way than each according to his own individual destiny, do you think it is at all sensible for him to feel either indignation or fear over destiny and death? Above all else, try on your own account to cultivate an attitude of indifference to the unknown in your affairs, since you can rest assured that I for my part have no such worries.

39 THE ELDER

1 The Elder to the chosen Lady and her children, whom I truly love, and not I alone but all those who have realized the truth, **2** through the truth that remains among us and will be with us for all time. **3** Grace, mercy and peace will be ours from God the Father and from Jesus Christ the Son of the Father in truth and love.

4 I was overjoyed to discover that some of your children are living in the way of truth, as we have been commanded by the Father. **5** I now ask you, Lady, not as if writing to you with a new command, but with the one we have had from the beginning, that we should love one another. **6** Love means living according to His commands; this is His command, as you have heard it from the beginning, that you live in love. **7** I write this because many impostors have gone out into the world, not acknowledging Jesus Christ coming in flesh; this is indeed what is meant by an impostor and Antichrist. **8** Look to yourselves, so as not to lose what we have achieved, but

ἀλλὰ μισθὸν πλήρη ἀπολάβητε. **9** πᾶς ὁ προάγων καὶ μὴ μένων ἐν τῆι διδαχῆι τοῦ Χριστοῦ θεὸν οὐχ ἔχει· ὁ μένων ἐν τῆι διδαχῆι, οὗτος καὶ τὸν πατέρα καὶ τὸν υἱὸν ἔχει. **10** εἴ τις ἔρχεται πρὸς ὑμᾶς καὶ ταύτην τὴν διδαχὴν οὐ φέρει, μὴ λαμβάνετε αὐτὸν εἰς οἰκίαν καὶ χαίρειν αὐτῶι μὴ λέγετε· **11** ὁ λέγων γὰρ αὐτῶι χαίρειν κοινωνεῖ τοῖς ἔργοις αὐτοῦ τοῖς πονηροῖς.

12 πολλὰ ἔχων ὑμῖν γράφειν οὐκ ἠβουλήθην διὰ χάρτου καὶ μέλανος, ἀλλὰ ἐλπίζω γενέσθαι πρὸς ὑμᾶς καὶ στόμα πρὸς στόμα λαλῆσαι, ἵνα ἡ χαρὰ ἡμῶν πεπληρωμένη ἦι. **13** ἀσπάζεταί σε τὰ τέκνα τῆς ἀδελφῆς σοῦ τῆς ἐκλεκτῆς.

40 BASILEIOS (PONTUS, c. A.D. 360)

(*Epistles* 10, πρὸς ἐλευθέραν)

τέχνη τίς ἐστι περιστερῶν θηρευτικὴ τοιαύτη. ὅταν μιᾶς ἐγκρατεῖς γένωνται οἱ τὰ τοιαῦτα σπουδάζοντες χειροήθη τε ταύτην καὶ ὁμόσιτον ἑαυτοῖς ἀπεργάζονται, τότε μύρωι τὰς πτέρυγας αὐτῆς χρίσαντες ἐῶσι συναγελασθῆναι ταῖς ἔξωθεν. ἡ δὲ τοῦ μύρου ἐκείνου εὐωδία τὴν αὐτόνομον ἐκείνην ἀγέλην κτῆμα ποιεῖται τῶι κεκτημένωι τὴν τιθασόν. πρὸς γὰρ τὰς εὐπνοίας καὶ αἱ λοιπαὶ συνεφέπονταί τε καὶ εἰσοικίζονται. τί δὲ βουλόμενος ἐντεῦθεν ἄρχομαι τοῦ γράμματος; ὅτι λαβὼν τὸν υἱὸν Διονύσιον, τὸν τότε Διομήδην, καὶ τῶι θείωι μύρωι τὰς τῆς ψυχῆς αὐτοῦ πτέρυγας διαχρίσας ἐξέπεμψα πρὸς τὴν σὴν σεμνοπρέπειαν, ὥστε καὶ σὲ αὐτὴν συναναπτῆναι αὐτῶι καὶ καταλαβεῖν τὴν καλιὰν ἣν παρ' ἡμῖν ἐπήξατο ὁ προειρημένος. ἐὰν οὖν ταῦτα ἴδοιμι ἐπὶ τῆς ἐμῆς ζωῆς καὶ τὴν σὴν σεμνοπρέπειαν πρὸς τὸν ὑψηλὸν βίον μεταθεμένην, πολλῶν προσώπων ἀξίων τοῦ Θεοῦ δεησόμεθα τὴν κεχρεωστημένην τίμην ἀποπληρῶσαι αὐτῶι.

41 BASILEIOS (CAESAREA, OCTOBER/NOVEMBER A.D. 368)

(*Epistles* 26)

Καισαρίωι τῶι ἀδελφῶι Γρηγορίου. χάρις τῶι Θεῶι, τῶι τὰ ἑαυτοῦ θαυμάσια καὶ ἐν σοὶ ἐπιδεικνυμένωι καὶ ἐκ τοσούτου

to receive your full reward. **9** Anyone who leads on and does not remain faithful to the teaching of Christ does not have God; but he who remains faithful to his teaching has both the Father and the Son. **10** If anyone comes to you and does not bring this teaching, do not welcome him into your house, do not even pass the time of day with him, **11** because anyone who wishes him well becomes a collaborator in his evil work.

12 Although I have much to write to you I do not want to do so with paper and ink, but hope to visit you and speak to you face to face, so that our joy may be complete. **13** The children of your chosen sister send you their greetings.

40 BASILEIOS (*TO THE WIDOW*)

There is a technique for catching doves that works like this. When professionals have caught a single dove and tamed it and made it used to taking food from them, then they smear its wings with perfume and allow it to flock with the doves out in the wild. The fragrance of the perfume brings the wild flock into the hands of the tame dove's owner, because the rest of them, attracted by the fragrant scent, follow the tame one and enter the dove-cote along with it. What is my reason for beginning my letter like this? It is because I have snared your son Dionysios, Diomedes that was, and smearing the wings of his soul with the perfume of God I have sent him out to your Ladyship, so as to induce you too to fly with him and enter the nest which he, the aforementioned, has built amongst us. If I were to live to see this sight, and saw your Ladyship converted to our exalted life, I shall need many lives worthy in God's eyes in order to discharge in full the debt of honour that will then be owing to Him.

41 BASILEIOS

To Caesarius, the brother of Gregorios. Thanks be to God, who has shown forth his wondrous deeds in you too and preserved you

θάνατου διασώσαντί σε τῆι τε πατρίδι καὶ ἡμῖν τοῖς προσήκουσι.

λείπεται δὴ οὖν μῆ ἀχαρίστους ἡμᾶς ὀφθῆναι μηδ' ἀναξίους τῆς τοσαύτης εὐεργεσίας, ἀλλὰ κατὰ δύναμιν τὴν ἡμετέραν διαγγέλλειν τοῦ Θεοῦ τὰ παράδοξα καί, ἧς ἔργωι πεπειράμεθα φιλανθρωπίας, ταύτην ἀνυμνεῖν· καὶ μὴ λόγωι μόνον ἀποδιδόναι τὴν χάριν, ἀλλὰ καὶ ἔργωι τοιοῦτον γενέσθαι οἷον καὶ νῦν εἶναι πειθόμεθα, τεκμαιρόμενοι τοῖς περὶ σὲ θαύμασι. καὶ ἔτι μειζόνως τῶι Θεῶι δουλεύειν παρακαλοῦμεν, προσθήκαις ἀεὶ τὸν φόβον συναύξοντα καὶ εἰς τὸ τέλειον προκόπτοντα, ἵνα φρόνιμοι οἰκόνομοι τῆς ζωῆς ἡμῶν ἀποδειχθῶμεν, εἰς ἣν ἡμᾶς ἡ ἀγαθότης τοῦ Θεοῦ ἐταμιεύσατο. εἰ γὰρ καὶ πᾶσιν ἡμῖν πρόσταγμά ἐστι παραστῆσαι ἑαυτοὺς τῶι Θεῶι ὡσεὶ ἐκ νεκρῶν ζῶντας, πῶς οὐχὶ μᾶλλον τοῖς ὑψωθεῖσιν ἐκ τῶν πυλῶν τοῦ θανάτου; τοῦτο δ' ἂν μάλιστα, ὡς ἐμαυτὸν πείθω, κατορθωθείη, εἰ βουληθείημεν ἀεὶ τὴν αὐτὴν ἔχειν διάνοιαν ἣν εἴχομεν ἐπὶ τοῦ καιροῦ τῶν κινδύνων. πάντως γάρ που εἰσήιει ἡμᾶς τοῦ βίου τὸ μάταιον καὶ ὡς οὐδὲν πιστὸν τῶν ἀνθρωπίνων οὔτε πάγιον, οὕτω ῥαιδίας ἐχόντων τὰς μεταπτώσεις. καί πού τις μεταμέλεια μὲν ἔκ γε τῶν εἰκότων ἐνεγίνετο ἡμῖν ἐπὶ τοῖς φθάσασιν, ὑποσχέσεις δὲ περὶ τῶν ἐφεξῆς, εἰ περισωθείημεν, Θεῶι δουλεύειν καὶ ἑαυτῶν ἐπιμέλεσθαι κατὰ πᾶσαν ἀκρίβειαν. εἰ γάρ τινα ἡμῖν ἔννοιαν ὁ τοῦ θανάτου κίνδυνος ἐπικείμενος ἐνεδίδου, οἶμαί σε ἢ ταῦτα ἢ ἐγγύτατα τούτων ἀναλογίζεσθαι τηνικαῦτα. ὥστε ἀναγκαίου ὀφλήματος ἐκτίσει ὑπεύθυνοι καθεστήκαμεν.

ταῦτα, ὁμοῦ μὲν περιχαρὴς ὢν τῆι τοῦ Θεοῦ δωρεᾶι, ὁμοῦ δὲ καὶ φροντίδα ἔχων ὑπὲρ τῶν μελλόντων, ἀπεθάρσησα ὑπομνῆσαι τὴν τελειότητά σου. σὸν δέ ἐστιν εὐμενῶς καὶ ἡμέρως προσέσθαι ἡμῶν τοὺς λόγους, ὡς καὶ ἐν ταῖς κατ' ὀφθαλμοὺς ὁμιλίαις σοι ἦν σύνηθες.

from such mortal peril for your country and for us, your nearest and dearest.

It devolves on us not to be seen to be ungrateful or unworthy of so great a benefaction, but to do all in our power to proclaim God's marvels and to sing the praises of the loving kindness we have experienced in very deed. Moreover, one should not give thanks in word alone, but should in deeds too become the sort of person that I am convinced you are even now, judging by the marvels that have attended you. I exhort you to serve God yet more devotedly, ever augmenting your fear of him with new additions and advancing towards perfection, so that we may be revealed to all as prudent stewards of the life for which God's goodness has spared us. If it is in any case enjoined on all of us to 'present ourselves to God as if brought to life from the dead', how can this not apply still more strongly to those who have been lifted from the gates of death? The best chance of success in this, I am convinced, would be if we were willing to maintain at all times the same frame of mind as we had in our hour of danger. For then, certainly, the vanity of life and the absence of anything reliable or sound in human affairs, which can change so very easily, came home to us. And in all probability, surely, we found within us a certain repentance for past actions, and promises about future actions, if we were to survive, that we would serve God and take care of ourselves with the utmost strictness. If ever the impending danger of death gave us cause for reflection, then I am sure that on this occasion these thoughts or others very like them went through your mind. We are then liable for the repayment of a binding debt.

Such is the reminder I have made so bold as to offer your Excellency, simultaneously overjoyed as I am at God's bounty, and concerned for the future. It is for you to attend to my words graciously and gently, as is your habit also when we meet face to face.

42 EUSEBIUS HIERONYMUS (ROME,
AUTUMN A.D. 384)

(Epistles 23: *Ad Marcellam de exitu Leae)*

1 Cum hora ferme tertia hodiernae diei septuagesimum secundum psalmum, id est tertii libri principium, legere coepissemus, et docere cogeremur tituli ipsius partem ad finem secundi libri, partem ad principium tertii libri pertinere – quod scilicet 'defecerunt hymni Dauid, filii Iesse' finis esset prioris, 'psalmus' uero 'Asaph' principium sequentis – et usque ad eum locum peruenissemus in quo iustus loquitur: 'dicebam: si narrauero sic, ecce generationem filiorum tuorum praeuaricatus sum', quod in Latinis codicibus non ita habemus expressum, repente nobis nuntiatum est sanctissimam Leam exisse de corpore. ibique ita te palluisse conspexi, ut uere aut pauca aut nulla sit anima quae fracto uase testaceo non tristis erumpat. et tu quidem, non quod futuri incerta esses dolebas, sed quo triste funeri obsequium non dedisses. denique in mediis fabulis rursum didicimus reliquias eius iam Ostiam fuisse delatas. **2** quaeras quo pertineat ista replicatio? respondebo tibi uerbis apostoli 'multum per omnem modum'. primum, quod uniuersorum gaudiis prosequenda sit quae calcato diabolo coronam iam securitatis accepit; secundo, ut eius uita breuiter explicetur; tertio, ut designatum consulem de suis saeculis detrahentes esse doceamus in tartaro. equidem conuersationem Leae nostrae quis possit digno eleuare praeconio? ita eam totam ad Dominum fuisse conuersam ut monasterii princeps, mater uirginum fieret; post mollitiem uestium sacco membra triuisse; orationibus duxisse noctes, et comites suas plus exemplo docuisse quam uerbis. humilitatis tantae tamque subiectae, ut quondam domina plurimorum ancilla hominis putaretur, nisi quod eo Christi magis esse ancilla dum domina hominum

42 EUSEBIUS HIERONYMUS (*TO MARCELLA ON THE DEATH OF LEA*)

1 When today at about Tierce we had begun to read the seventy-second psalm, that is the beginning of the third book, and I was obliged to explain that part of the title itself belongs to the end of the second book and part to the beginning of the third – I mean that 'the hymns of David, son of Jesse, are ended' was the conclusion of the previous book, but 'a psalm of Asaph' the beginning of the next – and we had reached the passage where the righteous man says: 'I said: "if I speak thus, lo I have transgressed against the generation of your children",' which in the Latin manuscripts we find differently translated, news was suddenly brought to us that the most holy Lea had departed the body. Thereupon I saw you grow so pale that truly no soul (or very few) would not shatter its vessel of clay and burst out in its grief. You for your part were grieved not through any uncertainty about the future but because you had not been able to perform your sad duties at her funeral. Then, even as we continued our conversation, we received a second message that her remains had already been taken to Ostia. **2** Do you ask why it matters to repeat all this? I will answer you in the words of the apostle, 'it matters much in every way'. First, because she who has trampled the devil underfoot and has now received the crown of salvation should be escorted on her way by universal rejoicing; secondly, so that I may give a brief account of her life; third, so that we can drag the consul designate down from his worldly pomp and preach that he is in Hell. Who indeed can commend our Lea's comportment in the manner it deserves? She had turned so completely to the Lord that she became the superior of a convent, a mother of virgins [nuns]; in place of the soft clothes she wore before, she mortified her limbs with sack-cloth; she spent her nights in prayer and taught her companions more by her example than by her words. She was a woman of such meek humility that, though once the mistress of many, she would be thought to be someone's maidservant, were it not that in ceasing to be seen as a mistress of men, she thereby appears all the more as Christ's maidservant.

non putatur. inculta uestis uilis cibus neglectum caput, ita tamen ut cum omnia faceret ostentationem fugeret singulorum, ne reciperet in praesenti saeculo mercedem suam. **3** nunc igitur pro breui labore aeterna beatitudine fruitur: excipitur angelorum choris, Abrahae sinibus confouetur, et cum paupere quondam Lazaro diuitem pur-puratum et non palmatum consulem, sed sacratum, stillam dig-iti minoris cernit inquirere. o rerum quanta mutatio! ille, quem ante paucos dies dignitatum omnium culmina praecedebat, qui quasi de subiectis hostibus triumpharet Capitolinas ascendit arces, quem plausu quodam et tripudio populus Romanus excepit, ad cuius interitum urbs uniuersa commota est, nunc desolatus est, nudus, non in lacteo caeli palatio, ut uxor commentitur infelix, sed in sordentibus tenebris continetur. haec uero, quam unius cubi-culi secreta uallabant, quae pauper uidebatur et tenuis, cuius uita putabatur amentia, Christum sequitur et dicit: 'quaecumque au-diuimus, et uidimus in ciuitate dei nostri', et reliqua. **4** quapropter moneo et flens gemensque contestor ut, dum huius mundi uiam currimus, non duabus tunicis, id est duplici uestiamur fide, non calciamentorum pellibus, mortuis uidelicet operibus, praegraue-mur, non diuitiarum nos pera ad terram premat, non uirgae, id est potentia saecularis, quaeratur auxilium, non pariter et Christum habere uelimus et saeculum, sed pro breuibus et caducis aeterna succedant, et cum cottidie – secundum corpus loquor – praemo-riamur, in ceteris non nos perpetuos aestimemus, ut possimus esse perpetui.

43 AURELIUS AUGUSTINUS
(HIPPO REGIUS, *c*. A.D. 405)

(*Epistles* 245)

Domino delectissimo et uenerabili fratri et consacerdoti Possidio et qui tecum sunt fratribus Augustinus et qui mecum sunt fratres in

Her clothing was plain, her food simple, her hair unkempt, but only in such a way that, in all she did, she avoided ostentation in any individual detail, so as not to receive her reward in this world alone. **3** Now therefore in return for a short-lived labour she enjoys eternal bliss: the chorus of angels welcome her, she is cherished in the bosom of Abraham, and in the company of the once poor Lazarus she sees a rich man in his purple and a consul, not yet indeed clothed in his palm-embroidered robe but already designate, seeking in vain for a drop of water from her little finger! What a change of condition! He who a few days ago stood higher than the highest pinnacle of rank, who ascended the citadel of the Capitol as if triumphing over defeated enemies, whom the people of Rome welcomed with no little applause and stamping of feet, at whose death the whole city was moved to grief, is now abandoned and naked, lodged not in the milky palace of the heavens, as his unfortunate wife falsely claims, but in squalid darkness. But this woman, whose fortress was the solitude of one small cell, who seemed poor and lowly, whose life was reckoned folly, follows in Christ's train and says: 'whatsoever we have heard, that we have seen in the city of our God', and the rest. **4** For which reason I counsel you and beseech you with tears and groans that, as we hasten along the road of this world, we should not clothe ourselves in two coats, that is in a double faith, that we should not be encumbered by leather shoes, that is by dead works, that a sack of riches should not weigh us down to the ground, that we should not seek the aid of a staff, that is of temporal power, that we should not wish to possess both Christ and this world equally, but that things eternal should take the place of what is transitory and fragile, and as each day – in the physical sense, I mean – we die in anticipation, we should not reckon ourselves everlasting in other respects, so that we may indeed live for ever.

43 AURELIUS AUGUSTINUS

From Augustine and the brothers who are with me, to my dearest Lord and venerable brother and fellow-priest Possidius and the

domino salutem. **1** magis quid agas cum eis qui obtemperare nolunt, cogitandum est, quam quem ad modum eis ostendas non licere quod faciunt. sed nunc epistula sanctitatis tuae et occupatissimum me repperit et celerrimus baiuli reditus neque non rescribere tibi neque ad ea quae consuluisti, ita ut oportet, respondere permisit. nolo tamen de ornamentis auri uel uestis praeproperam habeas in prohibendo sententiam, nisi eos qui, neque coniugati neque coniugari cupientes, cogitare debent quo modo placeant deo. illi autem cogitant quae sunt mundi, quo modo placeant uel uiri uxoribus uel mulieres maritis, nisi quod capillos nudare feminas, quas etiam caput velare apostolus iubet, nec maritatas decet; fucari autem pigmentis, quo uel rubicundior uel candidior appareat, adulterina fallacia est, qua non dubito etiam ipsos maritos se nolle decipi, quibus solis permittendae sunt feminae ornari secundam ueniam, non secundum imperium. nam uerus ornatus maxime Christianorum et Christianarum non tantum nullus fucus mendax uerum ne auri quidem uestisque pompa, sed mores boni sunt. **2** execranda autem superstitio ligaturarum, in quibus etiam inaures uirorum in summis ex una parte auriculis suspensae deputantur: non ad placendum hominibus sed ad seruiendum daemonibus adhibentur. quis autem possit speciales nefariarum superstitionum prohibitiones in scripturis inuenire, cum generaliter apostolus dicat: nolo uos socios fieri daemoniorum, et iterum: quae enim consonantia Christi ad Belial? nisi forte, quia Belial nominauit et generaliter societatem daemoniorum prohibuit, licet Christianis sacrificare Neptuno, quia nihil proprie de Neptuno uetitum legimus. moneantur interim miseri, ut, si obtemperare nolunt praeceptis salubrioribus, saltem sacrilegia sua non defendant, ne maiore se

brothers who are with you, greetings in the Lord. **1** You need to think harder about what to do to those who refuse to obey than about ways of showing them that what they are doing is forbidden. But at this moment your Holiness's letter finds me extremely busy, and the letter-carrier's immediate departure allows me neither to decline to write back to you, nor to give you the kind of answer your enquiry deserves. None the less, in the case of personal adornment with gold or fine clothes, I do not want you to come to any precipitate decision in the way of prohibiting it, except for those who, neither married nor desiring to be married, ought to devote their thoughts to pleasing God. Those of whom you speak, however, 'have worldly concerns, how as men they may please their wives' or 'as women their husbands' – except that not even married women may decently uncover their hair, given that the apostle commands them to veil their heads. However, colouring the face with make-up, so as to make it seem rosier or whiter than it really is, is a dishonest counterfeit, which I have no doubt even husbands themselves do not want to be taken in by; and they are the only people for whom women should be permitted to adorn themselves, and that as a concession not a command. For the true adornment of the most Christian men and women is not so much the absence of deceptive make-up, and also of ostentatious gold jewelry and clothing, but good morals. **2** On the other hand, the superstitious use of amulets on threads – even men's ear-rings, hanging from the top of the ear on one side, should be considered an instance of this – is an abomination: these are not used to please human beings but to serve demons. Who could expect to find particular prohibitions against wicked superstitions in the scriptures, when the apostle declares generally 'I do not want you to become associates of demons', or again 'what agreement can there be between Christ and Belial?' Unless perhaps, because he named Belial and prohibited association with demons in general terms, Christians may still sacrifice to Neptune, because we read no specific prohibition regarding Neptune! Let the wretches be warned in the meantime that, if they refuse to obey more salutary instructions, they should at least refrain from

scelere implicent. quid autem cum eis agendum sit, si soluere inaures
timent et corpus Christi cum signo diaboli accipere non timent?
de ordinatu autem, qui in parte Donati baptizatus est, auctor tibi
esse non possum; aliud est enim facere, si cogaris, aliud consulere
ut facias.

44 M. TULLIUS CICERO (ROME, APRIL 52 B.C.)

(Ad familiares 5.18 = 51 SB)

M. Cicero s.d. T. Fadio. **1** etsi egomet, qui te consolari cupio, consolandus ipse sum, propterea quod nullam rem grauius iam diu
tuli quam incommodum tuum, tamen te magno opere non hortor solum sed etiam pro amore nostro rogo atque oro te colligas
uirumque praebeas et qua condicione omnes homines et quibus
temporibus nos nati simus cogites. plus tibi uirtus tua dedit quam fortuna abstulerit, propterea quod adeptus es quod non multi homines
noui, amisisti quae plurimi homines nobilissimi. ea denique uidetur condicio impendere legum, iudiciorum, temporum ut optime
actum cum eo uideatur esse qui quam leuissima poena ab hac re
publica discesserit. **2** tu uero, qui et fortunas et liberos habeas et
nos ceterosque necessitudine et beneuolentia tecum coniunctissi-
mos, quique magnam facultatem sis habiturus nobiscum et cum
omnibus tuis uiuendi, et cuius unum sit iudicium ex tam multis
quod reprehendatur, ut quod una sententia eaque dubia potentiae
alicuius condonatum existimetur, omnibus his de causis debes istam
molestiam quam lenissime ferre. meus animus erit in te liberosque
tuos semper quem tu esse uis et qui esse debet.

defending their sacrilegious actions, lest they implicate themselves in graver offence. What can be done with them, if they are afraid to take off their ear-rings yet are not afraid to receive the body of Christ while wearing the badge of the devil? About the ordination of one baptized into the Donatist faction, I cannot take the responsibility of recommending you to do it; it is one thing for you to do it if you have no alternative, quite another for me to advise you to.

44 M. TULLIUS CICERO

M. Cicero to T. Fadius, greetings. **1** Even though I, who desire to console you, am myself in need of consolation, because it is a long time since I have resented anything more deeply than your present misfortune, yet I earnestly exhort you, and more than that entreat and implore you in the name of our mutual affection, to compose yourself and show yourself to be a man, and reflect on both the terms to which mankind universally is born, and the times to which we ourselves have been. Your worth has given you more than chance has taken away, in that you have attained what few 'new men' have, and lost no more than many of the highest rank. To put it squarely, we seem to be faced by circumstances in the laws, the courts, and conditions in general, in which it is the man who leaves public life with the lightest sentence who will be reckoned to have come off best. **2** You still have your fortune and your children; you have me and your other friends, bound to you by the closest ties of intimacy and goodwill; you are to have every opportunity of sharing your life with me and all your friends; the judgement given against you is the only one out of many to be criticized, in that it is held to have been a concession to the political pre-eminence of a particular individual, passed by a single vote in suspicious circumstances. For all these reasons you must bear your troubles as cheerfully as possible. My own feelings for you and your children will always be what you wish them to be, and what they ought to be.

45 P. OVIDIUS NASO (TOMI)

(Epistulae Ex Ponto 4.11)

Gallio, crimen erit uix excusabile nobis,
    carmine te nomen non habuisse meo.
tu quoque enim, memini, caelesti cuspide facta
    fouisti lacrimis uulnera nostra tuis.
atque utinam rapti iactura laesus amici   5
    sensisses ultra, quod quererere, nihil!
non ita dis placuit, qui te spoliare pudica
    coniuge crudeles non habuere nefas.
nuntia nam luctus mihi nuper epistula uenit,
    lectaque cum lacrimis sunt tua damna meis.   10
sed neque solari prudentem stultior ausim,
    uerbaque doctorum nota referre tibi,
finitumque tuum, si non ratione, dolorem
    ipsa iam pridem suspicor esse mora.
dum tua peruenit, dum littera nostra recurrens   15
    tot maria ac terras permeat, annus abit.
temporis officium est solacia dicere certi,
    dum dolor in cursu est et petit aeger opem.
at cum longa dies sedauit uulnera mentis,
    intempestiue qui mouet illa, nouat.   20
adde quod (atque utinam uerum tibi uenerit omen!)
    coniugio felix iam potes esse nouo.

46 EIRENE (?OXYRHYNCHUS, 2 ND CENTURY A.D.)

(P. Oxy. 115)

Εἰρήνη Ταοννώφρει ʽκαὶʼ Φίλωνι εὐψυχεῖν. οὕτως ἐλυπήθην καὶ
ἔκλαυσα ʽἐπὶʼ τῷ εὐμοίρῳ ὡς ἐπὶ Διδυμᾶτος ἔκλαυσα, καὶ πάντα
ὅσα ἦν καθήκοντα ἐποίησα καὶ πάντες οἱ ἐμοί, Ἐπαφρόδειτος καὶ
Θερμούθιον καὶ Φίλιον καὶ Ἀπολλώνιος καὶ Πλαντᾶς. ἀλλ᾽ ὅμως
οὐδὲν δύναταί τις πρὸς τὰ τοιαῦτα. παρηγορεῖτε οὖν ἑαυτούς.
εὖ πράττετε. Ἀθὺρ α´.

Reverse: Ταοννώφρει καὶ Φίλωνι.

45 P. OVIDIUS NASO

Gallio, it would lay me open to a charge on which I could scarcely defend myself if you were not to have been celebrated in my verses. For I remember that you too, with your tears, tended the wounds inflicted on me by heaven's lance. Oh if only, once damaged by the loss of the friend torn from you, you had felt no further cause for grief! Such was not the will of the gods, who in their cruelty thought it no crime to strip you of your chaste wife. The letter informing me that you were in mourning has just reached me, and it was with tears in my eyes that I read of your loss. But I would not make so bold as to offer you consolation when you are so much wiser than I, or to repeat to you the words of the learned that you know so well: and in any case I suspect that even if the power of reason has not put a term to your grief by now, then the lapse of time has. While your letters make their way to me, and mine on their way back traverse such expanses of sea and land, a whole year slips by. Offering words of consolation is a task for a specific period of time, when grief is runnning its course and seeking remedies for its pain. But when the long march of days has soothed the heart's wounds, anyone who touches on them out of time only reopens them. What is more – oh if only this has reached you as a prediction come true! – you may even now be happily remarried.

46 EIRENE

Eirene to Taonnophris and Philo, take heart. I was as distressed and I wept as much over the departed as I did over Didymas, and I kept all the proper observances, along with all my family, Epaphroditos and Thermouthion and Philion and Apollonios and Plantas. Even so, there is nothing anyone can do in the face of such events. Comfort each other, then. Fare well. 1 Hathyr.

Reverse: To Taonnophris and Philo.

47 LIBANIOS (ANTIOCH, spring 365)

(*Epistles* 142 Norman = 1508 Foerster)

Σελεύκωι. **1** Ἐδάκρυσα ἐπὶ τοῖς γράμμασι καὶ πρὸς τοὺς θεοὺς ἔφην· "τί ταῦτα, ὦ θεοί;" δοὺς δὲ καὶ τῶν ἄλλων οἷς πιστεύω μάλιστα τὴν ἐπιστολὴν κἀκείνους ταὐτὸν εἶδον παθόντας πρὸς τὴν ἐπιστολήν. ἐλογίζετο γὰρ ἕκαστος, ὧν ἄξιος ὢν τυχεῖν ἐν οἷς ἠνάγκασαι διάγειν. **2** ἐγὼ δὲ οἷς κἀκείνους καὶ ἐμαυτὸν παρεμυθησάμην ἐρῶ· καὶ γὰρ σοὶ τοῦτο ἀρκέσειν οἶμαι.

εἰσῆλθέ με Ὀδυσσεὺς ἐκεῖνος, ὃς ἐπειδὴ τὴν Τροίαν κατήνεγκεν, ἐκομίζετο διὰ τῆς θαλάσσης, ὡς οἶσθα, ἡμεῖς δὲ οὔτε κλάδων ἐπὶ τὰ αἰδοῖα δεόμεθα μηδ' αὖ δεηθείημεν οὔθ' ὑπὸ τῶν οἰκετῶν τυπτόμεθα καθαρός τέ σοι πάσης παροινίας ὁ οἶκος. **3** εἰ δ' εἴργηι πόλεων καὶ τῶν ἐν ἐκείναις λουτρῶν, ἐνθυμοῦ, πόσοι παρὸν ἐν πόλει διατρίβειν ἐν ἀγροῖς αἱροῦνται τὰς ἡδονὰς ἡδίους τῶν ἐκεῖ θορύβων κρίνοντες. εἰ δὲ ἦσθα Ἀχιλλεὺς καὶ ἐχρῆν σε ἐν Πηλίωι συνεῖναι τῶι Κενταύρωι, τί ἂν ἔδρας; ἀποδρὰς ἂν εἰς τὰς πόλεις ὤιχου συμφορὰν τὸ ὄρος ἡγούμενος; **4** μή, πρὸς Διός, ὦ Σέλευκε, μὴ κόπτε σαυτὸν μηδ' ἀμνημόνει τῶν στρατηγῶν ἐκείνων, οἳ ἄρτι τὰ τρόπαια στήσαντες, ὁ μὲν ἦν ἐν δεσμοῖς, οἱ δὲ ἔφευγον. οὐδὲ γὰρ ὅπως πονοῖμεν, ἐκεῖνα ἐμανθάνομεν, ἀλλ' ὅπως ἐν τοῖς δεινοῖς ἐκεῖθεν κουφιζοίμεθα. **5** σὺ δ' ἔχων καιρὸν εἰς ἐπίδειξιν ἀνδρείας ὀδύρηι καὶ τοὺς Πέρσας οὐ δείσας τὰ δένδρα ἥγηι δεινὸν καὶ τὸν μὲν ἥλιον τὸν περὶ τὸν Τίγρητα ἤνεγκας, σκιὰν δὲ ἔχων ἐκ φύλλων ἐν Πόντωι τῶν ἐν ἄστεσιν ἀγορῶν ἐπιθυμεῖς καὶ φὴς εἶναι μόνος· ὃ ἥκιστ' ἂν ἀνδρὶ φιλολόγωι συμβαίη. πῶς γὰρ ἄν σε καταλίποι Πλάτων καὶ Δημοσθένης καὶ ὁ χορὸς ἐκεῖνος, οὓς ἀνάγκη μένειν, ὅπουπερ ἂν ἐθέληις; **6** τούτοις τε οὖν διαλέγου καὶ τὸν πόλεμον ὃν ὑπέσχου σύγγραφε, καί σου τὰ παρόντα οὐχ ἅψεται βλέποντος εἰς ἄθλον

47 LIBANIOS

To Seleukos. **1** I burst into tears when I read your letter and cried out to the gods, 'You gods, what does this mean?' I gave the letter to those of the others whom I particularly trust and saw that they too were affected by it in the same way: each of them reflected on the disparity between what you deserve and the circumstances in which you are now compelled to live. **2** I shall tell you the terms in which I consoled both them and myself, in the belief that this will content you.

My thoughts turned to Odysseus of old, who wandered the seas, as you know, when he had sacked Troy; we by contrast have no need of branches to preserve our modesty (nor may we ever!), nor are we being assaulted by our own servants, and your household is free from any kind of drunken excess. **3** If you are barred from towns and their baths, just reflect how many positively choose to live in the country even though it is open to them to live in town, because they reckon that the pleasures of the one are superior to the hubbub of the other. If you had been Achilles and had to live with the Centaur on Mt Pelion, what would you have done? Would you have gone running off back to town because you thought the mountain would be your ruin? **4** No, Seleukos, in heaven's name do not torture yourself! Remember the generals of old who ended up so soon after celebrating their victories, one in prison and the others in exile. We didn't learn these stories in order to give ourselves pain but in order to draw comfort from them in our times of trouble. **5** You have the opportunity for a display of courage, but all you can do is lament. The Persians could not frighten you, yet you dread the forests; you bore the blazing sun by the Tigris, but now that you have the leafy shade of Pontus, you long for city squares and claim that you are living in solitude. That is the last thing that could happen to a man of culture. How could Plato and Demosthenes and all that company, who are bound to stay with you wherever you may wish, ever desert you?

6 So commune with them, and write your history of the war as you promised, and your present circumstances will get no

οὕτω μέγαν. τοῦτο καὶ Θουκυδίδηι τὴν φυγὴν ἐποίησεν ἐλα-
φράν, καὶ διῆλθον ἄν σοι τὸ πᾶν, εἰ μὴ ἠπίστω καλῶς. 7 πάνυ
γε ἡγοῦ τῆι γραφῆι χαριεῖσθαι πᾶσιν ἀνθρώποις. εἶδες μὲν γὰρ
ἔργα μετὰ πολλῶν, μόνωι δὲ σοὶ τῶν ἑωρακότων ἀξία τῶν ἔργων
ἡ φωνή.

48 GREGORIOS OF NAZIANZOS (c. 385/9)

(Epistles 222)

Θέκληι. 1 ὥρμησα μὲν καὶ αὐτὸς πρὸς τὴν σὴν εὐλάβειαν, καίπερ
ἀσθενοῦντος ἡμῖν τοῦ σώματος, ἐπισκεψόμενός τε ὁμοῦ καὶ τῆς
καρτερίας ἐπαινεσόμενος, ἣν ἐπὶ τῶι μακαριωτάτωι ἀδελφῶι σου
φιλοσοφεῖς· τοῦτο γὰρ οὐκ ἀμφίβολον. 2 ἐπειδὴ δὲ ὑπό τινος
περιστάσεως ἐκωλύθην, ἀναγκαίως ἦλθον ἐπὶ τὰ γράμματα καὶ
συμφιλοσοφήσω σοι διὰ βραχέων τὰ σά.
3 πόθεν ὁ καλὸς Σακερδὼς ἡμῖν, ὁ γνήσιος τοῦ Θεοῦ
παραστάτης καὶ νῦν καὶ πρότερον; ἐκ Θεοῦ. ποῦ δὲ νῦν Σακερδώς;
πρὸς Θεόν, οὐκ ἀηδῶς ὑποχωρήσας, εὖ οἶδα, τῶι φθόνωι καὶ τοῖς
τοῦ πονηροῦ παλαίσμασι. 4 πόθεν δ' ἡμεῖς; οὐκ ἐκεῖθεν; ποῦ δ'
ἡμεῖς ἀναλύσομεν; οὐ πρὸς τὸν αὐτὸν Δεσπότην; καὶ εἴθε μετ'
ἴσης τῆς παρρησίας. τοῦ αὐτοῦ προσκυνηταὶ καὶ παρήχθημεν
καὶ μεταχθησόμεθα, ὀλίγα ἐνταῦθα κακοπαθήσαντες, ὥς γε πρὸς
τὴν ἐκεῖθεν ἐλπίδα, καὶ ἴσως ἵνα γνῶμεν τὴν χάριν, ἐξ ὧν ἐνταῦθα
πεπόνθαμεν. 5 πατήρ, μήτηρ, ἀδελφός, οἱ προειληφότες, τί τοῦτό
ἐστιν; ἀριθμὸς ἐπαινετῶν ὁδοιπόρων. τούτοις ἀκολουθήσει καὶ
Θέκλα μετὰ μικρόν, ἡ τοῦ Θεοῦ δούλη καὶ ἀπαρχὴ τῶν καλῶν, ὀλί-
γον ὑπομείνασα, ὅσον ἐκείνους τε τιμῆσαι τῆι καρτερίαι καὶ πολλοῖς ὑπόδειγμα γενέσθαι τῆς περὶ ταῦτα φιλοσοφίας. 6 ἐπαινῶμεν
οὖν τὴν αὐτὴν δεσποτείαν καὶ δεχώμεθα τὴν οἰκονομίαν τῶν πολλῶν ὑψηλότερον.

grip on you as you set your eyes on such a splendid prize. That is what made Thucydides' exile easy for him to bear, and I would tell you the whole story if you didn't already know it well. **7** You should be in no doubt that in writing your work you will put all mankind in your debt. Many others witnessed the events along with you, but you alone of all the witnesses have the eloquence to do them justice.

48 GREGORIOS OF NAZIANZOS

To Thekla. **1** I started out for your Holiness in person, in spite of my poor state of bodily health, so as to visit you and at the same time to praise you for the truly philosophical fortitude you are showing over your dear departed brother, for that you are doing so cannot be doubted. **2** But since circumstances conspired to hold me back, I was compelled to resort to a written letter, and will briefly share some philosophical reflections on your position with you.

3 Whence did the noble Sacerdos come to us, God's true servant now and in time gone by? From God. Where is Sacerdos now? With God, having removed himself, not without pleasure I am sure, from the reach of envy and the wiles of the Evil One. **4** Whence did we come? Was it not from there? Where shall we end our journey? Will it not be with the same Lord and Master? May it only be with the same assurance! It was as worshippers of the same God that we were put on to the earth and that we shall be taken from it, after enduring sufferings that are trifling in comparison to the hopes we have of the hereafter, perhaps in order that we may appreciate God's grace to us from what we have suffered in this life. **5** Father, mother, brother, they who have gone before us, what are they? A band of travellers who deserve our praises. Thekla too will travel with them before long, God's true handmaid and the first fruits of the company of the virtuous, after a short wait, long enough only to honour them by her fortitude and be an example to many of the proper philosophical attitude in such circumstances. **6** Let us then praise this same Power, and let us welcome its Providence in a more enlightened way than the multitude.

ταῦτα ἔχε νῦν ἀνθ᾽ ἡμῶν καὶ τούτοις σύνεσο τοῖς λογισμοῖς, εἰ
καὶ κρείττονας παρὰ σεαυτῆι ἀνευρίσκεις. **7** εἰ δέ σε καὶ κατ᾽ ὄψιν
ἰδεῖν καταξιωθείημεν μετὰ παντὸς τοῦ σοῦ καὶ περὶ σὲ πληρώη-
ματος, πλείων ἡ χάρις τῶι εὐεργέτηι.

49 ANONYMUS (MODEL LETTERS,
4–5 CENTURY A.D.)

(*P.Bon.* 5, cols. III.3–13 and IV.3–13 = *CPL* 279, col. 2)

Lic[i]nn[i]um amicum tibi	1	Λικίννιον φίλον σου
[ue]rum		γνήσιον
obitum com·pertus sum		τεθνηκότα ἔμαθον
q]uem parum memorem		ὃν ὀλίγον ἐμνημονευ[κό]τα
ob·sequi · tui [fu]isse	5	τῆς σῆς ὑπεικίας γεγο[νέ]ναι
doleo · quidem		λυποῦμαι μὲν
[s]et hortor te		ἀλλὰ παρορμῶ σε
[u]t fortiter feras:		εὐσταθῶς ἐνεγκεῖν
tabulas enim suppremorum		διαθήκας μὲν γὰρ ἐσχάτων
[h]omin[e]s quidem faciunt	10	ἄνθρωποι μὲν ποιοῦσιν
[s]et ordinant fata		διατάσσουσιν δὲ μοῖρα[ι]

50 L. SERGIUS CATILINA (NOVEMBER 63 B.C.)

(Sallust, *Catilina* 35)

L. Catilina Q. Catulo. **1** egregia tua fides, re cognita, grata mihi
magnis in meis periculis, fiduciam commendationi meae tribuit.
2 quam ob rem defensionem in nouo consilio non statui parare:
satisfactionem ex nulla conscientia de culpa proponere decreui,
quam me dius fidius ueram licet cognoscas. **3** iniuriis contumeli-
isque concitatus, quod fructu laboris industriaeque meae priuatus
statum dignitatis non obtinebam, publicam miserorum causam pro
mea consuetudine suscepi, non quin aes alienum meis nominibus
ex possessionibus soluere possem – et alienis nominibus liberalitas
Orestillae suis filiaeque copiis persolueret – sed quod non dignos
homines honore honestatos uidebam meque falsa suspicione alien-
atum esse sentiebam. **4** hoc nomine satis honestas pro meo casu
spes relicuae dignitatis conseruandae sum secutus. **5** plura quom
scribere uellem, nuntiatum est uim mihi parari. **6** nunc Orestillam

Accept this letter now in my stead and ponder these thoughts, although you find still more effective ones within yourself. **7** If I were privileged to see you face to face as well, along with all your household (entourage), my gratitude to our Benefactor would be still greater.

49 ANON

I have learned that your true friend Licinnius is dead. That he should be so forgetful of your deference distresses me, but I exhort you to bear it bravely (steadfastly). Men may draft their last wills and testaments, but it is the Fates that are their Executors.

50 L. SERGIUS CATILINA

Lucius Catilina to Quintus Catulus. **1** Your outstanding loyalty, already demonstrated in deed rather than word, and welcome to me in this time of great personal danger, permits me to make this claim on your protection with confidence. **2** For this reason, I have determined not to make any formal defence for my change of plan; but I have decided to offer you an explanation – though not one springing from any guilty conscience on my part – the truth of which, as God is my witness, you may easily recognize. **3** Stung by the wrongs and slanders heaped upon me, because deprived of the due reward of all my hard work and energy and so unable to maintain the level of my prestige, I followed my natural inclination and took up the shared cause of the oppressed, not because I was unable to repay the debts standing to my name from my own property – Orestilla in her generosity could have discharged other people's too from her own and her daughter's resources – but because I saw unworthy individuals raised to positions of honour while I myself was cast aside on baseless suspicions. **4** For this reason I have pursued hopes of preserving what prestige remains to me by means that, considering my present condition, are honourable. **5** I should like to write at greater length, but news has come that I am about to be attacked. **6** I now

commendo tuaeque fidei trado; eam ab iniuria defendas, per liberos
tuos rogatus. haueto.

51 PHALARIS

(*Epistles* 66)

Τηλεκλείδηι. **1** ἰδίαι τινὶ χρώμενος γνώμηι πρὸς πολλοὺς ἤδη
τῶν ἐμῶν ἑταίρων διείλεξα, τοῦτ᾽ ἴσως διαπραττόμενος ὃ καὶ
γέγονεν, εἰς ἐμὲ κομισθῆναι τοὺς λόγους, ὡς οὐκ ἐχρῆν με μετὰ
τὸν δημιουργὸν τοῦ ταύρου Περίλαον ἄλλους κατεργάσασθαι
τῶι τρόπωι τῆς αὐτῆς αἰκίας· τὸν γὰρ ἴδιον λύειν ἔπαινον.
ἐγὼ
δὲ οὔτε τῆς ἐπὶ Περιλάωι τιμωρίας ἐπαινούμενος ἐπιστρέφομαι
(τιμωρὸς γὰρ οὐκ ἐγενόμην ἐπαίνου χάριν), οὔτε τῆς ἐπὶ τοῖς
ἄλλοις κολάσεως διαβαλλόμενος ἄχθομαι· δόξης γὰρ αἰσχρᾶς ἢ
καλῆς ἄμυνα κεχώρισται. **2** εὖ μέντοι καὶ τοῦτο ἴσθι, ὅτι τοῦ
μέλλειν καὶ ἄλλους τινὰς ἐν τῶι ταύρωι διαφθείρεσθαι χάριν ἐκολασάμην αὐτόν, ἐπεὶ τῆς τοῦ χαλκοῦ κατασκευῆς ἕνεκα δωρεᾶς
οὐκ ἀπωλείας ἦν ἄξιος. δίκαιον μὲν οὖν ἐκείνωι τὰς περὶ τούτων
αἰτίας καὶ τοῖς εἰς τοῦτο τύχης ἥκειν βιαζομένοις ἀνακεῖσθαι· εἰ δὲ
καὶ εἰς ἡμᾶς ἀναφέροιντο ὑπὸ τῶν ἀγνωμόνως κρινόντων, οὐκ
ἀχθόμεθα, ἕως ἔχομεν ἀξίους ἀποδεικνύναι τῆς κολάσεως τοὺς
ἀναιρουμένους. ἀρξάμενοι γὰρ ἀπὸ τοῦ πρώτου κολασθέντος,
ὃν ὑπὲρ ἁπάντων ἀνθρώπων, μᾶλλον δ᾽ αὐτῆς τῆς ἀνθρωπίνης
φύσεως ἐπυρπόλησα, τὸν αὐτὸν τρόπον τῆς ἐξετάσεως ἐπὶ πάντων ποιήσασθε. **3** εἰ γὰρ τὴν ἐπὶ Περιλάωι κόλασιν ὡς δικαίαν
ἐπαινεῖτε, καὶ τῶν ἄλλων, ὅσους ὑπὲρ ἀλλοτρίων ἐκολασάμην
ἀδικημάτων, οὐ δήπου μέμφοισθ᾽ ἂν προσηκόντως, οὐδὲ ὅσων
ἀνηρήκαμεν ἐκσπόνδων ἐμοὶ γεγενημένων δι᾽ οὓς ἐμηχανήσαντο
ὀλέθρους. ἦπου σφόδρα γε ἂν ἄβουλος εἴην, εἰ τοὺς ὑπὲρ ἄλλων
κακούργους, ἐάν με καὶ εὖ ποιῶσι, τιμωρούμενος τοὺς εἰς ἐμαυτὸν
ἐπιβουλεύοντας ἀζημίους ἐάσαιμι, καὶ τὴν δύσκλειαν ὑπὲρ τῶν μὴ
προσηκόντων ἐπὶ τῶι φοβερὸς δοκεῖν εἶναι τοῖς ἐπιβουλεύουσιν

consign and entrust Orestilla to your faithful care; defend her from harm, I beg you, as you value your own children's lives. Farewell.

51 PHALARIS

To Telekleides. **1** Acting on some private plan of your own, you have now held conversations with many of my companions, perhaps angling for what has indeed come about, that your words should be reported to me. You say that after doing to death the maker of the bull, Perilaos, I should not have continued by tormenting others in the same way, because by so doing I am undoing the good name I won myself. Just as I pay no attention to the praise accorded me for taking vengeance on Perilaos (because I did not turn avenger to win praise), so I am not distressed to be censured for the punishment I have meted out to others either. Self-defence is entirely separate from good or bad reputation. **2** Let me assure you of this also, that it was because others too were destined to perish in the bull that I punished Perilaos, since as far as his working of the bronze is concerned he deserved a reward rather than death. It is right then that the blame attaching to these cases should fall on him and on those who force their way to such a depth of ill-fortune; but if incompetent judges were to assign it to me, I do not mind, as long as I am able to demonstrate that those being disposed of deserve their fate. Starting from the first to be punished, whom I incinerated on behalf of all mankind, or rather on behalf of humanity itself, I challenge you and your kind to review all of the cases on the same criteria. **3** Because if you praise the punishment of Perilaos as just, then you could surely not properly find fault with those inflicted on the rest, whom I punished for other, unrelated offences, nor on those whom I made away with for breaking faith with me by plotting my assassination. I would be a complete fool if, while taking vengeance on those offending against others, even if they treat me well, I let those who plot against me go unpunished, and, while accepting an evil reputation over individuals who have nothing to do with me personally so as to intimidate plotters, I were to shrink from doing

ἀναδεχόμενος ὑπὲρ τῶν ἰδίων κινδύνων ὀκνήσαιμι. πέπαυσο δὴ
καὶ σεαυτῶι κἀμοὶ πράγματα παρέχων.

52 C. PLINIUS SECUNDUS (?ROME, c. A.D. 107)

(Epistles 9.2)

C. Plinius Sabino suo s(alutem). **1** facis iucunde quod non solum
plurimas epistulas meas uerum etiam longissimas flagitas; in quibus
parcior fui partim quia tuas occupationes uerebar, partim quia ipse
multum distringebar plerumque frigidis negotiis quae simul et auo-
cant animum et comminuunt. praeterea nec materia plura scribendi
dabatur. **2** neque enim eadem nostra condicio quae M. Tulli, ad
cuius exemplum nos uocas. illi enim et copiosissimum ingenium
et par ingenio qua uarietas rerum qua magnitudo largissime sup-
petebat; **3** nos quam angustis terminis claudamur etiam tacente me
perspicis, nisi forte uolumus scholasticas tibi atque, ut ita dicam,
umbraticas litteras mittere. **4** sed nihil minus aptum arbitramur,
cum arma uestra cum castra, cum denique cornua tubas sudorem
puluerem soles cogitamus. **5** habes, ut puto, iustam excusationem,
quam tamen dubito an tibi probari uelim. est enim summi amoris
negare ueniam breuibus epistulis amicorum, quamuis scias illis con-
stare rationem. uale.

53 M. AURELIUS ANTONINUS, M. CORNELIUS FRONTO (?BAY OF NAPLES, A.D. 139/40)

(Ad M. Caesarem 3.7–8)

Magistro meo. **1** quom tu quiescis et quod commodum ualetudini sit
tu facis, tum me recreas. et libenter et otiose age. sentio ergo: recte
fecisti quod brachio curando operam dedisti. **2** ego quoque hodie a
septima in lectulo nonnihil egi, nam εἰκόνας decem ferme expediui.

the same where my own peril was in question. Stop making trouble for yourself and for me.

52 C. PLINIUS SECUNDUS

C. Plinius to his dear Sabinus. **1** I am most gratified that you should demand not only very frequent letters from me but also very long ones. If instead I have been somewhat sparing with them, it has been partly out of consideration for your being so very busy, and partly because I myself was under great strain from some largely tedious pieces of business that simultaneously both monopolize the mind and crush it. Besides, I did not have at my command the subject-matter to write more about. **2** For I am not in the same situation as Cicero, whose example you encourage me to follow. He had abundantly at his disposal both the most fertile of natural talents, and the range and weight of subject-matter to match it; **3** even without my telling you, you can discern how narrow the limits are that confine me, unless perhaps I decide to send you rhetorical and, so to say, armchair letters. **4** But I can think of nothing less appropriate, when I call to mind the weapons, the military encampments, the horns and trumpets, the sweat, the dust and the blazing heat that you and your comrades are now experiencing. **5** This is my apology, and I think it is a legitimate one, yet I am not sure that I wish you to find it acceptable. For it is a mark of the closest friendship to refuse to pardon short letters from one's friends, even though you may know that they have sound reasons. Farewell.

53 M. AURELIUS ANTONINUS, M. CORNELIUS FRONTO

To my master. **1** When you rest and do what is good for your health, then you refresh me too. Indulge yourself, be lazy. This then is my verdict: you have done the right thing in taking trouble to look after your arm. **2** I too have achieved something quite substantial today, on my couch since one o'clock: I have worked out nearly all the

⟨in⟩ nona te socium et optionem mihi sumo, nam minus secunda fuit in persequendo mihi. est autem quod in insula Aenaria lacus inest: in eo lacu alia insula est, et ea quoque inhabitatur. ἔνθε⟨νδ'⟩ εἰκόνα ποιοῦμεν. uale, dulcissime anima. domina mea te salutat.

* * *

Domino meo. 1 imaginem quam tu quaerere ais, meque tibi socium ad quaerendum et optionem sumis, num moleste feres si in tuo atque tui patris sinu id fictum quaeram? ut insula in mari Ionio siue Tyrrhenico siue uero potius in Hadriatico mari, seu quod aliud est mare, eius nomen maris addito – igitur ut illa in mari insula fluctus maritimos ipsa accipit atque propulsat, omnemque uim classium praedonum beluarum procellarum ipsa perpetitur, intus autem in lacu aliam insulam protegit ab omnibus periculis ac difficultatibus tutam, omnium uero deliciarum uoluptatumque participem – namque illa intus in lacu insula aeque undis alluitur, auras salubres aeque recepit, habitatur aeque, mare aeque prospectat – item pater tuus imperii Romani molestias ac difficultates ipse perpetitur, te tutum intus in tranquillo sinu suo socium dignitatis gloriae bonorumque omnium participem tutatur. igitur hac imagine multimodis uti potes ubi patri tuo gratias ages, in qua oratione locupletissimum et copiosissimum te esse oportet. nihil est enim quod tu aut honestius aut uerius aut libentius in omni uita tua dicas quam quod ad ornandas patris tui laudes pertinebit. postea ergo quamcumque εἰκόνα huic addidero, non aeque placebit tibi, ut haec quae ad patrem tuum pertinet: tam hoc scio quam tu nouisti. quam ob rem ipse aliam εἰκόνα nullam adiciam, sed rationem qua tute quaeras ostendam. et, amem te, tu quas εἰκόνας in eandem rem demonstrata ratione quaesiueris et inueneris, mittito mihi ut, si fuerint scitae atque concinnae, gaudeam.

ten similes. For the ninth I co-opt you as my ally and adjutant, as it turned out less than successfully as I tried to follow it through. It is the one about the lake on the island of Aenaria: in the lake there is another island, and it too is inhabited. *C'est de ça que je fais l'image.* Farewell, sweetest friend. My Lady sends her greetings.

* * *

To my Lord. **1** As for the simile which you say you are lost over, and co-opt me as your ally and adjutant to search for – will you take it amiss if I think to find it figured in your and your father's embrace? Just as the island in the Ionian or Tyrrhenian sea – or indeed the Adriatic sea instead, or some other sea, just add its name – just as that island in the sea itself receives and repels the sea's waves, and itself endures every assault of fleets, pirates, sea-monsters and storms, while protecting the other island in the lake and keeping it safe from all dangers and difficulties, yet a partner in all its own pleasures and delights – for that inner island like it is washed by the waves, like it receives the health-giving breezes, like it is inhabited, and like it looks out over the sea – in just the same way, your father himself endures the dangers and the difficulties of the Empire of Rome, whilst guarding you safely within, in the calm of his embrace, as his partner in rank, glory and all that is his. This simile, then, you may employ in many different ways when you are thanking your father, in the kind of speech in which it is incumbent on you to be particularly rich and ample. There is nothing in the whole of your life that you will say more honourably or more truthfully or more gladly than what pertains to the expression of your father's praises.

After that, whatever simile I may add, you will not like it so much as this one relating to your father. I know this as well as you do. So I will add no further simile myself, but rather explain the method by which *you* may search them out. Then, if you please, once you have had the method revealed to you, send me whatever similes you may think up and discover for yourself, for me to delight in if they prove to be well conceived and elegantly executed.

2 iam primum quidem illud scis, εἰκόνα ei rei adsumi ut aut ornet quid aut deturpet aut aequiparet aut deminuat aut ampliet aut ex minus credibili credibile efficiat. ubi nihil eorum usus erit, locus εἰκόνος non erit. postea ubi re⟨i⟩ propositae imaginem scribes, ut, si pingeres, insignia animaduerteres eius rei cuius imaginem pingeres, item in scribendo facies. insignia autem cuiusque rei multis modis eliges, τὰ ὁμογενῆ, τὰ ὁμοειδῆ, τὰ ὅλα, τὰ μέρη, τὰ ἴδια, τὰ διάφορα, τὰ ἀντικείμενα, τὰ ἑπόμενα καὶ παρακολουθοῦντα, τὰ ὀνόματα, ⟨τὰ⟩ ..., τὰ συμβεβηκότα, τὰ στοιχεῖα, et fere omnia ex quibus argumenta sumuntur: de quibus plerumque audisti, cum Θεοδώρου locos ἐπιχειρημάτων tractaremus. eorum si quid memoriae tuae elapsum est, non iniutile erit eadem nos retractare ubi tempus aderit. in hac εἰκόνι, quam de patri tuo teque depinxi, ἕν τι τῶν συμβεβηκότων ἔλαβον, τὸ ὁμοῖον τῆς ἀσφαλείας καὶ τῆς ἀπολαύσεως. nunc tu per hasce uias ac semitas, quas supra ostendi, quae⟨res⟩ quonam modo Aenariam commodissime peruenias.

3 mihi dolor cubiti haud multum sedatus est. uale, domine, cum ingenio eximio. dominae meae matri tuae dic salutem. 4 τὴν δὲ ὅλην τῶν εἰκόνων τέχνην alias diligentius et subtilius persequemur; nunc capita rerum adtigi.

54 M. AURELIUS ANTONINUS, M. CORNELIUS
FRONTO (? ROME, A.D. 139–61)

(*Ad Ant. imp.* 2.4–5 = 3.7–8 van den Hout)

Magistro meo sal. 1 quom salubritas ruris huius me delectaret, sentiebam non mediocre illud me deesse, uti de tua quoque bona ualetudine certus essem, mi magister. id uti suppleas, deos oro. rusticatio autem nostra μετὰ πολιτείας prorsus negotium illud est ueitae

2 Now, in the first place, you are well aware that a simile is applied in order to adorn something, or denigrate it, or furnish a comparison for it, or belittle it, or aggrandize it, or to make it credible when it was not before. Where none of these operations is in question, there will be no place for a simile. Secondly, when you are composing a simile for a subject you have in mind, just as, if you were painting, you would notice the distinguishing characteristics of the thing you were painting, so too when writing. Now, there are various ways in which you will pick out a given thing's distinguishing characteristics: by reference to members of the same class, things of the same appearance, wholes, parts, individual traits, divergences, opposites, consequences and concomitants, names, < ... >, accidental attributes, elements, and just about everything on which an argument can be based. You heard a good deal about this when we were studying Theodorus on commonplaces of argument. If any of it has slipped from your memory, there will be some point in our going over the same ground again when there is time. In the simile I developed about your father and you *j'ai pris un des accidents, la ressemblance en sécurité et en profit*. It is now for you to work out, following the ways and paths I showed you a moment ago, how to reach Aenaria in the most convenient way.

3 The pain in my elbow has not abated much. Farewell, my Lord, man of rare talent. Give my greetings to my Lady your mother. **4** *L'art entier des images* we will follow up more conscientiously and in finer detail on another occasion; this time I have only touched lightly on the major headings.

54 M. AURELIUS ANTONINUS, M. CORNELIUS FRONTO

To my master, greetings. **1** Delightful though the healthy air is here in the country, I feel that I am lacking something very important, namely the assurance of your own good health, master. I pray the gods that you may make this good. Our country break, taking the cares of state with us, is just the same old busy city life all over again.

togatae. quid quaeris? hanc ipsam epistulam paululum me porgere non sinunt instantes curae, quarum uacatio noctis demum aliqua parte contingit. **2** uale mi iucundissime magister. Ciceronis epistulas, si forte electas totas uel dimidiatas habes, impertias, uel mone, quas potissimum legendas mihi censeas ad facultatem sermonis fouendum. ualeas.

* * *

Domino meo. quinctus hic dies est ut correptus sum dolore membrorum omnium, praecipue autem ceruicum et inguinum. memini me excerpsisse ex Ciceronis epistulis ea dumtaxat quibus inesset aliqua de eloquentia uel philosophia uel de republica disputatio; praeterea si quid elegantius aut uerbo notabili dictum uideretur, excerpsi. quae in usu meo ad manum erant excerpta, misi tibi. tres libros, duos ad Brutum, unum at Axium, describi iubebis, si quid rei esse uidebitur, et remittes mihi, nam exemplares eorum excerptorum nullos feci. omnes autem Ciceronis epistulas legendas censeo, mea sententia uel magis quam omnes eius orationes: epistulis Ciceronis nihil est perfectius.

55 BASILEIOS (CAESAREA, A.D. 373)

(*Epistles* 135)

Διοδώρωι, πρεσβυτέρωι Ἀντιοχείας. **1** ἐνέτυχον τοῖς ἀποσταλεῖσι βιβλίοις παρὰ τῆς τιμιότητός σου. καὶ τῶι μὲν δευτέρωι ὑπερήσθην, οὐ διὰ τὴν βραχύτητα μόνον, ὡς εἰκὸς ἦν τὸν ἀργῶς πρὸς πάντα καὶ ἀσθενῶς λοιπὸν διακείμενον, ἀλλ' ὅτι πυκνόν τε ἅμα ἐστὶ ταῖς ἐννοίαις, καὶ εὐκρινῶς ἐν αὐτῶι ἔχουσιν αἵ τε ἀντιθέσεις τῶν ὑπεναντίων καὶ αἱ πρὸς αὐτὰς ἀπαντήσεις· καὶ τὸ τῆς λέξεως ἁπλοῦν τε καὶ ἀκατάσκευον πρέπον ἔδοξέ μοι εἶναι προθέσει Χριστιανοῦ, οὐ πρὸς ἐπίδειξιν μᾶλλον ἢ κοινὴν ὠφέλειαν συγγράφοντος. τὸ δὲ πρότερον, τὴν μὲν δύναμιν ἔχον τὴν αὐτὴν ἐν τοῖς πράγμασιν, λέξει δὲ πολυτελεστέραι καὶ σχήμασι ποικίλοις καὶ διαλογικαῖς χάρισι κεκομψευμένον, πολλοῦ μοι ἐφάνη καὶ

What more need I say? Pressing duties forbid me to continue this very letter even for a little; it is only for a part of the night that I am allowed any rest from them.

2 Farewell, my dearest of masters. If by any chance you have some selected letters of Cicero, either complete letters or excerpts, please lend them to me, or else advise me which you think I ought particularly to read in order to nurture my command of style. I pray for your good health.

* * *

To my Lord. It is now four days since I was seized by pain in all my limbs, but especially in the neck and groin. As I recall, I excerpted from Cicero's letters only such passages as contained some discussion of eloquence or philosophy or politics; also, if there was anything I thought was phrased particularly elegantly, or in striking vocabulary, I excerpted it. I am sending you what I have to hand for my own personal use. If you think it worth while, have the three books, two to Brutus and one to Axius, transcribed and return them to me, as I have not made any copies of those excerpts. However, I judge that all Cicero's letters should be read, more even than his complete speeches, in my view; there is nothing more perfect than Cicero's letters.

55 BASILEIOS

To Diodoros, presbyter of Antioch. **1** I have read the books that your Honour sent me. I very much enjoyed the second, not only because of its brevity, as is natural for someone whose approach to everything must from now on be idle and feeble, but because it is densely packed with ideas, and at the same time presents both our opponents' objections and the replies they require very clearly. Its simple and unlaboured style seemed to me appropriate to the aims of a Christian, writing for general edification rather than in order to show off. The first of the two books, however, equally effective in its subject-matter, but tricked out with richer diction and varied figures of speech and the graces appropriate to a dialogue, seemed to me to

χρόνου πρὸς τὸ ἐπελθεῖν καὶ πόνου διανοίας πρὸς τὸ καὶ συλλέξαι
τὰς ἐννοίας καὶ παρακατασχεῖν αὐτὰς τῆι μνήμηι δεόμενον. αἱ γὰρ
ἐν τῶι μεταξὺ παρεμβαλλόμεναι διαβολαὶ τῶν ὑπεναντίων καὶ
συστάσεις, εἰ καὶ γλυκύτητάς τινας ἐπεισάγειν δοκοῦσι διαλεκ-
τικὰς τῶι συγγράμματι, ἀλλ᾽ οὖν τῶι σχολὴν καὶ διατριβὴν
ἐμποιεῖν διασπῶσι μὲν τὸ συνεχὲς τῆς ἐννοίας καὶ τοῦ ἐναγωνίου
λόγου τὸν τόνον ὑποχαυνοῦσιν.

ἐκεῖνο γὰρ πάντως συνεῖδέ σου ἡ ἀγχίνοια, ὅτι καὶ τῶν ἔξωθεν
φιλοσόφων οἱ τοὺς διαλόγους συγγράψαντες, Ἀριστοτέλης μὲν
καὶ Θεόφραστος, εὐθὺς αὐτῶν ἥψαντο τῶν πραγμάτων διὰ
τὸ συνειδέναι ἑαυτοῖς τῶν Πλατωνικῶν χάριτων τὴν ἔνδειαν.
Πλάτων δὲ τῆι ἐξουσίαι τοῦ λόγου ὁμοῦ μὲν τοῖς δόγμασι μάχεται,
ὁμοῦ δὲ καὶ παρακωμωιδεῖ τὰ πρόσωπα, Θρασυμάχου μὲν τὸ
θρασὺ καὶ ἰταμὸν διαβάλλων, Ἱππίου δὲ τὸ κοῦφον τῆς διανοίας
καὶ χαῦνον, καὶ Πρωταγόρου τὸ ἀλαζονικὸν καὶ ὑπέρογκον. ὅπου
δὲ ἀόριστα πρόσωπα ἐπεισάγει τοῖς διαλόγοις, τῆς μὲν εὐκρινείας
ἕνεκεν τῶν πραγμάτων κέχρηται τοῖς προσδιαλεγομένοις, οὐδὲν
δὲ ἕτερον ἐκ τῶν προσώπων ἐπεισκυκλεῖ ταῖς ὑποθέσεσιν· ὅπερ
ἐποίησεν ἐν τοῖς Νόμοις.

2 δεῖ οὖν καὶ ἡμᾶς τοὺς οὐ κατὰ φιλοτιμίαν ἐρχομένους ἐπὶ
τὸ γράφειν, ἀλλ᾽ ὑποθήκας καταλιμπάνειν ὠφελίμων λόγων
τῆι ἀδελφότητι προελομένους, ἐὰν μέν τι πᾶσι προκεκηρυγ-
μένον ἐπὶ αὐθαδείαι τρόπου πρόσωπον ὑποβαλλώμεθα, τινὰ
καὶ ἀπὸ προσώπου πεποιημένα παραπλέκειν τῶι λόγωι, εἴπερ
ὅλως ἐπιβάλλει ἡμῖν διαβάλλειν ἀνθρώπους τῶν πραγμάτων
ἀφεμένοις. ἐὰν δὲ ἀόριστον ἦι τὸ διαλεγόμενον, αἱ πρὸς τὰ
πρόσωπα διαστάσεις τὴν μὲν συνάφειαν διακόπτουσι, πρὸς οὐδὲν
δὲ πέρας χρήσιμον ἀπαντῶσι.

ταῦτα εἶπον ἵνα δειχθῆι ὅτι οὐκ εἰς κόλακος χεῖρας ἀπέστειλας
σου τοὺς πόνους, ἀλλὰ ἀδελφῶι τῶι γνησιωτάτωι ἐκοινώνησας
τῶν καμάτων· εἶπον δὲ οὐ πρὸς ἐπανόρθωσιν τῶν γεγραμ-
μένων, ἀλλὰ πρὸς φυλακὴν τῶν μελλόντων. πάντως γὰρ ὁ
τοσαύτηι περὶ τὸ γράφειν ἕξει καὶ σπουδῆι κεχρημένος οὐκ
ἀποκνήσει γράφων· ἐπειδὴ οὐδὲ οἱ τὰς ὑποθέσεις παρέχοντες

require a great deal of time to read and a great deal of mental effort also to grasp its ideas and commit them to memory. The slanders and assaults of our opponents, inserted at intervals along the way, though they may seem to introduce a certain dialogic attractiveness into your composition, certainly slow down and delay the flow and so interrupt the sequence of thought and slacken the polemical tension of your argument.

In your sagacity, you are of course well aware that those too of the pagan philosophers who wrote dialogues, Aristotle and Theophrastus, began straight in on their main subject-matter because they were conscious of their own lack of Platonic graces. Plato, such is the power of his writing, simultaneously grapples with ideas and satirizes personalities, attacking Thrasymachus' brashness and impetuosity, the triviality and windiness of Hippias' thinking, and Protagoras' bluster and pretension. Where he introduces figures without a determinate character into his dialogues, he uses these extra interlocutors in order to clarify the subject-matter, and he wheels nothing more besides from these figures into his dramas. This is what he did, for example, in the *Laws*.

2 So we too who approach the task of writing not in a spirit of personal ambition, but with the aim of bequeathing helpful and instructive discourses to our brethren, must, if we are adopting some character notorious for the stubborn individuality of his ways, weave some traits derived from his personality into our composition as well – always assuming that it is incumbent on us to leave the issues to one side and attack personalities in the first place. But if the figure participating in the dialogue has no determinate character, then *ad hominem* confrontations disrupt the continuity and achieve no useful purpose.

I say this so as to demonstrate that you have not entrusted the fruits of your labours to the hands of a mere flatterer, but have shared your toil with the truest of brothers. I speak not with a view to the correction of what you have written, but to put you on your guard for the future; for come what may someone who manifests such aptitude and enthusiasm for the business of writing will not be

ἀπολήγουσιν. ἡμῖν δὲ ἀρκέσει μὲν ἀναγινώσκειν τα ὑμέτερα· τοῦ δὲ δύνασθαι γράφειν τι τοσοῦτον ἀποδέομεν, ὅσον μικροῦ δέω λέγειν καὶ τοῦ ὑγιαίνειν, ἢ τοῦ καὶ μετρίαν σχολὴν ἄγειν ἀπὸ τῶν πραγμάτων. ἀπέστειλα δὲ νῦν διὰ τοῦ ἀναγνώστου τὸ μεῖζον καὶ πρότερον ἐπελθὼν αὐτὸ ὡς ἐμοὶ δυνατόν. τὸ δὲ δεύτερον παρακατέσχον, βουλόμενος αὐτὸ μεταγράψαι, καὶ μὴ εὐπορῶν τέως τινὸς τῶν εἰς τάχος γραφόντων. μέχρι γὰρ τοσαύτης ἦλθε πενίας τὰ ἐπίφθονα Καππαδοκῶν.

56 THEON (ALEXANDRIA, 2 ND CENTURY A.D.)

(P. Mil. Vogliano 11)

Θέων Ἡρακλείδηι ἑταίρωι εὖ πράττειν. ὥσπερ ἐγὼ πᾶσαν εἰσφέρομαι σπουδὴν τὰ χρήσιμα κατασκευάζειν βυβλία καὶ μάλιστα συντείνοντα πρὸς τὸν βίον, οὕτως καὶ σοὶ καθήκειν ἡγοῦμαι μὴ ἀμελῶς ἔχειν αὐτῶν πρὸς τὴν ἀνάγνωσιν, οὐ τῆς τυχούσης εὐχρηστίας ἐξ αὐτῶν περιγινομένης τοῖς ἐσπουδακόσιν ὠφελεῖσθαι. τὰ δὲ πεμφθέντα ἐστὶν διὰ Ἀχιλλᾶ τὰ ὑποτεταγμένα. ἔρρωσο, ἐρρώμην δὲ καὶ αὐτός· ἄσπασαι [ο]ὓς προσήκει.

ἐγρ(άφη) ἐν Ἀλεξανδρείαι
 Βοήθου περὶ ἀσκήσεως γ΄ δ΄
 Διογένους περὶ γάμου
 Διογένους περὶ ἀλυπίας
 Χρυσίππου περὶ γονέων χρήσεως
 Ἀντιπάτρου περὶ οἰκετῶν χρήσεως α΄ β΄
 Ποσειδωνίου περὶ τοῦ προτρέπεσθαι γ΄.

Reverse: παρὰ Θέωνος Ἡρακλείδηι φιλοσόφωι.

57 FLAVIUS CLAUDIUS IULIANUS
(CONSTANTINOPLE, JANUARY A.D. 362)

(Epistles 23 Wright = 9 Bidez = 107 Weis)

377d Ἰουλιανὸς Ἐκδικίωι ἐπάρχωι Αἰγύπτου. ἄλλοι μὲν ἵππων, ἄλλοι δ᾽ ὀρνέων, ἄλλοι δὲ θηρίων ἐρῶσιν· **378a** ἐμοὶ δὲ βιβλίων κτήσεως ἐκ παιδαρίου δεινὸς ἐντέτηκε πόθος. ἄτοπον οὖν

deterred from it, and there will be no shortage of people to provide you with your subject-matter either. I shall be content to read your compositions, but as for being able to write anything myself, I am as far from it as I am from (I might almost say) being of sound health, or from having even a modicum of leisure free from business.

I am returning to you the first, longer volume straight away via my secretary, as I have read it to the best of my ability. I am retaining the second as I wish to have a copy made and do not at the moment have access to a tachygrapher. Such is the state of destitution into which we Cappadocians, once so envied, have now sunk!

56 THEON

Theon to his friend Herakleides, greetings. Just as I devote every effort to obtaining books that are profitable and especially relevant to life, so I think it is incumbent on you too not to be casual about reading them, as it is no ordinary benefit that accrues from them to those keen on self-improvement. The list below details what I am sending you via Achillas. Good health to you; I too am well. Pass on my greetings as appropriate.

> Written in Alexandria.
>> Boethos *On Ascetic Training* Books 3 and 4
>> Diogenes *On Marriage*
>> Diogenes *On Freedom from Pain*
>> Chrysippos *On the Treatment of Parents*
>> Antipatros *On the Treatment of Slaves* Books 1 and 2
>> Poseidonios *On Moral Exhortation* Book 3.

Reverse: From Theon to Herakleides, the philosopher.

57 FLAVIUS CLAUDIUS JULIANUS

377d Julianus to Ekdikios, Prefect of Egypt. Some people have a passion for horses, others for birds, others for wild animals; **378a** the 'dread longing' that has become ingrained in me ever since I was a small child is for the possession of books. So it would be absurd if

εἰ ταῦτα περιίδοιμι σφετερισαμένους ἀνθρώπους, οἷς οὐκ ἀρκεῖ τὸ χρυσίον μόνον ἀποπλῆσαι τὸν πολὺν ἔρωτα τοῦ πλούτου, πρὸς δὲ καὶ ταῦτα ὑφαιρεῖσθαι ῥαιδίως διανοουμένους. ταύτην οὖν ἰδιωτικήν μοι δὸς τὴν χάριν, ὅπως ἀνευρεθῆι πάντα τὰ Γεωργίου βιβλία. **378b** πολλὰ μὲν γὰρ ἦν φιλόσοφα παρ' αὐτῶι πολλὰ δὲ ῥητορικά, πολλὰ δὲ ἦν καὶ τῆς τῶν δυσσεβῶν Γαλιλαίων διδασκαλίας· ἃ βουλοίμην μὲν ἠφανίσθαι πάντα, τοῦ δὲ μὴ σὺν τούτοις ὑφαιρεθῆναι τὰ χρησιμώτερα, ζητείσθω κἀκεῖνα μετ' ἀκριβείας ἅπαντα. ἡγεμὼν δὲ τῆς ζητήσεως ἔστω σοι ταύτης ὁ νοτάριος Γεωργίου, ὃς μετὰ πίστεως μὲν ἀνιχνεύσας αὐτὰ γέρως ἴστω τευξόμενος ἐλευθερίας· **378c** εἰ δ' ἀμωσγέπως γένοιτο κακοῦργος περὶ τὸ πρᾶγμα, βασάνων εἰς πεῖραν ἥξων. ἐπίσταμαι δὲ ἐγὼ τὰ Γεωργίου βιβλία, καὶ εἰ μὴ πάντα, πολλὰ μέντοι· μετέδωκε γάρ μοι περὶ τὴν Καππαδοκίαν ὄντι πρὸς μεταγραφήν τινα, καὶ ταῦτα ἔλαβε πάλιν.

58 M. VALERIUS MARTIALIS (ROME, A.D. 96–7)

(*Epigrams* 2, *praef.*)

Val. Martialis Deciano suo sal. 'quid nobis' inquis 'cum epistola? parum enim tibi praestamus, si legimus epigrammata? quid hic porro dicturus es quod non possis uersibus dicere? uideo quare tragoedia atque comoedia epistolam accipiant, quibus pro se loqui non licet: epigrammata curione non egent et contenta sunt sua, id est mala, lingua; in quacumque pagina uisum est, epistolam faciunt. noli ergo, si tibi uidetur, rem facere ridiculam et in toga saltantis inducere personam. denique uideris an te delectet contra retiarium ferula. ego inter illos sedeo qui protinus reclamant.' puto me hercules, Deciane, uerum dicis. quid si scias cum qua et quam longa epistola negotium fueris habiturus? itaque quod exigis fiat. debebunt tibi si qui in hunc librum inciderint, quod ad primam paginam non lassi peruenient.

I were to look on while they are appropriated by individuals whose great passion for wealth cannot be satiated by gold alone, and who plan to filch them too without a second thought. So please, as a personal favour to me, see to it that all of Georgios' books are sought out. **378b** He had many philosophical books in his library and many books on rhetoric, and many besides relating to the doctrines of the impious Galilaeans. These last I should prefer to be destroyed in their entirety, but so as to avoid the more beneficial volumes being done away with alongside them, let all of them too be scrupulously traced. Georgios' secretary should take charge of this search for you: give him to understand that if he hunts for them faithfully, he will win his freedom as a reward, **378c** but that if he should prove dishonest in any way in this matter, he will suffer for it under torture. I know the contents of Georgios' library, many of them at any rate, even if not all: when I was in Cappadocia he lent me some of them to copy, and got them back from me.

58 M. VALERIUS MARTIALIS

Valerius Martialis to his friend Decianus, greetings. 'What,' you say, 'do we need an epistle for? Are we not doing you enough of a favour by reading your epigrams? And in any case, what are you going to say here that you can't say in verse? I can see why tragedy and comedy offer scope for an epistle, because they aren't allowed to speak for themselves; but epigrams need no crier and are content with their own, malicious, voice: on whatever page they see fit, they are their own epistle. So, please, don't commit the absurdity of bringing on a character dancing in a toga. The thing is, ask yourself whether you like the idea of a cane against a retiarius. I'm seated with the set who voice their disapproval straight away.' You know, Decianus, I believe you're right! What if you knew what sort of a letter you *were* going to have to deal with, and how long it was going to be? So, let your demand be granted. If anyone ever reads this book, they'll owe it to you that they don't reach the first page tired out.

59 IULIUS POLLUX (?ATHENS, *c*. A.D. 175)

(*Onomastikon* 1.1)

Ἰούλιος Πολυδεύκης Κομμόδωι Καίσαρι χαίρειν. ὦ παῖ πατρὸς ἀγαθοῦ, πατρῶιόν ἐστί σοι κτῆμα κατ' ἴσον βασιλεία τε καὶ σοφία. τῆς δὲ σοφίας τὸ μέν τι ἐν τῆι τῆς ψυχῆς ἀρετῆι, τὸ δ' ἐν τῆι χρείαι τῆς φωνῆς. τῆς μὲν οὖν ἀρετῆς ἔχεις τὸ μάθημα ἐν τῶι πατρί, τῆς δὲ φωνῆς, εἰ μὲν ἦγεν αὐτὸς σχολήν, παρεῖχεν ἄν σοι τὸ ἡμῶν ἐλάχιστα δεῖσθαι· ἐπεὶ δ' ἐκεῖνον ἡ σωτηρία τῆς οἰκουμένης ἀπασχολεῖ, ἔγωγ' οὖν ἕν γέ τι σοι πρὸς εὐγλωττίαν συμβαλοῦμαι. ὀνομαστικὸν μὲν οὖν τῶι βιβλίωι τὸ ἐπίγραμμα, μηνύει δὲ ὅσα τε συνώνυμα ὡς ὑπαλλάττειν δύνασθαι, καὶ οἷς ἂν ἕκαστα δηλωθείη· πεφιλοτίμηται γὰρ οὐ τοσοῦτον εἰς πλῆθος ὁπόσον εἰς κάλλους ἐκλογήν. οὐ μέντοι πάντα τὰ ὀνόματα περιείληφε τουτὶ τὸ βιβλίον· οὐδὲ γὰρ ἦν ῥάιδιον ἑνὶ βιβλίωι πάντα συλλαβεῖν. ποιήσομαι δὲ τὴν ἀρχὴν ἀφ' ὧν μάλιστα προσήκει τοὺς εὐσεβεῖς, ἀπὸ τῶν θεῶν· τὰ δ' ἄλλα ὡς ἂν ἕκαστον ἐπέλθηι τάξομεν. ἔρρωσο.

60 PHALARIS

(*Epistles* 78)

Στησιχόρωι. **1** Νικοκλῆς ὁ Συρακούσιος (οὐκ ἀγνοεῖς δ' ἴσως ὃν λέγω, διὰ γὰρ ἐπιφάνειαν οἰκείαν οὐκ ἔστι τῶν ἀγνοηθῆναι δυναμένων ὑπὸ Στησιχόρου) γυναικὸς ἀποθανούσης αὐτῶι μέγα προσφάτως καὶ περιττὸν περιτέθειται πένθος. εἰκότως· ἔτυχε γὰρ τὴν αὐτὴν ταύτην ἀδελφιδῆν ἔχων καὶ γυναῖκα. οὗτος ὁ Νικοκλῆς (ἤιδει γάρ, ὡς ἔοικεν, ὅσοις πρὸς ἀλλήλους κεχρήμεθα πόθοις) πέμψας πρός με Κλεόνικον τὸν ἀδελφὸν αὐτοῦ ἠξίου ὅπως σου δεηθείην ἔπαινον ἐν ποιήσει διαθέσθαι περὶ τῆς ἀνθρώπου. καὶ γάρ, ὡς πυνθάνομαι Συρακουσίων πᾶσαν τε τὴν ἄλλην ἀρετήν, πρὸς δὲ καὶ τὴν ἀνωτάτω σωφροσύνην, αὐτῆι μαρτυρούντων, οὐκ ἔστιν ἀνάξιος ὑπὸ τοῦ σοῦ στόματος ὑμνηθῆναι. **2** πεφύλαξαι μὲν οὖν γράφειν εἰς τοὺς κατὰ σεαυτὸν ἀνθρώπους, ἵνα μὴ δόξηι σού τις ὠνίαν εἶναι τὴν ποίησιν· ἔστι δὲ Κλεαρίστη, φιλότης, οὐδὲ

59 JULIUS POLLUX

Julius Pollux to Commodus Caesar, greetings. O son of a noble father, kingship and wisdom alike are your paternal inheritance. Of wisdom, part lies in the virtue of the soul, and part in the use of the voice. As far as virtue is concerned, you have your model in your father; as for the voice, if he himself had the leisure, he would ensure that you had minimal need of me. But since he is preoccupied with the preservation of the inhabited world, I can make you at least this one contribution to the cultivation of eloquence.

'*Vocabulary*' then is the title of this work; it sets out which words are synonyms and thus interchangeable, and which words denote what; I have striven not so much for quantity as for elegant selection. This book does not however contain all words, as it would be no easy task to encompass everything in a single volume. I will begin where the pious most properly should, with the gods; the rest I will arrange as each item occurs to me. Farewell.

60 PHALARIS

To Stesichoros. **1** Nikokles of Syracuse (you are perhaps not ignorant of the man I mean, for thanks to his distinguished family he is not one of those who could go unknown to Stesichoros) has recently, with the death of his wife, been enveloped in a great and overbearing grief. He has good reason: it so happens that the same woman was both his niece and his wife. This Nikokles (knowing, apparently, the strength of our reciprocal affection) has sent his brother Kleonikos to ask me to request you to compose a verse encomium of his wife. And indeed, as I discover from the people of Syracuse, who bear witness to her possession of all the virtues, above all the most perfect chastity, she is not unworthy of being celebrated by your voice. **2** You have been careful not to write in praise of the men of your own times, so as to avoid anyone gaining the impression that your poetry is for sale; but Kleariste, dear friend, is not of our own times either,

αὐτὴ καθ᾽ ἡμᾶς, εἰς τὸ χρεὼν ἀπηλλαγμένη. μὴ δὴ τὸ σύνηθές σου τῆς γνώμης προβαλλόμενος ἀποστραφῇς μου τὴν δέησιν· οὐδὲ γὰρ εἰκὸς ἀτυχῆσαι παρὰ Στησιχόρου Φάλαριν αἰτησάμενον, οὐχ ὅτι χάριτας ὀφείλεις ὑπέρ τινος, ἀλλ᾽ ὅτι τὴν πεπιστευμένην δόξαν ἀξιοῦμεν ὑπὸ σου βεβαιωθῆναι. δὸς δή μοι προφανῶς χάριν τῆς σαυτοῦ φύσεως ἀφθόνως, αἰτουμένωι μὲν ἃ δώσεις εἰς ἐμαυτόν, ληψομένωι δὲ εἰς φίλον.

3 λοιπόν, εἴγε νενεύκας ἐπὶ τὴν χάριν, Κλεαρίστην γράφε Συρακουσίαν τὸ γένος, Ἐχεκρατίδου πατρός, ἀδελφιδῆν οὗ γεγράφαμεν καὶ γυναῖκα, ἑκκαίδεκα συνεζηκυῖαν ἔτη, τριακοστὸν δὲ ζήσασαν, δυοῖν παίδων μητέρα, τεθνηκυῖαν δὲ ἐκ διαφθορᾶς. τὰ μὲν κεφάλαια τῶν ὑποθηκῶν ταῦτα, ἐπιπνευσθείσης δὲ εἰς τὰ κατὰ μέρος τῆς γράφης ὑφ᾽ ὧν κατέχηι θεῶν, καί σου τὴν ἱερὰν καὶ ὑμνοπόλον κεφαλὴν ἡ Μουσῶν συγγένεια κοσμήσειεν ἄλλαις τε ὑμνωιδίαις καὶ τῆι νῦν ὑφ᾽ ἡμῶν εἰς Κλεαρίστην ἐπεσταλμένηι.

now that she has gone to meet her destiny. Do not excuse yourself on the grounds of your normal policy and reject my request. For, apart from anything else, it is not reasonable that Phalaris should make a request of Stesichoros and fail to have it granted, not because you owe me thanks for anything, but because I am asking simply for confirmation from you of a reputation that is already securely attested. Grant me openly and ungrudgingly the gift of your talent; I ask only for what you will bestow on me for my own sake, though it is on behalf of a friend that I will accept it.

3 Well then, if you are now inclined to do me this favour, record Kleariste as Syracusan by birth, daughter of Echekratidas, cousin and wife of the man I have mentioned, married to him for sixteen years, thirty years of age, mother of two children, and dead of a miscarriage. These are the main points of your brief; may the details of your composition be inspired by the goddesses by whom you are possessed, and may the sisterhood of the Muses adorn your holy, praise-singer's head with other songs of praise and, above all, the one we have now commissioned you to write in honour of Kleariste.

B PUBLIC LIFE AND OFFICIAL CORRESPONDENCE (**61–70**)

61 AMENNEUS (?224 B.C.)

(P.Grenf. ii.14 (b))

Ἀ[μ]εννε[ὺς] Ἀσκληπιάδει χαίρειν. [κα]θότι σ[υ ἔ]γραψας,
ἑτοιμάκαμεν ἐπὶ τὴν παρουσίαν τὴν Χρυσίππου [τοῦ ἀρ-
χισωματο]φύλακος καὶ διοικητοῦ λευκομετώπους δέκα, χῆνας
ἡμέρους π[έν]τε, ὄρνιθας πεντήκοντα· [ἄγ]ρια χῆνες πεντήκοντα,
ὄρνιθας διακόσια[ι], περ[ι]στριδεῖς ἑκατόν· συνκεχρήμε[θ]α δὲ
ὄνους βαδιστὰς πέντε καὶ τούτων τάς [...]ς, ἑτοιμάκαμεν δὲ καὶ
τοὺς τεσσαράκοντα ὄνους [τοὺς σ]κ[ε]υοφόρους· γινόμ[εθα] δὲ
πρὸς τῆι ὁδοιπόίαι. ἔρρω[σο (ἔτους)] κβ´ Χοίαχ δ´.

Reverse: Ἀσκληπιάδει. (ἔτους) κβ´ Χοίαχ ζ´. Ἀμεννεὺς ξενίων τῶν
ἡτοιμασμένων.

62 ATTALOS III OF PERGAMUM (PERGAMUM,
8 OCTOBER 135 B.C.)

(Inschr. Perg. 248 = 66 Welles)

Βασιλεὺς Ἄτταλος Κυζικηνῶν τῆι βουλῆι καὶ τῶι δήμωι
χαίρε[ιν. Ἀθή]ναιος ὁ Σωσάνδρου υἱός, τοῦ γενομένου ἱερέως τοῦ
καθηγεμόνος Δ[ι]ονύσου καὶ συντρόφου τοῦ πατρός μου, ὅτι μὲν
ἡμῶν ἐστι συγ[γ]ενὴς οὐ πείθομαι ὑμᾶς ἀγνοεῖν, εἴ γε ὁ Σώσανδρος
γήμας τὴν Ἀθηναίου θυγατέρα τοῦ Μειδίου, ὃς ἦν Ἀθήναιος ἀνεψ-
ιὸς τοῦ πατρός μου, τοῦτον ἐγέννησεν, ὧι καὶ γενομένωι ἀξίωι τοῦ
οἴκου ἡμῶν τὸ μὲμ πρῶτον Ἄτταλος ὁ θεῖός μου σὺγ καὶ τῆι ἐμῆι
γνώμηι ζῶντος ἔτι τοῦ Σωσάνδρου ἔδωκε διὰ γένους ἱερωσύνην
τὴν τοῦ Διὸς τοῦ Σαβαζίου τιμιωτάτην οὖσαμ παρ᾽ ἡμῖν, ὕστερον
δὲ μεταλλάξαντος τοῦ Σωσάνδρου διὰ τὴμ περὶ αὐτὸν οὖσαν
καλοκαγαθίαν καὶ περὶ τὸ θε[ῖ]ον εὐσέβειαγ καὶ τὴν πρὸς ἡμᾶς
εὔνοιαγ καὶ πίστιγ καὶ τῆς τοῦ καθηγεμόνος Διονύσου ἱερωσύνης
ἠξιώσαμεν αὐτόν, κρίναντες αὐτὸγ καὶ ταύτης ἄξιον τῆς τιμῆς
καὶ πρεπόντως προστήσησθαι μυστ[ηρί]ων τηλικούτωγ κἀγὼ
καὶ Ἄτταλος ὁ θεῖός μου, ὡς διασαφεῖται ἐν τῶ[ι] ιη´ ἔτει τῆς
ἐκείνου βασιλείας. εἰδὼς οὖν ὅτι πρὸς μητρὸς καὶ ὑμ[έ]τερός ἐστι

61 AMENNEUS

Amenneus to Asklepiades, greetings. In accordance with your written instructions, we have prepared for the visit of Commander of the Bodyguard and Finance Minister Chrysippos ten white-brows, five domestic geese and fifty fowls; as for wild birds, fifty geese, two hundred fowls, and one hundred young pigeons. We have borrowed five riding-donkeys along with their [. . .], and we have also readied the forty baggage-donkeys. We are proceeding with the road-making. Farewell. Year 22, Choiach 4.

Reverse: To Asklepiades. Year 22, Choiach 7. Amenneus, about the hospitality prepared.

62 ATTALOS III OF PERGAMUM

King Attalos to the Council and People of Kyzikos, greetings. I am sure that you are not unaware that Athenaios son of Sosandros, created priest of Dionysos the Guide and a Royal Page of my father's, is our relative, since Sosandros married the daughter of Athenaios son of Meidias (the Athenaios who was my father's cousin) and so became his father. To him in the first place as one worthy of our house, while Sosandros was still alive, my uncle Attalos with my approval gave the hereditary priesthood of Zeus Sabazios, which is in great honour with us; subsequently, after Sosandros had passed away, because of the goodness attending him, and his piety towards the divine, and his goodwill and fidelity towards us, we deemed him worthy of the priesthood of Dionysos the Guide as well, judging (my uncle Attalos and I) that he deserved the honour, and would preside in seemly fashion over the celebration of such important mysteries; this is on public record in the eighteenth year of his reign. Therefore, since I knew that on his mother's side he is a fellow-citizen

πολίτης, ἔκρινα ἐπιστεῖλαι ὑμῖμ πέμψας καὶ τὰ λοιπὰ προστάγ-
ματα καὶ φιλάνθρωπα τὰ γραφέντα ὑφ' ἡμῶμ περὶ τούτου ὅπως
εἰδῆτε ὡς ἔχομεμ φιλοστοργίας πρὸς αὐτόν.
δ', Δίου ζ. Μένης ἐκ Περγάμου.

63 MITHRIDATES OF PONTUS (88/7 B.C.)

(*SIG*³ 741 III = 73 Welles)

Βασιλ[εὺς Μιθριδ]άτης Λεωνίππω σατράπη [χαί]ρειν· ἐπεὶ
Χα[ιρ]ήμω[ν Πυ]θοδώρου ἐκχθρότατα κα[ὶ] πολεμιώτα[τα
πρ]ὸς τὰ ἡμέτερα πράγματα δια[κείμε]νος ἀπ' ἀρχ[ῆ]ς τε τοῖς
ἐκχθίστοις πολεμίοις [συνή]ει, νῦν τε τὴ[ν] ἐ[μὴ]ν παρουσίαν
ἐπιγνοὺς τούς [τε υἱ]οὺς Πυθόδω[ρ]ον καὶ Πυθίων[α] ἐξέθετο
καὶ αὐ[τὸς πέ]φευγεν, κήρ[υ]γ[μα] ποιῆσαι ὅπως ἐάν τις
ζῶντ[α ἀ]γάγη Χαιρήμ[ο]να ἢ Πυθόδωρον ἢ Πυθίων[α], λάβη
[τάλαν]τα τεσσαράκοντα, ἐὰν δέ τ[ι]ς τὴν κεφαλήν τινος [αὐτῶν]
ἐνένκη, λάβη τάλαντα εἴκοσι.

64 C. OCTAVIUS CAESAR IMPERATOR
(ROME, 39/8 B.C.)

(Document 12 Reynolds)

Αὐτοκράτωρ Καῖσαρ θεοῦ 'Ιουλίου υἱὸς 'Εφεσίων ἄρχουσι
βουλῆ δήμω χαίρειν· εἰ ἔρρωσθε εὖ ἂν ἔχοι, ὑγιαίνω δὲ καὶ
αὐτὸς μετά τοῦ στρατεύματος. Σόλων Δημητρίου υἱὸς πρεσ-
βευτὴς Πλαρασέων καὶ 'Αφροδεισιέων ἐνεφάνισέν μοι ὅσα ἐν τῶ
πολέμω τῶ κατά Λαβιῆνον ἡ πόλις αὐτῶν πέπονθεν ὅσα τε
διηρπάγη δημόσιά τε καὶ ἰδιωτικά, περὶ ὧν πάντων 'Αντωνίω
τε τῶ συνάρχοντι ἐντολὰς δέδωκα ὅπως ὅσα ἂν δύνηται
ὃ ἂν εὕρη ἀποκαταστήση αὐτοῖς· ὑμεῖν τε ἔκρεινα γράψαι
ἐπεὶ ἔχετε πόλιν εὔκαιρον ἐπιβοηθεῖ[α]ν αὐτοῖς ἐὰν σώματος
ἢ ἑτέρου τινὸς τῶν ἰδίων ἐπιλαμβάνονται. ἀπηγγέλη δέ μοι
ὅτι ἐκ τῆς διαρπαγῆς Ἔρως χρυσοῦς ὃ ὑπὸ τοῦ πατρὸς τῆ
'Αφροδείτη ἦν ἀνατεθεὶς εἰς ὑμᾶς ἀνενήνεκται καὶ ὡς ἀνάθημα
τῆ 'Αρτέμιδι τέθειται. ὑμεῖς οὖν καλῶς ποιήσετε καὶ ἀξίως

of yours too, I decided to write you a letter, sending also the other decrees and benefactions which we have put in writing concerning him, so that you may know in what affection we hold him.

Year 4, Dios 7. Menes (brought the letter) from Pergamon.

63 MITHRIDATES OF PONTUS

King Mithridates to the satrap Leonippos, greetings. Since Chairemon son of Pythodoros, by disposition most hateful and hostile to our state, has from the beginning consorted with our bitterest enemies, and now learning of my arrival has removed his sons Pythodoros and Pythion to a place of safety and himself taken flight, issue a proclamation that if anyone should apprehend Chairemon or Pythodoros or Pythion alive, he may receive forty talents, and that if anyone should bring in the head of any of them, he may receive twenty talents.

64 C. OCTAVIUS CAESAR IMPERATOR

Imperator Caesar, son of the god Julius, to the Magistrates, Council and People of Ephesos, greetings. It would be good if you are well; I myself am also in good health, together with the army. Solon son of Demetrios, ambassador for the people of Plarasa and Aphrodisias, has informed me how much their city suffered in the war against Labienus, and how much public and private property was looted, in connection with all of which I have commissioned my colleague Antonius to restore to them to the best of his ability whatsoever he may find; I have decided to write to you as well since you have a city that is well placed to assist them if they lay claim to a slave or some other item of private property. I have been informed that as a result of the looting a gold Eros, which had been dedicated to Aphrodite by my father, has found its way to you and been consecrated as a dedication to Artemis. You will then be doing right and acting

ὑμῶν ἀποκαταστήσαντες τὸ ὑπὸ τοῦ πατρός μου ἀνάθημα
τῇ Ἀφροδείτῃ δεδόμενον· καὶ γὰρ οὐ χαρίεν ἀνάθημα Ἔρως
Ἀρτέμιδι. ἀνάγκη γάρ μοι Ἀφροδεισιέων ποιεῖσθαι πρόνοιαν οὓς
τηλικαῦτα εὐεργέτηκα ἦν καὶ ὑμᾶς ἀκούειν νομίζω.

65 THE STRATEGOS OF THE PANOPOLITE NOME
(17 SEPTEMBER A.D. 298)

(*P.Beatty Panop.* 1.213–16)

νυκτοστρατήγοις. δι᾽ ὧν ἐπέθ[ηκε πρός] με γραμμάτων ὁ
κύριός μου ὁ διασημότατος ἡγούμενος τῆς Θηβαΐδος Ἰούλιος
Ἀθηνόδωρος ἐκέλευσεν ἐκ παν[τὸς τρό]που ἀναζητηθῆναι Νῖλ[ον
χα]λκέα ἀπὸ τῆς Ἑρμοντιθῶν πόλεως, ἀναγκαῖον ὄντα πρὸς
τὴν τῆς φαβρίκος ἐργασίαν, καὶ παρασταθῆναι καὶ παρ[απεμφ]
θῆναι μετὰ τῶν ἐργαλί[ων πρὸς τ]ὸ μεγαλῖον αὐτοῦ. κατὰ
τὸ ἀναγκαῖον ἠπίχθην ἐπιστῖλαι ὑμῖν ὅπως τοῦτον ἀνευρόντες
παραστήσητε· ἵν[α μὴ ἀμε]λήσαντες κ[[ο]]ινδύνω ὑ[ποστήση]ται.
Λιε′′ καὶ Λιδ′′ καὶ Λζ′′ Θὼθ κ́. σεσημίωμαι.

66 C. PLINIUS SECUNDUS, M. ULPIUS TRAIANUS
AUGUSTUS (BITHYNIA–ROME, NOV.–DEC.
A.D.? 109)

(Pliny, *Epistles* 10.33–4)

C. Plinius Traiano Imperatori. 1 cum diuersam partem prouinciae circumirem, Nicomediae uastissimum incendium multas pri-
uatorum domos et duo publica opera, quamquam uia inter-
iacente, Gerusian et Iseon absumpsit. 2 est autem latius sparsum,
primum uiolentia uenti, deinde inertia hominum quos satis
constat otiosos et immobiles tanti mali spectatores perstitisse;
et alioqui nullus usquam in publico sipo, nulla hama, nullum denique instrumentum ad incendia compescenda. et haec
quidem, ut iam praecepi, parabuntur; 3 tu, domine, dispice
an instituendum putes collegium fabrorum dumtaxat hominum
CL. ego attendam, ne quis nisi faber recipiatur neue iure

worthily of yourselves if you restore the dedication given by my father to Aphrodite; Eros is, after all, not a dedication to gladden Artemis' heart. I make this request because I am under an obligation to exercise on behalf of the people of Aphrodisias, on whom I have conferred such extensive benefits, the forethought of which I believe you too are coming to hear.

65 THE STRATEGOS OF THE PANOPOLITE NOME

To the night-watch. In his dispatches to me the most eminent Governor of the Thebaid, Julius Athenodorus, has ordered that all possible steps should be taken to search out one Nilos, a smith from the city of Hermonthis, who is needed for work in the arsenal; he is to be detained and sent under escort to his Highness, together with his tools. I am obliged to hasten to write to you with the order to find and detain this man, lest by disregarding these orders you should place yourselves in jeopardy.

Year 15 and year 14 and year 7. 20 Thoth. Signed.

66 C. PLINIUS SECUNDUS, M. ULPIUS TRAIANUS AUGUSTUS

C. Plinius to Emperor Trajan. **1** While I was making a tour in another part of the province, an enormously devastating fire in Nicomedia consumed a large number of private dwellings and two public buildings, the Gerousia and the Iseum, even though there was a street between them. **2** The reason for the fire's spreading more widely than might have been expected lay first in the violence of the wind, and secondly in the spinelessness of the local populace who, it has been established, did nothing in the face of such a catastrophe but stood idly by and watched the whole time. In any case, there was not a single pump available anywhere for public use, no bucket, indeed no tools of any kind for fighting fires. As far as the tools are concerned, I have already given the orders, and they will be provided; **3** but please decide, Sir, whether you think that an artificers' guild of not more than 150 men should be set up. I will see to it that membership is open only to artificers, and that the privilege once granted is not misused for other

concesso in aliud utantur; nec erit difficile custodire tam paucos.

* * * *

Traianus Plinio. 1 Tibi quidem secundum exempla complurium in mentem uenit posse collegium fabrorum apud Nicomedenses constitui. sed meminerimus prouinciam istam et praecipue eas ciuitates eius modi factionibus esse uexatas. quodcumque nomen ex quacumque causa dederimus iis, qui in idem contracti fuerint, hetaeriae eaeque breui fient. 2 satius itaque est comparari ea, quae ad coercendos ignes auxilio esse possint, admonerique dominos praediorum, ut et ipsi inhibeant ac, si res poposcerit, adcursu populi ad hoc uti.

67 FLAVIUS CLAUDIUS IULIANUS
(CONSTANTINOPLE, JANUARY A.D. 362)

(*Epistles* 21 Wright = 10 Bidez = 60 Weis)

Αὐτοκράτωρ Καῖσαρ Ἰουλιανὸς Μέγιστος Σεβαστὸς Ἀλεξανδρέων τῶι δήμωι. **378c** εἰ μὴ τὸν Ἀλέξανδρον τὸν οἰκιστὴν ὑμῶν καὶ πρό γε τούτου τὸν θεὸν τὸν μέγαν τὸν ἁγιώτατον Σάραπιν αἰδεῖσθε, **378d** τοῦ κοινοῦ γοῦν ὑμᾶς καὶ ἀνθρωπίνου καὶ πρέποντος πως οὐδεὶς εἰσῆλθε λόγος; προσθήσθω δὲ ἔτι καὶ ἡμῶν, οὓς οἱ θεοὶ πάντες, ἐν πρώτοις δὲ ὁ μέγας Σάραπις, ἄρχειν ἐδικαίωσαν τῆς οἰκουμένης· οἷς πρέπον ἦν τὴν ὑπὲρ τῶν ἠδικηκότων ὑμᾶς φυλάξαι διάγνωσιν. ἀλλ' ὀργὴ τυχὸν ἴσως ὑμᾶς ἐξηπάτησεν καὶ θυμός, ὅσπερ οὖν εἴωθεν

τὰ δεινὰ πράττειν, τὰς φρένας μετοικίσας;

εἶτα τῆς ὁρμῆς ἀνασταλέντες, τοῖς παραχρῆμα **379a** βεβουλευμένοις καλῶς ὕστερον ἐπηγάγετε τὴν παρανομίαν, οὐδὲ ἠισχύνθητε δῆμος ὄντες τολμῆσαι ταὐτά, ἐφ' οἷς ἐκείνους ἐμισήσατε δικαίως; εἴπατε γάρ μοι πρὸς τοῦ Σαράπιδος, ὑπὲρ ποίων ἀδικημάτων ἐχαλεπήνατε Γεωργίωι; τὸν μακαριώτατον Κωνστάντιον ἐρεῖτε δήπουθεν ὅτι καθ' ὑμῶν παρώξυνεν,

purposes. Keeping control over such a small group will not be difficult.

* * * *

Trajan to Pliny. **1** Following precedents set in a number of other places, you have had the idea that an artificers' guild could be established in Nicomedia. But let us remember that the whole of that province, and especially those cities, has been plagued by interest-groups of this kind. Whatever name we give to people brought together for a shared purpose, and for whatever reason, those groups inevitably become political factions before long. **2** It is enough therefore to provide the equipment that can be of use in extinguishing fires, and to instruct the owners of property to fight the fires themselves and, if circumstances demand, to summon the general public to come running for the purpose.

67 FLAVIUS CLAUDIUS JULIANUS

Imperator Caesar Iulianus Maximus Augustus to the people of Alexandria. **378c** Even if you have no respect for your founder Alexander, nor before him for the great and most holy god Sarapis, **378d** how is it that no thought even for common humanity or common decency entered your heads? Add to that also 'or for me', whom all the gods, and foremost among them the great Sarapis, appointed to rule the inhabited world; it was to me that you should have left the verdict over those who had wronged you. But perhaps you were led astray by anger and passion, which indeed habitually

    Displaces sense and does dread deeds?

Did you really then relent from your impulsiveness, only to supplant **379a** your first, sensible decision with illegal violence later? Had you no shame at daring to do as a people the very things for which you so justifiably hated your enemies? Tell me in the name of Sarapis, what crimes had Georgios committed, that you were so angry with him? I imagine that you will say that he incited the

εἶτα εἰσήγαγεν εἰς τὴν ἱερὰν πόλιν στρατόπεδον, καὶ κατέλαβεν
ὁ στρατηγὸς τῆς Αἰγύπτου τὸ **379b** ἁγιώτατον τοῦ θεοῦ τέ-
μενος, ἀποσυλήσας ἐκεῖθεν εἰκόνας καὶ ἀναθήματα καὶ τὸν ἐν τοῖς
ἱεροῖς κόσμον. ὑμῶν δὲ ἀγανακτούντων εἰκότως καὶ πειρωμένων
ἀμύνειν τῶι θεῶι, μᾶλλον δὲ τοῖς τοῦ θεοῦ κτήμασιν, ὁ δὲ ἐτόλμησεν
ὑμῖν ἐπιπέμψαι τοὺς ὁπλίτας ἀδίκως καὶ παρανόμως καὶ ἀσεβῶς,
ἴσως Γεώργιον μᾶλλον ἢ τὸν Κωνστάντιον δεδοικώς, (ὃς) ἑαυτὸν
παρεφύλαττεν, εἰ μετριώτερον ὑμῖν καὶ πολιτικώτερον, ἀλλὰ μὴ
τυραννικώτερον πόρρωθεν προσφέροιτο.

379c τούτων οὖν ἕνεκεν ὀργιζόμενοι τῶι θεοῖς ἐχθρῶι
Γεωργίωι, τὴν ἱερὰν αὖθις ἐμιάνατε πόλιν, ἐξὸν ὑποβάλλειν αὐτὸν
ταῖς τῶν δικαστῶν ψήφοις· οὕτω γὰρ ἐγίνετο ἂν οὐ φόνος οὐδὲ
παρανομία τὸ πρᾶγμα, δίκη δὲ ἐμμελής, ὑμᾶς μὲν ἀθώιους πάν-
τηι φυλάττουσα, τιμωρουμένη μὲν τὸν ἀνίατα δυσσεβήσαντα,
σωφρονίζουσα δὲ τοὺς ἄλλους πάντας ὅσοι **379d** τῶν θεῶν ὀλιγ-
ωροῦσιν καὶ πρόσετι τὰς τοιαύτας πόλεις καὶ τοὺς ἀνθοῦντας
δήμους ἐν οὐδενὶ τίθενται, τῆς ἑαυτῶν δὲ ποιοῦνται πάρεργον
δυναστείας τὴν κατ' ἐκείνων ὠμότητα.

παραβάλετε τοίνυν ταύτην μου τὴν ἐπιστολὴν ἧι μικρῶι
πρώιην ἐπέστειλα, καὶ τὸ διάφερον κατανοήσατε· πόσους μὲν
ὑμῶν ἐπαίνους ἔγραφον τότε; νυνὶ δὲ μὰ τοὺς θεοὺς ὁ φίλων
ὑμᾶς ἐπαίνειν οὐ δύναμαι διὰ τὴν παρανομίαν. **380a** τολμᾶι δῆμος ὥσπερ οἱ κύνες ἄνθρωπον σπαράττειν, εἶτα οὐκ αἰσχύνεται
καὶ φυλάττει καθαρὰς τὰς χεῖρας ὡς προσάγειν πρὸς τοὺς θεοὺς
αἵματος καθαρευούσας; ἀλλὰ Γεώργιος ἄξιος ἦν τοῦ τοιαῦτα
παθεῖν· καὶ τούτων ἴσως, ἐγὼ φαίην ἄν, χείρονα καὶ πικρότερα·
καὶ δι' ὑμᾶς ἐρεῖτε· σύμφημι καὶ αὐτός· παρ' ὑμῶν δὲ εἰ λέγοιτε,
τοῦτο οὐκέτι **380b** συγχωρῶ. νόμοι γὰρ ἡμῖν εἰσιν, οὓς χρὴ
τιμᾶσθαι μάλιστα μὲν ὑπὸ πάντων ἰδίαι καὶ στέργεσθαι· πλὴν
ἐπειδὴ συμβαίνει τῶν καθ' ἕκαστόν τινας παρανομεῖν, ἀλλὰ τὰ

late Constantius of blessed memory against you, and that he then brought an army into the holy city, with the result that the General of Egypt **379b** seized the god's most holy precinct and looted it of its statues and dedicatory offerings, and of the decorations adorning the shrines. And when you quite reasonably took this amiss and tried to defend your god, or rather your god's property, the General dared to order his legionaries against you, in contravention of all justice, legality and piety, acting perhaps more in fear of Georgios than of Constantius (for Constantius was keeping a careful eye on himself, in the hopes of being able to deal with you from a distance in a moderate and civil rather than a tyrannical manner).

379c It was then because you were angry with Georgios, the gods' enemy, that you once again defiled the holy city, when you had the choice of submitting him to a jury's verdict. This latter course of action would have resulted not in murder and lawlessness, but in the seemly execution of justice, which would have kept you safe and free from any retribution yourselves, inflicted due punishment on the impious perpetrator of inexpiable crimes, and chastened all such others as might **379d** despise the gods, and in addition hold such cities as yours and their flourishing communities in contempt, while regarding cruelty towards them as an incidental achievement of their power.

So, pray compare this letter of mine with the one I sent you a short time ago, and observe the difference. How highly I praised you in the former! But now, by the gods, I who am in the habit of praising you cannot do so because of your lawless behaviour. **380a** Can a people bring itself to tear a man apart like a pack of dogs, and then feel no shame, and does it keep its hands pure, so as to be able to bring them before its gods pure of blood? But Georgios deserved to suffer such a fate. Indeed; I myself would say he perhaps deserved a worse and more painful one. And you will say he deserved it because of you. So say I too. But when you add that he deserved to suffer it at your hands, then I cease **380b** to agree. We have laws, which ought ideally to be held in respect and cherished personally by all; but when certain individuals do chance to act illegally, all the same

κοινά γοῦν εὐνομεῖσθαι χρὴ καὶ πειθαρχεῖν τοῖς νόμοις ὑμᾶς καὶ μὴ παραβαίνειν ὅσαπερ ἐξ ἀρχῆς ἐνομίσθη καλῶς.

εὐτύχημα γέγονεν ὑμῖν ἄνδρες Ἀλεξανδρεῖς, ἐπ' ἐμοῦ πλημμελῆσαι τοιοῦτό τι ὑμᾶς, ὃς αἰδοῖ τῆι πρὸς τὸν θεὸν καὶ διὰ τὸν θεῖον τὸν ἐμὸν καὶ ὁμώνυμον, ὃς ἦρξεν 380c αὐτῆς τε Αἰγύπτου καὶ τῆς ὑμετέρας πόλεως, ἀδελφικὴν ὑμῖν εὔνοιαν ἀποσώζω. τὸ γὰρ τῆς ἐξουσίας ἀκαταφρόνητον καὶ τὸ ἀπηνέστερον καὶ καθαρὸν τῆς ἀρχῆς οὔποτ' ἂν δήμου περιίδοι τόλμημα μὴ καθάπερ νόσημα χαλεπὸν πικροτέρωι διακαθᾶραι φαρμάκωι. προσφέρω δ' ἐγὼ ὑμῖν δι' ἅσπερ ἔναγχος ἔφην αἰτίας τὸ προσηνέστατον, παραίνεσιν καὶ λόγους, ὑφ' ὧν εὖ οἶδ' ὅτι πειθήσεσθε μᾶλλον, εἴπερ 380d ἐστέ, καθάπερ ἀκούω, τό τε ἀρχαῖον Ἕλληνες καὶ τὰ νῦν ἔτι τῆς εὐγενείας ἐκείνης ὕπεστιν ὑμῖν ἀξιόλογος καὶ γενναῖος ἐν τῆι διανοίαι καὶ τοῖς ἐπιτηδεύμασι ὁ χαρακτήρ.

προτεθήτω τοῖς ἐμοῖς πολίταις Ἀλεξανδρεῦσιν.

68 BASILEIOS (CAESAREA, autumn a.d. 373)

(*Epistles* 102)

τοῖς Σαταλεῦσι πολίταις. ἐγὼ τάς τε ἰδίας ὑμῶν παρακλήσεις καὶ τὰς τοῦ λαοῦ παντὸς δυσωπηθεὶς καὶ ἐδεξάμην τὴν φροντίδα τῆς καθ' ὑμᾶς ἐκκλησίας καὶ ὑπεσχόμην ὑμῖν ἐνώπιον Κυρίου μηδὲν ἐλλείψειν τῶν εἰς δύναμιν ἐμὴν ἡκόντων. διὸ ἠναγκάσθην, κατὰ τὸ γεγραμμένον, οἷον τῆς κόρης τοῦ ἐμοῦ ὀφθαλμοῦ ἅψασθαι. οὕτως τὸ ὑπερβάλλον τῆς καθ' ὑμᾶς τιμῆς οὐδενός μοι συνεχώρησεν εἰς μνήμην ἐλθεῖν, οὐ συγγενείας, οὐ τῆς ἐκ παιδὸς συνηθείας τῆς ὑπαρχούσης μοι πρὸς τὸν ἄνδρα, πρὸ τῶν παρ' ὑμῶν αἰτηθέντων· ἀλλὰ πάντων μὲν τῶν ἰδίαι μοι ὑπαρχόντων πρὸς αὐτὸν εἰς οἰκειότητος λόγον ἐπιλαθόμενος, μὴ ὑπολογισάμενος δὲ μηδὲ τοῦ στεναγμοῦ τὸ πλῆθος ὃ καταστενάξει μου ὁ λαὸς ὁ τὴν προστασίαν αὐτοῦ ζημιωθείς, μὴ πάσης αὐτοῦ τῆς συγγενείας τὸ δάκρυον, μὴ μητρὸς αὐτοῦ γηραιᾶς καὶ ἐπὶ μόνηι τῆι παρ' αὐτοῦ θεραπείαι σαλευούσης τὴν θλίψιν εἰς καρδίαν λαβών, πάντων

the community as a whole must preserve due form – and you must obey these laws and not contravene enactments that were wisely established in the first place.

It is your good luck, people of Alexandria, to have committed such an offence in my reign, since I nourish for you a brotherly goodwill, out of reverence for your god and because of my uncle and namesake, who governed **380c** all Egypt together with your city. A ruler who wished his authority to be respected, and to exercise his power strictly and without compromise, would never look on inactive at a people's misbehaviour, but would purge it away with bitter medicine, as one would a serious disease. But what I am applying to you, for the reasons I have just mentioned, is the gentlest of medicines, words of advice, which I know for sure you will be the more ready to heed, if **380d** you are indeed, as I am told, Hellenes by remote origin, and if the noble stamp of that distinguished ancestry still remains in your character and habits to any appreciable degree.

Let this message be put on public display to my citizens, the people of Alexandria.

68 BASILEIOS

To the people of Satala. Discountenanced by your individual appeals and by those of the whole congregation, I both accepted the responsibility of looking out for your Church and promised you before the Lord that I would not fail you in anything that lay within my power. Thus I was compelled, in the words of Scripture, as it were to lay hands on the pupil of my eye: to such an extent did my extraordinary respect for you prevent me from calling anything else to mind – not our kinship, not the companionship I had enjoyed with the man since boyhood – before your request. Forgetting all the personal bonds of intimacy I had with him, taking no thought for the volume of lamentation that will be unleashed by my congregation when it is made to suffer the loss of his leadership, nor for the tears of all his family, nor taking to heart the prostration of his old mother whose only stay in life is his tender care – with

ὁμοῦ τοιούτων ὄντων καὶ τοσούτων ἀλογήσας ἑνὸς ἐγενόμην
τοῦ τὴν ὑμετέραν ἐκκλησίαν κατακοσμῆσαι μὲν τῆι τοῦ τη-
λικούτου ἀνδρὸς προστασίαι, βοηθῆσαι δὲ αὐτῆι ἐκ τῆς χρονίας
ἀπροστασίας εἰς γόνυ λοιπὸν κλιθείσηι καὶ πολλῆς καὶ δυνατῆς
χειραγωγίας εἰς τὸ διαναστῆναι δεομένηι. τὰ μὲν οὖν ἡμέτερα
τοιαῦτα· τὰ δὲ παρ᾽ ὑμῶν ἀπαιτοῦμεν λοιπὸν μὴ ἐλάττονα φανῆ-
ναι τῆς ἡμετέρας ἐλπίδος καὶ τῶν ὑποσχέσεων ἃς πεποιήμεθα τῶι
ἀνδρί, ὅτι πρὸς οἰκείους καὶ φίλους αὐτὸν ἐξεπέμψαμεν, ἑκάστου
ὑμῶν ὑπερβαλέσθαι τὸν ἕτερον ἐν τῆι περὶ τὸν ἄνδρα σπουδῆι καὶ
ἀγάπηι προθυμουμένου. ὅπως οὖν ἐπιδείξησθε τὴν καλὴν ταύτην
φιλοτιμίαν καὶ τῶι ὑπερβάλλοντι τῆς θεραπείας παρακαλέσητε
αὐτοῦ τὴν καρδίαν, ὥστε λήθην μὲν αὐτῶι ἐγγενέσθαι πατρίδος, λήθην δὲ συγγενῶν, λήθην δὲ λαοῦ τοσοῦτον ἐξηρτημένου
τῆς προστασίας αὐτοῦ ὅσον παιδίον νεαρὸν τῆς μητρώιας θηλῆς.
προαπεστείλαμεν δὲ Νικίαν, ὥστε τὰ γενόμενα φανερὰ καταστῆ-
σαι τῆι τιμιότητι ὑμῶν καὶ προλαβόντας ὑμᾶς ἑορτάζειν καὶ εὐ-
χαριστεῖν τῶι Κυρίωι τῶι δι᾽ ἡμῶν καταξιώσαντι τὴν εὐχὴν ὑμῶν
ἐκπληρωθῆναι.

69 AURELIUS AUGUSTINUS
(HIPPO REGIUS, A.D. 402)

(Epistles 65)

Domino beatissimo et uenerabiliter suscipiendo patri et consacerdoti seni Xanthippo Augustinus in Domino salutem. 1 officio deb-
ito meritis tuis salutans dignationem tuam tuisque me orationibus
ualde commendans insinuo prudentiae tuae Abundantium quen-
dam in fundo Strabonianensi pertinente ad curam nostram ordina-
tum fuisse presbyterum. qui cum non ambularet uias seruorum dei,
non bonam famam habere coeperat. quo ego conterritus non tamen
temere aliquid credens sed plane sollicitior factus operam dedi, si
quo modo possem ad aliqua malae conuersationis eius certa indicia peruenire. ac primo comperi eum pecuniam cuiusdam rusticani
diuino apud se commendato interuertisse, ita ut nullam inde posset
probabilem reddere rationem. deinde conuictus atque confessus est

no regard for such a mass of weighty considerations, I engrossed myself in the task of adorning your Church with the leadership of such a distinguished individual, and of rescuing it when it had been brought permanently to its knees from the protracted lack of a leader, and was in need of sustained and powerful guidance to recover. So much then for my actions. From you in your turn I request that your response should not fall short of my expectations and of the promises I have made this man, that I have dispatched him to devoted friends, each of whom strives to outdo the other in warmth and affection towards him. Make sure therefore to display this virtuous rivalry and to cheer his heart with the overwhelming warmth of your solicitude, so that he may come to forget his homeland, his relatives, and the congregation which depended on his leadership quite as much as a newborn child on its mother's breast. We have sent Nikias on in advance, so as to keep you informed of events, and so that you may in anticipation celebrate and give thanks to the Lord who has graciously granted that your prayer should be fulfilled through us.

69 AURELIUS AUGUSTINUS

To the elder Xanthippus, his most saintly lord and reverently cherished father and fellow-priest, Augustine sends his greetings in the Lord. **1** Greeting your Honour with the deference due to your merits and commending myself earnestly to your prayers, I beg to submit to the consideration of your Sagacity the case of one Abundantius, who was ordained priest in the manor of Strabonia, which belongs to my diocese. Because he did not walk in the ways of the servants of God, he began to acquire a bad reputation. This alarmed me; not however jumping to rash conclusions, though certainly placed more on my guard, I exerted myself to see if I could by some means obtain clear proof of immorality on his part. My first discovery was that he had embezzled the money of a certain countryman entrusted to him for religious purposes, and so was unable subsequently to give any satisfactory account of it. Secondly, it was proved – and he

die ieiunii natalis domini, quo etiam Gippitana ecclesia sicut ceterae ieiunabant, cum tamquam perrecturus ad ecclesiam suam 'uale' fecisset collegae suo presbytero Gippitano, hora ferme quinta, et cum secum nullum clericum haberet, in eodem fundo restitisse et apud quandam malae famae mulierem et prandisse et cenasse et in eadem domo mansisse. in huius autem hospitio iam quidam clericus noster Hipponiensis remotus erat; et hoc quia iste optime nouerat, negare non potuit, nam quae negauit, deo dimisi, iudicans quae occultare permissus non est. timui ei committere ecclesiam praesertim inter haereticorum circumlatrantium rabiem constitutam. et cum me rogaret ut ad presbyterum fundi Armenianensis in campo Bullensi, unde ad nos deuenerat, causa eius insinuata litteras darem, ne quid de illo atrocius suspicaretur, ut illic sic uiuat, si fieri potest, sine officio presbyterii correctior, misericordia commotus feci. haec autem me praecipue prudentiae tuae intimare oportebat, ne aliqua tibi fallacia subreperet.

2 audiui autem causam eius, cum centum dies essent ad dominicum paschae, qui futurus est VIII Id. Aprilis. haec propter concilium insinuare curaui uenerabilitati tuae, quod etiam ipsi non celaui, sed ei fideliter, quid institutum esset, aperui. et si intra annum causam suam, si forte sibi aliquid agendum putat, agere neglexerit, deinceps eius uocem nemo audiat. nos autem, domine beatissime et uenerabiliter suscipiende pater, si haec indicia malae conuersationis clericorum, maxime cum fama non bona eos coeperit comitari, non putauerimus nisi eo modo uindicanda quo in concilio constitutum est, incipimus cogi ea quae sciri non possunt, uelle discutere et aut incerta damnare aut uere incognita praeterire. ego certe presbyterum, ut qui die ieiunii, quo eiusdem loci etiam

himself confessed – that on the fast-day of the Lord's birthday, when the church of Gibba, like all the others, was keeping the fast, under pretence of returning directly to his own church, he said goodbye to his colleague, the priest of Gibba, at about 11 o'clock, and although he had no clergyman with him, he remained in the same manor, lunching and dining with a woman of ill repute and staying in the same house as her. However, one of our clergy of Hippo was already living away from home in this woman's guest-room; and since Abundantius knew this very well, he could not deny his guilt, though what he did deny I left to God, passing judgement only on what he was not in a position to conceal. I was afraid to let him remain in charge of a church, especially one situated in the midst of a baying pack of raging heretics. And when he asked me to send a letter giving an account of his case to the priest of the manor of Armenia in the district of Bulla, which was where he had come to us from, to avoid any worse suspicions about him being entertained, so that he could, if possible, live a reformed life there relieved of his priestly duties, I was moved to pity and did so. It was my duty to report this matter to your Sagacity in particular, to prevent any deception being practised on you.

2 I heard Abundantius' case one hundred days before Easter Sunday, which will fall on 6 April. I have taken care to inform your Reverence of these facts because of the decree of Council, which I did not conceal from him either but enlightened him as to exactly what procedure had been established. If he by any chance sees fit to take some action, yet fails to present his case within a year, no one thereafter may give him a hearing. For my part, my saintly lord and reverently cherished father, if I thought that this evidence of immoral conduct on the part of clergymen, especially when a bad reputation has begun to attach to them, deserved punishment only according to the form established at the Council, I should now start to be compelled to agree to discuss things that cannot be ascertained, and either to condemn him on indecisive evidence or to acquit him for want of any real proof. I at any rate came to the conclusion that a priest who, on a fast-day, which the local

ecclesia ieiunebat, 'uale' faciens collegae suo eiusdem loci presbytero apud famosam mulierem nullum secum clericum habens
remanere et prandere et cenare ausus est et in una domo dormire,
remouendum ab officio presbyterii arbitratus sum timens ei deinceps ecclesiam dei committere. quod si forte iudicibus ecclesiasti-
cis aliud uidetur, quia sex episcopis causam presbyteri terminare
concilio statutum est, committat illi, qui uult, ecclesiam suae curae commissam; ego talibus, fateor, quamlibet plebem committere
timeo, praesertim quos nulla bona fama defendit, ut hoc eis possit
ignosci, ne, si quid perniciosius eruperit, languens inputem mihi.

70 PHALARIS

(*Epistles* 84)

Μεσσηνίοις. **1** οὐκ ἠγνόουν ὅτι πέμψαντός μου τοῖς παρ' ὑμῖν
θεοῖς ἀναθήματα, τρίποδάς τε Δελφικοὺς καὶ στεφάνους χρυσοῦς
καὶ ἄλλα πολλὰ καὶ πολυτελῆ χαριστήρια τῆς σωτηρίας, δυοῖν
θάτερον ποιήσετε, ἢ τοῖς θεοῖς εὐσεβοῦντες ἀναθήσετε, ἢ τούτους ἀποστερήσαντες αὐτοὶ διανεμεῖσθε, ὅπερ δὴ καὶ δεδράκατε.
προσποιησάμενοι γὰρ ἐμοὶ λοιδορεῖσθαι, ὡς τῶν ἀναθημάτων
διὰ τὸν κτησάμενον οὐ καθαρῶν ὄντων, τοὺς θεοὺς ἱεροσυλήκατε.
τί γὰρ διαφέρει τὰ καθωσιωμένα περισπάσαντας ἀπενεγκεῖν ἢ
τὰ κατωνομασμένα τοῖς θεοῖς; ἐκείνων γὰρ ἀμφότερα ἦν καὶ οὐ
τῶν πεπομφότων. **2** ἡ μὲν οὖν παρ' ἐμοῦ χάρις εἰς τοὺς θεοὺς καὶ
ἡ παρ' ὑμῖν ἀσέβεια παντελής ἐστι· καὶ γὰρ ἐμὲ τὸν δεδωκότα
καὶ τοὺς ἁρπάσαντας ὑμᾶς ἴσασιν. ἀρκεῖ δέ μοι τοὺς τὰ τῶν θεῶν
λαβόντας ἐναργεῖς ὑμᾶς ὁρᾶν γεγονότας τῆι τῶν ἱεροσυληθέντων
ὀργῆι· σὺν γὰρ τοῖς ἄλλοις, δι' ὧν αὐτὰ κέρδος ἡγήσασθε,
προσωμολογήκατε μηδὲν εἶναι μυσαρὸν τῶν ἀπεσταλμένων, εἰ
μὴ τὰ αὐτὰ κειμήλια διττὰς ἔχει τύχας, ἂν μὲν ὑμεῖς αὐτὰ δι-
ανέμησθε, τὰς ἀμείνους, ἂν δὲ τοῖς θεοῖς κομισθῆι, τὰς χείρους.

church too was observing, said goodbye to his colleague, the local priest, and dared to stay with a woman of ill repute, and to lunch and dine and stay the night in the same house, with no clergyman accompanying him, ought to be removed from the office of priest, since I was afraid thereafter to entrust a church to his care. If the ecclesiastical court should happen to take a different view, seeing that the Council determined to employ six bishops to decide a case concerning a priest, let him who wishes entrust this man with a church that comes within his diocese. For my part, I confess I am afraid to entrust any congregation to people like that, especially if they have no good reputation to defend them, as a reason for excusing these delinquencies: I have no wish to suffer the distress of blaming it on myself, if some more pernicious trouble should erupt.

70 PHALARIS

To the Messenians. **1** I am well aware that, when I sent offerings to the gods of your city, Delphic tripods and gold garlands and many other precious thank-offerings for my deliverance, you would do one of two things – either set them up with due piety towards the gods, or rob the gods and divide the offerings among yourselves, which is precisely what you have done. With a show of abusing me, on the grounds that the offerings were impure because of their owner, you have sacrilegiously plundered the gods. After all, what is the difference between ripping away and carrying off what has been formally consecrated to the gods and doing so to what has been marked down for them? Both sets of items belonged to them, not to their senders. **2** Thus both my thank-offering to the gods and your impiety are complete and perfect; the gods know both me as the giver and you as the takers away. It is enough for me to see that you who took the gods' property stand revealed to the wrath of the victims of your sacrilege; because along with all your other reasons for thinking to have profited from it, you have also admitted that none of the items dispatched is polluted, unless one and the same treasure can have two fates, a better one if you share it out among

3 πρὸς δὲ τούτοις ἑαυτοὺς ἐλέγχετε περιφανῶς ἠσεβηκότας· οἱ μὲν γὰρ ἄρχοντες τοῦ ψηφίσασθαι πολέμια εἶναι τὰ χρήματα τὴν αἰτίαν ἐπὶ τὸν δῆμον ἀναφέρουσιν, ὑμεῖς δὲ ὁ δῆμος ἐπὶ τοὺς ἄρχοντας, καὶ τὸ πάντων δεινότατον τοὺς μὲν θεοὺς ὡς κακοὺς ἀνθρώπους προδότας ἂν γενέσθαι λέγετε, εἰ δῶρα παρὰ τυράννου λάβοιεν, τοὺς δὲ πολιτευομένους παρ' ὑμῖν, οἳ τρὶς οὐχ ἅπαξ Μεσσήνην ὡς Ἀκράγαντά μοι ὑπὸ χεῖρα πεποιήκεσαν ἄν, εἰ χρήματα αὐτοῖς αἰτοῦσι προείμην, οὐ κολάζετε. 4 τὸ δ' αἴτιον, ὅτι κοινωνεῖτε τῆς αὐτῆς προαιρέσεως καὶ οὐ δύνασθε τοῖς αἰτίοις ἐλευθέρως ἐπεξελθεῖν· πάντες γὰρ ἔνοχοι δωροδοκίας εὑρηθήσεσθε. οὐ μὴν ἀλλ' ἐγὼ μέν, ἵνα μὴ δοκῶ περὶ τῶν ἀναθημάτων λέγειν μήτε παρ' ἐμοὶ μεμενηκότων μήτε τοῖς θεοῖς ἀνατεθειμένων, οὐδεμίαν ποιήσομαι φροντίδα, μετελεύσονται δὲ ὑμᾶς ἀξίως τῶν τετολμημένων οἱ σεσυλημένοι καὶ περὶ ἐμοῦ καὶ περὶ ὧν εἰς αὐτοὺς ἠσεβήκατε. ἔρρωσθε· τὸ δὲ ἔρρωσθε διπλῆν παρέμφασιν ἔχον, ἀγαθοῦ καὶ κακοῦ, μὴ ἀγνοεῖτε ὅτι πρὸς τὸ χεῖρον γέγραπται.

yourselves and a worse one if it is presented to the gods. **3** What is more, you convict yourselves of manifest impiety; your magistrates cast the blame for the vote that the goods should be classed as an enemy's on you, and you the people cast it on your magistrates; and what is most shocking of all, you claim that the gods, like wicked humans, could turn traitor by accepting gifts from a tyrant, while at the same time refusing to punish those of your own citizens who, not once but three times, would have handed Messene over to my control just like Acragas, if I had paid out at their request. **4** The reason for this is that you all subscribe to the same principles and are not in a position freely to exact retribution from the guilty, because you will all be discovered to be receivers of bribes. All the same, so as not to give the impression of talking about the offerings that neither remained with me nor were dedicated to the gods, I will not concern myself over this; it is the victims of your depredations who will punish you in the manner your effrontery deserves, both in so far as it concerns me and in so far as it concerns the wrong that you have done to them. Farewell – but since 'farewell' has a two meanings, both good and ill, rest assured that it is here intended in the worse sense.

C EMBEDDED LETTERS (71-72)

71 PHOENICIUM

(Plautus, *Pseudolus* 23–77)

PSEUDOLUS. ut opinor, quaerunt litterae hae sibi liberos:
alia aliam scandit. CALIDORUS. ludis iam ludo tuo.
PS. has quidem pol credo nisi Sibulla legerit,   25
interpretari alium potesse neminem.
CALI. qur inclementer dicis lepidis litteris
lepidis tabellis lepida conscriptis manu?
PS. an, opsecro hercle, habent quas gallinae manus?
nam has quidem gallina scripsit. CALI. odiosus mihi es.   30
lege uel tabellas redde. PS. immo enim pellegam.
aduortito animum. CALI. non adest. PS. at tu cita.
CALI. immo ego tacebo, tu istinc ex cera cita;
nam istic meus animus nunc est, non in pectore.
PS. tuam amicam uideo, Calidore. CALI. ubi ea est, opsecro? 35
PS. eccam in tabellis porrectam: in cera cubat.
CALI. at te di deaeque quantumst – PS. seruassent quidem!
CALI. quasi solstitialis herba paullisper fui:
repente exortus sum, repentino occidi.
PS. tace, dum tabellas pellego. CALI. ergo quin legis?   40
PS. 'Phoenicium Calidoro amatori suo
per ceram et lignum litterasque interpretes
salutem impertit et salutem abs te expetit
lacrumans titubanti animo, corde et pectore.'
CALI. perii! salutem nusquam inuenio, Pseudole,   45
quam illi remittam. PS. quam salutem? CALI. argenteam.
PS. pro lignean salute ueis argenteam
remittere illi? uide sis quam tu rem geras.
CALI. recita modo: ex tabellis iam faxo scies
quam subito argento mi usus inuento siet.   50
PS. 'leno me peregre militi Macedonio
minis uiginti uendidit, uoluptas mea;
et priu' quam hinc abiit quindecim miles minas
dederat; nunc unae quinque remorantur minae.

71 PHOENICIUM

PS. It looks to me as if these letters are trying to have children: they're all over each other. CALI. You're making a joke of it now, as usual. **25** PS. So help me, unless the Sibyl happened to have read this, I don't reckon anyone else could make sense of it. CALI. Why are you being beastly about those dear little letters written on those dear little tablets by that dear little hand? PS. Here, do you mean the sort of hands hens have got? **30** It was certainly a hen wrote this stuff. CALI. You're being such a bore! Read it or give me the tablets back. PS. No, no, I'll read it. Give me your attention. CALI. I haven't got it. PS. Well fetch it then. CALI. No, I'll keep quiet; *you* fetch it from those wax tablets: *that's* where my heart is right now, not in my chest. **35** PS. Calidorus, I can see your girlfriend. CALI. *Please*, where is she? PS. There she is, stretched out full length, in the tablets, bedded in the wax. CALI. May every last single god and goddess – PS. Bless me! CALI. Like the midsummer grass I haven't lasted long, springing up suddenly and withering just as fast. **40** PS. Keep quiet while I read the tablets through. CALI. Well, get on with it then! PS. 'By this wax and this wood and these letters that are her messengers, Phoenicium bids good health to her beloved Calidorus, and begs for your help in return, heart and soul, with tears and trembling spirit.' **45** CALI. I've had it, Pseudolus: I don't know where to find the help to send her. PS. What sort of help? CALI. Silver. PS. You want to send her back silver help in return for her wooden wishes? I'd have a think about what sort of bargain that is, if I were you. CALI. Just go on reading; I'll see to it that you know soon enough from the tablets **50** how urgently I need to get hold of some money. PS. 'My darling, the pimp has sold me to a foreigner, a Macedonian officer, for twenty minas, and before he left here the officer had paid down fifteen; now it's only five minas that are keeping things waiting. Because of this the officer left a token

ea caussa miles hic reliquit symbolum　　　　　　　　55
expressam in cera ex anulo suam imaginem,
ut qui huc adferret eius similem symbolum
cum eo simul me mitteret. ei rei dies
haec praestituta est, proxuma Dionysia.'
CALI. cras ea quidem sunt: prope est exitium mihi,　　60
nisi quid mi in ted est auxili. PS. sine pellegam.
CALI. sino, nam mihi uideor cum ea fabularier;
lege: dulce amarumque una nunc misces mihi.
PS. 'nunc nostri amores, mores, consuetudines,
iocu', ludus, sermo, suauisauiatio,　　　　　　　　　65
compressiones artae amantium corporum,
teneris labellis molles morsiunculae,
nostrorum orgiorum * * * * *-iunculae,　　　　　　67ª
papillarum horridularum oppressiunculae,
harunc uoluptatum mi omnium atque ibidem tibi
distractio, discidium, uastities uenit,　　　　　　　70
nisi quae mihi in test aut tibist in me salus.
haec quae ego sciui ut scires curaui omnia;
nunc ego te experiar quid ames, quid simules. uale.'
CALI. est misere scriptum, Pseudole. PS. oh! miserrume.
CALI. quin fles? PS. pumiceos oculos habeo: non queo　75
lacrumam exorare ut exspuant unam modo.
CALI. quid ita? PS. genu' nostrum semper siccoculum fuit.

72 TIMARCHIDES

(Cicero, *Verrines* 2.3.154–7)

154 Venio nunc ad epistulam Timarchidi, liberti istius et accensi;
de qua cum dixero, totum hoc crimen decumanum peroraro. haec
epistula est, iudices, quam nos Syracusis in aedibus Aproni cum
litteras conquireremus inuenimus. missa est, ut ipsa significat, ex
itinere, cum Verres iam de prouincia decessisset, Timarchidi manu
scripta. Recita. EPISTVLA TIMARCHIDI. 'Timarchides Verris
accensus salutem dicit.' iam hoc quidem non reprehendo quod

here, **55** a picture stamped in wax from his ring, so that as soon as someone brought another token like it, the pimp could send me off with him straight away. The day's been fixed, the day before the Dionysia.' **60** CALI. And the Dionysia's tomorrow. I'm as good as dead unless you can help me somehow. PS. Let me finish reading. CALI. All right; it makes me feel as if I'm talking to her. Read away: it's a bittersweet drink you're mixing me. PS. 'Now all our love, our ways together, the things we used to do, **65** our jokes and games, our conversations, our kisses, the close embraces of our loving bodies, our soft lips' gentle nibblings, the [rapturous celebration] of our secret rites, the sweet squeezing of pointy breasts – unless you can rescue me or I you, all these pleasures are going to be **70** shattered and scattered and swept away for you and me alike. I've made sure to tell you everything I know; now I shall find out how much you really love me and how much is just a sham. Farewell.' CALI. It's a pathetic letter, Pseudolus! PS. Utterly pathetic! **75** CALI. So why aren't you crying? PS. I've got eyes made of pumice: I can't get them to shed a single drop however much I plead. CALI. Why's that? PS. My kind's always been dry-eyed.

72 TIMARCHIDES

154 I come now to the letter by the defendant's freedman and orderly Timarchides; when I have dealt with it I shall have brought this whole treatment of the produce-tax charges to an end. This is the letter, gentlemen, that I found in Apronius' house in Syracuse during my search for documents. As its contents show, it was sent after Verres had ended his term as governor of the province, while Timarchides was on the move, and it is written in his own hand. Read it out. [*Timarchides's letter is read out.*] 'Verres' orderly Timarchides sends his greetings.' I have no fault to find with him

adscribit 'accensus'; cur enim sibi hoc scribae soli sumant, 'L. Papirius scriba'? uolo ego hoc esse commune accensorum, lictorum, uiatorum. 'fac diligentiam adhibeas, quod ad praetoris existimationem attinet.' Commendat Apronio Verrem, et hortatur ut inimicis eius resistat. bono praesidio munitur existimatio tua, siquidem in Aproni constituitur diligentia atque auctoritate. 'habes uirtutem, eloquentiam.' **155** quam copiose laudatur Apronius a Timarchide, quam magnifice! cui ego illum non putem placere oportere qui tanto opere Timarchidi probatus sit? 'habes sumptum unde facias.' necesse est, si quid redundarit de uestro frumentario quaestu, ad illum potissimum per quem agebatis defluxisse. 'scribas, apparitores recentis arripe; cum L. Volteio, qui plurimum potest, caede, concide.' uidete quam ualde malitiae suae confidat Timarchides, qui etiam Apronio improbitatis praecepta det. iam hoc 'caede, concide'! nonne uobis uerba domo patroni depromere uidetur ad omne genus nequitiae accommodata? 'uolo, mi frater, fraterculo tuo credas.' consorti quidem in lucris atque furtis, gemino et simillimo nequitia, improbitate, audacia. 'in cohorte carus haberere.' quid est hoc 'in cohorte'? quo pertinet? Apronium doces? quid? in uestram cohortem te monitore an sua sponte peruenerat? 'quod cuique opus est, oppone.' qua impudentia putatis eum in dominatione fuisse qui in fuga tam improbus sit? ait omnia pecunia effici posse: dare, profundere oportere, si uelis uincere. non hoc mihi tam molestum est Apronio suadere Timarchidem, quam quod hoc idem patrono suo praecipit. 'te postulante omnes uincere solent.' **156** Verre quidem praetore, non Sacerdote, non Peducaeo, non hoc ipso Metello. 'scis Metellum sapientem esse.' hoc uero ferri iam non potest, inrideri uiri optimi, L. Metelli, ingenium et contemni ac despici a fugitiuo Timarchide. 'si Volteium habebis, omnia ludibundus conficies.' hic uehementer errat Timarchides, qui aut Volteium pecunia corrumpi putet posse, aut Metellum unius arbitratu gerere praeturam, sed errat coniectura domestica. quia multos et per se et per alios multa ludibundos apud Verrem effecisse uidit, ad omnis eosdem patere aditus arbitratur. facilius uos efficiebatis ludibundi quae uolebatis a Verre,

for adding 'orderly'; why should clerks alone claim the privilege, as in 'L. Papirius the clerk'? I'd like the practice to be extended to orderlies, lictors and errand-boys. 'Be sure to make an effort, as far as the good name of the governor is concerned.' He commends Verres to Apronius and encourages him to oppose his enemies. Your reputation is indeed in safe hands if it depends on Apronius' care and standing. 'You are brave and eloquent.' **155** What rich and splendid praise this is for Apronius from Timarchides! Can I believe that there is anyone who oughtn't to think well of a man who comes so highly recommended by Timarchides? 'You have money to spend.' If there is any surplus from your grain profits, it ought necessarily to trickle down to your agent sooner than anyone else. 'Get hold of the new clerks and servants; L. Volteius is very powerful – make common cause with him, then strike out and make a killing.' See how confidently Timarchides trusts in his own villainy, that he gives even Apronius advice on how to misbehave. That 'strike out and make a killing', for instance! Don't you think that he is trotting out some of his old employer's dicta – suitable for all kinds of depravity – from his own private store? 'Please, my brother, trust your own dear brother.' Yes, your partner in moneymaking and theft, your identical twin in depravity, vice and daring. 'The staff would count you as a bosom friend.' What is that about 'the staff'? What is the point of that remark? Are you trying to teach Apronius something he doesn't already know? Was it as a result of your advice or on his own initiative that he had joined? 'Put everyone in the way of what he needs.' What unscrupulousness do you think he would have shown from a position of power, when even on the run he can be such a villain? He says you can do anything with money: you need to give it, no lavish it, if you want to win. I am not so offended that Timarchides is urging Apronius to this course of action, as that he is giving the very same instructions to his patron. 'Usually, when you bring a prosecution, all your clients win their cases.' **156** Yes, under Verres as governor, but not under Sacerdos, not under Peducaeus, not under the very same Metellus. 'You know Metellus is a clever so-and-so.' This is quite intolerable, that the character of the distinguished L. Metellus should be mocked and belittled by the runaway Timarchides. 'If you have Volteius, it will be child's play for

quod multa eius ludorum genera noratis. 'inculcatum est Metello et Volteio te aratores euertisse.' quis istuc Apronio attribuebat, cum aratorem aliquem euerterat, aut Timarchidi, cum ob iudicandum aut decernendum aut imperandum aliquid aut remittendum pecuniam acceperat, aut Sextio lictori, cum aliquem innocentem securi percusserat? nemo; omnes ei tum attribuebant quem nunc condemnari uolunt. **157** 'obtuderunt eius auris te socium praetoris fuisse.' uidesne hoc quam clarum sit et fuerit, cum etiam Timarchides hoc metuat? concedesne non hoc crimen nos in te confingere, sed iam pridem ad crimen aliquam defensionem libertum quaerere? libertus et accensus tuus, et tibi ac liberis tuis omnibus in rebus coniunctus ac proximus, ad Apronium scribit uulgo esse ab omnibus ita demonstratum Metello, tibi Apronium in decumis socium fuisse. 'fac sciat improbitatem aratorum; ipsi sudabunt, si di uolunt.' quod istuc, per deos immortales, aut qua de cause excitatum esse dicamus in aratores tam infestum odium atque tantum? quantam iniuriam fecerunt Verri aratores ut eos etiam libertus et accensus eius tam irato animo ac litteris insequatur?

neque ego huius fugitiui, iudices, uobis epistulam recitassem, nisi ut ex ea totius familiae praecepta et instituta et disciplinam cognosceretis.

you to finish the business.' This is a serious mistake on Timarchides' part, if he thinks either that Volteius can be corrupted with a bribe or that Metellus conducts his governorship to suit one individual's wishes, but it is a wholly characteristic mistake for him to make. Because he saw many people under Verres achieving great things with no effort both through his own offices and through others, he concludes that the same approach will work with all governors. You and your like found it such child's play to get what you wanted from Verres because you knew many of his kind of tricks. 'It has been impressed on Metellus and Volteius that it was you who ruined the tenant farmers.' Who ever gave the credit to Apronius, when he ruined some tenant farmer, or to Timarchides, when he took a bribe for getting a verdict passed or a decision reached or a decree issued or something waived, or to Sextius the lictor, when he beheaded some innocent person with his axe? No one: everyone gave the credit to the man they now want to be condemned. **157** 'They have dinned it into his ears that you were the governor's associate.' Can you see how obvious this is and was, Verres, when even Timarchides is afraid of it? Do you grant that this is not a charge we have trumped up against you, but one to which your freedman has for some time since been looking for a defence? Your freedman and orderly, your and your children's close associate and right-hand man in everything, writes to tell Apronius that it has openly been proved to Metellus by everybody that you were Apronius' partner in the land-tax business. 'Make sure he knows about the tenant farmers' dishonesty; gods willing, they will be the ones to sweat.' Good God, what is this? What explanation shall we offer for such bitter hatred being unleashed against the tenant farmers? What wrong did tenant farmers do to Verres, that even his freedman and orderly should hound them by letter with such venom?

Gentlemen, the only reason I have read you this runaway's letter is to allow you to learn from it the principles, habits and methods of the whole entourage.

D EPISTOLARY THEORY (73–76)

73 DEMETRIOS

(De elocutione 223–35)

223 ἐπεὶ δὲ καὶ ὁ ἐπιστολικὸς χαρακτὴρ δεῖται ἰσχνότητος, καὶ περὶ αὐτοῦ λέξομεν. Ἀρτέμων μὲν οὖν τὰς Ἀριστοτέλους ἀναγράψας ἐπιστολάς φησιν ὅτι δεῖ ἐν τῶι αὐτῶι τρόπωι διάλογόν τε γράφειν καὶ ἐπιστολάς· εἶναι γὰρ τὴν ἐπιστολὴν οἷον τὸ ἕτερον μέρος τοῦ διαλόγου. **224** καὶ λέγει μέν τι ἴσως, οὐ μὴν ἅπαν· δεῖ γὰρ ὑποκατασκευάσθαι πως μᾶλλον τοῦ διαλόγου τὴν ἐπιστολήν· ὁ μὲν γὰρ μιμεῖται αὐτοσχεδιάζοντα, ἡ δὲ γράφεται καὶ δῶρον πέμπεται τρόπον τινά. **225** τίς γοῦν οὕτως ἂν διαλεχθείη πρὸς φίλον, ὥσπερ ὁ Ἀριστοτέλης πρὸς Ἀντίπατρον ὑπὲρ τοῦ φυγάδος γράφων τοῦ γέροντός φησιν· εἰ δὲ πρὸς ἁπάσας οἴχεται γᾶς φυγὰς οὗτος, ὥστε μὴ κατάγειν, δῆλον ὡς τοῖσγε εἰς Ἅιδου κατελθεῖν βουλομένοις οὐδεὶς φθόνος· ὁ γὰρ οὕτω διαλεγόμενος ἐπιδεικνυμένωι ἔοικεν μᾶλλον, οὐ λαλοῦντι. **226** καὶ λύσεις συχναὶ ὁποῖαι (αἱ τοῦ διαλόγου) οὐ πρέπουσιν ἐπιστολαῖς· ἀσαφὲς γὰρ ἐν γράφηι ἡ λύσις, καὶ τὸ μιμητικὸν οὐ γραφῆς οὕτως οἰκεῖον, ὡς ἀγῶνος, οἷον ὡς ἐν τῶι Εὐθυδήμωι· τίς ἦν, ὦ Σώκρατες, ὧι χθὲς ἐν Λυκείωι διελέγου· ἢ πολὺς ὑμᾶς ὄχλος περιειστήκει· καὶ μικρὸν προελθὼν ἐπιφέρει· ἀλλά μοι ξένος τις φαίνεται εἶναι, ὧι διελέγου· τίς ἦν; ἡ γὰρ τοιαύτη πᾶσα ἑρμηνεία καὶ μίμησις ὑποκριτῆι πρέπει μᾶλλον, οὐ γραφομέναις ἐπιστολαῖς. **227** πλεῖστον δὲ ἐχέτω τὸ ἠθικὸν ἡ ἐπιστολή, ὥσπερ καὶ ὁ διάλογος· σχεδὸν γὰρ εἰκόνα ἕκαστος τῆς ἑαυτοῦ ψυχῆς γράφει τὴν ἐπιστολήν. καὶ ἔστι μὲν καὶ ἐξ ἄλλου λόγου παντὸς ἰδεῖν τὸ ἦθος τοῦ γράφοντος, ἐξ οὐδενὸς δὲ ὡς ἐπιστολῆς.

228 τὸ δὲ μέγεθος συνεστάλθω τῆς ἐπιστολῆς, ὥσπερ καὶ ἡ λέξις. αἱ δὲ ἄγαν μακραὶ καὶ προσέτι κατὰ τὴν ἑρμηνείαν ὀγκωδέστεραι οὐ μὰ τὴν ἀλήθειαν ἐπιστολαὶ γένοιντο ἄν, ἀλλὰ συγγράμματα τὸ χαίρειν ἔχοντα προσγεγραμμένον, καθάπερ τοῦ Πλάτωνος πολλαὶ καὶ ἡ Θουκυδίδου. **229** καὶ τῆι συντάξει μεντοι λελύσθω μᾶλλον· γελοῖον γὰρ περιοδεύειν, ὥσπερ οὐκ ἐπιστολήν, ἀλλὰ δίκην γράφοντα· καὶ οὐδὲ γελοῖον μόνον,

73 DEMETRIOS

223 Since epistolary form also calls for a plain style, we will discuss it too. Artemon, who edited Aristotle's letters, says that one ought to use the same style in writing letters as in writing a dialogue, as the letter is like one of the two sides to a dialogue. **224** There is perhaps something in what he says, but it is not the whole truth; the letter should be somewhat more formal in its composition than the dialogue, as the latter represents someone speaking impromptu, whereas the former is written down and sent as a kind of gift. **225** At any rate, who ever would converse with a friend in the same way as Aristotle writes to Antipater on behalf of the old man in exile? 'If this man has journeyed to every country in the world, with no hope of recall, it is plain that we cannot begrudge a return home to Hades to those who wish it.' Someone who converses like this gives the impression of making a speech rather than chatting. **226** Frequent sentence-breaks, such as are characteristic of dialogue, are not right for letters: abrupt breaks in a piece of writing create obscurity, and imitation of live conversation is not as appropriate for writing as it is for debate. In the *Euthydemus*, for instance: 'Who was it you were talking to yesterday in the Lyceum, Socrates? There was a really large crowd surrounding you.' And a little further on he adds, 'I get the impression he was a stranger, the man you were talking to; who was he?' This kind of stylistic level and mode of representation is in all respects more appropriate to a performer than to written letters. **227** The letter should be strong on characterization, like the dialogue; everyone in writing a letter more or less composes an image of his own soul. One can indeed see the writer's character in any other kind of writing too, but in none so clearly as in the letter.

228 The length of a letter should be restricted, just as should its stylistic range. Those that are too long, and in addition rather pretentious in style, would not count as letters in the true sense, but as treatises with 'Dear So-and-so' attached, like many of Plato's and that one of Thucydides'. **229** Sentence-structure should be loose; it is ridiculous to construct elaborate periods as if one were composing

ἀλλ' οὐδὲ φιλικόν (τὸ γὰρ δὴ κατὰ τὴν παροιμίαν τὰ σῦκα σῦκα λεγόμενον) ἐπιστολαῖς ταῦτα ἐπιτηδεύειν. **230** εἰδέναι δὲ χρὴ ὅτι οὐχ ἑρμηνεία μόνον, ἀλλὰ καὶ πράγματά τινα ἐπιστολικά ἐστιν. Ἀριστοτέλης γοῦν, ὃς μάλιστα ἐπιτετευχέναι δοκεῖ τοῦ ἐπιστολικοῦ, τοῦτο δὲ οὐ γράφω σοι, φησίν, οὐ γὰρ ἦν ἐπιστολικόν. **231** εἰ γάρ τις ἐν ἐπιστολῆι σοφίσματα γράφοι καὶ φυσιολογίας, γράφει μέν, οὐ μὴν ἐπιστολὴν γράφει. φιλοφρόνησις γάρ τις βούλεται εἶναι ἡ ἐπιστολὴ σύντομος, καὶ περὶ ἁπλοῦ πράγματος ἔκθεσις καὶ ἐν ὀνόμασιν ἁπλοῖς.

232 κάλλος μέντοι αὐτῆς αἵ τε φιλικαὶ φιλοφρονήσεις καὶ πυκναὶ παροιμίαι ἐνοῦσαι· καὶ τοῦτο γὰρ μόνον ἐνέστω αὐτῆι σοφόν, διότι δημοτικόν τί ἐστιν ἡ παροιμία καὶ κοινόν, ὁ δὲ γνωμολογῶν καὶ προτρεπόμενος οὐ δι' ἐπιστολῆς ἔτι λαλοῦντι ἔοικεν, ἀλλὰ ⟨ἀπὸ⟩ μηχανῆς. **233** Ἀριστοτέλης μέντοι καὶ ἀποδείξεί που χρῆται ἐπιστολικῶς, οἷον διδάξαι βουλόμενος, ὅτι ὁμοίως χρὴ εὐεργετεῖν τὰς μεγάλας πόλεις καὶ τὰς μικράς, φησίν· οἱ γὰρ θεοὶ ἐν ἀμφοτέροις ἴσοι, ὥστ' ἐπεὶ αἱ χάριτες θεαί, ἴσαι ἀποκείσονταί σοι παρ' ἀμφοτέρois. καὶ γὰρ τὸ ἀποδεικνύμενον αὐτῶι ἐπιστολικὸν καὶ ἡ ἀπόδειξις αὐτή.

234 ἐπεὶ δὲ καὶ πόλεσίν ποτε καὶ βασιλεῦσιν γράφομεν, ἔστωσαν τοιαῦται ἐπιστολαὶ μικρὸν ἐξηρμέναι πως. στοχαστέον γὰρ καὶ τοῦ προσώπου ὧι γράφεται· ἐξηρμένη μέντοι οὐχ ὥστε σύγγραμμα εἶναι ἀντ' ἐπιστολῆς, ὥσπερ αἱ Ἀριστοτέλους πρὸς Ἀλέξανδρον καὶ πρὸς τοὺς Δίωνος οἰκείους Πλάτωνος.

235 καθόλου δὲ μεμίχθω ἡ ἐπιστολὴ κατὰ τὴν ἑρμηνείαν ἐκ δυοῖν χαρακτήροιν τούτοιν, τοῦ τε χαρίεντος καὶ τοῦ ἰσχνοῦ.

74 L. ANNAEUS SENECA

(*Epistles* 75.1–4)

Seneca Lucilio suo salutem. **1** minus tibi accuratas a me epistulas mitti quereris. quis enim accurate loquitur nisi qui uult putide loqui?

not a letter but a speech for the courts; indeed it is not just ridiculous to do this in a letter, but against the spirit of friendship – remember the proverbial saying about 'calling a spade a spade'.

230 We should be aware that there are such things as proper epistolary topics, as well as proper epistolary style. Aristotle at least, who is acknowledged to have been particularly successful as a letter-writer, says, 'I shall not write to you about this, as it is not appropriate matter for a letter.' **231** If someone were to write about logical problems or questions of natural science, he might indeed write, but it would not be a letter that he was writing. The aim of a letter is to convey friendly feelings succinctly, and to express a simple subject in simple terms.

232 The beauty of a letter lies in the feelings of warm friendship it conveys and the numerous proverbs it contains; this should be the only element of philosophy in it, because a proverb is something everyday and accessible, whereas someone who produces senten-tious maxims and exhortations seems no longer to be chatting by letter but pontificating *ex cathedra*. **233** Aristotle, however, does ad-mittedly produce epistolary versions of formal argumentation; for instance, wanting to prove that one ought to confer benefits equally on great cities and on small, he says: 'The gods are equal in both, so – since the Graces are goddesses – equal gratitude will be stored up for you in both.' This is legitimate, because the point he is arguing for is appropriate to a letter, and so is the argumentation itself.

234 Sometimes we write to cities and kings: this kind of letter ought to be in some way slightly more elaborate, as one should adapt to the person being written to, but not so elaborate as to become a treatise rather than a letter, like Aristotle's letter to Alexander and Plato's to Dion's friends.

235 To sum up, the letter should be stylistically a combination of the two styles, the elegant and the plain.

74 L. ANNAEUS SENECA

Seneca to his friend Lucilius, greetings. **1** You complain that the letters you receive from me are less carefully written than they might

qualis sermo meus esset si una desideremus aut ambularemus, in-
laboratus et facilis, tales esse epistulas meas uolo, quae nihil habent
accersitum nec fictum. **2** si fieri posset, quid sentiam ostendere
quam loqui mallem. etiam si disputarem, nec supploderem pedem
nec manum iactarem nec attollerem uocem, sed ista oratoribus
reliquissem, contentus sensus meos ad te pertulisse, quos nec exor-
nassem nec abiecisem. **3** hoc unum plane tibi adprobare uellem,
omnia me illa sentire quae dicerem, nec tantum sentire sed amare.
aliter homines amicam, aliter liberos osculantur; tamen in hoc
quoque amplexu tam sancto et moderato satis apparet adfectus.
non mehercules ieiuna esse et arida uolo quae de rebus tam magnis dicentur (neque enim philosophia ingenio renuntiat), multum
tamen operae impendi uerbis non oportet. **4** haec sit propositi nostri summa: quod sentimus loquamur, quod loquimur sentiamus;
concordet sermo cum uita.

75 C. IULIUS VICTOR

(*Ars rhetorica* 27, pp. 447–8 Halm)

Epistolis conueniunt multa eorum, quae de sermone praecepta
sunt. epistolarum species duplex est, sunt enim aut negotiales aut
familiares.

negotiales sunt argumento negotioso et graui. in hoc genere
et sententiarum pondera et uerborum lumina et figurarum insignia conpendii opera requiruntur atque omnia denique ora-
toria praecepta, una modo exceptione, ut aliquid de summis
copiis detrahamus et orationem proprius sermo explicet. si quid
historicum epistola comprehenderis, declinari oportet a plena
formula historiae, ne recedat ab epistolae gratia. si quid etiam
eruditius scribas, sic disputa, ut ne modum epistolae corrumpas.

be. Quite true – who but a man who wants to speak like a tiresome pedant speaks carefully? I want my letters, which have nothing recondite or elaborate about them, to be like my conversation, were we sitting around or strolling together – unstudied and natural. **2** Were it possible, I should prefer to show you what I think rather than express it in words. Even if I were arguing, I wouldn't stamp my foot or gesticulate or raise my voice, but would leave all that to the orators, and would be content to avoid making my ideas seem either too grand or too trivial as I conveyed them to you. **3** The one thing I want absolutely to get you to accept is that I think everything I say, and don't only think it, but adhere to it warmly. Men kiss their mistress and their children in different ways, yet even in such a chaste and restrained embrace as the latter their affection is clear enough. I certainly don't want what is said about such weighty matters to be dull and dry (philosophy does not turn its back on the assistance of literary talent), but it is not appropriate to expend great effort on mere words. **4** Our aim should be, in brief, to say what we think and think what we say; words and life should be in harmony.

75 C. JULIUS VICTOR

Many of the instructions given for conversation hold also for letters. There are two types of letter, official and private.

Official letters are concerned with serious matters of business; what is required for this type are – in concise form – weighty maxims, brilliant diction, and striking figures of speech, in brief all that is enjoined by rhetorical teaching, with just the one qualification, that we should hold back a little from employing its full resources and that our message should unfold at the appropriate stylistic level. If you are going to include some historical matter in a letter, then you should diverge a little from the full procedure for historical writing, to avoid a diminution in epistolary charm. Or again, if you were to write something in more learned vein, you should present the argument in such a way as not to spoil the good proportions required for a letter.

in familiaribus litteris primo breuitas obseruanda: ipsarum quoque sententiarum ne diu circumferatur, quod Cato ait, ambitio, sed ita recidantur, ut numquam uerbi aliquid deesse uideatur: unum 'te' scilicet, quod intelligentia suppleatur, in epistolis Tullianis ad Atticum et Axium frequentissimum est. lucem uero epistolis praefulgere oportet, nisi cum consulto clandestinae literae fiant, quae tamen ita ceteris occultae esse debent, ut his, ad quos mittantur, clarae perspicuaeque sint. solent etiam notas inter se secretiores pacisci, quod et Caesar et Augustus et Cicero et alii plerique fecerunt. caeterum cum abscondito nihil opus est, cauenda obscuritas magis quam in oratione aut in sermocinando: potes enim parum plane loquentem rogare, ut id planius dicat, quod in absentium epistolis non datur. et ideo nec historia occultior addenda nec prouerbium ignotius aut uerbum curiosius aut figura putidior; neque dum amputatae breuitati studes, dimidiatae sententiae sit intelligentia requirenda, nec dilatione uerborum et anxio struendi labore lux obruenda. epistola, si superiori scribas, ne iocularis sit; si pari, ne inhumana; si inferiori, ne superba; neque docto incuriose, neque indocto indiligenter, nec coniunctissimo translatitie, nec minus familari non amice. rem secundam prolixius gratulare, ut illius gaudium extollas: cum offendas dolentem, paucis consolare, quod ulcus etiam, cum plana manu tangitur, cruentatur. ita in litteris cum familiaribus ludes, ut tamen cogites posse euenire, ut eas litteras legant tempore tristiore. iurgari numquam oportet, sed epistolae minime. praefationes ac subscriptiones litterarum

In private letters the first rule to follow is brevity: even the individual sentences should not be allowed, in Cato's phrase, to cast their net too wide or carry on too long, but equally they should be cut back only in such a way that there never seem to be any words missing: for example, in Cicero's letters to Atticus and Axius, one very often finds just one 'you', which has to be supplemented from the sense of the sentence.

Letters ought to be crystal clear, except when the writing is secret by deliberate design, and such writing, even though cryptic to everyone else, should nevertheless be clear as day to its recipients. It is a common practice for correspondents to agree a special secret code between them, as Caesar and Augustus and Cicero and many others did. But when there is no need for secrecy, then obscurity is to be avoided even more than it is in oratory or conversation: you can always ask someone who is not speaking clearly to 'say that more clearly', but the same possibility is not available with letters from people who are not physically present. For the same reason, you should not include obscure stories from history or less well-known proverbs or recondite vocabulary or pedantic figures of speech; nor, as you strive for brevity and conciseness, should the sense of an abbreviated sentence need to be sought for, nor should clarity be overwhelmed by the delayed positioning of words or by the anxious effort that needs to be expended on construing.

If you are writing to a superior, your letter should not be droll; if to an equal, it should not be cold; if to an inferior, it should not be too haughty; nor carelessly written if to a learned correspondent, nor cursorily written if to a close friend, nor lacking warmth if to someone not so close. Be profuse in congratulating someone on a success, so as to increase his joy; but when you encounter someone who is grieving, console him in few words, because the wound bleeds even when touched with the flat of the hand. Joke with your friends in your letters only within the limits imposed by the reflection that their circumstances may be sadder when they read them. It is never right to be abusive, but least of all in a letter.

computandae sunt pro discrimine amicitiae aut dignitatis, habita ratione consuetudinis. rescribere sic oportet, ut litterae, quibus respondes, prae manu sint, ne quid, cui responso opus sit, de memoria effluat. obseruabant ueteres karissimis sua manu scribere uel plurimum subscribere. commendatitias fideliter dato aut ne dato. id fiet, si amicissime dabis ad amicissimum, et si probabile petes et si impetrabile. graece aliquid addere litteris suaue est, si id neque intempestiue neque crebro facias: et prouerbio uti non ignoto percommodum est, et uersiculo aut parte uersus. lepidum est nonnumquam quasi praesentem alloqui, uti 'heus tu' et 'quid ais' et 'uideo te deridere': quod genus apud M. Tullium multa sunt. sed haec, ut dixi, in familiaribus litteris; nam illarum aliarum seueritas maior est.

in summa id memento et ad epistolas et ad omnem scriptionem bene loqui.

76 'LIBANIOS'

(De forma epistolari, 1–4, 46–51)

1 ὁ μὲν ἐπιστολικὸς χαρακτὴρ ποικίλος τε καὶ πολυσχιδὴς ὑπάρχει, ὅθεν καὶ τῶι γράφειν βουλομένωι προσήκει μὴ ἁπλῶς μηδ᾽ ὡς ἔτυχεν ἐπιστέλλειν, ἀλλὰ σὺν ἀκριβείαι πολλῆι καὶ τέχνηι. ἄριστα δ᾽ ἂν ἐπιστεῖλαι δυνηθείη τις εἰ γνοίη τί τέ ἐστιν ἐπιστολὴ καὶ τί λέγειν ὅλως ἐν αὐτῆι θέμις καὶ εἰς πόσας προσηγορίας διαιρεῖται.

2 ἐπιστολὴ μὲν οὖν ἐστιν ὁμιλία τις ἐπιγράμματος ἀπόντος πρὸς ἀπόντα γινομένη καὶ χρειώδη σκόπον ἐκπληροῦσα, ἐρεῖ δέ τις ἐν αὐτῆι ἅπερ ἂν παρών τις πρὸς παρόντα. **3** διαιρεῖται δὲ εἰς συχνάς τε καὶ παμπόλλας προσηγορίας· οὐ

Headings and conclusions to letters should be calculated according to the differences in the degree of friendship or of rank involved, with due regard for conventional practice. When replying, you should do so with the letter you are replying to before you, in case anything that needs an answer escapes your memory. The ancients were in the habit of writing to their closest friends, or at least in most cases of adding a subscription, in their own hand. Letters of recommendation should be written honestly or not at all; this condition will be met if you write them in the warmest terms to a very close friend, and if what you are asking for is reasonable and realistic.

Adding a phrase or two in Greek to a letter is an elegant touch, provided that you do not do it in the wrong place or too often; it is also very suitable to use a well-known proverb, or a line or phrase of poetry. It is elegant sometimes to address your correspondent as if he were physically present, as in 'hey, you!' and 'what's that you say?' and 'I see you scoff'; there are many expressions of this kind in Cicero. But all this, as I have said, applies to private letters; the other kind have greater dignity.

In conclusion, remember to cultivate a good style not only in your letters but in everything that you write.

76 'LIBANIOS'

1 The letter is a heterogeneous form with many separate kinds, so it is appropriate for the intending writer to compose his letters not naïvely or casually, but with great meticulousness and skill. The ability to compose in the best epistolary style follows from knowledge of what a letter is, what in general it is conventionally appropriate to say in it, and into how many types it is divided.

2 A letter, then, is a kind of written conversation that takes place between two parties who are in different places, and fulfils some practically useful purpose; one will say in it just what one would say if face to face with the addressee. **3** It is divided into many, indeed a plethora of types; it does not follow that because 'the letter'

γὰρ ἐπειδὴ ἐπιστολὴ προσαγορεύεται ἑνικῶι ὀνόματι, ἤδη καὶ
πασῶν τῶν κατὰ τὸν βίον φερομένων ἐπιστολῶν εἷς τις ἐστι
χαρακτὴρ καὶ μία προσηγορία, ἀλλὰ διάφοροι, καθὼς ἔφην.
4 εἰσὶ δὲ αἱ πᾶσαι προσηγορίαι, αἷς ὁ ἐπιστολιμαῖος ὑποβά-
λλεται χαρακτὴρ αἵδε· α΄ παραινετική, β΄ μεμπτική, γ΄ παρακλ-
ητική, δ΄ συστατική, ε΄ εἰρωνική, ϛ΄ εὐχαριστική, ζ΄ φιλική, η΄
εὐκτική, θ΄ ἀπειλητική, ι΄ ἀπαρνητική, ια΄ παραγγελματική, ιβ΄
μεταμελητική, ιγ΄ ὀνειδιστική, ιδ΄ συμπαθητική, ιε΄ θεραπευτική,
ιϛ΄ συγχαριστική, ιζ΄ παραλογιστική, ιη΄ ἀντεγκληματική, ιθ΄ ἀν-
τεπισταλτική, κ΄ παροξυντική, κα΄ παραμυθητική, κβ΄ ὑβριστική,
κγ΄ ἀπαγγελτική, κδ΄ σχετλιαστική, κε΄ πρεσβευτική, κϛ΄
ἐπαινετική, κζ΄ διδασκαλική, κη΄ ἐλεγκτική, κθ΄ διαβλητική, λ΄
ἐπιτιμητική, λα΄ ἐρωτηματική, λβ΄ παραθαρρυντική, λγ΄ ἀναθετ-
ική, λδ΄ ἀναφαντική, λε΄ σκωπτική, λϛ΄ μετριαστική, λζ΄ αἰνιγ-
ματική, λη΄ ὑπομνηστική, λθ΄ λυπητική, μ΄ ἐρωτική, καὶ μα΄ μικτή.

[5-45]

46 αὗται μὲν οὖν αἱ πᾶσαι προσηγορίαι, εἰς ἃς ἐπιστολὴ
διαιρεῖται. δεῖ δὲ τὸν ἀκριβῶς ἐπιστέλλειν ἐθέλοντα μὴ μόνον
τῆι τῆς ὑποθέσεως μεθόδωι χρῆσθαι, ἀλλὰ καὶ φράσεως ἀρετῆι
τὴν ἐπιστολὴν κατακοσμεῖν καὶ ἀττικίζειν μὲν μετρίως, μὴ
μέντοι γε πέρα τοῦ προσήκοντος κομψολογίαι χρῆσθαι· 47 ἡ
γὰρ ὑπὲρ τὸ δέον ὑψηγορία καὶ τὸ τῆς φράσεως ὑπέρογκον καὶ τὸ ὑπεραττικίζειν ἀλλότριον τοῦ τῶν ἐπιστολῶν χαρακτῆρος καθέστηκεν, ὡς πάντες οἱ παλαιοὶ μαρτυροῦσι, Φιλόστρατος ὁ Λήμνιος μάλιστά φησι· δεῖ γὰρ τὴν τῆς ἐπιστολῆς φράσιν τῆς
μὲν συνηθείας ἀττικωτέραν εἶναι, τοῦ δὲ ἀττικισμοῦ συνηθεστέραν
καὶ μήτε λίαν ὑψηλὴν μήτε ταπεινὴν ἄγαν, ἀλλὰ μέσην τινά.
48 κοσμεῖν δὲ δεῖ τὰς ἐπιστολὰς σαφηνείᾳ τε μάλιστα καὶ συν-
τομίᾳ μεμετρημένῃ καὶ ἀρχαϊσμῶι λέξεων· σαφήνεια γὰρ ἀγαθὴ
μὲν ἡγεμὼν παντὸς λόγου, μάλιστα δ᾽ ἐπιστολῆς.

49 χρὴ μέντοι μήτε συντομίαι σαφήνειαν διαφθείρειν, μήτε
σαφηνείας φροντίζοντα ληρεῖν ἀμέτρως, ἀλλὰ τοῦ συμμέτρου
στοχάζεσθαι τοὺς ἀκριβεῖς τοξότας μιμούμενον. ὥσπερ γὰρ οὔτε
τὸ τὸν προκείμενον τοῖς τοξόταις σκοπὸν παρέρχεσθαι οὔτε τὸ

is designated by a single name, there is also a single style and type that embraces everything acknowledged as a letter in everyday life. As I have said, they are of different types. **4** Here is a complete list of the headings under which the letter form can be subsumed: (i) advice; (ii) blame; (iii) request; (iv) recommendation; (v) irony; (vi) thanks; (vii) friendship; (viii) entreaty; (ix) threat; (x) denial; (xi) command; (xii) repentance; (xiii) reproach; (xiv) sympathy; (xv) conciliation; (xvi) congratulation; (xvii) contempt; (xviii) counter-accusation; (xix) reply; (xx) provocation; (xxi) consolation; (xxii) insult; (xxiii) news; (xxiv) indignation; (xxv) representation; (xxvi) praise; (xxvii) instruction; (xxviii) refutation; (xxix) slander; (xxx) reproof; (xxxi) enquiry; (xxxii) encouragement; (xxxiii) consultation; (xxxiv) declaration; (xxxv) mockery; (xxxvi) jesting [?]; (xxxvii) coded communication; (xxxviii) suggestion; (xxxix) grief; (xl) love; (xli) mixed type.

[**5–45**: definitions of the forty-one types of letter.]

46 That, then is a complete list of the categories into which the letter is divided. Anyone who wishes to be meticulous in letter-composition must not only adopt the appropriate procedure for his subject-matter, but also trick his letter out in a distinguished style and Atticize moderately, though not fall into an inappropriate pretentiousness of speech. **47** Unnecessary loftiness of speech, excessive solemnity of style and hyper-atticism are foreign to the letter, as all classical authors testify, but Philostratus of Lemnos above all emphasizes: epistolary style should be more Attic than everyday speech, but more everyday than Atticism, and neither too elevated nor too mean, but somewhere in between the two. **48** Clarity, moderate brevity and archaizing diction should be letters' principal adornments: 'clarity is a good guide in all kinds of writing, but above all in the letter'.

49 However, one should neither impair clarity with brevity, nor babble on interminably out of concern for clarity, but imitate good marksmen in aiming for the right measure. The man who is naturally gifted with a good aim does not overshoot the target set up for

ἐντὸς τοῦ σκοποῦ τοξεύειν καὶ πολὺ τοῦ προσήκοντος ἀποδεῖν ἀν-
δρός ἐστιν εὐφυοῦς καὶ στοχαστικοῦ, ἀλλὰ μόνον τοῦ συμμέτρως
στοχαζομένου τοῦ σκόπου καὶ τοῦτον βάλλοντος, οὕτως οὔτε τὸ
πέρα τοῦ προσήκοντος ληρεῖν οὔτε τὸ βραχυλογίαν ἀσπάζεσθαι
δι' ἀπορίαν καὶ τὸ σαφὲς ἐπικρύπτειν τῶν ἐπιστάλσεων ἀν-
δρός ἐστι λογίου, ἀλλὰ μόνου τοῦ μετ' εὐφραδείας τῆς συμ-
μετρίας στοχαζομένου καὶ τὸ λεγόμενον καλῶς σαφηνίζοντος.
50 τὸ οὖν μέγεθος τῆς ἐπιστολῆς ὡς πρὸς τὰ πράγματα, καὶ οὐ
πάντως τὸ πλῆθος καθάπερ κακίαν ἀτιμάζειν καλόν, ἀλλὰ δεῖ καί
τινας ἐπιστολὰς ἀπομηκύνειν ἐν καιρῶι πρὸς τὴν ἀπαιτοῦσαν
χρείαν, πληρώσει τε τὴν ἐπιστολὴν χάρις ἱστορίων καὶ μύθων
μνήμη καὶ παλαιῶν συγγραμμάτων καὶ παροιμίων εὐστόχων καὶ
φιλοσόφων δογμάτων χρῆσις, οὐ μέντοι γε ταύτην διαλεκτικῶς
προσενεκτέον.

51 τοσαῦτα μὲν περὶ ἐπιστολιμαίου χαρακτῆρος εἰρηκὼς καὶ
τοῖς λεχθεῖσιν ἀρκεῖσθαι κρίνας τοὺς συνετοὺς καὶ τὰς ἐπιστολὰς
αὐτὰς ἐκθήσω, ἑκάστηι οἰκείαν ἁρμόσας προσηγορίαν. προσήκει
μέντοι τῶι γράφειν βουλομένωι πρὸ τοῦ κατ' ἐπίσταλσιν χαρακτῆρος μὴ ληρεῖν, μήτε μὴν ἐπιθέτοις ὀνόμασι χρῆσθαι, ὡς ἂν μὴ
κολακεία τις καὶ δυσγένεια προσῆι τῶι γράμματι, ἀλλ' οὕτως
ἀπάρχεσθαι ὁ δεῖνα τῶι δεῖνι χαίρειν. οὕτω γὰρ ἅπαντες οἱ
ἐπὶ σοφίαι τε καὶ λόγοις διαπρέψαντες παλαιοὶ φαίνονται πε-
ποιηκότες, καὶ δεῖ τὸν βουλόμενον ἐκείνων ζηλωτὴν γενέσθαι
κατόπιν αὐτῶν βαίνειν.

[52-92]

the archers, nor does he shoot at the space between him and it and so fall far short of where he ought to reach; success belongs uniquely to the man who takes well-measured aim at the target and strikes it. In just the same way, the eloquent man does not babble on at inappropriate length, nor does he embrace brevity from ignorance of how to express himself, and so obscure the clarity of his missive; success belongs uniquely to the man who aims at the right length in correct style and conveys a clear message with panache. **50** The length of the letter, then, should be determined by its subject-matter. It is not right always to scorn length as if it were a vice; given the right occasion, some letters demand to be extended, to meet the needs of the moment. Length can be achieved in a letter by means of entertaining stories and mythological references, and the use of classic works of literature, apposite proverbs, and philosophical doctrines, although these last should not be employed in the style of formal argumentation.

51 Having said this about letter form, and judging that what I have said will suffice intelligent readers, I shall now append the letters themselves, affixing its proper heading to each. The intending writer, before employing any given epistolary type, should not ramble on nor use additional honorific appellations, so as to avoid giving his letter a tone of ignoble flattery; he should begin thus, 'So-and-so to So-and-so, greetings.' This is what all classic authors distinguished for their wisdom and eloquence manifestly did, and anyone who wishes to imitate them must follow in their footsteps.

[**52–92**: examples of the forty-one types of letter]

COMMENTARY

A I PRIVATE LETTERS: GENERAL

The fourteen letters in this first section send news, make requests and issue instructions of various kinds in the sphere of private life and business, without falling into any of the more specific thematic and functional categories singled out in Sections **A II–A VIII** below. They divide into three groups. First, five 'naïve' letters, preserved by chance, on lead and on papyrus, dating from between the beginning of the fifth century B.C. and the early fourth century A.D., and coming from the Black Sea region, Athens and Egypt; all derive from relatively lowly social milieux and are concerned with everyday commercial and domestic matters. Secondly, five letters from more sophisticated correspondents of the first century B.C. and the first two centuries A.D., mainly in or near Rome (though one again comes from the shores of the Black Sea); all of these are known to us because, unlike the first group, they were deliberately put into the public domain either by their authors or by a later editor. Both stylistically and in the concerns they revolve round, these belong to a noticeably more exalted social context. Finally, four 'pseudepigraphic' letters of news and instructions, written at only vaguely specifiable dates between the second century B.C. and (perhaps) as late as the sixth century A.D., but all purporting to be by correspondents of the archaic and classical periods of Greek history, and all written in an elegant literary style.

Very crudely, the first two groups consist of 'real' letters – written documents actually sent, whether or not we now possess the original, or instead a copy (of a copy of a copy . . .) of an edited version – whereas the items in the third group are 'fictitious', but it may not be helpful to make too much of this distinction: see Introduction, 3–4. Similarly, there are variations of 'literariness' between the different items in the second, 'literate' group, in which the last two are notably more stylistically self-conscious than the first three, and the last one breaks with 'normal', utilitarian epistolary practice in its choice of verse rather than prose form (and may indeed never have been 'sent' in the standard way). All these letters can however be read for the pleasure (and occasionally the puzzlement) of trying to reconstruct the circumstances in which they were sent, and a full picture of the events and persons to which they only allude (whether this allusiveness is being consciously manipulated by the letter-writer or not). All give the sense of letting the reader in on a more personal, intimate dimension of the ancient world and historical events than is available from more formal written sources (again, whether or not this sense has been purposefully contrived).[1] And all invite the reader to form impressions and construct stories around the character projected – consciously or unconsciously, calculatingly or inadvertently – by the correspondent.

A number of themes and topics recur in these fourteen items: several of the correspondents request letters in return, or comment on their own performance in this respect; news is frequently given or requested about family members; several write, wholly or partly, to request the dispatch of some item or items that they need for use or show; several send news of their own and others' health; separation and exile crop up more than once, as do court-cases and tyrants. A good many of these are something like standard epistolary topics: see Introduction, 35–42. At the same time, connections can also be made with other sections of this anthology: with letters of consolation (**A VI**; cf. **7**, **8**, **10**); with letters of recommendation (**A IV**; cf. **5**, **8**); with moral exhortation (**A V**; cf. **11**, **12**); and with letters of public as opposed to private business (Section **B**).

1 Achillodoros, *SEG* 26.845.3 (the 'Berezan letter'). The earliest surviving Greek letter (*c.* 500 B.C.), scratched on a thin rectangle of lead, measuring 153 × 65 × 1 mm, and found in 1970 in the remains of an ancient rubbish-pit on the island of Berezan in the estuary of the River Bug (Hypanis). Since it was found tightly rolled, with the address marked on the outside surface, it seems never to have been read, or even to have reached its destination.

Contents and context. Berezan (ancient name unknown) seems to have been some kind of out-station of the Milesian colony of Borysthenes, founded in the sixth century B.C., and it is in this frontier region on the north shores of the Black Sea that the events dealt with by the letter must have unfolded. What those events add up to, however, is made tantalizingly unclear by a

---

[1] In comparison with modern private correspondence, however, it might be felt that real informality and friendly intimacy are missing from these letters: those on papyrus are just too simple and functional, while those by educated correspondents, subsequently published, are too stiffly self-conscious. Ancient and modern standards of informality differ.

combination of Achillodoros' allusiveness, his vague use of personal pro-
nouns, and his miswritings (or more likely those of the scribe to whom he
dictated his message). Achillodoros, who seems to be a merchant or commercial agent, writes to instruct his son Protagoras to inform a third party,
Anaxagoras, of a dispute that has arisen between him and one Matasys, in
which Anaxagoras too is somehow involved. It is clearly a serious business
for Achillodoros, who has not only lost his (?) ship, but is also under threat
of being enslaved on what he makes out to be a spurious pretext. But what
is the precise nature of the dispute, and of the relationship and past dealings
between Achillodoros, Matasys and Anaxagoras? And where exactly are
the protagonists located at the time of writing? Is Achillodoros, up country,
writing to Protagoras and Anaxagoras on the coast at Borysthenes? Or is
he himself at Borysthenes (or on Berezan), writing to the others back in
Miletus? In the last sentence of the letter, Achillodoros issues another instruction, and offers some further information, which may or may not relate
to the dispute with Matasys. The instruction is clear enough in outline, but
the information that follows can be read in several substantially different
ways. The text printed here, although dividing up the words and adding
accents and breathings, does not attempt to clear up all the problems and
awkwardnesses: the spelling mistakes are retained, and the disputed words
in the last sentence are left as written, with some possible interpretations
given in the commentary.

Dialect and orthography. Achillodoros' message is written in capital letters,
without word-breaks (though words are not split over line-ends), accents or
breathings; it uses the East Greek (Ionic) dialect of Miletus and a version
of the spelling conventions current at the time. Thus η is written for long
α ('Αναξαγόρης, 'Αρβινάτηισιν), εο for ευ (ἐλεόθερος), ε for ει (ἀδικῆται,
ἔναι, λέγεν), ο for ου (δολόται), ἑωυτόν for ἑαυτόν, and there is psilosis
(absence of aspiration: ἀπήγησαι, ὁ, ἐλεότερος). See Chadwick (1973) 35;
Buck (1955) 142–3, 183–9. Note also the treatment of final -ν before a
following guttural (κ) or labial (μ, π): μιγ καί, τὴμ πόλιν (cf. below, 298).

Bibliography. Vinogradov *(*1971), with photographs, and (1995); Bravo (1974);
Chadwick (1973); Miller (1975); Merkelbach (1975); Boardman (1980)
225–66 (with map); Wilson (1998).

Ὦ Πρωταγόρη ... ἐπιστέλλε̄: Ach., although the sender of the message, is referred to throughout in the third person; the turn of phrase

perhaps reflects a feeling that sending a message by letter is like sending one via a living messenger, who would naturally report the sender's wishes thus (this seems better than supposing that the hidden first-person speaker is the scribe who wrote the message for Ach.). For comparable formulations in other early letters, cf. Amasis in Hdt. 3.40 (Ἄμασις Πολυκράτει ὧδε λέγει), Darius, *SIG* 22 (Meiggs and Lewis, *Greek Historical Inscriptions*, 12: βασιλεὺς βασιλέων Δαρεῖος ὁ Ὑστάσπεω Γαδάται δούλωι τάδε λέγει) and Mnesiergos in item **2** below; cf. also Introduction, 37.   **Πρωταγόρη**: like 'Anaxagoras' a name more familiar to us from a famous later bearer, also Ionian Greek; of the other names in the letter, 'Matasys' is of non-Greek origin, while 'Achillodoros' may have special connections with the area of Olbia (Bravo (1974) 135 ff.; cf. Russell (1992) 216, on Dio Chrys. 36.9). **ἐπιστέλλε͞** 'sends (as instructions/commands)', not 'writes (in a letter)'; the specialized, epistolary sense of ἐπιστέλλω/ἐπιστολή is not being used here (and may not yet be available at this date); cf. **2.1** n.   **δο͞λο͞ται** (= δουλοῦται) 'is making a slave of him, trying to enslave him'. The subject, in spite of the previous clause, is Matasys – the first of many unsignalled changes of subject-/object-reference in the letter. Confusion of this kind is characteristic of untrained storytellers, who do not find it easy 'to tell a plain tale plainly', particularly when (as in this case) their mood is indignant or querulous (cf. **15** below).   **φορτηγεσίο͞**(= φορτηγεσίου): φόρτον + ἄγω + -εσιον; probably 'cargo-carrier' (but ship or wagon?) rather than 'licence to carry'.   **φησὶ γὰρ κτλ**: Matasys is trying to make out that Ach. is a slave, but the precise logic of his case, as Ach. reports it, is obscure. One possible reading is that Matasys has had his property taken from him by Anaxag. and is trying to seize Ach. in compensation, but others can be envisaged instead.   **Ἀναγόρης**: the first of a number of spelling mistakes in the letter; the others are ἑωυτι for ἑωυτῶι τε, Ματασιν and Ματατασυ for Ματάσυι (but see Chadwick (1973) for a different correction), and ἀδεφεύς (= ἀδελφούς).   **ἀναβῶι** = ἀν-αβοᾶ.   **ἔναι οὐδὲν … οὐδὲν ἔναι**: emphatic repetition; Dover (1997) finds parallels in a mixture of early documents, both high and low style: Lysias 1. 17; *Ath. pol.* 2. 11; Anaxag. D–K 59 B 12; and (later) *P.Oxy.* 3070. **αὐτοὶ οἴδασιν κτλ**: i.e. (dismissively and indignantly) 'that's their business, not mine, so I don't deserve to be caught up in it'.   **τῆ γυναικί**: presumably Ach.'s wife rather than Anaxag.'s? The omission of the final iota of τῆι may be a simple slip, or a vulgarism.   **ιεσσιν**: probably οἵ ἔσιν, 'who are'.   **ἐν Ἀρβινάτηισιν**: could be either 'in Arbinatae'

(place) or 'among the Arbinatae' (people).   τὴμ πόλιν: presumably
Borysthenes; if this second instruction is connected with the first (which it
need not be) the point may be to get Ach.'s dependants to a place where they
can appeal to effective authorities to protect them and/or rescue Ach. from
Matasys.   αὐτὸς κτλ: very obscure because of (possible) mis-spelling,
uncertainty over word-division, and unclear letter forms. Chadwick's reconstruction gives 'but Euneurus himself (?another son of Ach.) will come to
him and go straight (<ἰ>θύωρα) on down (i.e from further up-country than
Ach. down to Olbia)'. Merkelbach suggests 'he himself, going to the Neuri
(a Scythian tribe mentioned in Herodotus 4.17), will go down to Minthyora
(place or person?).' Bravo offers 'but the ship-guard himself will come to
him (Anaxagoras) and go down to Thyora'. Consensus seems some way
off.   Ἀχιλλοδώρō τό: asserting ownership rather than authorship;
the possessive genitive in predicate position invites the reader to supply
'is'; τό is used demonstratively (Smyth §1099–1117). There is then a slight
pause between μολίβδιον and παρά, indicated by the fact that the final
nu of μολίβδιον is not converted into a mu.   μολίβδιον 'piece of lead',
'leadlet'. Ach.'s use of the word can be taken to suggest either that he knows
no word directly corresponding to 'letter' (cf. note on ἐπιστέλλε above), or
that he is specially concerned to ensure that this valuable piece of writing
material remains in his or his family's possession for future reuse. But it
should be noted that, even when a word for 'letter' had become available
in ἐπιστολή/αί, letters continued to be referred to with words denoting the
material used (cf. e.g. the later use of ὄστρακον to refer to a letter written
on a potsherd (e.g. O. Claud. 138.9 and 145.4–10), and see Introduction, 37).

2 Mnesiergos, SIG³ III 1259. A second letter on lead, measuring
40 × 70 mm, dating from the 4th century B.C. and found at Chaidari
near Daphni in Attica. Written in capitals without word-break, accents
or breathings. Like the Berezan letter, it too may never have reached its
intended destination.

Dialect and orthography. The dialect of the letter is Attic (nb -ττ- for -σσ-), with
some eccentric features (βόλεστε, ἰς). By the same orthographic conventions
as are also seen in the Berezan letter, ε stands for ει, and o for ου, and final
nu can be modified by a following guttural.

Bibliography. Wilhelm (1904); Crönert (1910).

ἐπέστειλε 'bids', 'sends instructions to' (cf. **1.1** n.); here, however, the following infinitives bring us closer to standard epistolary formulae of only slightly later times. See Exler 32–3 and Introduction, 34–5.   **καὶ αὐτὸς κτλ:** again, a later standard formula seems already more or less to have crystallized here; cf. Greek εἰ ἔρρωσαι, εὖ ἂν ἔχοι, κἀγὼ δὲ ὑγιαίνω (and equivalents, e.g. *P.Cairo Zen.* 59060; *P.Petr.* 2.11; *P.Goodspeed* 4; cf. Exler 103–6) and Latin s.u.b.e.e.q.u. = 'si uales bene est ego quidem ualeo' (cf. *OLD ualeo* 2c).   **εἴ τι βόλεστε:** a courtesy formula (cf. e.g. Claud. Terent., *P.Mich.* VIII 468 [**5** below]; Cic. *Ad fam.* 14.7 (= 155 SB).3 [**8** below]). βόλεστε = βούλεσθε; βόλομαι is more familiar from Ionic than Attic documents, -εστε from N. and W. Greek.   **εὐτελεστας**: careless misspelling (haplography) for εὐτελεστάτας.   **σισυρωτάς:** a σισύρα was a piece of sheep or goat-skin shaped for use as a cloak, but with the hair left on it for warmth, so that it could also be used as a blanket (cf. Ar. *Vesp.* 738 (with MacDowell *ad loc.*), *Av.* 122); Mnesiergos wants completely plain, unworked skins.   **κατύματα:** misspelling for καττύματα (κασσύματα), 'pieces of stitched leather, shoe soles.'   **τυχόν:** accusative absolute (Smyth §2076–8).   **φέρ̄εν:** infinitive for imperative (Smyth §2013).   **ις = εἰς;** apparently a phonetic spelling (cf. Allen (1974) 66; M–S 48).   **τὸν κέραμον τὸγ χυτρικόν:** it was normal practice in Athens to use the names of goods and produce to refer to the different sections of the market in which they were sold (e.g. Ar. *Lys.* 557–8); thus here 'to the earthenware pot' may mean 'to the potters' section of the Athens market'. But the reference could as well be to a workshop or market somewhere else.   **Θρασυκλῆι:** for -ει, as often in Attic inscriptions of the period (M–S 39).   **θυῖῶι:** crasis for τῷ υἱῷ.

3 Apollonios, *P.Oxy.* 2783. A letter on a sheet of papyrus (150 × 270 mm), found at Oxyrhynchus in Egypt, and written some time in the middle of the third century A.D. After a conventionally courteous opening, the writer settles into a sequence of tetchy and vividly phrased complaints and criticisms relating to the family business (involving olive oil, camels and misbehaving cattle). For the economic background, see Bowman (1990) 90–120, esp. 101 ff.

Language and orthography. Like the letters on lead, this too was written in capitals without word-break, accents or breathings. The spelling is frequently phonetic, reflecting contemporary pronunciation: ε for αι, and vice versa, and ι or η for ει (cf. Allen (1974) 66, 75–6); τάμροι seems to represent a nasalization of the pronunciation 'av' for αυ (Allen (1974) 76); in ἀνήκασαι the writer has misplaced his augment (as if ἀναγκάζω were a compound verb formed ἀνα-κάζω) and dropped the nasal **γ**; mute final iota is usually omitted, but written adscript (not subscript) when included. In the verb, weak aorist replace strong aorist terminations (e.g. ἔβαλας; cf. Mayser I. 2, 144). On the language of this and the other papyrus letters in this anthology, see also Horrocks (1997) chs. 4 and 6 (esp. 61–3, 107–27).

Bibliography. Oxyrhynchus Papyri 36 (1970) 79–81 (J. E. Rea).

Ἀπολλώνιος κτλ: the commonest of all opening formulae in papyrus letters (Exler 24–7, 62–4). **τῶ ἀδελφῶι:** Artemas may or may not be literally Apollonios' brother; in papyrus letters the word can also be used of more distant relations, or close friends; cf. e.g. Bagnall (1993) 205. **πρὸ μὲν παντὸς κτλ:** again formulaic (Exler 108–10; cf. **4** and **5** below), though the wish that follows is more often specifically for the correspondent's health than the more general form of words that is found here. **τὰ ἐν βίω κτλ:** probably best taken with κάλλιστα predicative: 'that you may have the things in (your) life at the best'. **μετεβαλόμην:** specialized commercial use of the verb: LSJ B.2.b ('order to be paid, remit'). **ἀπὸ μέρους:** adverbial, 'in part'. **ἐξ δὶς ἔβαλας:** on the face of it, a metaphor for good luck (cf. Fraenkel on Aesch. *Ag.* 33, τρὶς ἕξ); but in the context, Apollonios does not seem to be congratulating Artemas. Either, then, he is being heavily sarcastic, or there is some context in which two sixes is not in fact a particularly good throw of the dice (perhaps when three dice are being used, as is envisaged in the *Agamemnon* passage). See Rea *ad loc.* **ὅθεν κτλ:** somewhat obscurely phrased, but apparently again sarcastic, advising Artemas to try his hand at some other kind of deal, as he doesn't seem to be very good with olive oil. **λαμμβάνις** = 'buy, make your purchases', LSJ II.1.g. **ὡς ἐμοῦ κτλ:** ὡς + gen. abs., 'as on the basis that', K–G II 2, 93–5. **κατακόπτοντος:** used metaphorically in comedy to mean either 'make mincemeat of' or 'bore' (LSJ κατακόπτω I.6–7); here presumably either 'running me down' (verbally) or 'squandering my resources'. **χείρω** adverbial / n. pl. form. **τῶν πρώτων:** LSJ πρότερον B.III.3.a. **ἀπαρτί:** LSJ III.2 (a sense lost sight of by the Rev. Suppl., s.v. III); a later Greek (*koine*) usage (in classical authors, the word means 'exactly' or 'absolutely'). **οὐκ ὀφίλις** (= ὀφείλεις) **κτλ:** i.e. Artemas lacks the sympathetic understanding of other people's feelings and reactions characteristic of a normal, healthy human being; for ἄνθρωπος in this sense (= Lat. *homo*, as in Cic. *Q. fr.* 2.10(9 = 14SB).3), cf. Men. *Sam.* 17 and fr. 484 and Jocelyn (1973).   **τῆς Κόπτου:** either 'from' or 'for'; Koptos (Lat. Coptus, modern Qus) was a town on the Nile, between Panopolis and Thebes.   **αὐτοματάρις:** Latin *automatarius*, a maker of mechanical devices – mainly toys rather than machines for serious use – such as are described in Heron of Alexandria's *Automaticopoetica* (1st century A.D.).   **κατάρατοι:** colourful and colloquial, cf. Ar. *Pax* 33, *Lys.* 530, *Ran.* 178.   **στρηνιῶσι:** ditto, cf. Antiph. 82, Sophil. 6, Diph. 132 (all Middle and New comedians).   **προῆλθα:** probably in the specialized legal sense (LSJ II), but not certainly.   **ἵνα μὴ κτλ:** cf. Ovid, *Tr.* 5.13.32 (**10** below) and, for brevity as a proper quality of letters, Dem. *Eloc.* 228 (**73** below) with Cugusi (1983) 74–5 and (1989) 406. **ἐρρῶσθαί σεχομαι:** a slip for ἐρρῶσθαί σε εὔχομαι, one of the commonest closing formulae: Exler 69–77.   **τὸν τύφλον:** presumably an animal.

4 Kopres, *P.Oxy.* 2601. Another papyrus letter (70 × 266 mm) found at Oxyrhynchus, and dating from the early fourth century, probably from the early years of the Great Persecution of Christians that took place in the reign of the Emperor Diocletian. The writer, a Christian, reports back to his 'sister' on the progress of a court-case concerning some land.

Language and orthography. Written again in capitals without accents, breathings, or word-division (with the closing words, from καὶ Ἀσενά, written in the margin and on the reverse of the sheet), and many of the same vulgarisms of spelling and verb-formation as in **3** (misplaced augment in ἐκατηχήσαμεν, *but* ἀναγκάζω correctly spelled); note also the redundant εἰ .. ἐάν in the conditional.

Bibliography. Oxyrhynchus Papyri 31 (1966) 167–71 (P. J. Parsons).

Κοπρῆς κτλ: a common Greco-Egyptian name, perhaps originally given to foundlings ('those from the rubbish-heap'). Sarapias, called his 'sister', is likely to be his wife: cf. Bagnall (1993) 204–5 and n. on ἀδελφῶι in **3** above. On the order of names in the introductory formula, see Introduction, 34; later Christian practice preferred to put the nominative second.   **πρὸ μὲν πάντων κτλ:** cf. **3** and **5**.   **ὁλοκληρῖν (-εῖν):** a verb known only from papyrus letters, though the corresponding noun (below) is also found in Hellenistic and later literary texts.   παρὰ τῷ κυρί(ῳ) θ(ε)ῷ: Kopres here uses a slightly botched form of a distinctively Christian *nomen sacrum* abbreviation (cf. Reynolds and Wilson (1991) 223, 225; van Groningen (1963) 45–7).   προσερχόμενοι: technical legal sense (cf. **3** προῆλθα), LSJ 1.5.   θύειν: to demonstrate that they were not Christians; but this letter shows that the requirement could easily be circumvented.   ἀποσυστατικόν: neut. of an adj. that can also be used of letters of introduction, here used as a noun, 'a representative-making'; ἀποσυνίστημι = 'appoint as representative' or 'introduce'; Kopres' 'brother' was clearly not a Christian but had no objection to acting for one. ἐκατηχήσαμεν: general term for 'instruct', not only in legal contexts, first found in Hellenistic Greek.   εἰ . . . ἐάν: a curious repetition, as if Kopres either remembers only after the sentence has started that he needs the indefinite form of 'if', or is hazy about the distinction between εἰ and ἐάν; either way, an unsophisticated use of language.   ι ̄: according to Parsons, the traces of ink on the papyrus suit ιβ′ (12) better than ια′ (=11) or ιγ′ (=13).   Ἀσενᾶ: a masculine name, perhaps of Jewish origin (cf. II Esdras 2.50).   λευκωμάτιον: diminutive of λεύκωμα ('white patch', a disease of the eye), hesitantly restored by Parsons.   ἐγὼ γὰρ κτλ: surprisingly emphatic; if Kopres is writing from Alexandria, he may have witnessed impressive cures by the doctors of the city; alternatively, he may have a religious cure in mind.   ἔρρωσθαι κτλ: cf. **3**.   ἀσπάζομαι κτλ: another sequence of stereotyped formulae: Exler 115.   ϙθ: the numeral 99, Christian code for 'amen' by isopsephy – (α = 1) + (μ = 40) + (η = 8) + (ν = 50); cf. Irenaeus *Haer.* 1.16.

5 Claudius Terentianus, *P.Mich.* VIII 468.

One of an archive of fifteen papyrus letters in Greek and Latin found at Karanis in Egypt, dating from the early 2nd century A.D., and belonging to a Roman soldier called Claudius Tiberianus. Ten of them, including this one (220 × 230 mm), are letters to him by his son (or protégé), Claudius Terentianus.

Content and context. At the time of writing of this letter, Terentianus is a marine in the Alexandrian fleet (cf. *P.Mich.* VIII 467. 13–17). He records the dispatch of assorted items to his father (location unknown; not Karanis, which is where Tiberianus retired to as a veteran), and he asks for others to be sent to him. He hopes to transfer to the army, and seems to be appealing to his father, himself a *speculator*, or 'scout' (469, 472) to use his army contacts on his behalf. Subsequent letters (476–8) show that he was successful in his ambition, whether or not with his father's assistance.

Collectively, the letters raise interesting questions about the composition and cultural background of Tiberianus' and Terentianus' family. The two soldiers have Roman names, but Terentianus' sister bears the Greco-Egyptian name Tasoucharion, and he several times uses the word 'father' not only of Terentianus, but also of a second individual, Ptolemaios. He writes to Tiberianus both in Greek and in Latin, with a much more marked tendency for his Latin usage to be influenced by Greek than vice versa. We seem to see a mixed Roman-cum-Greco-Egyptian family, in which at least the two male members in military service are bilingual, but for which Greek is the first language at home: cf. **21** and **26** below. Which of Tiberianus and Ptolemaios is Terentianus' natural father, and which an older man to whom he has some special relationship of respect or obligation, is hard to decide.

Orthography and style. Comparison with other letters in the archive shows that this letter was written by a scribe, from Terentianus' dictation. The spelling shows many signs of everyday, non-educated usage ('vulgar Latin'). Note particularly: dropping of unstressed syllables (*uetranum, amicla, singlare*); substitution of b for u and l for r (*imboluclum, glabalum, pulbino*); substitution of d for t (*ud, ed*); interchange of vowels (*itarum, commandaticiae; nese, nesi, sene; con; ualunt*); omission, erroneous insertion and substitution of final m (*unu, aute, speraba; im mensem, pluriam; con, illan*); and omission of initial h (*abes*). There are also one or two more learned or scholastic touches: *mihi* as well as *mi*, the spelling '*sequrum*' for '*securum*'. In morphology, note *hunc* for *hoc*, the future participle of the 3rd. decl. in -*iturus*, '*pluria(m)*' for '*plura*' and (if this is a matter of analogy rather than pronunciation) '*ualunt*'. In word-usage, *aute(m)* is becoming the all-purpose particle and *ille* the all-purpose pronoun. See further Grandgent (1907); Palmer (1954) 148–80; Adams (1977); Väänänen (1981).

Bibliography. Youtie and Winter (1951) 16–74; Pighi (1964); Davis (1973); Adams (1977); Väänänen (1981) 178–9, 208–10; Alston (1995).

plurimam salutem: standard Latin formula. Many of T.'s epistolary formulae are, however, translated from the Greek, beginning with **ante omnia etc.**, for which cf. **3** and **4** above.   **que** = *quae*.   **maxime**

uota sunt: Professor Kenney suggests that the use of the plural *uota* gives these words a literary ring (comparing Ovid, *Am.* 2.5.2–3); T. may consciously be copying a high-style phrase he has heard somewhere or other.   **scias:** T.'s regular usage, in place of higher-style *scito, scire te uolo*.   **imboluclum** = *inuolucrum*: a cloth bag which could be closed by stitching the ends together; the stitching acts as a kind of seal (if it has been unpicked, the package has been tampered with).   **concosutum:** a misspelling (by dittography) of *consutum*.   **amicla par unu:** the syntax is characteristic of lists (and comes well from one military man to another), 'cloaks, one pair'.   **sabana:** transliterated from Greek; σάβανον = 'linen cloth, towel'.   **glabalum:** *grabatulum* (again a Greek word, but also used in (e.g.) Apul. *Met.* 1.16): the omission of a syllable may be just a slip, or phonetic spelling.   **me iacentem:** probably meant as abl. abs. (but cf. Adams (1977) 59–60); *iacentem* here has the special sense of 'lying *ill*', *OLD* 2c.   **liburna:** the *Neptune*, as we learn from the previous letter in the series.   **singlare:** opp. *duplex*, 'double thickness'.   **hunc:** for *hoc*.   **mater:** who is apparently in Alexandria, not where Tiberianus is presently stationed.   **suntheseis, phialas:** more transliterated Greek, 'sets, *suites*' and 'goblets'.   **quinarias:** precise meaning unclear, but an indication of measure ('five-size' – diameter? capacity?).   **panes Alexandrinos:** seasoned with cummin, cf. Pliny, *NH* 20.163.   **ista:** abl., the *gallinaria*.   **subtalares:** not reaching up as far as the ankle.   **udones:** socks or slippers.   **nucleatae:** lit. 'stoned, pitted'; so perhaps referring to buttons or decorative bosses on the boots.   **im mensem:** *in mense*.   **dalabram:** *dolabram*.   **optionem . . . abstulisse:** presumably on the occasion already referred to; T. here goes into reported speech, but forgets to include an introductory verb (e.g. *scias*).   **bona re:** *bonam rem*, 'good fortune, good state'; the periphrastic **habere . . . acceptam** is well on the way to the perfect tense as formed in French or Italian.   **uice** 'situation', *OLD* 3; but the papyrus is hard to read at this point.   **do:** a slip for *domo*.   **hic autem etc.:** an interesting comment to set beside section **IV** below (see esp. **26**).   **nesi si:** *OLD nisi* 7.   **aiutaueret:** *aiutauerit*, sc. with money.   **Carpum:** from the (Greek) name perhaps a slave (cf. Trimalchio's Carpus in *Sat.* 36).   **inuentus est Dios:** T. forgets that he is in indirect speech. The story here is tantalizingly hard to reconstruct: is Dios a member of a family known to Tib. who had gone missing, and Carpus a slave sent to look for him (so Youtie and Winter

1951)?   **(denarios):**   the scribe here uses a star-shaped mark to stand for the noun.   **pater:**   presumably the Ptolemaios named elsewhere in the correspondence.   **perbene...recte esse:**   has a colloquial ring: *recte esse* (idiomatic for 'all well at home') is already an informal phrase, well suited to an epistolary context (eg. Pliny 3.17.1, 6.2.10; Cic. *Att.* 12.23 (= 262 SB).3, *Q. fr.* 3.2 (= 22).3, *Ad fam.* 9.9 (= 157).1 [Dolabella]); *perbene* increases the effect, both in itself (cf. Plaut. *Aul.* 185, *Men.* 1142, *Rud.* 164) and in the doubling up of adverbs it brings.   **Aprodisia:**   phi is often transcribed as 'p' in Latin papyri. The mixture of Latin and Greco-Egyptian names in this list of salutations is indicative of the social milieu; the preponderance of Latin names perhaps reflects the army context. For the naïve style of the list (an extended sequence of names and formulaic phrases linked by simple 'and'), cf. **46** below.   **nostrous:**   *nostros*, perhaps influenced by the Greek accusative plural masculine.   **bene ualere:**   T. again uses Greek formulae in the concluding salutation: ἔρρωσθαί σε εὔχομαι πολλοῖς χρόνοις εὐτυχοῦντα δι' ὅλου, cf. Exler 76.

6 M. Tullius Cicero, *Ad Atticum* 1.10 (= 6 SB). A letter of assorted news and requests, written by Cicero to his friend T. Pomponius Atticus in late May or early June 67 B.C., just before the elections for the praetorships for the following year. Cicero was forty at the time: the prosecution of Verres, which had established him as a public figure, was three years in the past; the consulship, and the defeat of the Catilinarian conspiracy, was to follow four years later. Atticus (110–32 B.C.) – Cicero's friend since boyhood, literary adviser and most faithful correspondent – had been living in Athens for nearly twenty years.

Cicero Attico sal.: given as the opening formula in some of the MSS of the *Ad Att.*, but probably an editorial addition and not what C. originally wrote (A. is not addressed by his cognomen 'Atticus' in the body of a letter until 50 B.C.).   **1 Tusculano:**   C.'s country villa at Tusculum, in the hills some twelve miles S.E. of Rome.   **Ceramico:**   the 'Potters' Quarter', long known as one of the most agreeable addresses in Athens (cf. Thuc. 2.34).   **uerum tamen:**   resumptive, after the parenthesis.   **sorore:**   Pomponia, married to C.'s brother Quintus (see below).   **eum:**   indefinite, 'someone'.   **tam pauca:**   in spite of the apology, the letter turns out to be of respectable length; for the sensitivity about short measure, cf. **52** and **54** below.   **2 de nostro amico placando:**

the identity of this 'friend', and the reason for which he had taken offence, are unknown. **contendam ab:** *OLD* 7, 'press for something from someone'. **officio:** the obligations placed on one by a given post or relationship, in this case, friendship; *fore in* in this idiom = 'keep within the bounds of, live up to'. **in . . . potestate:** not as strong as Eng. 'in my power'. **3 signa etc.:** items acquired by Atticus on C.'s behalf, already mentioned in previous letters (5, 6, 8, 9 (= 1, 2, 4, 5 SB) in Bk I); *Hermeraclas* are herms (square-section pillars topped by portrait-busts) bearing portraits of Heracles. **imponas:** sc. *naui*. **οἰκεῖον** 'at home, suited, appropriate'; the use of scattered words and phrases of Greek is a feature of Cicero's epistolary style (as presumably also of educated Roman speech of the time); cf. Julius Victor in **75** *ad fin.* **eius loci:** the villa as a whole (cf. 1.6 (= 2 SB).2); C. uses the periphrasis out of real or feigned modesty. **palaestrae gymnasique:** the well-appointed Greek-style villa had an exercise yard with associated rooms and halls used for cultural rather than athletic activity (meetings, talks, reading); for the function of the Greek gymnasium as more than just an athletic facility, see Jones (1940) 220–6; Walbank (1981) 182–4. C. had, or would eventually have, two gymnasia in his villa, a Lyceum and an Academy. **scribebam:** epistolary tense (see Introduction, 36). **mando** 'commission you (to find)', *OLD* 5. **putealia:** panels to decorate a well-head, decorated with carved figures (*sigillum*, dimin. of *signum*). **tectorio:** fine, moulded plaster, stucco. **atrioli:** the diminutive indicates size (a secondary entrance-hall attached to the main one), but also adds a flavour of affection and/or modesty. **4 despondeas . . . amatorem:** joking metaphor, personifying the library as a nubile female; for book-collecting as an epistolary topic, cf. **54**, **56**, **57** below. **uindemiolas:** the metaphor and the diminutive are again humorous, lit. 'little crop of grapes (*uindemia*)'; C. casts himself as the poor but worthy suitor who has to save long and hard for the marriage that will bring him security. **5 fratre:** Quintus Tullius Cicero (*c.* 102–43 B.C.), at this stage yet to begin his public career in earnest. **praegnans:** the child was Quintus junior (66–43 B.C.); Quintus senior and Pomponia were to divorce in 44. **6 comitiis:** for the praetorships of 66. **permisisse:** sc. *rem*, 'the matter, the decision'. **eum . . . quasi:** *eum* here is equivalent to *talem* (G–L §308 R1), and *quasi* introduces a kind of consecutive clause; the sequence *eum . . . quasi* conflates *talem . . . quem* ('the kind of man to . . .') and *tam . . . quasi* ('so . . . that it is as if . . .'). **offendes:** *OLD offendo* 3b. **Tulliola:** affectionate diminutive; C.'s daughter Tullia (*c*.79–45 B.C.) was about twelve when this letter was written, and within four years of her first marriage (see also **8** below). **diem ... sponsorem:** another humorous metaphor, this time legal. Atticus has promised a present and not yet produced it (cf. 1.8 (= 4 SB).3); C. has 'gone surety' for his good intentions.

7 M. Tullius Cicero, *Ad Atticum* 3.7 (= 52 SB). An altogether more sombre letter than **6**, both in content and in style, written when a deeply depressed and disconsolate Cicero was on his way into exile, in consequence of his execution without trial of some of the Catilinarian conspirators in 63. On the topic of exile in C.'s letters in general, see Hutchinson (1998) ch. 2; for the historical background, Scullard (1982) 118–23.

1 Brundisium: mod. Brindisi; C. had left Rome (probably) on 19 March, and had made for several different ports as his plans altered; he was now staying on the estate of M. Laevius Flaccus. **post diem etc.:** cumbersome, but standard idiom. **Epiro:** on his estate near Buthrotum (Butrint), on the coast opposite Corcyra (Corfu). **ualde:** somewhat colloquial, more at home in letters and dialogues than in formal speeches or essays. **ut:** depends on the preceding *hortaris*; the clause repeats A.'s invitation, and C.'s response begins with *primum*. **Autronio etc.:** exiled Catilinarian conspirators, whom C. had no desire to meet. **quadridui:** sc. *uiam abest*, 'is distant by a journey of four days'. **hostes:** more exiled Catilinarians. **interpretentur:** an amendment to the bill banishing C. had specified a distance of 400 or 500 miles (the sources differ) from Rome, within which it was a criminal offence to give him shelter; much would depend on how distances were calculated. **2 quod me:** A. had been sending C. a series of consolatory-hortatory letters. **spes ea:** presumably that, by leaving Rome as he did, before being condemned by name, he would take the heat out of the situation, and give his friends and allies a chance to rally to his assistance. **inuidorum:** a consistent accusation in C.'s musings on his downfall, directed particularly against the orator Hortensius, who had advised him to leave. **reliqua tempora:** i.e. death will, eventually, put an end to C.'s misery, but in the meantime nothing can cure it. **3 Candauia:** mountain district in Illyria, some 70 miles from the coast at Dyrrachium (mod. Durazzo); C. intends to travel by the Via Egnatia. **quem quidem ... scio:** C.'s feelings about his brother are set out

more fully in *Att.* 3.9.1 and 3.10.2, where he explains his unwillingness
to inflict the pain and shame of his present fortunes on Quintus, and
distract him from his own pressing concerns (he was on his way back
from his term as governor of Asia, and threatened with prosecution).
ut = quo modo, 'how'.   **maximum ... miseriarum:** this declaration stands out not only for its uncompromising gloom, summing up C.'s
whole present experience as utterly wretched, but also for the sustained al-
literation/assonance (12x *m*, even though some might be elided in pronunciation), reinforced by the etymological/semantic echo between *miserrimum*
and *miseriarum*.   **saepius ... plura:**   a standard epistolary apology,
but with special force under the circumstances.

8 M. Tullius Cicero, *Ad familiares* 14.7 (= 155 SB). A letter from
Cicero to his wife, written soon after their daughter Tullia had given birth
to a son, and at the outbreak of the civil war between Caesar and Pompey.
C. himself was on his way to join Pompey and the Consuls in Thessalonica.
For the historical background, see Scullard (1982) 123–7, 138–44.

Terentiae: C.'s wife since *c.* 80 B.C., and mother of Tullia and Marcus
junior; she had supported him through the period of his exile, but soon
after the time this letter was written their relationship began to de-
teriorate, and they divorced in 46.   **suae:**   *OLD* B7.   **1 Tulliolam:**   affectionate diminutive. For Tullia see also **6** above; she was
now married to her third husband, P. Cornelius Dolabella, but given
the unsettled times was staying with her mother in the family property
at Cumae. Her son, born in May (cf. *Att.* 10.16.5, 10.18.1), died shortly
afterwards.   **eieci:**   medical technical term.   **causae:**   predicative dative, or partitive genitive.   χολὴν ἄκρατον: Greek was the
language of medical science. It was standard medical theory, going back
to the 5th century Hippocratics, that a healthy state of the body depended on an even blend of the four humours (black and yellow bile,
blood and phlegm), in which each softened and diluted the others, and
that a concentration of any of them in unmixed form spelled trouble. For
the writer's health as an epistolary topic, see also **9, 10** and **53–4** below.
medicinam fecisse: colloquial use of *facere*; *medicina* = 'cure, treatment', not 'medicine'.   **deo:**   Aesculapius.   **pie ... caste:**   both
a compliment to Terentia, and an expression of C.'s keenness that
the offering should be properly made.   **2 ualde:**   cf. on **7** above.

conscendi ... scripsi: epistolary tenses (Introduction, 36). **quo** = *ut.* **commodissime ... esse:** idiomatic use of *esse* + adv. to express the idea of staying in/at a place. **3 uillis iis:** presumably belonging either to the family or to friends and clients. **utere:** future; C.'s usage suggests that if he had wanted an imperative he would have used the future form *utitor*. **Arpinati:** at Arpinum, some 70 miles E. of Rome, Cicero's home town. **carior:** as a result of Pompey's blockade. **Cicero bellissimus:** Marcus junior, now sixteen; the diminutive is again affectionate, and the use of the adjective without a noun (e.g. *puer*) in apposition to *Cicero* colloquial. **etiam:** this was an unexpected extra letter, only made possible by a delay in sailing.

9 M. Cornelius Fronto, *Ad M. Caesarem* 5.55. A letter to the future emperor Marcus Aurelius from his old tutor (cf. **53** and **54** below), written some time between A.D. 154 and 156, when the orator, advocate, literary scholar and ex-consul Fronto was going on for sixty years of age and Marcus (who was to become emperor in 161) about thirty-five. F. had recently been appointed proconsul of Asia, but had been unable to take up the position through ill health (perhaps the very attack described here). See Birley (1966) chs. 3–5 (esp. 143–5).

Language and style. Highly literary; true to his stylistic ideals (see Introduction, 15) F. writes with great care over interesting choice of words (see notes below), word-order, sound-effects, rhythm and sentence-structure, even in such a short letter as this. Rhythmically, every sentence (indeed every colon) ends with an identifiable clausula (cf. Russell (1990) xxiii–xxv): e.g. the spondees of *destillatum gluttiui* and *focilatus totus sum*, and the double cretic in *clarius clamito*. Notable structural features are the taste for tricola, as in the first, second, fifth and penultimate sentences; the use of asyndeton; and the careful mixture of longer and shorter sentences. Prominent sound-effects include the three alliterative pairs *micularum minimum*, *clarius clamito* and *uehiculo uectari*, the paronomasia *uixero ... uidero*, and the assonances of u, l and t in *cum ... gluttiui*.

1 cholera: not the disease now called 'cholera', but a set of symptoms attributed to disorders of the bile (χολή, cf. **8** above); in modern terms what F. describes here might be diagnosed as a mild stroke (though van den Hout (1999) ad loc. more luridly suggests a combination of stroke, gastro-enteritis and heart-attack!). Reports on the writer's health are a regular epistolary topic (cf. **8**, **10**, **53–4**), but Fronto embraces it with more gusto than many. **singultirem:** relatively rare (as opposed to *singultare*) and not used by late republican and Augustan authors. **suspirio:** frequently used in medical contexts (e.g. Sen. *Ep.* 54.1, Luc. 4.328; Pliny, *NH* 20.100), but not confined to them. **uenae … uenarum:** careful repetition, to emphasize the cause–effect relation between the two events. **pulsu:** an important diagnostic aid in ancient as in modern medicine (cf. e.g. Galen's *De pulsu*, 8.453ff. Kühn), although the idea of the circulation of the blood was unknown in antiquity. **animo male fieret:** colloquial expression for fainting: Donatus on Ter. *Adelph.* 655, Plaut. *Rud.* 510, Lucr. 3.596; its presence in the comedians and Lucretius ('archaic' writers) will have made it particularly attractive to F. **ne balneo … data:** puzzling at first sight, as the doctors surely had *time* to go to work between F.'s regaining consciousness and nightfall; I follow a suggestion from Professor Kenney, that *tempus aut occasio* is F.'s pleonastic way of saying καιρός, the crucial moment the doctor waits for to administer his treatment. **frigida:** sc. *aqua*. **micularum minimum:** besides the archaizing colloquial alliteration, the two words reinforce each other semantically ('*smallest* of *tiny* crumbs'); the diminutive *micula* is again rare, and not found before the 1st century A.D. **destillatum:** *OLD* 2; 'sprinkle, moisten', rather than the more usual intransitive sense ('drip down'). **gluttiui:** another lovingly chosen item, found also in Plautus and the Elder Pliny, and much used in medical writing. **ita etc.:** rather jaunty after the alarming symptoms just described; Haines in his Loeb text suggested adding ⟨*sensim*⟩. **focilatus:** relatively rare; found in Varro, Seneca, Pliny, Suetonius and the *Laus Pisonis*. **uehiculo uectari:** a form of 'etymological figure', as both noun and verb derive from the same root. **silicem:** hard stone, particularly as used for road-making (*silicarius* = 'paver'). **tum uixero etc.:** a Ciceronianism; cf. *Att.* 2.24 (= 44 SB).5 *respiraro si te uidero*. **quom:** archaic spelling for *cum*. **sei:** archaic spelling for *si*. **desiderantissime:** superl. of the pres. ptc. in a passive sense, as also on inscriptions.

10 P. Ovidius Naso, *Tristia* 5.13. A verse letter to an unnamed friend, pleading reproachfully for some communication. At the apparent time of writing (cf. *Trist.* 5.10.1–2) O. was coming to the end of his third year of exile at Tomi on the Black Sea. Exile, as a subject for witty play in epistolary form, had featured in the experiences O. had created for his *Heroides*, written in happier times; now he was writing from and about his own experience.

Form. Tristia 5.13 is one of a book of fifteen or sixteen elegies (depending on whether or not the second is divided into two), ranging between 24 and 80 lines in length; six others similarly take the form of verse letters, preparing the way for O.'s next work, the more consistently epistolary *Ex Ponto*. Whether any of them was ever sent as an individual missive is open to question; it may well be that they only made their way to Italy in the collective guise of a finished book of poetry. In any case, they repay reading both as individual pieces and as elements in a shaped collection. 5.13 stands out for the thoroughness of its reworking of epistolary formulae and topics in elegiac dress (cf. Introduction 24–5), as also for its use of literary reminiscence to appeal more effectively to the recipient's (and the reader's) sympathy.

Bibliography. Evans (1983) ch. 5; Davisson (1985) 238–46; Williams (1994) 122–8.

1 Hanc . . . mittit . . . salutem: recalls the standard opening formula (*salutem dicit*), but with the substitution of *mittere* for *dicere*, drawing attention to the distance that separates O. from his addressee, and his inability to communicate directly in speech (cf. 27–30 and 34). The specification of the place of writing is likewise epistolary; the omission of the addressee's name is not.   **3 aeger enim etc.:** wishes for his friend's health lead on, again in familiar epistolary manner (Exler 103–6; Cugusi (1989) 407), to news of O.'s own, via the not-so-usual paradox of *mittere si quisquam*.   **traxi . . . mentis:** the ability of state of mind to affect bodily health and vice versa is a commonplace of ancient physiological thinking: see Max. Tyr. *Or.* 28.2 (with Trapp (1997) ad loc.).   **5–6 uror . . . frigore:** the paradox underlines the wretchedness of the conditions O. now has to live in (cf. again 27–30).   **7 si tamen etc.:** echoes the epistolary formulae *si uales, ualeo* and *si uales, bene est, ego quidem ualeo* (Cugusi (1989) 386; cf. **2** above). O. seeks both to console himself and to win admiration for the warmth and generosity of his friendly feelings. **8 fulta:** idiomatic with *ruina*: *OLD* 1 a.   **9** O. now turns to his main concern, the failure of his friend to write. This too is a standard epistolary topic: e.g. Cic. *Ad fam.* 14.2 (= 7 SB), Pliny 1.11, 3.17; Cugusi (1989) 408. **ingentia pignora:** not so much promises, verbal guarantees, as actions, practical help that guarantees both the friend's affection and further aid in the future.   **10 numeros omnes:**   *omnes* is the usual accompaniment to *numeri* in this sense, 'successive parts/stages (of a whole)', *OLD* 12. **11 quod ... epistola:**   internal object to *peccas*, 'in that ... '; G–L §525. **12 rem ... uerba ... :**   summing up epigramatically the *a fortiori* argument of the last six lines: if you can do the greater thing, then you can (and should) do the lesser too. Like any good suppliant, O. puts pressure on his friend by emphasizing how much he has already done, and so how little more is being asked for, and how well within his power it is (cf. Bremer (1981) 196, with Cal. *H.* 4.226 and Virg. *Aen.* 6.117). The *res–uerba* antithesis is taken up and developed in 25ff. below.   **13–14** mix insistence that the friend is (shamingly) at fault (*emenda, correxeris;* cf. 11 *peccas*) with encouragement that the adjustment can easily be made (*unum, nullus*), and colours the whole thought with an allusion (in *nullus ... naeuus*) to Horace *Sat.* 1.6.66–7 (also encouraging: Hor. ad loc. owns up to a few blemishes; the friend, if he writes, will not even have that many, and so will be able to claim a higher rank than Hor. in the annals of literary friendships).   **15–16** Calculated generosity: the friend will feel all the more guilty if he does not in fact qualify for this escape-clause. Comment on the uncertainties of delivery is again a standard epistolary topic: Cic. *Att.* 1.13 (= 13 SB).1, 4.15 (= 90).3, 15.17 (= 394).1; *Ad fam.* 14.4 (= 6).5.   **16 missa ... tamen:**   jussive perfect subjunctive with concessive force ('let it none the less have been sent'), Woodcock §112; cf. G–L §264.   **19–23** More calculated (and potentially shaming) flattery.   **21–3** A pair of ἀδύνατα ('impossibilities'), reinforcing the appeal of O.'s expression of confidence in his friend. The two locations specified (and their characteristic products) measure not only the physical distance between O. and civilization, but also the spiritual distance between his past and present circumstances, and the artistic distance between his present poetic activity and his past glories. Besides sun and warmth, thyme and Hybla hint at honey, and its function as an image for poetic activity (Pind. *O.* 10.98, *N.* 3.77, *I.* 5.54; Hor. *Odes* 4.2.27ff.; etc.); for cold as an image of poetic or intellectual sterility, cf. Virg. *Geo.* 2.483–4 and *OLD frigidus* 8. **21 absinthia:**   Pontic wormwood (Artemisia Pontica); for its bitter taste, cf. Lucr. 1.936 and 2.444, and for its largely medicinal uses, Pliny, *NH* 27.18.45–52.   **24 fati stamina:**   the image is that of the threads of life spun by the Fates; cf. Cat. 64.305ff.   **nigra:**   black colouring for an ill-fated life (cf. *Ibis* 244, *Trist.* 4.1.64; and contrast the golden thread of Petron. *Sat.* 29.6); in other uses of the image, all human threads are

black, because all human beings must die (Hor. *Odes* 2.3.15–16).   **27**
utque solebamus etc.:   a reminiscence of Callim. *Epig.* 2 Pf. ('They
told me, Heraclitus . . . '); again with protreptic intent, an appeal to recover
what can be recovered of the good old days together, which are made to
glow more brightly by association with a famously commemorated literary
friendship. O., of course, casts himself as the Callimachus of this relationship.   **29–30** Expansion and concretization (*ferat ac referat, charta
manusque*) of the commonplace of letters as written conversations, for which
see Dem. *Eloc.* 223 ff. (**73** below) and Thraede (1970) 39–47 (Cicero) and
52–61 (Ovid); and cf. **16** below. Correspondence can be only a pale imitation of the old conversations (*tacitas, uices*), but it can at least be sustained and
conscientious (*ferat ac referat, peragant*).   **31–4** O. ends as he began, with
elegiac transformation of standard epistolary procedure. The closing salutation comes in its proper place, but it is self-consciously signposted as the
last word, and as proper epistolary procedure (*quo semper finitur epistula verbo*).
Also familiar from 'real' letters is the inclusion of a concluding comment on
the length of the letter (*paucis, satis*), cf. e.g. Cic. *Att.* 2.25 (= 45 SB).2, 3.1
(= 46), 3.2 (= 48); *Ad fam.* 3.2 (= 65).2, 4.8 (= 229).2; Pliny 2.5.13, 5.7.5;
and compare **3** above for the introduction of such a comment by a negative
clause of purpose.   **33 accipe:**   balances *mittit* in line 1.   **uerbo:**
resonates against *uerba* in 12 (and 27–30): O. has written, even if the friend
has not.   **34 aque etc.:**   another piece of calculating generosity, highlighting both O.'s nobility and his plight.   **distent:**   further emphasis
on distance, separation and absence, cf. 1–2 and 21–2 above.

11 Phalaris, *Ep.* 49. A letter purportedly written by the 6th-century (B.C.)
tyrant of Acragas, setting a correspondent straight on the realities of his lot.
As in the following letter, Phalaris is made to portray himself with clear-
eyed resignation as living proof of the unhappiness of the tyrant's life. See
further Introduction, 27–9.

Ἐπιστράτωι: the recipient also of *Ep.* 127, where he is identified as
an enemy whom P. has already pardoned three times.   συνελὼν ἐν
βράχει: the familiar emphasis on brevity as a virtue of letter-writing; cf.
3 and **10** above. True to his promise, P. duly proceeds to sum up his existence in eight parallel clauses enclosed by the protasis and pithily ironic
apodosis of a conditional clause. The display of telling brevity is, of course,
a large part of the point of the letter (the other main element being the

piquant spectacle of a notorious tyrant's confession of his own wretchedness).   **τὸ κτλ:** article + (acc. and) infin., extending down to τὸν
ἐν τυραννίδι βίον; Smyth §§ 2025–30 and 2037.   **περίστασιν** 'hos-
tile/adverse circumstances, difficult situation', common in Hellenistic and
later Greek: LSJ ii.b.   **ἐκπεσεῖν:** for the passive of ἐκβάλλειν, as frequently (LSJ 3). Although historical tradition asserts that P. was a native-
born Acragantine, the letters consistently claim him as originally an
Astypalaean (cf. esp. *Ep.* 119).   **φθαρῆναι:** for φθείρεσθαι = 'go mis-
erably' or 'wander', see Denniston on Eur. *El.* 234; the usage is picked up
by Atticizing writers in the Imperial period: Dio 7.95, 40.7; Alciphron 1.13,
1.24; Plutarch *Ant.* 24; etc. (cf. LSJ ii.4).   **ἐπιβουλεύεσθαι:** the well-
known and inevitable fate of tyrants, cf. Plato *Resp.* 9.578d–598a, Xen. *Hiero*
2.8–18 (etc.).

12 Phalaris, *Ep.* 69. A letter from Phalaris to his wife Erytheia, asking
her to send their son Paurolas to him on a visit. He insists that his intentions
are noble and generous, and that he has reason on his side. But is this P. the
moral paragon, or P. the scheming tyrant, ready to put on any mask in order
to achieve his ends? The reader is challenged here either to admire the love
and generosity a good man can show even in his own misfortune (and to
feel indignant on his behalf in the face of his wife's unworthy suspicions),
or to be shocked by the cunning with which he seeks to gain control of
his son, and cheat his wife of one of her last remaining consolations (and
so to hope on her behalf that she will not fall for his blandishments) – or
indeed, to wonder anxiously which of these readings is the right one. A
longer letter than **11**, and more rhetorical in style (e.g. in its use of antithesis
and rhetorical question).

Ἐρυθείαι: the recipient also of *Ep.* 18, where she is warmly praised for her
devotion in bringing up her son after P.'s exile and, Penelope-like, resisting
invitations to remarry (cf. 51, where P. tells another correspondent that she
was poisoned by one of the disappointed suitors). The name is a grand
one, borne originally by one of the mythological Hesperides.   **τὸν...**
βίον: cf. **11** above.   **Παυρόλαν:** recipient of assorted fatherly advice in *Epp.* 19, 20, 40, 67 and 68. The name means 'Little One' (παῦρος).
ἀποτομώτατον: in this metaphorical sense ('severe, austere, brusque'),
more common in later than in classical usage. The idea that the father not
the mother is the true parent has a long pedigree: cf. Aesch. *Eum.* 657ff.

οὐ διὰ μακρᾶς: apparently for the more usual οὐ διὰ μακροῦ (sc. χρό-νου), although the feminine would more naturally suggest distance (sc. ὁδοῦ).   ἀναγκαιοτέρους: LSJ II.5.   περιουσιάζειν: Hellenistic coinage, not found in Classical authors.   ἐν ὑμῖν τοῖς φιλτάτοις: perhaps imitated from Thuc. 3.57.3.   ἐναπερείσασθαι: 'settle on'; a hellenistic coinage, not found before Polybius; the double preposi-tional prefix is particularly characteristic of later Greek word-formation. πρόσφατον: neut. as adv. ὑπομιμνῄσκει: cf. the case of Antigonos in Plut. Apophth. 182b, also 'put in mind' of a home truth by sickness. προθεσμίαν: sc. ἡμέραν, 'appointed day, predetermined time, set term'. For the thought, cf. Musonius, fr. 22, Sen. Ep. 12.8, Aurelius 2.5, 2.11.1, 5.29. Κρήτηθεν: Erytheia and Paurolas have apparently moved from Asty-palaea since P.'s banishment.   τὸ πιστόν κτλ: the use of the article + neut. adj. formula has a Thucydidean ring; cf. Thuc. 1.68.1, 2.40.5 (with dependent genitive); 6.72.4 (ditto). For the whole phrase, cf. also Max. Tyr. 32.4 τὸ ἐχεγγυώτατον ἡδονῆς πρὸς σωτηρίαν ('the best guarantee that pleasure promotes survival').

13 *Epistulae Socraticorum* 17. One of a collection of pseudepigraphic epistles, supposedly written to and by Socrates and his friends and disciples (see Introduction, 29). In this example, purportedly written soon after the Master's execution, one devotee writes (from an unspecified place of exile, perhaps Megara) to report to another (on Chios) that the Athenians have had second thoughts, and are seeking to make amends; Sykutris (1933) 67 tentatively identifies the writer as Aeschines (the Socratic, not the orator). For the view of Socrates and his execution embodied here, cf. Ferguson (1970) 187 ff.; Libanios *Apol. Soc.* (tr. Russell (1996) 17ff.), Max. Tyr. *Orr.* 3, 8–9 and 18–21 (tr. Trapp [1997]), Diog. Laert. 2.43, with Giannantoni (1990) 97–8. In a manner typical of such 'historical' pseudepigrapha, the letter seeks both to evoke the classic accounts of the people and events at issue, and to give the impression of taking the reader beyond and behind the official version.

Bibliography. Sykutris (1933), esp. 67–9.

πρὸς ἡμᾶς τοὺς ἐκείνου φίλους along with πρὸς σε ... διαμαχόμενος fol-lowing, establishes that writer and recipient did not stand in exactly the same relationship to Soc.: the former was one of the intimate circle, the latter a (respectful) rival and opponent in philosophical debate. For some possible identities for them, see below. **Πρόδικον … Πρωταγόραν … περὶ ἀρετῆς:** the sophists P. and P. were celebrated sparring-partners of Soc., and Virtue his great topic; if a particular debate is called to mind by the juxtaposition of these thinkers with this topic, it is that recorded in the *Protagoras*. **ἦι … ὅπως:** seem *prima facie* simply to repeat each other; but perhaps **ἦι** can be taken as 'in what place', viz. in the soul. **δόξαν:** accus. absol., 'because it seemed good to, was decided by'. But the writer's grasp of Athenian procedure is faulty: the decision was that of the sovereign Assembly; the Eleven only saw to the execution of the sentence. **ἔγραψα:** epistolary tense (Introduction, 36). **οἴκοι … ἐν Χίωι:** the only Chiot recorded among Soc.'s interlocutors is the sophist Euthydemos, who features in Plato's *Euthyd.*, so he may well be the addressee of the letter (particularly if confused with the other, Athenian, Euthydemos of Xenophon *Mem.* 4.2–3 and 5–6). **ἀφυπνώσαντες:** another Hellenistic coinage (conjectured by Hercher for MS ἀνύπνωσαν ὑπνώσαντες): cf. **11** and **12** above. The image perhaps picks up on the way Plato's Soc. characterizes the Athenians as slumberers in *Apol.* 30e–31a. **Ἄνυτόν τε καὶ Μέλητον:** as usual in later accounts of Soc.'s trial and death, the third prosecutor, Lycon, drops out of sight. The story of A.'s and M.'s trial and execution, though found already in Diod. Sic. 14.37.7 (from Ephoros?), is fiction: M.'s actual fate is unknown, but A. (the principal prosecutor) lived to become Archon in 384. Plutarch, *Inv. et od.* 538a says that they were shunned by their fellow citizens as if polluted, and eventually committed suicide; Diog. Laert. 6.9–10 has yet another story, involving Antisthenes. **προκαλεσάμενοι:** technical term in Athenian law ('issue a challenge', LSJ II.2), here apparently misused for 'prosecute' or 'put on trial'. **κακοῦ:** Soc.'s execution was an evil not only because he was innocent, but also because he was Apollo's protégé (cf. e.g. Max. Tyr. 3.1 and 8, Libanios *Apol. Soc.* 181, building on Plato *Apol.* 20e ff. and *Phdo* 60e–61b), and because of the divine retribution that allegedly followed (Max. 3.8; Liban. *Apol.* 183; *Argum. in Isoc. Bus.*, pp. 187–8 Mathieu-Brémond). **αὐτοῖν:** dual; a learned, archaizing touch (cf. **τὼ πονηρὼ ἄνδρε ἐκείνω** below). **κατηφεῖς:** conjectured by Hercher for MS ἀληθεῖς. **γάρ:** picks up the preceding αὗται, introducing the more detailed specification (Denniston 59). **ἄρα:** retrospective realization (Denniston 36–7). **ἀποκτιννύναι:** the use of ἀποκτείνυμι in place of the commoner ἀποκτείνω is another touch of learned style; in the context, probably specifically Platonizing (P. uses the -νυμι form more frequently in both *Grg.* [8:5] and *Phdo* [4:1]).

τὸν πλάτανον ... τὸν κύνα: a well-known fact about Soc., satirically connected by his defenders with the impiety charge (e.g. Max. Tyr. 18.6, looking to *Grg.* 461a (etc.) and *Phdr.* 236de).   ἀνηρώτα ... ὅτι: pregnant construction, as if ἀνηρώτα had been ἤλεγχε (what is described here is the celebrated Socratic elenchus, cf. Plat. *Apol.* 21b ff.).   εἶτα δὲ κτλ: implicit refutation of the charge of corrupting the young; for the counter-claim that the young would have been still worse without him, cf. Xen. *Mem.* 1.2.24–7.   καθοσονοῦν: (καθ' ὁσονοῦν), LSJ ὅσος, IV.6.   συγγενέσθαι: construe with κατ' ἔρωτα (= ἐπιθυμῶν). προσελθὼν διελέγετο: the young man behaves like a bereaved relative or lover; cf. Prop. 3.16.21–4. At the same time, his 'night with Socrates' is a kind of distant echo of Alcibiades' in Plato *Smp.* 218b ff. The closest parallel for this story elsewhere is told in the article on Socrates in the *Suda* (in which one Cyrsas of Chios (n.b.?) sleeps by the grave and sees Soc. in a dream).   Μεγαράδε: where a number of Soc.'s pupils, including Aeschines, had withdrawn after his execution (cf. *Epp.* 15–16); it may be from here that we are to imagine the letter being sent.   τοσοῦτον διάστημα: acc. of extent (Smyth §1581), depending on the idea of motion towards in ἀφικνοῦνται.   κοινόν ... ʽ Ελλήνων: cf. again Plut. *Inv. et od.* 538a; the treatment of M. and A. as an affront to Hellenic civilization rather than just to Athens reflects the viewpoint of a later period than the purported time of writing (cf. e.g. Apuleius *Met.* 10.33.2–3).   ἀνασεσοβημένοι: for the diaspora of Soc.'s pupils after his death, cf. Libanios *Apol.* 175–6. So many were involved that this detail does not really help to identify the correspondent. The author of the letter may well have other, later expulsions of philosophers in mind too (e.g. the expulsion from Rome under Vespasian, Dio Cass. 65.13).

14 Chion of Heraclea, *Ep.* 17. Chion's last letter, purportedly written on the eve of his successful attempt on the life of the tyrant Klearchos of Heraclea, at the Dionysia of 353/2 B.C. A correspondent's last letter, whether or not consciously written as the last, bears a special authority and interest for the reader. For Chion's letters, the only extant example of an ancient epistolary novel, see Rosenmeyer (2001) ch. 9, and Introduction, 30–1.

Πλάτωνι: C. had been a pupil of Plato's in Athens; *Ep.* 5 records his first impressions on meeting.   1 θεραπόντων: for slaves delivering letters, cf. **6** and **7** above. The names are well omened: 'Pylades' recalls Orestes'

faithful companion in the assassination of Clytemnestra and Aegisthus,
'Philokalos' means 'Lover of nobility'.   ἐξέπεμψα: epistolary tense
(Introduction, 36).   πολιτευσάμενος: LSJ B.VI (a sense found chiefly
in vernacular and later Greek). See esp. *Ep.* 16, to Klearchos, in which C.
insists (quite falsely) that his philosophical convictions make any kind of political action impossible, let alone assassination.   τὰ τῶν δορυφόρων:
periphrasis, meaning little more than 'the bodyguards' (cf. τὰ τῶν συνωμοτῶν below); the usage is classical (Plato *Leg.* 657d, Soph. *Phil.* 497), but
here sounds rather mannered.   συνωμοτῶν: according to the historical sources, C. had either one or two accomplices, named as Leonides and
either Antitheus or Euxenon.   2 ἀναιρεθήσομαι: the conspirators
were cut down by Klearchos' bodyguard after the assassination.   μετὰ
παιᾶνος: goes closely in sense with νικητηρίων, as a paean is properly a
song of victory (first sung by Apollo after the defeat of Pytho, Callim. *Hymn*
2.97ff.). The connection with Apollo is particularly appropriate to a pupil of
Socrates and Plato: cf. *Phaedo* 84e ff. and Riginos (1976) 9–32. C.'s 'victory'
is of course principally his heroic deed, but we perhaps catch also an echo
of the idea that death itself is something to be celebrated by the philosopher, whose true home is not in this world (*Phdo* 85ab; cf. Metrodorus fr.
49 Körte, Diog. Oen. 2 II 7ff. Chilton, [Plato], *Axiochus* 365b, Dio Chrys.
30.43).   καταλύσας: to the knowledgeable reader, there is an irony
here: C. did indeed bring off the assassination successfully, but that did
not put an end to the tyranny, which was continued by Klearchos' brother
Satyros.   ἐναργεστέραν ... ὄψιν: the vision *is* a dream (cf. τούτου
τοῦ ὀνείρατος below), but one of exceptional vividness. For ἐναργής, cf.
Burnet on Plato, *Crito* 44b4 ('so distinct that [its] interpretation is not in
doubt'). The vision itself is closely modelled on Socrates' in *Crito* 44ab
(just as, in *Ep.* 16, C.'s prosopopoea of Hesychia echoed Soc.'s of the Laws
in *Crito* 50a ff.).   γυνή: unidentified by C. (just as Soc. in *Crito* loc.
cit. does not name the figure who appeared to him); the reader however
will perhaps think of Philosophy or Virtue (cf. Xen. *Mem.* 2.1.22, Virtue
in Prodicus' *Choice of Heracles*). Whatever her identity, the figure has the
standard basic attributes of an allegorical representation of a good quality;
cf. Gera (1995) 241–3.   θεῖόν τι χρῆμα: Atticizing usage, cf. Xen.
Cyrop. 1.4.8, Ar. *Nub.* 2 with scholion.   ἀναδεῖν ... ταινίαις: another
image of (athletic) victory; the olive wreath is distinctive of the Olympic
games.   κέκμηκὰς ... ἀναπαυσόμενος: like a victorious athlete; but
of course κέκμηκα can also mean 'am dead' (LSJ II.5).   καὶ σύ: looks

mainly to *Phdr.* 244 (which has to be read in a de-ironized form for the purpose) and *Tim.* 71a–72b; cf. also *Apol.* 33c. None of the Platonic passages, however, goes so far as to say that the soul *always* foresees truly.   **3**
μακαριώτατον . . . ἤ: for the conflation of superlative with comparative (perceived as an Atticism by later writers) see K–G 1 22–3.   **καλὸν κτλ:**   a kind of self-consolation, in which C. as it were anticipates the contents of the encomia he will receive after his death.   **τι:** adverbial acc.
μείζων γὰρ κτλ: a *sententia* in characteristic syntactic form, with the commendatory adj. in first position, followed by the topic-noun and a defining relative clause. For the question at issue (the importance of disinterestedness), cf. Sen. *Ben.* 6.12–13 (citing Kleanthes).   **εὐδαιμονοίης . . . γῆρας:** there is perhaps a hidden barb here, addressed by the author to the reader over his character's head. P. did indeed live to a ripe old age, but managed to do so (in part) by *failing* to do anything constructive about the tyrant in his life, Dionysius.   **προσαγορεύσω:**   slightly illogical tense (as in the Eng. translation); the future as it were carries over from 'I *will* never address you again' to 'I *am* addressing you for the last time.' Alternatively, C. here, forgetting the standard epistolary conventions for tenses (Introduction, oo), treats his address to Plato as something that will not happen until Plato reads the letter.   **ὕστατ(α), ὡς πείθομαι:**   heroic resolution, but also elegant style: C. ends with a double cretic ($- \smile - - \smile -$) clausular rhythm. C. could be read here as tacitly adapting the epistolary topic of unwritten letters (complained of or apologized for – Introduction, 36): announcing the imminence of one's own certain death is the best of all excuses for failing to write any more.

A II PRIVATE LETTERS: AFFAIRS OF THE HEART

Love-letters provide a particularly clear case of the importance of letters in contracting, maintaining, defining and negotiating relationships (Introduction, 40–2). This section contains eight letters to and from spouses and lovers, in which (as not in **4**, **8** and **12** above) their emotions towards each other are on display: one naïve item on papyrus from second-century A.D. Egypt; one sophisticated message, worked up for publication, from first-century Rome; and six fictitious missives (including two pairs) from the first to third centuries. For another lover's letter, see also **71** below. Separation, actual or threatened, is not surprisingly a major recurring theme; see also the headnote to **A I** above, and Introduction, 38.

It is worth remembering that none of the women in these letters speaks for herself; all of them are seen through the eyes of, or invented by, male writers.

15 Serenos, *P.Oxy.* 528. A letter on a sheet of papyrus (180 × 128 mm), found at Oxyrhynchus and written some time in the 2nd century A.D. The writer expresses his longing for his wife ('sister'), who has gone away in circumstances that the letter does not wholly clarify.

Language and orthography. Again, written in capitals without word-break, accents or breathings. As in **1–5** above, the spelling is careless, and often phonetic: besides features already seen in those letters, Serenos (or the scribe writing for him) adds the use of υ for οι (e.g. πυῶ, ὑ λόγυ), uncertainty over long and short o and over double consonants and digraphs (ξ, ψ), the treatment of unstressed short i (ἐδοῦ), and the double misspelling of ποσάκις. In morphology and usage, notable features include the low/late form of the second person pronoun (ἐσοῦ), the conjunctions ἀφ' ὡς and ἀφ' ὅτε, oscillation between aorist and perfect in past time, the missed agreement (and misspelling) in δυναμένου, and the uncertain handling of reported speech (cf. **1** above).

Bibliography. *Oxyrhynchus Papyri* 3 (1903) 263–5 (B. P. Grenfell, A. S. Hunt); *Select Papyri* 1 (Loeb) 326–9; Montserrat (1996) 7, 70, 116.

ἀδελφῆι: probably his wife; cf. **4** above with Lewis (1983) 43–4, Bagnall (1993) 204–5. **πλαῖστα:** unusual misspelling, as it seems to give the wrong sound (short e rather than long i [ει]); for the formula, cf. **4** and **5**. **πρὸ μὲν παντὸς κτλ:** formulaic, cf. **3–5**. **ὄψας:** slip for ὀψίας; for the gen. with κατά here, rather than the more usual acc., LSJ A.II.6. **τὸ προσκύνημά σου πυῶ:** another formula, cf. Exler 108–10. Thoeris was an Egyptian goddess, usually represented in the form of a pregnant hippopotamus, and with special concern for pregnant women. Does this indicate something about the circumstances of Isidora's absence? **γινόσκειν σε θέλω:** formulaic again, cf. **4**. **ἀφ' ὡς:** apparently ἀπό (from) + ὡς (when), cf. ἀφ' ὅτε below; standard educated Greek would be ἀφ' οὗ. **πενθῶ:** apparently a slip for πενθῶν, rather than a reversion from participial clause to main verb. **Φαῶφι:** the month running from Sep. 28 to Oct. 27 by the modern calendar; Hathyr ran from Oct. 28 to Nov. 26. **ἐσοῦ:** extended form of the second-person pronoun, formed by analogy with the first person; a late usage (Jannaris 532; Browning (1983) 62). **ἥλιμε = ἥλιμμαι**. Abstention from washing and anointing are standard tokens of grief (most often seen in mourning for the dead); and one month (the period S. specifies) is standard for such measures. **δυναμένου:** for δυναμένας, but wrong gender and final letter dropped. **αὐτήν:** another slip, for αὐτῆ(ι). **ἔδωκα:** sc. to someone to deliver; cf. the use of *dare* in Lat. (*OLD* 10). **ὁ Κόλοβος . . . πεπύηκεν:** direct quotation from Isidora's letter, introduced by the notion of saying in λόγων κὲ γράματων; naïve diction, as is the preservation of direct speech after ὅτι in the next clause. S.'s naïvely allusive style (like Achillodoros' in **1**) makes it difficult to be sure what the story is. There is at least a nice tangle of claim and counter-claim, with S. telling Isidora what Kolobos said she said about him, as reason to dispute what she has said about Kolobos. **φάσειν =** φάσιν (LSJ II.5). **κατέστακε:** transitive pf. (with short α) as found in 4th century and later texts, with loss of the aspirate (confusion with the aorist?). **πλύν =** πλοῖον. **πιστευθῶ μου τὴν ἐμβόλην:** obscure, both in sense and in syntax; it isn't clear whether S. is using πιστεύεσθαι in the rarer sense of 'be trusted', with μου τὴν ἐμβόλην as acc. of respect, or in the sense of 'be entrusted with', with τὴν ἐμβόλην as retained acc. and a redundant (construction-confusing) μου. **ἐμβολήν:** LSJ I.3 seems to be the operative meaning, but this does not wholly clarify what S.'s position is, and what he is worried about. **⟦φ⟧πιστευθῶ:** the writer (S. or a scribe?) originally began with a φ (more trouble with aspirates), but crossed it out. **ἔρχηι κτλ:** absence of an initial εἴτε gives a colloquial parataxis. By the standards of many papyrus letters, S. ends abruptly (even if there was a final ἔρρωσο on part of the papyrus now missing) and on a strikingly querulous note.

16 C. Plinius Secundus, *Ep.* 6.7. A letter from Pliny to his third wife Calpurnia, some years his junior, whom he married some time after 97. At the time of writing (cf. *Ep.* 6.4), she seems to have been convalescing by the sea in Campania, while he attended to his duties as Chair of the drainage-board (*curator aluei Tiberis*) in Rome. This decorously erotic letter (the references to impressions on the bed, the flames of desire, and pleasure laced with pain all echo clichés of love poetry) plays its own variations on the epistolary theme of written words as (inadequate) substitutes for face-to-face exchange.

uestigio: properly an impression left in something soft and yielding; here, the marriage-bed, a reference supported by the choice of the verb *collocare* (see *OLD* 6). For the imprint of the absent lover's body in love poetry, cf. Prop. 2.9.45, 2.29.35, Ov. *Her.* 10.53, *Am.* 1.8.97. **fomentis:** medical metaphor. **inuicem** 'for my part, just like you'; a gentle extension of the standard senses 'in turn', 'reciprocally', 'alternately'. However, in spite of the suggestion of symmetry of feeling, P. does seem to want to claim an edge in sensitivity: *C.*'s pangs may be alleviated by contact with P.'s books, but *his* are as much inflamed as soothed by her letters. **accendor:** for the image, cf. e.g. Prop. 2.34.86, Ov. *Am.* 1.1.26, 1.2.9–12, Virg. *Aen.* 4.2, 54. **litterae ... sermonibus:** cf. **10** above. **quam frequentissime:** for the request, cf. **10** and **5** above. **ita ... ut:** making a concession, but then limiting it severely ('only to the extent that ... also ... ', 'without precluding'): *OLD ut* 34. **delectet ... torqueat:** a conceit going all the way back to Sappho, fr. 130 L–P (γλυκύπικρον); cf. Theogn. 1353, Musaeus 166, Plaut. *Pseud.* 63, Cat. 68.18.

17 'Circe' and 'Polyaenus' (Petronius, *Sat.* 129.4–9, 130.1–6). An exchange of letters between Petronius' 'hero', Encolpius, here operating under a pseudonym, and a rich lady with low-life tastes, with whom he has attempted to begin an affair in the southern Italian town of Croton. For impotence as a literary theme, compare Ovid, *Am.* 3.7, on which Petronius clearly draws.

4 Circe Polyaeno: both names are pseudonyms and recall Homer's *Odyssey* (Polyaenus = πολύαινος, 'much-praised', an epithet of Odysseus in both epics, most notably in the (seductive) song of the Sirens, *Od.* 12.184). The whole episode is thus presented as a parodic replay of one of Od.'s adventures; the parody seems both to cast an ironic light on Encolpius and his lover (who are anything but epic heroes), and to suggest an amusedly eroticized reading of the *Odyssey* (compare for example the way Lucian in *Vera Historiae* 1.35 invents a nostalgic love-letter from Odysseus to Calypso, and the moral allegorization of Circe as sensual pleasure, Horace, *Epist.* 1.2.23–5 and Heraclitus *Alleg.* 72.2–3). See further Courtney (2001) 152–7 and 190–207. **quererer decepta:** lit. 'deceived, I'd be complaining (about it)'. **umbra:** slightly unusual metaphorical usage, combining the idea of shadow versus substance (cf. *OLD* 10) with that of a shadow encountered *in advance* of the solider object that casts it. **diutius** 'longer than usual', rather than 'too long'. **5 quid ... agas:** colloquial usage (*OLD* 21 f.), here with a medical nuance: C. is enquiring in good epistolary form (but also with malicious amusement) after her correspondent's health. **neruis:** *double entendre*, as also in *neruos tuos* further on; *nerui* can mean both 'sinews' in general, and (with reference to one particular 'sinew') 'virility:' see Adams (1982) 38. **6 narrabo:** colloquial usage, *OLD* 1 d. **paralysin:** another piece of Greek medical terminology, cf. **8** and **9** above. **tam magno periculo:** ablative of attendant circs. **medius:** euphemistic, Adams (1982) 46f. **7 genua manusque:** P.'s extremities, as opposed to the more central portion already affected; for the idea of the knees as a major seat of physical vitality, see Onians (1951) 174–86. **tubicines:** trumpeters, a standard ingredient in Roman funerals (cf. e.g. Hor. *Sat.* 1.6.43ff., Prop. 2.7.2, Pers. 3.103, Petron. 78.5–6). **8 quid ergo est:** *OLD quis* 14a. **Gitonem:** Encolpius' boyfriend and companion in misadventure in the *Satyrica*. **fratre:** *OLD* 3b. **9 minus** = *non*. **uale, si potes:** more wordplay, both with the senses of *possum* ('be able' and 'be potent') and between *potes* (in the second sense) and *uale*, converting the standard epistolary good wish into a taunt.

2 habes confitentem reum: an ironic quotation of Cicero *Pro Ligario* 2, itself a plea for mercy in the face of a powerful enemy. **proditionem feci etc.:** metaphorically, in failing C.; not a reference back to adventures of E. earlier in the novel. **3 ferro ... nudus:** further *double entendre*, as also in *instrumenta* and *arma* below (cf. Adams (1982) 19–22). **4 arma:** a variation on the theme of *militia amoris*, cf. e.g. Ovid, *Am.* 1.9. **hoc:** internal acc. with *turbauerit*. **6 ea:** abl. of comparison. **per quod:** for *id per quod*. **etiam:** i.e. C. is the last person you would think could inspire impotence. **placebo:** like C., E. ends with a *double entendre*.

18 Gemellos and Salakonis (Alciphron, *Epistles* 2.24–5). An exchange from Alciphron's second book of letters, all of which are from and to country people. A rich country-dweller remonstrates threateningly with a low-born town girl he has 'rescued' from a life of squalor; she rejects him and declares her intention of committing suicide. Between them, the two letters sketch out a whole amorous episode, and a clash of perceptions and expectations between its protagonists. The language throughout is literary and high style, not colloquial, and careful attention is given to rhythm at sentence-end (clausulae). See Rosenmeyer (2001) ch. 10, and Introduction, 32.

Γέμελλος: the name suits its possessor's amorous intentions (particularly as perceived by Salakonis), since *gemini* ('twins') in Latin (of which *gemellus* is the singular diminutive) can be a translation of Greek δίδυμοι = 'balls': see Adams (1982) 68.   Σαλακωνίδι is also a 'speaking name', reflecting the perceptions of the other party: σαλάκων = 'snob'. 'Young Ball' writes to 'Snobbess'. This kind of play with names is regular in Alciphron's letters.   1 ταῦτα: internal acc. w. ὑπερηφανεῖς.   ὑπερηφανεῖς: once in Homer (in part.), otherwise characteristic of Hellenistic and later Greek.   οὐκ ἐγώ κτλ: G.'s indignant outburst allows the reader to reconstruct the earlier stages of the relationship.   λάθραι τῆς μητρός: a situation (parental disapproval) familiar from New Comedy, on which Alciphron draws heavily (cf. **19** below).   ἀγαγόμενος ἔχω: the sequence of short syllables at sentence-end (outside the normal range of clausulae) perhaps expresses G.'s irritation; so also με διατελεῖς at the end of the next sentence.   **2 φρυάττηι:** lit. 'whinny', like a difficult, spirited horse; normally used metaphorically, as here, but the metaphor suits the rustic context well.   παιδισκάριον: double diminutive, given a contemptuous twist by the final element.   κιχλίζουσα: like φρυάττηι above, onomatopoeic; also connected by ancient etymologists with κίχλη, 'thrush', so again appropriate to the rustic setting. It is presumably not accidental that the same word had been used in Theoc. 11.78, there too of feminine reactions to an uncouth and unwelcome suitor (the Cyclops). μωκωμένη: more onomatopoeia; ancient etymologists connect the word (which is not found before the hellenistic period) with a noise made by camels.   κάχρυς ... φρύγειν: so as to separate grain from husk; hot, laborious, unpleasant work.   οἵ κακῶν: partitive gen. with adv. of place, Smyth §1439.

1 καὶ τὴν νύκτα κτλ: by making S. refer to a previous episode *not* alluded to in G.'s letter, Alciphron very economically enhances the reader's sense of the background to the exchange. For an upturned trough as a hiding-place (also in an erotic context), cf. Apul. *Met.* 9.3.2.   **2 κέκρικα:** bluff or earnest? In any case, the letter is thus identified as a suicide-note, and the words it contains gain resonance as (perhaps) the writer's last (cf. **14** and **34**).   κίναδος: lit. 'fox', but can be used more generally

of a monstrous or unpleasant creature; perhaps another touch of rustic naïvety. **3 μυχαιτάτου:** irreg. superl. of μύχιος, 'inward, inmost'; a recondite word, built into an exquisitely styled sentence (n.b. esp. the balance τοῦτο μέν . . . τοῦτο δέ . . . , the repeated use of neuter adj. + possessive gen., and the elegant enclosing of ἐκ τοῦ . . . δυσοσμίαν between noun and qualifying participle). There is a playful contrast (on Alciphron's part, not his character's) between this fine diction and the down-to-earth message it conveys ('I hate you: you're hairy and your breath smells!'). **σαλεύουσαν:** lit. 'riding at anchor' (ἐπί, 'on, held by'): LSJ II.2. **τῶι ἐκ τῆς πίττης ἐλαίωι:** a more elegant periphrasis for the technical term πισσέλαιωι, an oily liquid derived from raw pitch (Dioscorides 1.72.3; Pliny, *NH* 15.7.31; 23.96; 24.23.40); in context, the point is that it is (*a*) smelly and (*b*) medicinal (and apparently more often applied externally to livestock than to people) – in S.'s eyes, G.'s ideal partner needs to be diseased and as rank as he is. This final taunt also suggests an age difference between S. and G. (though perhaps one that seems greater to S. than it really is).

19 Glykera to Bakchis (Alciphron, *Epistles* 4.2). One of the letters from Alciphron's fourth book of letters, all of which are from or to *hetairai* (courtesans). The book as a whole draws heavily on material from New Comedy, both for the characters involved and the situations in which they find themselves; here the mistress of the greatest of the New Comic poets, Menander, duplicates the experiences of one of his heroines, worrying about the fidelity of her lover (and characterizes herself for the reader in the process). As in the preceding two letters, Alciphron writes with elegantly studied informality, combining a colloquial tone with close attention to sentence-structure and rhythm.

Γλυκέρα: well-known as Menander's lover (cf. Athenaeus 13.585 and 594d); the story of their affair (and eventual split) was probably originally concocted from the appearance of a G. in several of his plays (esp. *Perikeiromene*, but n.b. also frr. 87 and 280), although some scholars have argued for a real historical basis (see the note in Benner and Fobes (1949) 252–3, and Lefkowitz (1981) 113–14). *Epistles* 18 and 19 are an exchange between them. **Βακχίδι:** Bakchis of Samos, another famous courtesan, mentioned just before Glykera in Athenaeus 13.594bc, and also represented elsewhere in the *Epistles*: she is the sender of 4.3–5, and her death is lamented in 4.11 (cf. also 4.14). Both in Alciphron and in Terence's *Hecyra* she is distinguished for her generosity and good character. **1 Ἰσθμίων ... Κόρινθον:** the Isthmian games were celebrated every two years in honour of Poseidon; but their location, Corinth, had a reputation for luxury and loose living (cf. e.g. Max. Tyr. 32.3, 33.10), which surely hovers in the background of G.'s opening statement. **βεβούληται:** the pf. underlines the firmness of M.'s decision, presenting it as a settled state. **2 φιλοτιμίαν:** LSJ II. **ἑταιρίαν:** a kind of *double entendre*, as G.and B. are not simply colleagues, but fellow-*hetairai*. G.'s point is that being keen for M. to go on his visit, even though she knows that B. shares her professional interests and skills, suggests a noble lack of jealousy, and a firm confidence in her ability to keep her man. **3 χρηστοτέρωι ... βίου:** compare the sketch of B.'s character in 4.11. **ἐρωτικός:** the same claim is made about M. in the article on him in the *Suda*; it is probably based on the prominence of love (and love at first sight) in his plays, rather than on historical fact (cf. again Lefkowitz (1981) 113). **4 τὸ μὲν γάρ ... πείθομαι:** G. is still thinking of her own reputation (cf. φιλοτιμίαν above); the result here is a trifle catty. **5 δεήσει με κτλ:** ironic, as the readers of this letter know that she did end up in M.'s plays (cf. 4.19.4); for other ancient examples of the idea that an author's works are drawn simply and directly from his own experiences, see Lefkowitz (1981) *passim* (summary, 136-8). **Χρέμητος ... Φειδύλου:** stock names of old men in New Comedy (though Pheidon is more usual than Pheidylos): cf. Antiphanes fr. 189.22 K-A and Horace, *AP* 94.

20 Anon. (Philostratus, *Epist. Erot.* 39). A fictional love-letter by Philostratus. A love-sick exile threatened with a second 'exile' from his lover's affections pleads for kindness. Both the situation (the lover excluded) and the elaborately rhetorical manner in which he makes his case are reminiscent of elegy and epigram; together with the elegant style and close attention to clausular rhythm, they make the letter into a kind of prose-poem. It has a clearly marked ring-structure: (*a*) opening appeal (which also establishes the circumstances of writing): μηδέ ... δυνάμεως; (*b*) amplification ('proof' or 'sanction') of the appeal: ἔφευγε ... αἰδοῦς; (*c*) repetition of the appeal: ἀνάστησον ... κατελήλυθα. For further discussion of Philostratus' letters, see Rosenmeyer (2001) ch. 12, and Introduction, 32.

οὐκοῦν: Atticizing vocabulary. **φύσις:** a keynote of the lover's persuasive strategy, presenting his beloved's behaviour as not merely hurtful but positively unnatural.   **τὸ λάμπρον ... τῶι ἀλόγωι:**   more Atticizing diction (article plus neuter adj. to make an abstract noun); cf. **12** above. The references to chance and to the irrational exercise of power hint that the writer is the innocent victim of an arbitrary tyrant.   **ἔφευγε καί κτλ:**   the body of the letter consists of a catalogue of *exempla* from history, mythology and the natural world, all manipulated to demonstrate that an exile is to be cherished sooner than rejected. For this kind of ingenious piling-up of (often deliberately unexpected) instances, cf. e.g. Ovid in *Tristia* 2.361ff. (fellow-composers of love-poetry) and *Anacreontea* 21 (drinking as a natural law). **᾽Αριστείδης ... Δημοσθένης:**   famous examples from Athenian history in the great days of the fifth and fourth centuries (precisely the subject-matter favoured by the sophistic declaimers who were the subject of another of Philostratus' works; cf. Bowie (1970/74)).   **θάλαττα ... ἔαρος διώκοντος:**   for this series of natural examples, in which the cyclical processes of nature are read as parallels for some human event or relationship, compare Soph. *Ajax* 669–77 and Eur. *Phoen.* 538–48; the reference to the sea depends on the belief of some ancient theorists that it was the sun rather than (or as well as) the moon that caused the tides (Pliny, *NH* 2.212, Lucan 1.412–17, ps.-Plut. *Plac.* 897b).   **ἐδέξαντο καί κτλ:**   a concluding set of mythological *exempla*, all from the mythology of Athens, and embodying the image of the city as a helper of fugitives well known both from tragedy (Soph. *OC*; Eur. *Suppl.*, *Heracl.* and *Medea*) and from Funeral Orations (esp. those of Lysias, Hyperides and ps.-Demosthenes). Demeter's welcome in Attica, while searching for the abducted Persephone, was the subject of the foundation-myth of the Eleusinian mysteries (*Hom. Hymn. Dem.*, esp. 88ff.); Dionysus was welcomed by Icarius, whom he rewarded with the secret of wine-making (Apollodorus, *Bibl.* 3.14.7); the arrival of the children of Heracles, pursued by Eurystheus after the death of their father, is the subject of Eur. *Heracl.* The culminating reference to the Altar of Pity (for which see Pausanias 1.17.1 and Parker (1996) 232–3 with n. 55) provides the transition to the letter's concluding appeal.   **τρισκαιδεκάτου θεοῦ:**   for the practice of highlighting a divinity (or a ruler) by styling him/her 'thirteenth' (i.e. next in line after the Twelve Olympians), cf. Mynors on Virg. *Geo.* 1–42.   **οἶνου ... γάλακτος ... δακρύων ... αἰδοῦς:**   partitive gen., idiomatic with σπένδω as an alternative to the acc. **ἀνάστησον ... κατελήλυθα:**   careful sentence-structure, with a long, elaborate colon (ἀνάστησον ... σφαλείς) followed by something shorter and punchier (ἐάν ... κατελήλυθα); the long first unit takes the form of an increasing tricolon, with chiasmus between elements 1 and 2 (ἀνάστησον – ἐλέησον) and element 3 subdivided into two sub-units with homoeoteleuton (στερηθείς, σφαλείς). Rhythmically, the first unit ends with a double cretic (− ⌣ − − ⌣ −), the second with a sequence (− ⌣ ⌣ − ⌣ −) already used three times in the first half of the letter.   **κατελήλυθα:** both the tense (imagining the event, wishfully and/or persuasively, as *fait accompli*), and the placing are carefully calculated; κατέρχομαι is the technical term for an exile's return.

A III PRIVATE LETTERS: INVITATIONS

Five letters issuing invitations to a variety of gatherings: two brief 'naïve' examples from Egypt and Hadrian's Wall, a more elaborate and sententious example from the Emperor Julian, a characteristic summons from the tyrant Phalaris to a council of state, and a Horatian verse adaptation of the type for moralizing purposes. As a kind of letter standardly intended to create or continue a friendly relationship, the invitation is specially liable to expressions of warmth; the sender will often be particularly concerned to convey to the recipient how much he or she values and wishes for the other's company, how much care he or she will take over the guest's reception, and the depth of sympathy that already exists (or will be created) between them. This in turn can provide a platform for reflection on values, whether over the etiquette of hospitality and the proprieties of the table, or over other aspects of the shared priorities and ideals of those who are to meet. It may also be remarked that, unusually among forms of letter, the invitation looks in response not to a return communication (though that may often be expected as well), but to the physical arrival of the recipient. See also Introduction, 38–42.

21 Petosiris, *P.Oxy.* 112. An invitation written on a sheet of papyrus (750 × 850 mm), found at Oxyrhynchus and dating from the late 3rd or early 4th century A.D.

Language and style. Cf. note to **3** above. The language is, as often in invitations, largely formulaic, but enlivened by the eager (if unsubtle) repetition of the vocative **κυρία**.

Bibliography. Oxyrhynchus Papyri 1 (1898) 177–8 (B. P. Grenfell, A. S. Hunt).

χαίροις: the optative (expressing wish) provides an alternative formula to the imperatives χαῖρε and χαίρειν; cf. Exler 53, 67–8.
Σερηνία ... Πετοσείριος: Petosiris ('the one given by Osiris', cf. modern 'Theodore') is a very common Egyptian name; the genitive can be formed in -ιος, -ιδος or -εως. Serenia, a Latin name, is much more of a rarity (the papyri otherwise know 'Serena' and 'Serenilla'; 'Serenius' but not 'Serenia' is found in Latin inscriptions).   **ἐξελθεῖν:** inf. of purpose; 'come *out*' may suggest that Serenia lives in a larger centre of habitation than Petosiris (perhaps even Alexandria).   **γενεθλείοις τοῦ θεοῦ:** the reading favoured by the first editors of the papyrus over a possible alternative τοῦ Θεῶνος. For the Egyptian religious custom of celebrating gods' birthdays, see Perpillou-Thomas (1993) , citing e.g. *BGU* 149. 15 and 362. 8. 22–3.   **ἢ (= εἰ) πλοίωι ἢ ὄνωι:** the fact that travel by donkey is an option shows that the Serenia's journey would be a short one; cf. Bagnall (1993) 34–40, Lewis (1983) 140–4. For εἰ rather than πότερον in a double indirect question, see Smyth §2675c (citing Xen. *Anab.* 2.3.7).
ἐρρῶσθαί ... χρόνοις: another standard formula (Exler 76).

22 Claudia Severa, Vindolanda tablet II 291. An invitation written on a thin wooden diptych (223 × 96 mm), found at Vindolanda on Hadrian's Wall. This is one of a set of three letters sent to Sulpicia Lepidina, wife of Flavius Cerealis, prefect of the 9th Cohort of Batavians, which was stationed at Vindolanda between A.D. 97 and 102/3. The sender of this item, Claudia Severa, was the wife of Aelius Brocchus, also an officer. Both women belong to the educated equestrian class. The main body of the letter is the work of a scribe, but Severa writes the concluding greeting (*sperabo ... have*) in her own hand. These greetings, together with similar additions to two other of Severa's letters (nos. 292–3) constitute the earliest surviving securely identifiable sample of Latin handwriting by a woman.

Script and layout: The main body of the letter is written in an elegant cursive hand, with *apices* (') placed over some vowels, on a system not yet fully understood (cf. Bowman and Thomas (1994) 57–61). The concluding greetings, in Severa's own less-polished hand, are set off from the rest by being written in shorter, closer-spaced lines. There is no punctuation (apart from a point marking the abbreviation of Claudia) and there is no word-division.

Bibliography. Bowman and Thomas (1994) 256–9, with pl. XX (cf. 29–30); Bowman (1994), 54–7, 57, 74, 86–9, 92–3, 127, 153.

ad:　purpose, not motion: *OLD* 40. **diem′:**　it is not clear why the scribe
has written a *apex* after the 'm' of *diem*. 　　**sollemnem** 'celebrated according to time-honoured formula'; also applied to birthdays by Horace
(*Odes* 4.11) and Fronto (*ad Ant. Imp.* 1.2). 　　**libenter:**　translated here
with *rogo*, but could as well be taken with *facias*. 　　**facias:**　subj. after
verb of willing/desiring. With Severa's use of *facias ut* to add emphasis to
her invitation, compare Petosiris' πᾶν ποίησον and ὅρα μή in **21** above.
interuentu:　*OLD* 1; for another epistolary use, see Cic. *Att.* 4.2 (= 74
SB).5. 　　**factura:**　the future participle standing for the apodosis of a
conditional clause has a slightly mannered, literary feel to it; but this is
perhaps a case of a construction that had been taken into standard educated diction. 　　**uenies:**　the damaged word might also be restored as
facies, 'if you do so'. 　　**sperabo:**　unusual sense, but also found at Ter.
Eun. 193–5, and cf. *speratus* = 'longed for' (e.g. Plaut. *Amph.* 676). 　　**ita
ualeam:**　apparently reinforcing *karissima*, 'dearest to me as surely as I
hope to be healthy'; for this asseverative use of a wish, see *OLD ita* 17, and cf.
Cic.'s use of *ita ualeam* in *Ad fam.* 16.20 (= 220 SB).1 and *Att.* 5.15 (= 108).2.
haue = *ave* (the aspirated version is common); unusual at the end of a letter
(but cf. Sallust *Cat.* 35.6), and odd coming after *uale* – a sign of effusiveness
on Severa's part? 　　**Cerealis:**　standard use of unaccompanied gen. to
indicate 'wife of'.

23 Q. Horatius Flaccus, *Epist.* 1.5. A verse letter from the first book
of Horace's *Epistles* (for which see Introduction, 23–4), adapting the form
and topics of the letter of invitation. By envisaging a situation in which his
prospective guest (the patrician barrister Torquatus) is perceived to need
some persuading, H. opens up space for gentle moralizing on the value
of opportune relaxation, the good effects of wine wisely used, the virtues
of simple living without austerity, the proper organization of a party, and
friendship. The very first words, with their self-depreciating offer of simple
hospitality, challenge T. to show that he is no snob; the wine offered has
flattering family associations for him (see below); everything is ready and
tomorrow is a holiday, so he cannot plead either that he is putting H. to too
much trouble, or that business prevents him (1–11). His host wants to use his
money in this way, and positively welcomes the excuse for a party (12–20).
Every care will be taken to make it a congenial occasion (21–31). More sub-
tly, the whole message is personalized by being phrased in language that
plays with the technical terms of Torquatus' own profession as a lawyer. But

above all, Torquatus is being gently challenged to show that, for all his engagement in worldly business, he has the right priorities. H. thus offers both Torquatus and the reader ('eavesdropping' on the exchange, and reflecting on both parties to it) a model of sound values and committed friendship.

As another verse adaptation of letter-form, this poem can be compared with **10** above (Ovid). It shows fewer overtly epistolary features, declining to imitate the opening and closing formulae of the standard product; indeed, it is only with the penultimate line (*rescribe*) that it becomes unambiguously clear that it is envisaged as a written not a spoken message, physically dispatched to its recipient (but see n. on 11). It is also intriguing to compare the different relationships between sender and recipient reflected (constructed) in the two letters.

Bibliography. Williams (1968) 9–10, 103–31; Kilpatrick (1986) 61–5; Mayer (1994) 136–43; Eidinow (1995).

1 si potes: polite formula, also in invitations at Plaut. *Stich.* 619, *Poen.* 696; with the following *nec . . . times*, it issues a gentle challenge to T. not to scorn virtuous simplicity (for a grander version of which, Virg. *Aen.* 8.364–5). **Archiacis** 'by Archias', supposedly a maker of unpretentious furniture (or 'of Archias', if the reference is to Theban Archias (Nepos, *Vit. Pelop.* 3.2), who refused to open a (fatally important) letter at dinner, putting it under his cushion instead – the suggestion being that H. is offering temporary freedom from serious business).   **2 holus omne:** i.e. a very modest meal; *holus* is acc. with *cenare*, an archaic (and colloquial?) constr.; *omne* = 'pure, wholly', rare usage but cf. Plaut. *Rud.* 500.   **3 supremo . . . sole:** relatively late for a Roman dinner, in deference to T.'s busy schedule (but see also on 31 below); *sol* = 'day' is poetic (*OLD* 2c), *supremus* = 'the last part of' (*OLD* 3).   **Torquate:** a member of the patrician family of the Manlii Torquati, also addressed by H. in *Odes* 4.7.   **manebo** with personal obj. is colloquial (*OLD* 3b).   **4 uina:** poetic pl.   **iterum Tauro** sc. *consule*, a very unusual ellipse.   **diffusa:** poured from vat into jar, then sealed, with the names of the consuls of the year (26 B.C.) on the jar to indicate the vintage.   **4–5 palustres . . . Petrinum:** in Campania, in the Massic wine region; but the important point seems to be that the choice of this wine is a compliment to T., recalling the famous victory won by his ancestor T. Manlius at Trifanum near Sinuessa in 340 B.C. (Livy 8.11). **6 imperium fer:** the *imperium* is H.'s as 'master of the feast', but there is also a punning reference to T.'s family's proverbial taste for giving orders, the *imperia Manliana* (e.g. Cic. *Fin.* 2.32.105).   **7 iamdudum splendet etc.:** a sign of H.'s care as a host, but also (like the further details in 21–4) an inviting anticipatory glimpse of the promised party (cf. H. *Odes* 1.36, 3.29, 4.11). A clean hearth is aesthetically desirable (cf. Xenophanes, fr. 1.1 West), but might also have practical use at the time of year H. is writing.   **8 spes et certamina:** both T.'s, and those of his clients. **9 Moschi causam:** a major case, and so an indication of T.'s importance; Volcacius Moschus was a rhetorician from Pergamum unsuccessfully defended by T. and Asinius Pollio on a charge of poisoning (Sen. *Con.* 2.5(13).13, Tac. *Ann.* 4.43.5).   **nato Caesare:** causal abl. ('by reason of') with *festus*; Augustus' birthday fell on 21, 22 or 23 Sept.   **dat ueniam ... impune licebit:** phrases with a legal tinge to them (*OLD uenia* 2, *impune* 1).   **10 ueniam somnumque:** hendiadys.   **11** Another inviting glimpse of simple, honest pleasure to come. The anticipation of face-to-face conversation is an epistolary commonplace (cf. Cic. *Att.* 3.7 (= 52 SB).3 (= **7** above), Fronto *Ad Caes.* 5.5. (= **9** above)), just as extended conversation characterizes close friendship (cf. esp. Ovid *Tr.* 5.13 (= **10** above), 27–8, and Callim. *Epig.* 2).   **12 quo mihi fortunam:** idiomatic ellipse of the verb (as if e.g. *habeo*, although it is unlikely a Roman speaker would have a specific verb in mind), *OLD quo*[1] 2.   **conceditur:** another verb with legal overtones (cf. *concessio*). Roman law (as T. would know well) bracketed the spendthrift and the madman together, as both requiring the appointment of a guardian for their property; H. here teases T. by suggesting it is instead the miser who ought really to be paired with the madman.   **14 potare:** *heavy* drinking; H. continues his teasing, by suggesting that *he* at least is prepared to go to the opposite extreme, however much serious types like T. might disapprove.   **flores:** the normal accompaniment to after-dinner drinking, in garlands or scattered on table and guests.   **15 inconsultus:** another legal pun, 'ill-advised'/'lacking a legal consultant'.   **16 dissignat:** given in *OLD* s.v. *designo*.   **operta recludit:** the point is that wine inspires confidences and gives insight into your fellow drinkers' real characters, not that it betrays secrets in any reprehensible way: cf. Alcaeus, frr. 333, 366, Theognis 500. **17 spes ... inertem:** more symposiastic commonplaces, cf. Bacchyl. fr. 20b.7.   **21: procurare ... imperor:** rare use of the pass. of intr. *imperor*, with a reflexive sense; the vocab. suggests official duties (esp. those of an aedile).   **23 corruget** 'cause you to wrinkle '(in disgust)', perhaps a Horatian coinage; the emphasis on neatness and cleanliness picks up from 7 above. **24 ostendat tibi te:** perhaps suggesting not only careful polishing, but also trust and trustworthiness, an absence of distortion and concealment? **25 eliminet** 'broadcast', archaic and used in this sense only here. **25–6 par...pari:** a little more than just the promise of congenial company: both in proverbial wisdom and in physics, like rightly goes with like, and in the conventions of the symposium, all fellow-drinkers are equals. **27 Sabinum:** gramatically obj. of *detinet*, within the *nisi*-clause, but to be supplied also with *adsumam*. **28 umbris:** friends/associates brought by the guest himself, not invited personally by the host. **29 olidae:** perhaps colloquial. **caprae:** the feminine ('she-goat') is found here only as a metaphor for the smell of sweaty armpits; elsewhere the masculines *caper* and *hircus* are preferred (e.g. Cat. 69.6). **30 quotus** 'one of how many', 'the howmanyth'. **rescribe:** only with this word in the penultimate line is it made unambiguously clear that the whole poem is envisaged as a written message, brought by a messenger, who will wait for a written response; at the same time, there is another legal pun (cf. *OLD* 2b), maintaining the careful tailoring of the language of the message to its addressee and introducing the scene sketched in the final line. **30–1** A final exhortation to T. to indulge in a little (justifiable) selfishness, and to forget his professional scruples for a while. Although T'.s court day will have ended at sunset (cf. 3 above), there will still be clients to see at home; but the honest lawyer should be kind enough to himself to elude/cheat them (*falle*, another teasing pun) just this once. **31 postico:** instrumental abl., 'by (the use of)'.

24 Flavius Claudius Iulianus, *Ep.* 54. A brief and rather mannered letter from the Emperor Julian (Introduction, 16), inviting a friend to the inaugural celebrations for the new year's consuls. The reference to his recently acquired status must be to his elevation to the Imperial throne, which fixes the date as 361 or 362 (he died in 363). If it is 361, he is writing from Constantinople, and the celebrations are for the consuls for 362, Claudius Mamertinus and Flavius Nevitta; if it is 362, he is writing from Antioch, and is himself one of the consuls to be inaugurated. There are signs that Julian may be making use of a model letter from a handbook (cf. Introduction, 38, and **74–5** below).

Bibliography. Bidez (1960) 39, 65; Bouffartigue (1992) 228, 647.

Εὐστοχίωι: not securely identified.   **'Ησιόδωι ... ταραχή:** *Works and Days* 343–5: 'invite above all him who lives near you; for if something untoward happens at your place, neighbours come ungirt, but relations have to gird themselves'. J.'s paraphrase substitutes sympathetic feeling ('share our grief') for the more practical assistance H. envisages.   **ὡς συνησθησομένους:** fut. part. of purpose after verb of sending/summoning, Smyth §2065 (cf. also **μεθέξων** below).   **ἐγὼ δέ φημι κτλ:** the rhetorical device of *refutatio sententiae*, giving emphasis to a declaration by presenting it as an improvement on a similar statement by an acknowledged authority; cf. Soph. *Trach.* 4–5, with Easterling's note. J.'s correction, with its semi-philosophical stress on logical compatibility, means to draw attention to the superior value of friends over mere neighbours. To anyone who knows the full Hesiodic context, however, it risks falling flat, because *WD* 342 says precisely 'invite to dinner him who is friendly, and leave your enemy be'. This in turn suggests that J. himself may not know the full context, but be getting his allusion via a gnomology or a collection of model letters.   **οὐ νῦν μόνον:** presumably, 'not only now that I'm Emperor'.   **εἰ καὶ μηδέν ... σημεῖον:** a rather strained and clumsy way of saying that E. is indeed a true friend; J. means that he would not have kept his feelings for E. for so long had he not been absolutely convinced that they were reciprocated, and he would not have been convinced unless it were true.   **ὑπατείας:** here = not 'consulship', but the inaugural ceremony, the *processus consularis* (for the Republican/early Imperial form of which, see Scullard (1981) 52–4).   **δημόσιος δρόμος:** the *cursus publicus*, the Imperial message-system set up by Augustus, with relays of horses at 10–20 km intervals, grooms and wheelwrights, and an inn every 30–40 km: see Casson (1994) 182–90, Mitchell (1976), Levick (2000) 107–11. These facilities were available to officials and (occasionally) to private individuals, if furnished with a special pass; J.'s letter will either constitute such a pass itself, or be the means to one.   **παρίππωι:** lit. 'side-horse'; probably a pack-horse for luggage, rather than a change.   **ἐπεύξασθαι:** the prefix ἐπ(ι)- indicates both 'in addition to these practical measures' and 'to round off this letter'.   **'Ενοδίαν ...'Ενόδιον:** Hekate and Hermes, deities with a special concern for roads and travellers (Burkert (1985) 156–9, 171). Hekate is also invoked to protect a traveller by the *cursus publicus* at the end of *Ep.* 34; the fact that she was specially revered by Hesiod (*Theog.*

411–52) might suggest a deliberate attempt on J.'s part to match the end of his letter to its opening, but may be wholly coincidental. In any event, the use of two relatively obscure divine names fits well with J.'s devoted, classicizing paganism.

25 Phalaris, *Ep*. 39. Another letter from the tyrant (Introduction, 28), this time summoning a meeting of his most trusted friends at a moment of (unspecified) crisis. His words again portray him as the high-minded, noble, responsible ruler, but with (perhaps) a slipping of the mask in the final words. In general terms, the dramatic situation recalls episodes from Herodotus (e.g. Periander's consultation of Thrasybulus in 5.92f., or Polycrates' correspondence with Amasis in 3.40–3).

Πολυστράτωι: the recipient also of *Ep*. 140, but probably not the same as the co-recipient of 58, who is addressed as an enemy. **ἐπέσταλκα** 'have written with instructions to'; both the epistolary and the non-epistolary senses of the verb are in play here. **διὰ ταχέων:** stylistic variant for the more usual διὰ τάχους, substituting the n. pl. of the adj. for the abstract n. (Smyth §1003); cf. e.g. Thuc. 1.80.3, 3.13.2. **Ὀλυμπίων:** for the great temple of Olympian Zeus at Acragas, described by Diod. Sic. 13.82, and still visible in ruin, see Holloway (1991) 117–19. **μάλιστα εὐνουστάτων:** LSJ μάλα III.3. **ἐπιμέλειαν:** for the affairs of state, rather than for his friends: τὴν πρέπουσαν . . . ποιήσασθαι is to be taken closely with καὶ περί . . . λαβεῖν following, both clauses painting P. as the model of political prudence. **γνωμὴν λαβεῖν** seems to want to combine two senses, 'take thought (one's own)' and 'gather opinions (other people's)': LSJ II.1 and III.1.a. **ἀτόπου . . . ἐμαυτοῦ:** more characterization, of P.'s courage, determination, and scrupulousness towards his friends. **ἂν εἴποιτε:** good Classical usage would demand the subjunctive here; the opt. is either a scribal error (for the homophone εἴπητε) or a sign of the shaky grasp of 'correct' Attic syntax characteristic of later Greek authors (Schmid IV 620–1, cf. 1.97–8, 243–4, IV.89–90). **ἂν δοκῆι . . . :** noble acceptance of Fate/divine will. **ἐφιλοτιμήθημεν:** LSJ III; a further sign of P.'s great-heartedness (Ar. *Ethics* 1124b9–18). **ἥκετε:** the switch to the plural is notable in a letter to a single addressee. Perhaps explicable as an example of the plural used when an individual is regarded as the representative of a group (not a sign that the author has forgotten the dramatic situation): Smyth §1011. **ὃν . . . γινώσκετε:** on the surface, entirely complimentary, 'whom you know well to be

the good man I am'; but perhaps also a covert admission (by P. to
Polystratus, or by the author to the reader) that others know a very different
P. (see Introduction, 28).

A IV PRIVATE LETTERS: RECOMMENDATION

Most of the letters in this collection so far have been intended to maintain
or extend the relationship between the two correspondents alone. Letters
of recommendation, while again presupposing such a relationship, differ by
seeking also to create a new one, between the addressee and the individual
recommended by the writer. Since their function is to request a favour, both
to the writer and to the beneficiary of the recommendation, and since the
personal status and prestige of all three parties to the transaction is so often
at stake, such letters play an important role in the complex web of reciprocal
benefactions and conferrals of honour that was so central to the social and
political world of the élite in antiquity: see Lendon (1997) 48–9, 63–9. Each
one of them, besides requesting the preservation or the enhancement of
the beneficiary's status, also asserts the writer's own. Furthermore, since the
status in question is a social and even political matter rather than a purely
private one, this is a category of letter which falls on and problematizes the
boundary between 'private' and 'public' correspondence; compare letters
62 (Attalus) and **68** (Basil) below.

Given its obvious persuasive purpose, this is by some way the most
rhetorical kind of letter to be examined so far. Not surprisingly, it is also by
some way the most highly formalized, with its own distinctive commonplaces and clichés – perhaps most prominently the exhortation to treat the
subject of the recommendation as if he were the writer of the letter himself
(which in turn combines interestingly with the idea of the letter as substitute for face-to-face conversation). Cicero's letters of recommendation –
both occasionally in their wording, and in the fact that a whole book of
them was collected as *Ad fam.* 13 – show that this formalization was fully
acknowledged by the 1st century B.C. It brought with it a problem of a kind
familiar to writers of works of persuasion of all kinds: how to maintain the
desired effect once the clichés and formulae had come to be recognized
as such. On the letter of recommendation in general, see Cotton (1984)
and (1985); compare also the remarks of Terentianus (**5** above) and Julius
Victor (**75** below), and see Introduction, 39–42.

26 Aurelius Archelaus, *P.Oxy.* **32+.** A Latin letter on papyrus (355 × 105 mm), found at Oxyrhynchus and dating from the second century A.D. Archelaus, a Greek serving in the Roman army in Egypt, writes to recommend a fellow Greek to his (Roman) commanding officer; the friend, Theon, presumably hopes to enlist too. For content, context, and language, compare **5** above (Cl. Terentianus); and, for the military setting, **22**.

Language, orthography and style. A. composes in Latin, because he is writing to a native Latin speaker and because Latin is the language of army administration. He makes some attempt at formality, both in style and in his use of the proper formulae for recommendation (esp. in his recall of an earlier recommendation, his exhortation to treat Theon as if he were A. himself, and his assurance that Theon is the addressee's type). At the same time, his performance shows signs both of everyday ('vulgar') Latin usage, and of the influence of his own first language: examples of the former are *tales* for *talis*, omission of the initial aspirate of *(h)omo*, paratactic style (esp. in *reliquit enim . . . de actum nostrum* and *hanc epistolam . . . loqui*), substitution of *t* for *d* in *ad*, *quidquid* and *illud*, substitution of regular for irregular infinitive termination (*referere*), acc. for. abl. after *de*; for the latter, see esp. the n. on *estote . . . agentes*. Also characteristic of everyday Latin is the tendency to place verbs before their direct objects (*commendaueram Theonem, habeat introitum*, etc.).

Bibliography. *Oxyrhynchus Papyri* 1 (1898) 61–2 (and pl. VIII), 2 (1899) 318–19 (B. P. Grenfell, A. S. Hunt); Deissmann (1927) 163–6; Hunt and Edgar (1932) 320–2; Bruckner and Marichal (1967) 86–9; Watson (1969) 37–8; Davies (1989) 11–12.

Iulio Domitio: not otherwise known.　　　　**tribuno:** each legion had five tribunes, one senior and five junior (Webster (1985) 112–13; Davies (1989) 37; Le Bohec (1994) 38–9); even as one of the five juniors, D. will have been of equestrian rank, so considerably above A. in the social as well as the military hierarchy.　　　　**Aurelio Archelao:** the combination of names suggests an ethnic Greek family with some foothold in the Roman social/political establishment: cf. again Cl. Terentianus and his family (**5** above), and contrast Theon, who has just the single name, in the Greek/Egyptian style.　　　　**beneficiario:** a member of the headquarters staff, exempt from some ordinary legionary duties, who owes his position to the patronage of a particular officer (Watson (1969) 75–86;

Davies (1989) 43–6; Le Bohec (1994) 46–8); A. thus uses the word with some rhetorical/persuasive force, reminding D. of the bond that already exists between him and Domitius.   **pristine:**   only here, but Tertullian uses *pristinum* adverbially (*adu. Prax.* 1, p. 228.17).   **commendaueram:** epistolary plpf., but awkward with the pres. tenses following.   **ant oculos habeas:**   notable, because *ante oculos* (like Greek πρὸ ὀφθαλμῶν) normally means 'before the *mind's* eye'; here, it carries overtones of looking attentively and/or benevolently. The elision of *ante* is also unusual: phonetic spelling, but also the sign of someone working in a second language?   **tales omo** = *talis homo*.   **reliquit enim . . . et . . . et . . . :**   naïve polysyndeton, perhaps influenced by the fondness of simple Greek (e.g. NT) for sequences of καί . . . καί . . . καί . . . .   **securum fecit:**   seems to be something of a set phrase, cf. **5** above.   **at te:**   for the behaviour of *t* and *d*, Väänänen (1981) 69; Adams (1977) 25–9.   **referere** = *referre*; assimilation of the irregular verb to the standard 3rd conj. form.   **de actum nostrum:**   a little mysterious: does this refer just to T.'s recent good service to A., or to some further business between A. and D.? For the tendency of the acc. to displace other prepositional cases in later and vulgar Latin, see Adams (1977) 36–7, Väänänen (1981) 112.   **quitquit . . . :**   the text becomes fragmentary for some ten lines at this point; the space seems to have contained further (more detailed?) praise of T.'s qualities, and a reassertion of A.'s keenness to recommend him.   **estote . . . agentes:**   like Terentianus' (**5** above), A.'s final salutations are Greek formulae translated (e.g. *multis annis* = πολλοῖς ἔτεσιν, *cum tuis omnibus* = σὺν τοῖς σοῖς πᾶσιν: cf. Exler 75–7). *estote* (like *habeto, putato* following) is second ('future') imperative: this form is colloquial in earlier Latin (Plautus), rarer and more solemn (and/or literary) in the classical period and later, and felt as particularly appropriate in laws, maxims, recipes and the like (commands not necessarily expecting an immediate response); A.'s use may be either a sign that it survived in everyday usage, or (once more) that he is working in his second language, learned partly from literary and official texts.   **hanc epistulam . . . habeto . . . putato:**   another naïve parataxis (for '*as* you look on . . . imagine . . . '). The epistolary commonplace of the letter as equivalent to, or a substitute for, face-to-face conversation (cf. n. on **10**. 29–30 above) combines well with the equally commonplace encouragement, specific to recommendations, to treat the bearer of the letter as if he were its sender.

27 M. Tullius Cicero, *Ad fam.* **13.5 (= 319 SB)**. One of a set of letters to those in charge of the distribution of land to Caesar's veterans, written in 46–5 B.C. Having previously (and unsuccessfully) written on behalf of the Etrurian landowners as a group (*Ad fam.* 13.4 = 318 SB), C. now pleads for a particular individual. For the issue of land confiscation and distribution, see Brunt (1971) 294–344 (esp. 319–26).

Structure and strategy. C. begins (§1) with a disarming and ingratiating preamble, reminding his addressee of their friendship and flattering him on the importance of his present job, and the dedication with which he is discharging it. By stressing his own previous restraint, he both underlines the importance he wishes to attach to the present request and hopes to make Orca more inclined to grant it. The specifics then follow in §2–3: C. (*a*) emphasizes the length of his connection with Curtius, and his own past record of assistance; (*b*) sketches the details of the situation, with emphasis on the paradoxical nature of the fate that faces Curtius; and (*c*) concludes by re-emphasizing the restraint with which he is making the request, and asking for Curtius to be treated as if C. himself.

Q. Valerio: Q. Valerius Orca, securer of Sardinia for Caesar during the Civil War (*Bell. Civ.* 1.30–1), now in charge of land-distribution in Etruria; as praetor in 57 B.C., he had been one of those lobbying for C.'s return from exile (Cic. *pro red. in sen.* 23).   **leg(ato) pro pr(aetore):** a *legatus* was a senator appointed to the staff of a military commander or governor; as *pro praetore*, O. exercised the (legal and administrative) powers of a regular praetor, but outside the city of Rome, and outside the normal structure for the annual appointment of magistrates (cf. *OCD*[3] s.vv. *pro consule, pro praetore* and *legatus*).   **1 existimare** 'judge', *OLD* 2.   **committo** 'perpetrate, bring it about that', *OLD* 15b.   **2 C. Curtio:** otherwise unknown, probably the son of a professional prosecutor murdered during Sulla's dictatorship; that, and the accompanying loss of property, will be the *calamitas* C. refers to. Cf. Scullard (1982) 77–80.   **Sullani temporis:** the direct mention of Sulla is probably a deliberate persuasive move – O. is being encouraged not to be party to the same sort of brutality as gave Sulla his black reputation.   **Volaterrano:** sc. *agro*, 'territory, region'; V. = mod. Volterra, in Etruria; the area had already been subject to confiscations after the capture of Volaterrae by Sulla in 80 B.C.   **tamquam** 'as if, so to speak', acknowledging that a metaphor is being used (*OLD* 6); for shipwreck as image of personal

catastrophe, cf. **31** below.   **quem ordinem etc.:**   there was no formal property qualification for the senate at this period, but the position
demanded money all the same; *ordo* = 'rank, position', *OLD* 5.   **superior . . . inferior . . . Caesaris iussu . . . Caesaris beneficio:**   a
pointed pair of antitheses, aiming at underlining the cruelty and inconsistency of the fate Curtius is faced with.   **conuenit** 'is consistent', *OLD*
6.   **3 minus** = *non*.   **causa . . . gratia:**   a striking formulation of
the understanding on which C. writes, the reverse of what a modern petitioner would think legitimate. By the code of the late Republican ruling
class, it is still better to do the just thing because a friend asks you than to
do so simply because it is the right thing.   **in maiorem modum** 'in
a greater (sc. than usual') manner, *OLD modus* 11 d, G–L §297.2.   **quicquid . . . habere abs te:**   a slightly contorted development of the standard 'do it for x as if for me' formula, made more difficult by the postpone-
ment of *ut* and *cum*. Construe *ut . . . existimes* with *rogo* ('(and I beg you) to
take it that . . . '), *faceres* as conditional, and *id* as resuming *quicquid*. With
the future perfects *feceris* and *habuerit*, C. encourages O. to think forward
beyond the actual granting of the request to the satisfaction of knowing
that he has gratified a deserving friend.

28 M. Tullius Cicero, *Ad fam.* 13.15 (= 317 SB). A second letter
of recommendation by Cicero, of a subtler kind. Overtly, it recommends
young Precilius to Julius Caesar, now master of Rome. The concluding
reference to its unconventional nature might seem simply to acknowledge the heavy use of literary quotation in Greek, as a (flattering and
persuasive) compliment to Caesar's literary taste and learning: faced with
a specially deserving case, C. does all he can to revitalize the tired, familiar clichés of recommendation (cf. Hutchinson (1998) 13–15). Closer
attention to the content of the quotations, however, shows that there is
more to the communication than this: they carry a further message from
C. to Caesar not about Precilius, but about himself. This is an unconventional recommendation because its additional (even perhaps its main)
purpose is not to recommend but to reassure Caesar about C.'s own
loyalty, or at least his disinclination to be drawn into any further anti-
Caesarian activity, in an urbanely allusive way (so Shackleton Bailey, citing
Att. 13.37 (346 SB).2, 12.38 (278), 13.9 (317), *Ad fam.* 9.11 (250) as evidence
that C. was indeed under suspicion of subversive activity at the time of
writing).

In structure, the letter forms an elegant ring. It opens and closes with the overt object of the communication, recommendation of young Precilius, each time with the unusual nature of the message underlined; within that comes the message about C. himself, framed by references to Precilius' father.

1 Precilium: not otherwise known.   **unice:** underlines the warmth of C.'s recommendation, but also anticipates the final emphasis on the uniqueness of the letter itself.   **em:** colloquial interjection, used for drawing something to an interlocutor's attention; common in Plaut. and Ter.   **hic ille est de illis maxime qui ... solitus est** '*he's* the one who above all (out of the whole group of them) who ...', slightly redundantly phrased in that either *hic ille est maxime* or *hic est de illis maxime* would say the same on its own. C. looks back to events of 59 B.C. **ἀλλ ' ἐμόν κτλ:** Hom. *Od.* 7.258 and 9.33, of Calypso and Circe failing to persuade Od. to stay with them rather than returning home.   **proceres:** republicans like the Younger Cato, urging heroic defence of the old order.   **ἄλκιμος κτλ:** *Od.* 1.302, said by Athena to Telemachus.   **ὡς φάτο κτλ:** *Od.* 24.315, of Laertes reacting to the (false) news that his son Od. is still missing. C. means that he took the advice of the *proceres*, and suffered for it.
2 perustum ... incendere: telling juxtaposition of two different registers of fire imagery, to bring out the fatuity of the attempt, as C. now sees it. **μὴ μάν κτλ:** *Il.* 22.304–5, spoken by Hector on his way to the final duel with Achilles. C. quotes the same lines in a letter to Atticus of 49 (*Att.* 10.1 (= 190 SB).1).   **magniloquentia** refers both to H.'s high (epic) style, and to the matching nobility of the sentiments he expresses.
praecepta Εὐριπίδου: Euripides was the tragedian most read and quoted by subsequent generations, with a special reputation for the telling formulation of wise sayings (*sententiae*, γνῶμαι): cf. e.g. Quint. *Inst.* 10.1.67–8. C.'s contrast between him and the grander, but less-convincing, Homer to some extent recalls that between him and Aeschylus in Aristophanes *Frogs* (830–1481, esp. 907–47, 1434).   **μισῶ κτλ:** Eur. fr. 905 Nauck², from an unknown play. The Latin poet Ennius had translated the line in his tragedy *Medea*, and C. uses the translated version in *Ad fam.* 7.6 (= 27 SB).4 and *Off.* 3.62.   **ἅμα πρόσσω κτλ:** *Il.* 1.343, cf. *Od.* 24.452; said of the prudent leader, capable of using the past as a guide to future action.
αἰὲν ἀριστεύειν κτλ: *Il.* 6.208, 11.783, the classic statement of the hero's ambition to excel, quoted by C. also in a letter to his brother Quintus in

54 (*Q.Fr.* 3.5 (= 25 SB).4); both times in the original context, it is reported as uttered by father to son (Hippolochus to Glaucus, Peleus to Achilles). **3 humanitate . . . singularis:**   echoes the opening section of the letter (*humanitatem . . . singularem*, §1), as well of course as offering further flattery. **et ad id . . . commendationis meae:**   more tactful persuasion, as C. affects to believe that he is only giving Caesar an extra gentle nudge in a direction he is already inclined to take. *cumulum*, 'cap, crown, completion', comes neatly towards the end of a message.   **id quod . . . te uelle:** *uelle* here in its affective sense, as in *bene/male uelle*, *OLD* 15b.   **genere nouo . . . non uulgarem:**   see headnotes to this letter and section.

29 Q. Horatius Flaccus, *Epist.* 1.9. The shortest poem from the first book of the *Epistles* is not so much a proper letter of recommendation as a meditation on and a partial subversion of the tropes, etiquette and institution of such letters, with a message for all the parties involved. The actual recommendation is phrased in the baldest and most conventional of terms, and occupies only the final line. For the rest, H. expresses his doubts about his own standing with his addressee, and his ability to make an effective recommendation. This could be read either as a warning to those in Septimius' position not to expect too much of their intermediaries, and a lesson to those in H.'s about how not to abuse a patron's generosity; or, alternatively, as a particularly subtle way of working on an addressee, by ostentatiously not presuming too far, and by inviting amusement at the delicate position S.'s ambition has put the conscientious H. into. Remarkably, the poem has no overtly epistolary features (apart perhaps from the ghost of one in the choice of the metaphor *scribe* in the last line); what qualifies it as a letter is its function.

Bibliography. Kilpatrick (1986) 41–3.

1 Septimius: known otherwise only as the addressee of H. *Odes* 2.6, and (?) from a letter of Augustus to H. (Suet. *vita Horati* 31 Rostagni). **Claudi:**   Tiberius Claudius Nero, the future Emperor Tiberius; the use of his given name, Claudius, is respectful ('sir').   **nimirum:**   colloquial and ironic.   **unus:**   *OLD* 8.   **2 quanti . . . facias:**   *OLD facio* 18c; *quanti* is gen. of value.   **cum:**   *OLD* 9.   **3 scilicet:**   *OLD* 2; to be taken with *cogit*.   **4** *OLD mens* 4e, *domus* 6, *lego* ² 6; *dignum* attaches to *se* in a predicative construction ('*as* one who is worthy . . . ').   **5 cum:** *OLD* 6; supply *me* (from *coner*) with *fungi*. *censet* carries the implication that

S. may be mistaken in his belief (*OLD* 2).   **6 ualdius:**   colloquial.
7 excusatus abirem: both words carry overtones of release from formal and/or legal obligation (*OLD excuso* 3, *abeo* 7b).   **9 dissimula-**
tor: Greek εἴρων; the suggestion of devious or self-interested 'modesty'
is confirmed in the second half of the line.   **11** The contrast is between
rustic modesty (cf. Cic. *Ad fam.* 5.12 (= 22 SB).1) and urban self-assurance
(*OLD frons*² 3).   **12 ob amici iussa** excuses H. to T.: a friend's request obliges compliance as firmly as a direct command.   **13 scribe**
(*OLD* 7) is an unsurprising metaphor here, but is perhaps chosen as appropriate usage in an imitation of a written letter.   **tui gregis:**   *grex*
(lit. 'flock') used like this of a group or set with common interests (*OLD*
3a) is not necessarily dismissive; the use of the partitive gen. with a verb is
poetic.   **fortem ... bonumque:**   wholly conventional, cf. Cic. *Fam*
13.72 (= SB).2, Hor. *Odes* 4.4.29.   **crede:**   *OLD* 6.

30 C. Plinius Secundus, *Ep.* 4.4. A brief and formulaic recommendation by the younger Pliny, elegantly styled and apparently undisturbed
by any worries about its own effectiveness (perhaps, as Professor Mayer
suggests to me, because published only after a successful outcome). The
appearance of perfunctoriness probably does not reflect any intention on
P.'s part of damning his beneficiary with faint praise.

Sosio Senecione: Q. Sosius Senecio, *cos.* 99 and 107, a friend
of Plutarch and the Emperor Trajan: *PIR*¹ III, s 560, Jones (1971)
54–7.   **1 Varisidium Nepotem:**   otherwise unknown.   **diser-**
tum ... potentissimum est: P. expects that his preference will be
shared by S., another literary man. The whole sentence is itself carefully
composed in somewhat oratorical triads (three main units, with a trio of
adjs. in asyndeton in the central one).   **C. Caluisium:**   a business
associate and friend of P.'s, a wealthy landowner and town-councillor of
Comum; *PIR*² c 349.   **2 semestri tribunatu:**   a junior tribunate
(cf. **26** above), but its precise nature (half-pay? half a year's service?) is
not clear.   **splendidiorem** implies that Nepos is of equestrian rank
(*OLD* 4b).   **obligabis ...:**   a second carefully contrived rising tricolon, with anaphora of *obligabis*.   **ipsum ... quam nos:**   the familiar 'as if he were me' formula; cf. **26** and **27** above.   **idoneum:**
OLD 2.   **3 multa ... collocasse:**   yet more careful composition (two
units, with the second divided so as to give three overall; antithesis between
the two major units, and between the two sub-divisions of the second).

Nepos is urged as a special case ('as good as any candidate I've seen'), and
S. is reminded of his past generosity as an incentive to maintain the habit
(cf. n. on **10**.12 above).

31 Basileios, *Ep*. 147. One of three letters by St Basil (Introduction,
19) on behalf of a noble 'friend' (political ally) fallen on hard times (*Epp.*
147–9). An elegantly developed literary reference recommends the victim
and dignifies his plight, reminds the addressee of his responsibilities as a
cultivated and civilized individual, and stresses the bond of sympathy (and
class solidarity) between him and the writer of the letter. Compare **47**.2
(Libanius) for the use made of Odysseus as an exemplar of misfortune.

'Αβουργίωι: a wealthy layman and fellow native of Caesarea, to whom
Basil often appealed on behalf of unfortunate friends (cf. *Epp.* 33, 75,
178, 196, 304); he held high rank at the Imperial court, perhaps as *comes
rei priuatae* (minister in charge of the Emperor's private property) or
quaestor sacri palatii (official responsible for the drafting of imperial decrees):
PLRE I 5.   ἐπήιειν: LSJ ἔπειμι (B) 2.   τὸ ἕτερον μέρος: Hom.
is here regarded as the author of *Il.* and *Od.* alone, not the *Hymns* as
well.   πάθη: the emphasis on Od.'s adventures as tribulations suits
the use B. wants to make of him as a parallel to Maximus, but is in any
case conventional, taking its cue from *Od.* 1.4 (πολλά...πάθεν ἄλγεα).
μεταδιδάσκει: the compound verb, with its sense of 'teach (to believe)
differently' seems out of place; it might be better to read the simple verb
διδάσκει here, and the compound in the next sentence.   πάντα:
adverbial n. pl. acc.   Μάξιμον: *praeses* (governor) of Cappadocia
Prima in 372–3, accused of embezzlement and forced to flee to Caesarea
(*PLRE* I 585, Maximus 23). *Ep.* 148 also appeals on his behalf, and gives
a few more details of his story. Prosecution after a period of office was a
standing threat and the cultivation of influential 'friends' (like B.) was a
prudent form of insurance.   περιπέτεια: Aristotle's term for reversal
of fortune in tragedy (*Poet.* 1452a22, etc.), but (?) used here without any
specifically literary overtones.   στρατηγός...Κεφαλλήνων: cf. *Il.*
2.631–6 (Catalogue of Ships).   ῥάκεσιν: like Od. in disguise in his
beggar's rags on Ithaca, *Od.* 13.429ff.   Λαιστρυγόνας: the man-
eating giants of *Od.* 10.81–132: it is not known who B. is referring to in this
guise.   τάχα που: apologizes for and softens the metaphor: LSJ τάχα II,
που II.   Σκύλληι: *Od.*2 12.73–100, 222–59. Od.'s Scylla only yelped like a

new-born puppy; later artists and poets (e.g. Ov. *Met.* 14.59–67) pictured her with dogs around or in place of her lower limbs. B.'s 'Scylla' is canine in character (i.e. bestial, unrestrained, offensive, perhaps with overtones of sexual rapacity); as with the 'Laestrygonians', it is not known who Basil means here. **ὑπῆρξε:** LSJ III. **ἄφυκτον:** 'hard to escape from' or more loosely 'murderous'. **διανήξασθαι κλύδωνα:** in this and what follows, M. is implicitly compared to the Od. of *Od.* 5.312–7.154, swept from his raft, washed ashore on Scherie, and making supplication to Nausicaa and her parents, Arete and Alcinous: we have moved on from Od.'s adventures with monsters to the next stage of his story. **αἰδεσθῆναι τὴν κοινὴν φύσιν:** not to be so cruel as to be unmoved by the suffering of a fellow human being. **σκευωρηθεῖσαν:** depicts M. as the victim of scheming and trumped-up charges. **προαίρεσιν:** in its moral philosophical sense, the 'deliberate choice' of action that reveals your character: LSJ 2 and 7. **ἐμπαροινήσαντος:** another emotive word, depicting M.'s enemy as behaving with a drunkard's reckless violence and disregard for proper conduct; both this word and the phrase σκευωρηθεῖσαν ἐπήρειαν before it perhaps continue the letter's Odyssean vein by evoking the last stage of Od.'s adventures, his struggle with the (scheming, swaggering, drunken) Suitors. **εἰ δὲ μή … ἀρκοῦσα:** concluding the appeal with the suggestion of a second-best response is clever; it offers the addressee the chance to do something even if he cannot or does not want to grant the main request, but at the same time it puts him under some moral pressure not to be ungenerous, by doing less when he could do more.

A V PRIVATE LETTERS: INSTRUCTION AND EXHORTATION

The association of the letter with friendship, and of friendship with straight speaking (*parrhesia*), candid advice and the shared pursuit of enlightened values, make the letter an appropriate vehicle for moral instruction and exhortation. This section illustrates the potential of the letter to develop into a kind of miniature, individualized sermon, among both pagan and Christian correspondents. Of the dozen letters it contains, one (35) is a 'real', first-order letter, while three (36–8) are fully fictionalized examples, in which instruction is gained by listening in to the advice supposedly given by one correspondent to the other, but in reality planned all along for the reader; the remainder fall at different points in the middle ground between these poles, as worked-up versions of first-order correspondence subsequently released to a general readership. Among the Christian letters we see correspondents writing both as private individuals, with their own personal authority, and as holders of official or semi-official authority within the hierarchy of the Church. Pagan and Christian writers alike share a hostility to vulgar materialism and a devotion to the value of self-restraint and self-discipline (i.e. to the ideology of mainstream *philosophia*), but with some interesting variations in emphasis and presentation. See also Introduction, 18–21, 23–6, 40–2.

32 Q. Horatius Flaccus, *Ep.* 1.12. Another poem from Book 1 of Horace's *Epistles* (cf. **23**, **29**), responding to a friend's grumbles by advising him to count his blessings and remember his devotion to the lifestyle and interests of a philosopher. In imitation of epistolary form (cf. **35** below), H. breaks off from his topic two-thirds of the way through in order to recommend another friend and to include news of recent military and political developments.

Bibliography. Kilpatrick (1986) 83–8.

1 Agrippae: M. Vipsanius Agrippa, Augustus' close ally and son-in-law. **Iccius** is known also as the addressee of *Odes* 1.29, written some five years earlier, in which he is jovially reproached for thinking of abandoning his philosophy books for the spoils of war. He is now manager (*procurator*) of Agrippa's Sicilian estates, and apparently still torn – to H.'s (?malicious) amusement – between philosophy and profit. **2 si recte:** *recte* (emphasized by the displacement of *si*) = both morally 'correctly' and 'rightfully' as a matter of legal entitlement. **non est ut:** *OLD sum* 7. **3 tolle:** *OLD* 14c. **4 usus:** *OLD* 4: I. has the legal right to use A.'s property while he is its manager; H. also hints in his use of *fructibus* and *frueris* in 1–2 that I. in fact enjoys the still greater privilege of *usufructus*, the right to receive profits from the estate. I. would be well enough off, H. means, even if he had less than he in fact does. **5–6** Health is preferable to wealth, a conventional reflection (cf. Solon, fr. 241–4 W.); the thought that wealth *adds* nothing may echo the Epicurean notion that, once a state of physical and mental comfort is attained, anything else can only vary your pleasure, not increase it (Epic. *Key Doctrines* 18 = 21 E L–S). **7–10** move into more overtly philosophical territory, first with the mention of an abstemious diet, then more decisively with the suggestion that I.'s abstemiousness (*if* actual) may reflect a Stoic's conviction that moral virtue is the one truly good aim.   **7 in medio positorum:** *OLD medium* 4a; the genitive with *abstemius* is poetic usage.   **7–8 herbis ... et urtica:** simple fare, when freely chosen, is a mark of sound (anti-materialist) moral values (as also in **23**.2 above; cf. N–H on *Odes* 1.31.15); the *et* is epexegetic ('explanatory'), as *urtica* is a particular kind of *herba*.   **9 Fortunae riuus:** the image of the river suggests both Fortune's abundance (rivers are inexhaustible, and never cease flowing from their sources – ἀέναος, 'ever-flowing', is a traditional epithet), and its instability (rivers never stand still, cf. Heraclitus, frr. 12, 49a, 91 D–K; Max. Tyr. 1.2). *inauret* perhaps glances at gold-bearing rivers like the Pactolus, in which Midas washed off his (unlucky) golden touch (Ov. *Met.* 11.127–45).   **10 nescit:** *OLD* 3.   **11 una uirtute:** it is the mark of the philosopher to attach special importance to moral virtue, and specifically of the Stoic to regard it as the *sole* human good; in *Odes* 1.29.14, I. is identified as a reader of the Stoic Panaetius.   **12–20** H. praises I. for his continuing philosophical commitment, but hints that he may not be living up to his own ideals (or may be concentrating too much on dubiously relevant natural science to the exclusion of ethics).   **12 Democriti:** the fifth-century atomist Democritus is here used in the role (played elsewhere by Thales and Anaxagoras) of the contemplative philosopher who neglects his worldly affairs in pursuit of wisdom (for the story, see Cic. *Fin.* 5.87 and Diog. Laert. 9.38–9); his other identity, as the inspirer of Epicurus' atomism, may also be relevant.   **13 peregre ... sine corpore:** mental travels, like those of the philosopher contemplating the nature of the world and its processes, are preferable to physical travels in search of a wealth that will never satisfy. This image of the contemplating soul goes back to Plato (*Tht.* 173e), and was widely used (Jones (1926)); H.'s application seems to have an ironic twist.   **15 nil:** internal limiting acc. w. *sapias* (*OLD sapio* 6b).   **sublimia**, archaic for 'lofty, elevated', refers specifically to phenomena of the heavens (Gk τὰ μετέωρα).   **16–20** contain a series of indirect questions, dependent on *cures*, clarifying *sublimia* with specific examples. Interest in natural phenomena (cf. Virg. *G.* 2.477–81, Prop. 3.5.25–38, Lucretius *DRN* and (a generation later) Sen. *NQ*) was meant to be not an end in itself, but a means either to better understanding of the divine rationality of the world (Stoics, Platonists) or to the expulsion of superstitious fear (Epicureans). But is I. being reminded of what the true philosopher is interested in, or teased with the lofty irrelevance of his tastes to a truly virtuous life?   **17 stellae ... errent**

plays on the Greek terminology (ἀστέρες) πλάνητες, 'wanderers, wan-
dering stars'.   **18 obscurum:**   predicative.   **lunae . . . orbem** is
object of both *premat* and *proferat*.   **19 uelit . . . possit:**   *OLD uolo* 17,
possum 8b.   **rerum concordia discors:**   the oxymoron may recall
either the opposition of Love and Strife in the universe of Empedocles, or
the tension of opposites in Heraclitus' (frr. 8, 10, 51).   **20 Empedoc.**
of Acragas (in Sicily, where I. is based) was regarded, along with Democ.,
as one of the greatest Presocratic natural scientists, and seems to have been
particularly admired by Roman intellectuals of the 1st centuries B.C. and
A.D. (Lucr. *DRN* 1.716–33, Cic. *ND* 1.217, the lost *Empedoclea* of Sallustius).
His other image, as a type of the mad philosopher, follows from his supposed leap into the crater of Aetna, in an attempt to be thought immortal
(Hor. *AP* 464–6).   **20 Stertinium . . . acumen** (with *Stertinium* as adj.
not n.) is high-style periphrasis (= 'clever S.'); the whole line is mockingly
grandiose. Stertinius, depicted in *Sat.* 2.3.33–295 sermonizing on the mad-
ness of ordinary ambitions and praised in 296 as an 'Eighth Sage', was
a prolific contemporary Stoic; in Stoic thought, all human beings were
mad (and bad) except the perfect (Stoic) sage. H.'s question ('which is the
real lunatic?') again has an ironic edge.   **21–4** turn via another piece
of gentle mockery to other, more down-to-earth and (it is suggested) substantial matters: recommendation of a potential friend, who himself has
the right moral outlook, and good news from the wider world.   **21 tru-
cidas:**   jokingly, as in the thought of Empedocles (like that of Pythagoras) the human soul can transmigrate into fish and even plants (fr. 117
D–K).   **22 Grospho:**   a Sicilan *eques*, dedicatee of *Odes* 2.16.   **24**
The agricultural-financial metaphor is chosen to allude to I.'s job as land-
agent; the thought goes back to Xenophon's Socrates (*Mem.* 2.10.4), but had
become proverbial (Otto p. 89). The reference to the corn price (*OLD annona*
4) also looks forward to the poem's end.   **25–9** make a final paragraph
of assorted news, in good epistolary style (cf. e.g. **6**), which also picks up
the theme of agricultural abundance and offers a final encouragement to
I.: Roman arms and farms are doing well, so he stands to benefit too. The
lines have the ring of an official bulletin, echoing the language of annalistic
history.   **25 ne tamen** mark a contrast with what precedes, but not a
strong one; *tamen* corresponds, as often, to Greek δέ.   **loco:**   *OLD* 22.
Romana . . . res is deliberately close to Ennius' *res . . . Romana* (e.g. fr. 156
Sk.).   **26–8** list successes in West and East, dating to 21–19 B.C., cried up
in the manner of official propaganda: Agrippa's completion of the conquest

of Spain, Tiberius' (diplomatic) success in putting the Romans' favoured candidate on the throne of Armenia, Augustus' recovery of the legionary standards lost by Crassus to the Parthians at Carrhae in 53 B.C. In spite of the glowing language, only one of them was a purely military achievement. **27 Prahates** is the correct contemporary spelling of the Parthian king's name (commonly 'Phraates'): N–H on *Odes* 2.2.17.   **28 genibus:** abl. of respect w. *minor*.   **28–9** give a final vision of agricultural plenty: another stock element in official histories and imperial propaganda, but here simultaneously a return to earlier topics in the letter, and a message to I. that he has every reason for contentment.   **29 Italiae:** dat. of advantage.   **pleno . . . Copia cornu:** for Plenty's horn (the Cornucopia), see *LIMC* III 1.304, Otto p. 441 and Sellar and Yeatman (1936) 1–4.

33–34 L. Annaeus Seneca, *Epp.* **38, 61.** Two of Seneca's *Epistulae Morales* (Introduction, 25–6), in the first of which he discusses the proper style and tone for effective moral teaching, and thus establishes the appropriateness of the letter as a vehicle for it. In the second, he constructs a small sermon on the need to train one's material desires and to cultivate a serene acceptance of one's destiny. In both cases – as with S.'s epistles in general – overt epistolary form is limited to the opening and closing salutations, plus (in **33**) allusion to a preceding letter from the other correspondent, and (in **34**) a reference to the act of writing; but **33** suggests the further thought that letters and moral advice are linked by the idea of informal, intimate conversation (letters being written conversation and conversational style the best for moral instruction; cf. **74** below); and **34** plays on the idea of the special resonance and authority of the last letter of a correspondent's life (cf. **14** above).

Bibliography. (**33**) Jordan (1990) 139–70. (**34**) Sharples (1996) 82–4, 100–13.

33.1 commercium: *OLD* 4, applicable equally well to letters and to conversation.   **frequentemus:** *OLD* 4b.   **plurimum . . . minutatim** points up a paradox: quantity and volume do not achieve the best results.   **sermo:** informal speech and style (*OLD* 2, 6b), as opposed to high-style oratory. It was above all Socrates (as reported, and in part created, by Plato and Xenophon) who had made conversational style available for moral philosophical teaching, aimed at the betterment of the listener's character (soul, *animo*). Debates over the merits of alternative styles were frequent, from Plato's *Gorgias* onwards (cf. e.g. Sen. *Epp.* 40 and 100, Epictetus 3.23, Philo of Larissa in Stob. *Ecl.* 2.6.2).

disputationes: formal speeches are inferior for the purpose because they are inflexible (*preparatae*), and do not allow the hearer to question them, answer back, or even stop to think; furthermore, they are not tailored to the specific needs of the individual, because intended for a large audience. The thinking here again goes back to Plato (*Gorgias* and *Phaedrus*).

bonum consilium: philosophy in the mainstream thinking of the Hellenistic and Imperial periods was not a purely academic discipline but the 'art of life', essential teaching with the highly practical aim of helping people to lead a morally good and fulfilled existence. The philosopher was thus a counsellor whose words could be relevant in any and every situation: cf. e.g. Cicero *Tusc.* 5.2, Plutarch *An seni* 26.796de, Max. Tyr. 1. **clare:** of sound, not sight (*OLD clarus* 1). **aliquando etc.:** S. is not alone in allowing some usefulness to a more strident form of teaching: cf. Philo of Larissa in Stob. *Ecl.* 2.6.2, Max. Tyr. 1.7–8, 25.7. **impellendus** plays on the standard Greek term for speeches of moral exhortation, λό-γοι προτρεπτικοί. **contionibus:** grand, formal oratory: *contio* is a technical term in Roman public language, for a mass meeting of the people, or a speech made at it. **facilius ... efficacibus:** repeats the thought of *plurimum ... familiaritatis* in order to round off the paragraph.

2 seminis: the image of sowing the seeds of (philosophical) teaching in the soul is another commonplace, once more going back to Plato (*Phdr.* 276b, *Resp.* 491e) and beyond (Antipho fr. 60 D–K, Hippoc. *Law* 3). For some other developments of it in the literature of the Imperial period, see Philo Jud. *Agric.* 7.17ff., Plutarch, *Vit. Pud.* 529d, Epictetus 4.8.34ff., Herodes Atticus in Gellius *NA* 19.12.7–10, and Max. Tyr. 5.8, 10.4 and 15.5; and compare also the imagery of sowing in the New Testament, esp. Mark 4: 4–20. S.'s version of the image puts more stress on the innate power of the teacher's words than on the need for any answering effort from the pupil. **exiguum:** S.'s emphasis on the small size of the seed hints at the perception of the letter as particularly suited for moral teaching in virtue of its small scale. **uires** 'power, potency', *OLD* 23b. **explicat ... auctus** (*OLD* 4, 'physical bulk') **... diffunditur** suggest the emergence of the first shoots from the seed and their steady growth into a mature plant. **ratio** 'reasoned teaching' (cf. *OLD* 7) = Greek λό-γος. **patet ... crescit ... conualescunt ... exsurgunt** continue the imagery of natural growth. **excepit:** *OLD* 5. **condicio:** *OLD* 8. **multum ... angusta:** again repeats the central thought, first expressed in *plurimum ... minutatim.* **rapiat ... in se trahat**

perhaps constitute a shade more of a suggestion than *excepit* that some active effort is required on the part of the pupil; so too the closing words of the letter point to the capacity of the mind to make its own progress once given some external stimulus (cf. Max. Tyr. 5.8 and 10.8).   **rapiat:** *OLD* 13–14.   **reddet:** *OLD* 15 ('yield'), a final touch of agricultural imagery.

34 A letter that weaves together two major themes in ancient philosophical preaching, the control of material desires and the right ideas about death. S. urges the distinctively Stoic perception that it is crucially important to cultivate an attitude of willing acceptance of whatever Fate (= God = the Universe) brings; only thus can a human being be truly free, both from resentment of death and from discontent with material circumstances. Also noteworthy is the way in which S. uses himself as an example for Lucilius' edification (cf. Hadot (1986)). This is good pedagogical technique (S. presents himself, encouragingly, as a model of the right kind of effort, rather than of securely achieved virtue); at the same time, it is a flattering piece of self-characterization, setting S. in the great tradition of philosophical heroes. See further Introduction, 25–6, and above on **33–34**.

1 uoluimus uelle . . . uelim . . . uolui: the repetition of different parts of the verb (a form of polyptoton) establishes the right kind of desiring as a major topic of the letter.   **senex . . . puer:** the antithesis contains an implicit exhortation to Lucilius too to 'grow up'; for the thought, compare *Ep.* 27.2.   **ueteribus:** *OLD* 3b. S. both claims the credit for trying so single-mindedly to eradicate his failings and admits that, even at his age, the task is not yet completed.   **instar totius uitae dies** both reinforces the point about control of desire and prepares for the introduction of the topic of death.   **uel** (*OLD* 5) strengthens the sense of unquantifiable possibility.   **2 hoc animo . . . euocatura** focuses the general thought (that the good person is ready for death at any time) on the specific circumstances of the moment; by implication, it also raises the possibility that this very letter might never have been completed, and only ever read (if at all) as a half-finished fragment from the writer's desk (for which cf. 'Diogenes' in *Epistle* 22). The letter is thus presented as potentially S.'s last: the final declaration, and proof of his devotion to philosophical values to the end (for which cf. **14** above, Chion of Heraclea's last letter).   **exire:**

death is easily imaged (or euphemized) as a departure (*OLD exeo* 7, cf. *exitus*); if a specific image is in question, it could be either that of the actor leaving the stage (cf. Aurelius 12.36, w. Curtius (1953) 138), or that of the guest leaving the party (cf. Bion fr. 16 Hense, Lucr. *DRN* 3.938, Hor. *Sat.* 1.1.118–9, *Ep.* 2.2.214).   **pendeo:** *OLD* 12, cf. Eng. 'suspense'. **autem:** *OLD* 4b.   **libenter:** the emphatic word, making the central point that is expanded and explained in what follows (the antithesis of *uolenti* and *libens* with *repugnanti, seruitutis, nolit* and *inuitus* is marked). **3 repugnanti . . . uolenti:** the contrast is central to Stoic ethics: compare S.'s *ducunt uolentem fata, nolentem trahunt* in *Ep.* 107.11, where he is adapting Cleanthes *SVF* i.527, and the image of the dog tied to the cart, which has the choice only of following placidly or being dragged (*SVF* ii.975). **res:** *OLD* 17. Events will take their destined course whatever we think; it is up to us to adapt our attitude to suit them, not *vice versa*.   **4 ad mortem . . . praeparandi:** the idea that the good life (the life of philosophy) is above all a preparation for death is differently developed by different thinkers, from Plato *Phaedo* 67d onwards (cf. Rutherford (1989) 18, with n. 52). In S.'s Stoic version, the point is not that death paves the way to a better existence, but that life cannot be lived well in the here-and-now unless one's attitude to death is right.   **satis . . . sumus:** a carefully composed sentence, with the etymological echo between *instructa* and *instrumenta*, and the enclosing contrast of *satis* and *auidi sumus*.   **et semper uidebitur:** emphatic – material desires are *intrinsically* insatiable, so no true happiness is to be gained from the attempt to gratify them (cf. Plato, *Grg.* 492e–494e, Max. Tyr. 1.5, Oltramare (1926) 288); contentment follows from an attitude of mind (*animus*), not material abundance.   **erat:** the imperfect makes S.'s declaration of his own contentment still firmer: he has not just recently achieved a satisfying length of life, but had already done so long ago (because chronological length is not the point).   **plenus** again evokes the image of the satisfied dinner-guest (cf. on *exire* above).   **uale:** the standard formula is given an extra charge by the reference to death immediately preceding it, and once again raises the thought that this may be S.'s last.

35 Aquila, *P.Oxy.* 3069. A private letter on papyrus (100 × 222 mm), dating from the 3rd or early 4th century A.D. One Aquila writes to his friend Sarapion, congratulating him on his devotion to philosophical self-discipline and urging him to keep up the good work. The naming of a third like-minded individual, Kallinikos, begins to suggest something of an intellectual circle, as also does the careful style and refined vocabulary employed (in contrast to the less-refined style of e.g. **46**); compare **56** below. Aquila's high tone falters however in the last sentence, with the intrusion of more mundane domestic detail – a nice reminder that the writers of papyrus letters seldom stick to a single point per letter, even in the most solemn circumstances.

Hand and orthography. Although there is only one mark of punctuation (a rough breathing on ὁ), the hand is a careful one ('almost literary' says the first editor). In his spelling, A. twice makes the phonetic substitution of -ει- for -ι-, twice writes then crosses out a nu he judges superfluous, and spells ἔρρωσο with two double consonants instead of one; mute final iota is twice omitted and once written adscript.

Bibliography. Oxyrhynchus Papyri 42 (1974) 161–3 (P. J. Parsons).

Ἀκύλας: the standard Greek transliteration of the Roman *nomen* Aquila; of the other two men's names, one is pure Greek, while the other (Sarapion) is distinctively Greco-Egyptian (Sarapis being a Hellenized version of an Egyptian divinity whose cult was particularly developed by the Ptolemies, cf. *OCD*[3] s.v. and **67** below). The woman's name, Soteris, is also purely Greek (attested in, e.g., 4th-century Athenian inscriptions). For the mixture of derivations, cf. **5** above.   **ἥσθην** is a true past, rather than the so-called 'dramatic' aorist (Smyth §1937), but the use of this irregular principal part is still a sign of educated diction.   **ἥ (= ὡς) μάλιστα:** strengthened superlative (Smyth §1086), another token of the writer's educated style, as also is the attraction of the relative **ἧς** (Goodwin §1031 ff.).   **καὶ ἐν ... πράγμασιν:** it is not clear whether this is best taken with ποιῆ or with ἀφιστάμενος; in either case, the repetition of μάλιστα is stylistically awkward.   **ἀσκήσεως:** the deliberate, principled avoidance of superfluous luxury and exercise of self-control (cf. LSJ III, but the article is not a good one; see also *PGL* s.v. 3–5 and 9, *RAC* I 749–58): the philosopher keeps 'in training' by making sure that he puts his theoretical beliefs about what is and isn't valuable conscientiously into practice in his daily life.   **μή:** standard later Greek usage, in place of classical οὐ (Schmid I.145).   **ἐξαγόμεθα ὑφ' ἑαυτῶν:** i.e. by our wayward material desires.   **ἀνδραγάθει:** ἀνδραγαθία = manly virtue, manliness, however that is to be understood in specific cases – here, as adherence to the difficult values of philosophy. This form of the verb (as opp. to ἀνδραγαθίζομαι) is Hellenistic/Imperial rather than classical.   ἢ πλοῦτος ἢ ὥρα: money and sex (lit. 'youthful beauty', LSJ B.II), standardly understood as two of the most seductive distractions from the life of moral virtue. οὐδὲν … παρούσης: an echo of the formal philosophical doctrine (most closely associated with the Stoics) that conventional 'goods' have no value in themselves (L–S §58). φροῦδα: high-style diction, familiar from Atticizing writers (recommended in Moeris' Atticist lexicon, 211.26 Bekker), but not found in the NT, or elsewhere in non-literary papyri. ἐν … 'Αντινόου: sc. πόλει, the city founded by Hadrian in A.D. 130 in memory of the boyfriend drowned in the Nile. At around the time this letter was written, it became the capital of the region of Egypt known as the Thebaid.   τὸ σκυλάκιον: a nice epistolary change of topic, with (presumably unintended) bathos; cf. 6, 32, 43.   αὐτή: it is not clear whether this refers to Soteris, and means 'by herself' (LSJ I.3), or to an un-named further party, 'she herself' = 'the mistress of the household' (LSJ I.1). ἔρρωσσο … ἔρρωσσο: the repetition seeks to add warmth to the (rel-atively brief) closing formula.   φιλοσόφωι may acknowledge formal status enjoyed by S. (in the first and second centuries A.D., at least, philoso-phers could claim tax exemption, ateleia, cf. Millar (1977) 491–506), or it may be a simple compliment carrying no such official implications. φιλόσοφος on the papyri and in inscriptions seems sometimes to be used to mean 'man of culture' rather than strictly 'philosopher': see Preisigke (1925–31) s.v.

36 Diogenes, *Ep.* 6. A letter purporting to come from the fourth-century founder of Cynicism. Diogenes (*c.* 410–*c.* 321) writes to his friend and pupil Krates (*c.* 365–*c.* 285) with news of an edifying encounter. The episode he describes is a famous instance of his quest for the simplest, most self-sufficient lifestyle attainable (cf. e.g. Diog. Laert. 6.37), and was frequently depicted in Classicizing art of the 16th–19th centuries. See also Introduc-tion, 29–30.

1 χωρισθέντος: LSJ IV, a post-classical usage.   ἀνέβαινον ἐκ Πειραιῶς … Πάνοπος κρήνην: D. is here made to speak in tones bor-rowed from the Socrates of Plato's dialogues, echoing the narrative in-troductions of both *Lysis* (203a) and *Resp.* (327a, with a reversal of direction). Panops was supposedly an Athenian hero, commemorated near a postern gate in the city wall.   ὑπό: LSJ C.III.2.   πήρας: along with the staff (βακτήριον), the standard 'uniform' of the Cynic,

symbolizing his austere and self-sufficient style of life: cf. Diog. Laert. 6.22, Lucian *Vit. auct.* 9, *Pisc.* 1 and 45, Max. Tyr. 1.10, Branham and Goulet-Cazé (1996) 26–7.   **τῶν ... ἐργαζομένων:** partitive not possessive gen.   **κοίλας:** predicative.   **δόξαν:** acc. absol. of impersonal vb. **οὐκ ἡιδέσθην:** ἀναίδεια, shamelessness, was another mark of Cynic lifestyle (Dudley (1937) 29–31, Branham and Goulet-Caze (1996) 35), but normally referred to rather more outrageous behaviour than that D. is made to attribute to himself here.   **2 καὶ σοί:** constr. with ἐπέσταλκα. **οὐδὲν ... ἐπίστασθαι:** D.'s declared motivation for writing is also a token of the proper attitude for a teacher towards his pupil and friend, with whom he shares the quest for the good life. The reader is thus edified not only by the content of D.'s message (which is being shared with her/him as well as with Krates), but also its spirit.   **πειρῶ ... ἐμβάλλειν:** odd advice for one Cynic to give another, given that Cynics were so famous for living their lives in public; this looks like a lapse of imagination/characterization on the part of the author of the letter, betraying his own un-Cynic sense of respectability. πειρῶ is something like formulaic in this kind of horta-tory message: cf. **37** and **38** below. ἐμβάλλειν is used intransitively (LSJ II.1.b).   **τῶν κατὰ μέρος:** presumably neuter rather than masculine ('from separate individuals'); D. seems to be contrasting sporadic, piecemeal encounters in daily life with some notional educational experience in which one might learn the whole truth about the good life all at once.   **φύσις:** another catchword of Cynic (and other Hellenistic) moral philosophy. The good life *is* the life according to Nature (whatever it is that, according to the different schools of thought, Nature exemplifies and recommends): see (e.g.) Cic. *Fin.* 3. 62–8, Sen. *Ep.* 5.4, Long (1986) 179–84, Branham and Goulet-Cazé (1996) 28–45.   **δόξης:** *mistaken* human opinion, at vari-ance with the truth about life and the world (a usage going back to Plato, e.g. *Resp.* 475e ff.).   **ἐπὶ σωτηρίαι ... κατάγομεν:** the idea of philos-ophy as the saviour of mankind (from vicious living and the spiritual and material disaster supposed to follow from it) was the common property of all philosophical sects in the Hellenistic and Imperial periods: cf. e.g. Lucr. *DRN* 1.62–79, 3.1–30, Cic. *TD* 5.1–5, Max. Tyr. 1.2–3. ἐκβαλλομένην and κατάγομεν personify Nature as an exile, needing to be restored to her rightful home and status; cf. Hor. *Ep.* 1.10.24 and Otto s.v. *natura*.

37 Krates, *Ep.* 30. A letter purportedly from Krates to his wife and fellow-Cynic, Hipparchia (Diog. Laert. 6.96–8, Dudley (1937) 49–52). As in the preceding letter, the lesson K. here attempts to teach H. about the simple life is also a lesson to the reader; but at the same time, the letter is a small-scale dramatic re-creation of an early stage in a famously unconventional marriage, and stands in deliberate contrast to the normal style in which gifts of clothing and the like are described and acknowledged in everyday correspondence (cf. e.g. Terentianus in **5** *init*.).

Bibliography. Rosenmeyer (2001) 221–4.

ἐξωμίδα: a kind of tunic that leaves one shoulder bare – a poor man's garment, so in theory appropriate for a Cynic (cf. Sext. Emp. *Pyrrh.* 1.153), but even this seems to be too luxurious for the K. of this letter.   **καρτερίαι:** another Cynic watchword.   **εὖ γε ποιεῖς:** εὖ γε (εὖγε) is the Greek for 'bravo!' (e.g. Ar. *Clouds* 757).   **[αὐτή]** is probably a scribal error, mistakenly anticipating the **αὐτή** before **ὠρέχθης**, so should not be translated. **πειρῶ:** see n. on **36**.

38 Phalaris, *Ep.* 37. Another letter from the tyrant of Acragas (cf. **11, 12, 25** above), in which he responds to a friend's attempts at salutary advice with a noble and edifying re-assertion of his principled acceptance of his destiny. The sentiments are similar to Seneca's in **34**, but not presented in such overtly Stoic terms. The situation of the letter – a tyrant responds to advice from a friend – recalls such famous episodes from Herodotus as the correspondence of Polycrates and Amasis (3.39–43). The reader is left to speculate how specific or general the friend's exhortation was, and how closely related P.'s status as a (possibly hated) ruler.

1 Γοργίαι: a good archaic/classical Sicilian/S. Italian name: cf. not only the Sophist G., but also the G. for whom the lyric poet Ibycus wrote (*PMG* 289 + s226).   **νυνὶ μάλιστα:** either a reference to P.'s advanced years (cf. **25**), or a deliberately opaque reference, to tantalize the reader with the correspondents' possession of contextual knowledge that s/he lacks.   **εἴ τις … φυλάξασθαι:** both the possibility of prediction and its moral and practical implications were hotly debated in Hellenistic and later philosophy: the issues as they had crystallized by the 1st century B.C. are summarized in Cic. *De diuinatione*, while Lucian's *Charon* and *Juppiter confutatus* show that they were familiar enough to have become material for satire by the 2nd century A.D.   **2 ἐγὼ μέν:** μέν *solitarium* (Denniston 380–4); the answering δέ-clause (what anyone else may think) remains implicit.   **τοὺς**

λεγομένους . . . 'Ραδάμανθυν: the canonical trio (cf. e.g. Lucian *Phal* 1.7), first named together in surviving lit. as Underworld judges by Plato (*Ap.* 41a, *Grg.* 523e–524a).   οὔτε ἀθανάτους . . . εἱμαρμένην: the classics of mythology enshrined two contrasting perceptions: that all die, even the greatest of heroes (*Il.* 18.115–21), and that the greatest of heroes are allowed to cheat death (*Od.* 4.561–9, Hes. *WD* 156–73). It is up to the individual writer to choose which one suits his argument of the moment; the former is well-known as a *topos* of consolation literature (e.g. Lucret. 3.1024–52). πειρῶ: see n. on **36**.

39 The Elder (2 John). A letter from a Christian elder to a church (or churches), lightly disguised as a private letter to an individual. It is possible that it is meant as an open, circular letter rather than as a strictly occasional piece for just one incident in a particular church. The three NT letters of John, like John's Gospel, spring from and relate to a group of Christian communities of the late 1st century A.D., perhaps centred on Ephesus, which they show to have been experiencing severe problems over doctrine and authority. In this one the writer appeals for adherence to true Christian teaching (in the local 'orthodox' version, as also enshrined in John's Gospel and 1 John) and for resistance to the falsehoods of dissenters. The fact that it has been accepted into the NT canon implicitly endorses the writer's view of himself as the preserver of the truth against error; but it can legitimately be seen instead an attempt by just one party to an as-yet unsettled argument to secure the victory of *his* version of right doctrine over the competition.

Language and style. The writer uses standard colloquial Greek of the Imperial period, with heavy Christian colouring in his vocabulary and (perhaps) some Hebraism. See in general Horrocks (1997) 91–5. *Bibliography*. Smalley (1984) xxii–xxv, xxxii, 313–37 (devout); Lieu (1986) 5–100, 125–65 (scholarly); Chadwick (1967) ch. 2.

1 ὁ πρεσβύτερος: the writer identifies himself and his addressee not by name but by title/description. This may be (*a*) because that was how he was generally known; (*b*) for reasons of security, to avoid trouble with pagan authority; (*c*) to underline the fact that this is not a personal but a collective pastoral communication; or (*d*) for all of these reasons. πρεσβύτερος in early Christian Greek may possibly indicate a formal rank (*ODC*[3] s.v. 'Presbyter'), but can also refer unhierarchically to age and personal authority; the latter is more likely here.   **ἐκλεκτῆι κυρίαι:**   from the body of the letter, it becomes clear that the 'lady' is a Christian community (a local church) and her 'offspring' its congregation; ἐκλεκτῆι = 'chosen' in the Christian sense, by God (but the writer may be thinking in still more strongly exclusive, partisan terms, of his sect as elect even among soi-disant Christians).   **οὖς ἐγώ… 3 ἀγάπηι:** the extension of the specification of the addressee, and the salutation that follows, are distinctively Christian, differing from contemporary non-Christian formulae (Exler 24–60, 103–12; cf. **3–5, 15, 35**) both in length and in vocabulary and thought; for a teacher's view of such elaboration, see 'Libanius' in **76**.51.   **ἀγαπῶ:** a key word for Christian teaching in general and for the message of this letter in particular.   **ἐν ἀληθείαι:** here simply = 'really, truly', but paves the way for the more loaded insistence on (Johannine Christian) truth in what follows.   **2 τὴν μένουσαν…καὶ μεθ᾽ ἡμῶν ἔσται:** the anacoluthon (strict sequence would demand ἐσομένην) may reflect Hebrew phraseology; but similar anacolutha are not unknown in classical Gk (K–G II §490.4).   **3 ἔσται…ἀγάπηι:** the formula echoes and expands the standard greeting from Paul's epistles (the 'Pauline salutation'), but substitutes a confidently predictive future for his normally verbless wish. This can be seen as a Christian counterpart to the wishes for good health conventionally found at this point in a pagan letter (Exler 103–12; cf. **3–5**).   **4 ἐχάρην λίαν** also conforms to standard epistolary practice – reaction to news recently received (by letter or otherwise) from or about the other party to the correspondence (cf. **35**).   **περιπατοῦντας:** lit 'walking about'; here 'living' (Arndt-Gingrich 2a).   **5 καὶ νῦν** marks the transition from generalities and/or subsidiary matter to the main point of the letter.   **οὐχ ὡς…ἀπ᾽ ἀρχῆς:** the writer insists that, unlike the deviants he is about to mention, he is merely recalling his addressees to the simple truth as first revealed. ἀπ᾽ ἀρχῆς may refer either to the beginning of Christian teaching with Christ, or to the first preaching of his message to this community.   **ἵνα:** as often in later Gk, ἵνα + subj. here has no final sense, but stands for what in classical usage would be an infinitive construction; ἐρωτῶ in the sense of 'request' (= αἰτέω) is also post-classical usage, LSJ III.   **ἀγαπῶμεν ἀλλήλους:** the central Christian injunction. However, in the Johannine version used here (cf. John 13:34, 15:12, 17), as opposed to that of the Synoptic Gospels (Matth. 22:39, Mark 12:31, Luke 10:27), it enjoins loving solidarity *within* the group of true believers, rather than a universal love.   **6 ἐν αὐτῆι:** sc. ἀγάπηι rather than ἐντολῆι.   **7 ὅτι** instead of γάρ is post-classical usage.   **πλάνοι:** LSJ III (cf. 1.1),

but commoner as a noun in Christian than in pagan writing.   ἐξῆλθον
εἰς τὸν κόσμον: the words indicate propagandizing (missionary) activity
on the part of these 'deceivers'.   ἐρχόμενον ἐν σαρκί: the use of the
present part. is noticeable (*not* 'who *came* . . .'); tense and word-order seem
chosen so as to give a general characterization of Christ as the writer wants
this community to understand him, rather than a pointed reference either
to the historical fact or the doctrinal truth of the Incarnation.   οὗτός
ἐστιν ὁ κτλ: i.e. '*this* is what we mean when we talk of . . .' – the writer
refers to ideas he knows his addressees are familiar with, but may be in doubt
how to apply to present circumstances.   ἀντίχριστος: the word may
have been invented in the milieu from which this letter comes (it appears
in NT only in 1 and 2 John), but the idea was more widespread (and the
word was to enjoy a very successful career subsequently). The prefix ἀντι-
seems to indicate both one *opposed to* Christ and one seen as a (false) *substitute*
Christ. In early Christian thinking, the appearance of (an) antichrist(s) had
strong eschatological implications (cf. esp. 1 John 2:18ff. and 4:1f.).   **8**
εἰργασάμεθα . . . μισθόν: heavenly reward for the hard toil of Christian
faith and life; the economic imagery is familiar from elsewhere in NT (e.g.
Matth. 20:18) and the message 'don't throw it all away *now*' increases the
sense of eschatological urgency.   **9** ὁ προάγων: to be taken closely
with μὴ μένων, 'not remaining, but leading on' (with the implication that
such people urge others to follow their lead rather than acting purely for
themselves).   **10** εἴ τις ἔρχεται: suggests 'missionaries' coming from
some distance, rather than locals.   οἰκίαν may refer to local 'house
churches' rather than to purely private dwellings.   **12** πολλὰ ἔχων
κτλ begins the letter's closing movement. The epistolary *praeteritio* (**3**, **7**),
the contrast between written and (superior) spoken contact (**10**.29–30, **41**),
the anticipation of a meeting in the near future (**7**, **9**), the self-reflexive reference to the letter in terms of its physical materials (**10**.30), and the transmission of greetings from a third party (**5**), are all familiar elements from
ancient epistolography in general.   γενέσθαι πρὸς ὑμᾶς: γενέσθαι
εἰς + acc. is attested in classical Gk (Hdt. 5.38), but γενέσθαι πρός seems to
be Hellenistic usage.   στόμα πρὸς στόμα: lit. 'mouth to mouth', a
phrase influenced by Hebrew usage (Jer. 39.4).   τὰ τέκνα τῆς ἀδελφῆς:
if the κυρία and her children are a church and its congregation, then her
sister and her children will be another (? that with which the writer is more
immediately connected). The letter thus ends not with a personal note but
with an affirmation of a more general (Johannine) Christian solidarity.

40 Basileios, _Ep._ 10. A short letter from St Basil to a potential convert to Christianity, simultaneously both describing and attempting to enact the process of conversion. The elegant style and the self-conscious beauty of the image round which the letter is built depict (and flatter) the recipient as herself a woman of culture as well as high social status (and a very desirable catch for the Church).

τέχνη … θηρευτική: there is perhaps a gentle joke in applying such language, with its air of formal (even philosophical) definition, to a bird-catcher's trick; for the use of decoys in ancient bird-catching in general, see Pollard (1977) 104–9 (but without mention of this particular device). Basil's ornithological imagery has a special appropriateness for a Christian author, given the prominence of birds (and especially doves) as symbols in Christian art and writing (e.g. Mark 1:10, Matth. 10:16, Gen. 8.11; cf. _ODC_[3] and _Oxford Companion to Art_ s.v. 'Dove'). **Διονύσιον … Διομήδην:** the change took place on baptism; 'Dionysius' was a name borne by several distinguished early Christians, starting with the Areopagite, St Paul's Athenian convert (Acts 17:34). **τὰς τῆς ψυχῆς αὐτοῦ πτέρυγας:** B.'s choice of imagery allows him to work in a fleeting allusion to the famous image of the soul's wings from Plato's _Phaedrus_ (246d ff., cf. Trapp (1990) 148–55). By 'the perfume of God' B. means, principally, the signs of divine love and goodness now visible in the converted Dionysius' character; but one might detect also a secondary reference to his own evangelism (including this elegant letter), in which case the imagery will also recall the honeyed medicine-cup of pagan philosophical teaching (most famously, Lucret. 1.936ff.). **τὴν σὴν σεμνοπρέπειαν:** the use of abstract n. + possessive adj. as an honorific and form of address (familiar also in archaic/formal English) is a feature of later Greek and Latin style: see for this instance _PGL_ σεμνοπρέπεια 2, and more generally Zilliacus (1949), Dineen (1929) and O'Brien (1930). **ὥστε:** final rather than consecutive force: Smyth §2267, Goodwin §1452. **ὁ προειρημένος:** clumsy, given that the referent, D., has already appeared in the sentence by name, as well as in the pronoun αὐτῶι. **ὑψηλόν:** spiritually exalted (though the word fits the ornithological image too): _PGL_ 2. **μεταθεμένη:** often used for conversion in Christian writing: _PGL_ 3. **πολλῶν … ἀποπληρῶσαι:** a rather contorted way of expressing the value B. places on success in this particular conversion. προσώπων seems here to have its sense of 'person(ality)' (LSJ IV, *PGL* VIII), but with a suggestion also of the meaning 'character, role' (LSJ III.2, *PGL* V.C). B. is saying, hyperbolically, that he would need himself to lead a whole *series* of holy lives properly to thank God for his goodness in bringing about this conversion. The ideas of indebtedness and proper repayment come up also in the next letter (**41**).

41 Basileios, *Ep.* **26.** Another, longer letter from St Basil to a private individual. Taking his cue from a recent narrow escape from death (in the Nicaea earthquake of 11 October 368), B. exhorts his addressee to a renewed and intensified fidelity to Christian principle. The tone is once more respectful, but – perhaps because the addressee is a politically important male – without the ingratiating charm of the previous letter.

Καισαρίωι = *PLRE* I Caesarius 2: younger brother of Basil's lifelong friend Gregory of Nazianzos, commemorated in Gregory's *Or.* 7; initially distinguished as a doctor, he now enjoyed high office (perhaps as *comes thesaurorum*, Imperial Treasurer) in Bithynia; although he survived the earthquake referred to here, he died in office soon afterwards.   **χάρις τῶι Θεῶι:**   though it strikes a distinctively Christian note straight away (perhaps obliquely echoing the use of χάρις in the salutations of NT epistles, cf. **39**), this opening also conforms to older formulae, coming as it does at the point conventional for expressions of pleasure at good news recently received and/or wishes for the recipient's health (cf. **3–5** and **35** above). It perhaps also preserves a ghostly echo of the conventional χαίρειν omitted from the first sentence.   **θαυμάσια:**   a keynote of B.'s message (cf. παράδοξα, θαύμασι below): it is the *miraculousness* of C.'s escape that demands the kind of response B. urges on him.   **τῶι... προσήκουσι:** the article + participle clause, equivalent in function to a relative clause and specifying the grounds on which thanks are due, has something of the feel of prayer- and hymn-formula about it (cf. e.g. *Il.* 1.37–8, Alcaeus, frr. 34.5–8, 308 *PMG*); this continues in the next sentence in B.'s adaptation of the encomiastic commonplace that great deeds demand celebration and commemoration (cf. e.g. Plato, *Menex.* 236de, Xen. *Ages.* 1.1, [Dem.] *Epitaph.* (60) 1, Catull. 68.41 –4; B.'s choice of the verb ἀνυμνεῖν is significant), and may even be there already in an echo of hymnic χαῖρε (e.g. Alcaeus 308.1) in the opening χάρις.   **ἐπιδεικνυμένωι:**   B.'s choice of words (cf. ὀφθῆναι, διαγγέλλειν, ἀνυμνεῖν) emphasizes that C.'s escape is, or should be, a lesson to the world at large (if only the right people accept the responsibility for making it known). There is an element of reflexivity here: B.'s letter enacts its own advice, since it is itself a means of making God's goodness to C. more widely known.　**ἡμᾶς:**　from here on B. slides cleverly between the encouraging, inclusive 'we', and the more challenging 'you' that puts C. himself on the spot.　**καὶ μὴ λόγωι** introduces B.'s second and more important point *via* the time-honoured antithesis of word and deed: true gratitude demands action (in the form of *moral* improvement) as well as mere verbal expressions of thanks.　**δουλεύειν . . . φόβον . . . εἰς τὸ τέλειον προκόπτοντα:**　the third element here echoes pagan (specifically Stoic) moral philosophical terminology (LSJ προκόπτω II.3), but the first two strike a distinctively Christian note.　**φρόνιμοι οἰκόνομοι . . . ἐταμιεύσατο:** this 'economic' imagery (familiar also from much subsequent Christian writing) echoes that of the Gospels (esp. Luke 12:42; cf. *PGL* οἰκόνομος A.1). **ἐταμιεύσατο:**　LSJ II.4.　**παραστῆσαι . . . ζῶντας:**　a quotation from *Romans* 6:13; in a familiar rhetorical manoeuvre, B. suggests that a well-known general exhortation has particular force in present circumstances.　**τῶν πυλῶν τοῦ θανάτου:**　the image goes back to Homer's Ἀΐδαο πύλαι (*Il.* 5.646, etc.) and beyond, first appearing in Christian writing in Matth. 16:18.　**πάντως . . . μεταπτώσεις:**　B. produces his own variant of one of the oldest and most often repeated of Greek moral reflections: see the quotations assembled in [Plut.], *Consolatio ad Apollonium* 103b ff. It is intriguing that a famous early instance, Simonides fr. 521 (quoted by Stobaeus and in the Homeric scholia, and imitated by Horace), also relates to death in an earthquake.　**ἐπιμέλεσθαι** denotes care for one's moral character, rather than physical well-being or material circumstances. This loaded sense of the verb goes back to Plato's Socrates (e.g. *Phaedo* 115b; cf. Nehamas (1998) 157–68); B.'s use of it implicitly claims Christianity as a continuation and improvement of classical philosophy (cf. n. on **48**.1 below).　**ταῦτα . . . τελειότητά σου:**　B. sums up on a calculatedly tentative and deferential note (ἀπεθάρσησα), casting himself as the concerned and responsible adviser who is worried that he may offend, but is none the less convinced that he must speak out.　**τὴν τελειότητα:**　see n. on τὴν σὴν σεμνοπρέπειαν in **40**.　**σὸν . . . σύνηθες:**　further persuasive flattery, indicating to C. the response desired and assuring him that it accords with his natural and established standards of behaviour.　**ὡς καὶ ἐν ταῖς κατ' ὀφθαλμοὺς ὁμιλίαις:** the familiar comparison/contrast between face-to-face and written communication, in its standard position at the end of the letter: cf. **10** and **39** above.

42 Eusebius Hieronymus, *Ep*. 23. A letter from St Jerome (Introduction, 20) to the widow Marcella, one of a circle of aristocratic ladies to whom he served as spiritual guide and teacher of scripture during his residence in Rome in A.D. 382–5 (cf. Kelly (1975) 91–103). Using a (very) recent event as his cue, J. constructs a letter of consolation (cf. the following section) which is also a sermon on the superiority of spiritual over worldly values; central to its rhetorical structure is a comparison (*synkrisis, comparatio*) that combines eulogy of a recently deceased Christian with invective against a recently deceased pagan. Rhetorical polish is evident also in the attention given to rhythm: e.g. in the double cretic ($-\smile--\smile-$) clausulae (*ex*)*isse de corpore*, (*doce*)*amus in tartaro*, *quanta mutatio*, *cernit inquirere*; cf. Scourfield (1993) 233–42.

1 cum hora ferme tertia: the opening greeting (like the closing salutation) which presumably originally framed the letter, has been removed from the published version; that J. had a wider readership in mind from the start is suggested by the careful scene-setting, which goes into more detail than the recipient herself will have needed; cf. Scourfield (1993) 13–14. Tierce, the third hour, roughly = 9 a.m.; ancient time-reckoning divided day and night into twelve hours each, the length of one daylight or night-time hour (and its correlation to the modern 12–/24–hour clock) varying from one part of the year to another.   **psalmum . . . legere coepissemus . . . docere cogeremur** remind us not only of J.'s authority and role among his Roman circle, but of his distinction as translator and expounder of scripture in general. At the time of writing he had just completed his revisions of the Old Latin versions of both Psalms and Gospels: *ODC*[3] s.v. 'Old Latin Versions', Kelly (1975) 86–9 (cf. 157–9). In context, the point of going over this textual detail is to remind Marcella of her own access to the eternal truths by which Lea lived, and which contrast so strongly with the false values espoused by Praetextatus and his wife.   **secundi libri . . . tertii:**   the date of this division into five 'books' is not known. **defecerunt . . . Iesse:**   Ps 71:20; the final version of J.'s Vulgate translation (reflecting his subsequent use of the Hebrew original as opposed to the Greek Septuagint) reads '*laudes*' not '*hymni*'. But it seems that in any case J. tended, throughout his life, to quote scripture as often from the Old Latin versions, on which he had been brought up, as in his own renderings: Scourfield (1993) 10–11.   **Dauid . . . Iesse . . . Asaph:**   genitives; most Hebrew names in Greek and Latin translation do not decline.

dicebam ... praeuaricatus sum: Ps. 72:15.   **Latinis codi-cibus:**   the various Old Latin versions consulted for the first edition of his Vulgate.   **expressum:**   *OLD* exprimo 7.   **Leam:**   another high-born widow of Marcella's and J.'s circle, who had withdrawn from the world on her husband's death.   **ut uere ... erumpat:**   M. went *deathly* pale. With J.'s *uas testaceum* here, commentators regularly compare Paul's '*thesaurum in uasis fictilibus*' in 2 Cor. 4:7 (contrasting the splendour of the Gospel with the dowdiness of its human propagators), but it is better compared to pagan philosophical imagery contrasting the precious soul with its worthless bodily container: Philo *Spec. leg.* 1.215, *Post Cain.* 163–4, Aurelius 10.38, Cic. *Tusc.* 1.22.52, Dio Chrys. 12.59, Lucret. 3.440–3, 554–7.   **fabulis:**   *OLD* 1 a.   **2 multum ... modum:** Paul, Rom. 3:2.   **primum quod ... in tartaro:**   a carefully balanced trio of clauses, with two long units, contrasting in sense (*prosequenda, calcato diabolo, coronam securitatis* vs *detrahentes, in tartaro*), arranged around a shorter central element. The contrast between the first and third elements paves the way for the comparison between Lea and the consul designate that fills the second half of the letter.   **calcato diabolo:**   for the image, cf. Lucret. 1.78, Paul, Rom. 16:20.   **coronam ... securitatis:**   the victor's crown, here consisting of eternal salvation, 'won' by victory over the Devil and his works; the image is again familiar from both pagan and Christian writing: Lucret. 1.929, Max. Tyr. 1.6, *Tabula Cebetis* 21–2, James 1:2, 1 Peter 5:4; *PGL* στέφανος 3a, στεφανόω 3.   **designatum consulem:**   Vettius Agorius Praetextatus (*PLRE* 1.722–4), scholar, leading light of the 'pagan resistance' of the later 4th century, host to the discussion in Macrobius' *Saturnalia*, Praetorian Prefect of Italy, and consul elect in 384.   **saeculis**, if correct, must be taken in a version of its Christian sense, 'worldliness, (position of) worldly power' (cf. the instances of the word later in the letter), but the usage is odd and emendation may be called for; *sacculis*, 'moneybags', has been suggested, but is not very convincing.   **totam ... conuersam** punningly picks up the preceding *conuersationem*, as if it had been its near relative *conuersionem*.   **post mollitiem uestium:**   the catalogue of Lea's pious and ascetic practices that follows combines elements that would also be at home in pagan philosophical asceticism (simple food and clothing, indifference to externals, teaching by example, cf. **32–7** above) with more specifically Christian elements (prayer, humility, expectation of heavenly reward). J.'s ideas on (esp. female) asceticism are most fully set out in his *Ep.* 22

(to Eustochium, written in the same year); cf. Kelly (1975) 91–4; Rousseau (1978) 99–139; *ODC*[3] s.v. 'asceticism'.   **ancilla:** for the image of Christian servitude, cf. **41** above and (the foundational text) Luke 1:38.   **3 angelorum choris:** a common image in early Christian writing (though not in OT or NT): Arndt-Gingrich χορός 3, *PGL* 1. **Abrahae sinibus...Lazaro:** alluding to the story of Dives and Lazarus, Luke 16:19–31.   **palmatum:** clothed in the *tunica palmata*, the tunic embroidered with palm leaves worn by triumphing generals and (it appears here) consuls on their inauguration. For the inaugural ceremony (1 Jan.) see Ovid, *Fasti* 1.79–88, Scullard (1981) 52–4.   **stillam...inquirere:** like Dives, Luke 16:24.   **tripudio:** the word properly applied to a ritual dance in triple time (*tri-*), originally performed in honour of Mars (Livy 1.20.4), but was also used more generally of wild or outlandish dancing (e.g. Cat. 63.26); here it expresses Christian distaste for benighted pagan ritual.   **lacteo caeli palatio:** the Milky Way, regularly envisaged as the destination of the souls of the dead from at least the 4th century B.C. onwards: Heraclides Ponticus fr. 7 Wehrli, Cic. *Somn. Scip.* 8 with Macrobius *Com.* 1.15.1–7, Manilius 1.758ff.; the connection between the Milky Way and the celestial Palatine had been made previously by Ovid, *Met.* 1.168ff.   **commentitur:** not only vocally, but also in the inscription to the honorific statue set up to commemorate him, surviving as *CIL* vi.1779 (...*cura soforum, porta quis caeli patet*).   **uxor:** Fabia Anconia Paulina (*PLRE* 1 675, Paulina 4), also a devout pagan.   **secreta:** *OLD* 2a.   **amentia:** cf. Paul, 1 Cor. 1:18–23.   **quaecumque...nostri:** Ps. 47:9; the quotation, picking up the references to the Psalms at the start of the letter, signals that it is starting to move towards its close.   **4 mundi uiam etc.:** J.'s imagery in the peroration (most of it from the standard repertoire of both pagan and Christian moralists) takes its cue from the preceding ref. to Praetextatus' pomp; the near juxtaposition of *uiam* and *duabus/duplici* suggests the idea of a *choice* of roads (like that of Prodicus' Heracles, Xen. *Mem.* 2.1.21ff.), Lea's or P.'s.   **duplici...fide:** explained by *et Christum...et saeculum* below; *tunicis* glances back to P.'s *tunica palmata*.   **calciamentorum...operibus:** P.'s senatorial shoes (*calcei patricii*), taken as a symbol of activity contributing nothing to salvation. **praemoriamur:** like the good Platonist (*Phaedo* 64a ff.), the good Christian detaches herself from the world and its values even before death, in the expectation of a better (and eternal) life to come.

43 Aurelius Augustinus, *Ep.* 245. A letter of Saint Augustine (Introduction, 21), responding to a request for advice on an assortment of Church matters, but one made to him in his private capacity as friend and mentor, rather than in virtue of his formal position in the hierarchy. Some (relatively) temperate teaching about personal adornment, which can be compared with the simple-life values of the pagan writers included in this section, leads on to some more distinctively Christian concerns: a condemnation of magical amulets, and a difficult point about ordination. The letter instructs both by the substantial teaching contained in it, and by the spectacle (for the subsequent reader) of A. instructing a fellow bishop in how best to do his job.

Domino delectissimo . . . salutem: compare the extended salutation in **39**. Possidius, a former pupil of A.'s (and his eventual biographer), was now Bishop of Calama (Guelma, in Algeria); he had evidently recently tried to enforce a strict code of dress in his congregation and met with resistance; cf. Brown (1967) 264–9.   **1 magis . . . faciunt** (picked up below in *moneantur interim . . .*) corrects the emphasis in P.'s request for advice.   **sed nunc . . . permisit:**   for the reference to the circumstances of a letter's arrival, and of the composition of the reply, cf. **6** and **7** above.   **sanctitatis tuae:**   cf. n. on **40** τὴν σὴν σεμνοπρέπειαν.   **baiuli:**   in later Latin, 'courier' or 'pall-bearer', rather than the classical sense of 'porter.'   **de ornamentis etc.:**   as the references to Paul, 1 Cor. show, deciding what level of personal adornment was legitimate for the Christian was a perennial concern for the Church from the earliest period.   **quo modo placeant . . . mulieres maritis:**   part quotation, part paraphrase of 1 Cor. 7:32–4 (in a Latin version that coincides with that of Jerome's Vulgate, but is presumably taken from one of the older Latin translations; see *ODC*³ s.v. 'Old Latin Versions').   **apostolus iubet:** Paul, 1 Cor. 11.5–13.   **fucari . . . pigmentis:**   regularly condemned by Christian writers, but cf. also Xen. *Mem.* 2.1.22, Plato, *Gorgias* 465b, Eubulus fr. 98 (with Hunter ad loc.), Sen. *NQ.* 7.31.2 and [Lucian], *Amores* 41 for similar distaste among (male) pagan moralists.   **ueniam:**   *OLD* 1b.   **uerus ornatus . . . mores boni sunt:**   the standard (explicit or implicit) complement to condemnation of artificial adornment, cf. e.g. Plut. *Mor.* 141e, 'Crates' *Ep.* 9.   **2 ligaturarum:**   lit. 'tyings', magical amulets attached to the wearer with a piece of thread, for the use of which in both pagan and Christian contexts see Barb (1963) and Graf (1997).

inaures: in classical times, the wearing of ear-rings by men was taken as a sign of Eastern extraction (Xen. *Anab.* 3.1.31, Plaut. *Poen.* 981); it is not clear whether what A. condemns here was a fashion for ear-rings in general, or for a particular kind of magical amulet.   **ad seruiendum daemonibus:**   in early Christian thinking, all magic as well as all pagan cult was the work of malicious demons, seeking to seduce human beings away from true religion, cf. Daniélou (1973) 427–41 (with 31–5, 183–94). **apostolus:**   Paul, in 1 Cor. 10:20 and 2 Cor. 6:15 (both times in a Latin version different from the Vulgate).   **Belial** = the Devil: from a Hebrew word for 'worthlessness, wickedness' used in the OT in phrases like 'sons of Belial', and just the once in the NT, in the passage A. quotes from Paul.   **sacrificare:**   for the question of Christians and pagan sacrifice, cf. **4** above (though A. of course here speaks sarcastically).   **Neptuno:**   to judge from other references in A.'s works, still a significant cult deity in N. Africa at the time (or at least up until the prohibition of pagan sacrifice a decade or so before, in 391).   **moneantur interim:**   A. returns to the question with which he began, offering a temporary solution, pending the fuller and more considered answer he does not yet have time for.   **agendum sit:**   the deliberative subj. underlines A.'s own uncertainty.   **de ordinatu . . . facias:**   the sudden change of direction, with a new topic introduced briefly at the very end, is a familiar epistolary move (cf. e.g. **6**, **32**, **35**); A. employs it here to underline the seriousness of his reservations.   **in parte Donati:**   Donatism, the schismatic movement, named for its second head, which split N. African Christianity from *c.* 311 until its final condemnation in 411 (and survived in attenuated form up until the Arab conquest): see Brown (1967) 212–25, Chadwick (1967) 121–4 and 216–25.

A VI PRIVATE LETTERS: CONDOLENCE AND CONSOLATION.

Just as it is the mark of the true friend to advise and instruct, so it is also to condole and console (a process often involving an element of instruction) in times of misfortune. This function too produces a whole sub-genre of letter, linked also to the larger literary kind of consolation literature, the standard formulae and reflections of which it reproduces in characteristically concise and individualized form. Whatever the misfortune that gives rise to it (it may be exile, failure in the courts, or financial loss as well as bereavement that is in question), the letter of condolence focuses a major consideration in all written communication – the need for the writer to envisage the effect of his/her words on the recipient even as they are being written – in a particularly immediate way. It might also be observed that this is one area in which the standard epistolary *topos* of the superiority of face-to-face over written communication may not always be felt to be appropriate. Precisely by its calming distance, and by its physical identity as a tangible token of friendly concern, a letter may be felt in certain circumstances to perform its function better than the spoken equivalent; in addition, it may be re-read and preserved.

Among ancient texts, the most comprehensive collection of consolatory commonplaces is [Plutarch], *Consolatio ad Apollonium* (*Mor.* 101 f–122a). The etiquette of the letter of consolation is briefly discussed in Julius Victor's *Ars rhetorica* (**75** below), and in a number of actual letters (e.g. Cic. *Ad fam.* 4.13 = 225 SB, Sen. *Ep.* 99, Greg. Naz. *Ep.* 165). Models are given by Demetrius (*Typ. ep.* 5) and Libanius/Proclus (*Form. ep.* 21 and 24). See Kassel (1958), Mitchell (1968), Scourfield (1993) 15–34, Chapa (1998) 9–50.

44 M. Tullius Cicero, *Ad fam.* 5.18 (= 51 SB). A letter of condolence from Cicero to a political ally condemned to exile on unknown charges, written during the chaos of 52 B.C., when Pompey was both proconsul and sole consul, and had recently passed laws on bribery and political violence: see Scullard (1982) 123–7. The first half of the letter is taken up with consolatory commonplaces: the consoler's own grief, putting him in need of consolation himself (*consolari / consolandus*); the exhortation (*hortor*, *rogo atque oro*) to manly fortitude (*uirum . . . praebeas*); the reminder that what has happened simply exemplifies a general law and/or feature of the times (*qua condicione . . . cogites*); and the contrast of fortune with manly virtue (*uirtus / fortuna*). The second half of the letter deals briefly with the specifics of the recipient's case, enumerating the mitigating factors, but without any special colour or warmth. On C.'s letters of condolence in general, see Hutchinson (1998) 49–77.

Fadio: C.'s quaestor during his consulship (63 B.C.), who worked for his return from exile as tribune in 57.   **1 consolari . . . consolandus:** cf. **47** below.   **hortor:** cf. **49** below.   **uirumque praebeas:** cf. **47** and **49** below.   **qua condicione:** cf. **41** above.

uirtus . . . fortuna: for the contrast between irremediable circumstances and the moral worth of the person addressed, cf. **47** below, or (for irremediability alone) **46** and **49**. In the background to C.'s use of the idea here lies the (Stoic) philosophical contrast between external circumstances which are not under the individual's control and moral character which is : cf. (e.g.) Sen. *Ep.* 98.1–5, Epictetus, *Encheiridion* 1.   **homines noui . . . nobilissimi:** a *nouus homo* was the first member of his family to achieve senatorial rank, whereas a *nobilis* ('known man') belonged to a family long established in the governing class; cf. *OCD*³ s.v. *nouus homo, nobilitas*. Since many *homines noui* attained the ranks of quaestor and tribune, Shackleton Bailey suggests that C.'s words here imply that F. had become aedile or praetor in the years 55–53.   **optime actum cum eo:** *OLD ago* 37b.   **quam leuissima poena . . . discesserit:** this letter must have been written at about the time of C.'s unsuccessful defence of T. Annius Milo, another of his supporters driven into exile under Pompey's new legislation (8 April 52); *poena* is abl. of manner, G–L §399.   **2 quique . . . uiuendi:** suggests not that C. thinks there is a good chance that F.'s sentence will be overturned, but that the terms of his exile allowed him to remain in Italy.   **dubia** suggests an irregularity in the voting.   **potentiae:** personal as opposed to official power (*potestas*): *OLD* 1a. The choice of word reflects C.'s sense that Pompey's position did not conform to good republican precedent.   **alicuius:** Pompey.

45 P. Ovidius Naso, *Ex Ponto* 4.11. A message of consolation from the exiled Ovid (cf. **10** above), apparently dating from the last years of his life (Bks 1–3 of the *Ex Ponto* were published in A.D. 13, Bk 4 probably after his death in 17). Although lacking a regular initial or final salutation, the poem none the less describes itself as '*littera nostra*' (15), sent in response to an '*epistula*' recently received (9), and takes up the characteristically epistolary topic of the gap in space and time between sender and recipient, writing and reading (15–16). And although overtly declining to offer any extended, formal consolation (11–12), it does so in words that are themselves a consolatory commonplace, while also making a topic of the psychology and etiquette of consolation (17–20), and putting forward three further standard consolatory thoughts: the writer's own sympathetic grief (5–10), the healing effects of time and reason (13–14), and the possibility of mitigating factors (21–2). At the same time, while ostensibly consoling another,

O. manages once more to solicit sympathy for himself as well, both in the opening acknowledgement of his friend's past support (which he must now sadly repay), and in the reflections on epistolary distance.

1 Gallio: Junius Gallio (*praenomen* unattested), *PIR*² J 756, known as a friend of O. also from Sen. *Contr.* 3.7; a distinguished orator, and subsequently the adoptive father of Seneca's eldest son (Seneca the Younger's elder brother), he was himself to experience *relegatio* (as far as Lesbos) under Tiberius in A.D. 32 (Tac. *Ann.* 6.3.1–3).   **2 nomen:** *OLD* 11.
3–4 caelesti cuspide facta . . . uulnera: the sentence of banishment, ambiguously ascribed both to the blows of fortune and to the hostility of the god-like Emperor; *caelesti cuspide* picks up and varies O.'s recurrent image of himself as the victim of a thunderbolt from on high (Jupiter/Augustus), e.g. *Tristia* 1.1.81.   **4 fouisti:**   medical terminology, *OLD foueo* 3a. **7 non . . . placuit:** solemn diction, cf. Virgil's *dis aliter uisum*, *Aen.* 2.428.   **spoliare:**   the semantic echo of *rapti* (5) reinforces the parallel between O.'s exile and the death of G.'s wife, both cases of cruel 'snatching away'.   **10 lacrimis . . . meis** echoes *lacrimis . . . tuis* in 4, again underlining the parallel, and the reversal of roles between consoler and consoled; for the confession of tears on receipt of a letter, cf. **47** below.   **11–12**   O. protests his lack of qualification for the task of consoling G., and the inadequacy of consolatory commonplaces to one who already knows them well in virtue of his superior education; cf. Libanius in **47** below, Greg. Naz. *Ep.* 125, Julian *Ep.* 69, and Pliny, *Ep.* 1.12.13. *prudentem stultior* may hint at superior *philosophical* attainment on G.'s part, as both *prudens* and *stultus* are the Latin versions of Stoic technical terms (φρόνιμος, ἄφρων); *uerba doctorum* looks to classic formulations of consolatory topics in both philosophical and literary works (*OLD doctus* 1a and 3).   **13–14 ratione . . . mora:**   time heals eventually (Pliny *Ep.* 5.16.10, with Merrill's note), but the wise man can achieve the same effect more quickly by philosophical reflection (Sulpicius ap. Cic. *Ad fam.* 4.5 (= 248 SB).6, Cic. *Tusc.* 3.35, Sen. *Ep.* 63.12, [Plut.] *Cons. Apoll.* 112c, Basil *Ep.* 269, Jerome *Ep.* 60.15.1, with Scourfield (1993) 196–7).   **15–16 peruenit . . . permeat . . . abit:**   consoling reflection on the healing effect of time leads O. on to the distance, and communication-time, that separate him from G., and thus to his own plight as an exile as well as G.'s as a bereaved husband. The same ideas of distance, the passage of time, and the reciprocal movement of letters over the seas

are memorably combined in another consolatory context by Jerome, *Ep.* 60.19.2.   **17–20**   The lines both underscore O'.s tact as a friend, in his concern not to make matters worse by speaking out of time, and again draw attention to his own isolation: at his distance he cannot know either how things now stand with G. or how they will stand when his letter gets through. What is a concern to any sensitive correspondent (to get the tone and timing right) becomes more and more tricky the greater the intervening distance. Comparable thoughts on the danger of untimely (but premature, not belated) consolation can be found in [Plut.] *Cons. Apoll.* 102ab and Pliny, *Ep.* 5.16.10–11; cf. also the remarks of Julius Victor in **75** below.   **17 solacia dicere** is subj., *officium* predicate, and *temporis* possessive/characterizing gen.   **18 in cursu:** *OLD cursus* 8b.   **19 uulnera** again underlines the parallel between G. and O. (cf. *uulnera nostra* in 4).   **20 mouet:** *OLD moueo* 9a.   **21 utinam . . . uenerit:** the wish once more glances at O'.s own position: at his distance he cannot know whether G. has remarried or not. The perfect tense of the subj. *uenerit* envisages not only the arrival of the letter but also, by implication, the hoped-for remarriage as safely in the past by the time G. reads O.'s words. This final expression of hope for G.'s recovered happiness in some way stands in for a concluding epistolary salutation, just as the opening vocative, supported by *nomen . . . habuisse*, stood in for the standard initial greeting.   **uerum:** *OLD uerus* 6.

46 Eirene, *P.Oxy.* 115. A brief and efficient (not to say brisk) letter of condolence from second-century provincial Egypt. Relatively few such letters survive on papyrus, and all are similarly formulaic: Lewis (1983) 80–1, Chapa (1998). A second letter from the same correspondent to the same addressees, written a month later, survives as *P.Oxy.* 116; the sum of 340 drachmas, mentioned in this latter item, suggests that both parties to the correspondence were relatively prosperous.

Bibliography. Chapa (1998) 59–64, with illustration (Pl. II).

Ταοννώφρει: Onnophris ('the good being') is a title of Osiris; Ta- is the feminine determinative prefix.   **ἐπὶ . . . ἐπί:**   E. wavers in her choice of case to follow the preposition; the dative is the classically 'correct' option, but by this period was fading fast in normal usage: Browning (1983), 36–8, Horrocks (1997) 124–6 and index s.v.   **εὐψυχεῖν:**   the normal χαίρειν seems (usually) to have been felt inappropriate in letters of condolence: cf. *PSI* 1248 (εὐθυμεῖν) and *P. Ross.Georg.* 3.2 (εὖ πράσσειν), but contrast the (insensitive?) writer of *P. Princeton* 102, who sticks with χαίρειν; cf. Introduction, 34–5.   **τῶι εὐμοίρωι:** a conventional euphemism, also found in *P. Princeton* 102; cf. the more familiar ὁ μακαρίτης. The deceased is presumably T.'s and P.'s son.   **Διδυμᾶτος:** E.'s assertion of fellow-feeling would be all the closer if D. was her son, but this need not be the only possibility.   **ἦν καθήκοντα:** periphrasis (Smyth §1961) for the imperfect of καθήκει, 'it is appropriate'; as a noun (τὰ) καθήκοντα is a regular term for moral duty, in both philosophical and ordinary speech (LSJ II.2); cf. **56** below.   **Θερμούθιον, Φίλιον:** both feminine names, as such ('affectionate') neuter diminutives regularly are (cf. e.g. Delphium and Philematium in Plautus's *Mostellaria*); the catalogue of names linked by bare 'and' is characteristic of naïve epistolary style, cf. Terentianus in **5** above. **ἀλλ' ὅμως κτλ:** among the most well-worn of consolatory reflections. Hector in *Iliad* 6 is already using a version of it to calm Andromache (488–9); Socrates in Plato *Gorgias* 512e claims it as distinctively feminine (cf. Dodds *ad loc.*).   **ἑαυτούς** = ἀλλήλους, reflexive for reciprocal (Smyth §§1231–2).   **εὖ πράττετε:** like the initial εὐψυχεῖν, another variation (from the standard ἔρρωσθε or εὐτυχεῖτε) to suit the consolatory purpose of the letter; cf. *P. Ross.Georg.* 3.2 (εὐθύμει).   **Ἀθὺρ α΄** = Oct. 28; Hathyr was the third month of the Egyptian year, which began with 1 Thoth on Aug. 29.

47 Libanios, *Ep.* 142 Norman = 1508 Foerster. A letter from the rhetorician and man of letters Libanius (Introduction, 16–17) to a high-ranking friend exiled to Pontus and forbidden to enter cities. Writing as one educated man to another, L. urges him to draw comfort from his learning and to seek distraction in a literary project.

Σελεύκωι: *PLRE* I Seleucus 1 (818–19): a high-ranking official (*comes*, count, and high-priest of Cilicia) under the Emperor Julian, whom he accompanied on his ill-fated Persian campaign of 363. His prosecution and condemnation (for his pagan zeal in Julian's service) is referred to by L. also in *Ep.* 140 Norman = 1473 Foerster.   **1 ἐδάκρυσα:** cf. Ovid in **45** above, ll. 9–10.   **2 ἐμαυτὸν παρεμυθησάμην:** cf. Cicero in **44** above.   **Ὀδυσσεύς:** Od. like S. endured exile after military success; but his example also holds out the hope of an eventual restoration. Cf. **31**

above for the use of Od. as an exemplar of undeserved misfortune. Here, L.'s point is that, though there are similarities between the two, S. is not nearly as badly off as Od. **κλάδων:** like Od. approaching Nausicaa, *Od.* 6.127–9. **τυπτόμεθα:** as Od. was by Melanthios, *Od.* 17.233–5. **παροινίας:** like that committed by the Suitors in Od.'s palace. For the Suitors as exemplars of drunken misconduct, cf. (e.g.) Max. Tyr. 14.4, 30.5. **3 λουτρῶν:** an essential of civilized, sociable existence in the Romanized Greek world, but L.'s words perhaps glance also at bathing as a central element in scenes of hospitality in the *Od.*, and its consequent importance as a symbol of restoration and security (e.g. 6.211–38, 23.130–62). **παρόν:** acc. absol. of the impersonal πάρεστι (Goodwin §1569, Smyth §2076). **διατρίβειν:** to be taken with both παρόν and αἱροῦν-ται. **Ἀχιλλεύς:** Ach.'s education by Chiron on Mt Pelion is de-scribed in Pindar, *Nem.* 3.43–52, Statius, *Achilleid* 1.159–97 and Apollod. *Bibl.* 3.13.6. The choice of example, like that to follow, again flatters S. on his military distinction. **4 στρατηγῶν:** Miltiades (Hdt. 6.132–6, but tried rather than imprisoned), Themistocles (Thuc. 1.135–8) and Pausanias (Thuc. 1.128–35), remembered as subjects for declamation as well as char-acters from the historians (cf. in general Lucian *Rhet. Praec.* (41) 18, Russell (1983) 117–23). **οὐδὲ γάρ . . . κουφιζοίμεθα:** it is consoling to reflect that one's sufferings are shared, or exceeded, by the great characters of history or myth; for this consolatory use of *exempla* (which L. has already begun to tap in his previous mention of Odysseus) cf. [Plut.] *Cons. Apoll.* 106bc, Seneca, *Cons. Marc.* 2, Jerome, *Ep.* 60.5. **5 ἐπίδειξιν ἀνδρείας:** the standard exhortation to meet misfortune with virtuous endurance; cf. **45** above and **49** below. **τοὺς Πέρσας:** on Julian's eastern campaign of 363. **ἐκ φύλλων ἐν Πόντωι:** for the fame of the forests of Pontus, cf. (e.g.) Theophrastus, *Hist. plant.* 4.5.3, Pliny, *NH* 16.197. **φιλολόγωι:** LSJ 2, 'fond of learning and literature'. **χορός:** metaphorically, of any band, troupe or gang: LSJ 2; for the application to classic writers as a class, cf. Max. Tyr. 17.5. **οὓς ἀνάγκη μένειν:** for the thought, com-pare Cic. *Pro Archia* 16. **6 τὸν πόλεμον . . . σύγγραφε:** nothing more is heard of this projected history, in L.'s correspondence or anywhere else. **Θουκυδίδηι:** Thuc. *Hist.* 5.26, [Marcellinus], *Vit. Thuc.* 23–6, 31. **εἰ μὴ ἠπίστω καλῶς:** cf. Ovid to Gallio in **45** above, 11–12. **7 εἶδες κτλ:** L.'s closing compliment perhaps glances again at Thuc. 1.22.2–4 and 5.26.5, so underlining the flattering and consoling parallel between S. and his distinguished predecessor. The suggestion that literary fame may compensate for the loss of political status (spectacularly exemplified by Thuc., but by many others too) follows the familiar consolatory pattern of discerning powerfully redeeming factors in an apparently bleak situation (cf. Cicero to Fadius and Ovid to Gallio in **44** and **45** above).

48 Gregorios of Nazianzos, *Ep.* 222. Gregory (Introduction, 19–20) writes to console a Christian addressee on the death of her brother or husband. The consolation proper, framed by expressions of G.'s desire to visit and comfort the bereaved in person, dwells on the thought that the deceased has gone on to a better existence, which is the proper destiny of all the virtuous – a thought equally at home in pagan consolation, thanks above all to Plato, *Apol.* 40e ff. and *Phaedo* (cf. [Plut.] *Cons. Apoll.* 107f–109d). Compared to some of G.'s other letters of consolation (e.g. 31–4, 76, 165, 238), this one is remarkable for its simplicity and the absence of learned philosophical and literary allusions – perhaps because directed to a female rather than a male recipient (though contrast **40** above). It is none the less carefully composed, both in the rhetorical vigour of the central section, and in the use made of literal and metaphorical journeying, and the idea of reunions briefly delayed, to link that central section with its surrounding frame.

Θέκληι: known only from this letter and one or two others of G.'s. The same name is borne by a number of early Christian saints, most notably Thekla of Iconium, supposedly converted by St Paul.   **1 τὴν σὴν εὐλάβειαν:** cf. n. on τὴν σὴν σεμνοπρέπειαν in **40** above; εὐλάβεια is standard Christian Greek for 'piety' or 'godly fear', *PGL* 1c and 2. **ἀσθενοῦντος:** this letter was written within a few years of G.'s death, when he was perhaps between 55 and 60 years of age.   **καρτερίας:** a keynote of both pagan and Christian exhortation, repeated in (5) below; cf. **44, 47** and **49.**   **μακαριωτάτωι:** LSJ μακάριος 1.3; *PGL* E; cf. Irene's εὐμοίρωι in **46.**   **ἀδελφῶι:** it is not clear, from this letter or the others in which T. and Sacerdos feature (210 (?), 223), whether they were literally brother and sister, or husband and wife.   **φιλοσοφεῖς** (cf. **2** συμφιλοσοφήσω, **5** φιλοσοφίας): Christian usage transferred the notion of 'philosophy' from pagan schools of thought to Christian revelation and living – as the true philosophy to which even the best of the pagans had only approximated: see *PGL* φιλοσοφία B, φιλοσοφέω B, and Daniélou (1973) 47–73.   **2 ἀναγκαίως:** in standard epistolary manner, as also at the end of the letter, G. characterizes his written communication as a second-rate substitute for face-to-face contact; cf. (e.g.) **10**, **16** and **39** above.   **3 Σακερδῶς:** the Latin word for 'priest', used as a proper name.   **παραστάτης:** 'servant' (*PGL* 2) rather than the classical 'comrade' (LSJ II).   **φθόνωι** could in theory refer either to human ill-will or to the Devil's; the position of the gen. τοῦ πονηροῦ makes the former more likely here.   **4 ἀναλύσομεν** makes overt the image of life as a journey already implicit in the use of the locatives πόθεν and ποῦ, and the verb of motion ὑποχωρήσας; cf. **5** ὁδοιπόρων and ἀκολουθήσει. **παρρησίας** has its Christian rather than its classical sense here, *PGL* II.A.3 and III.A.   **προσκυνηταί:** not attested in classical Greek (contrast προσκυνέω and προσκύνησις), but standard Christian usage for 'worshipper', *PGL* 3.   **5 προειληφότες:** euphemistic, *PGL* προλαμβάνω 8. **ἀπαρχή:** the 'choice' or 'flower', as what is offered as first fruits must be the best: *PGL* B.3, cf. LSJ 2.   **ὅσον:** followed by the infin., Smyth §2003, 2497.   **6 ὑψηλοτέρον:** *PGL* ὑψηλός 2; cf. Basil in **40** above. **ἀνθ' ἡμῶν:** as at the opening of the letter, G. characterizes his written message as an (inferior) substitute for his presence in person.   **λογισμοῖς:** reasoned/reasonable advice (cf. **45**.13) as opposed to unreasoning grief. **εἰ καὶ κρείττονας:** a gesture of modesty on G.'s part, and another compliment (as in οὐκ ἀμφίβολον at the beginning) to T.'s own faith and virtue.   **7 κατ' ὄψιν:** cf. **39** ad fin. for both the phrase and the thought. **καταξιωθείημεν:** by God.   **τοῦ σοῦ καὶ περὶ σέ** sounds pleonastic, but perhaps distinguishes between T.'s immediate household and the other members of her Christian congregation.   **πληρώματος:** generally 'company', 'crew', 'complement' (*PGL* πλήρωμα A.8–9, LSJ 3), or more specifically in Christian usage 'congregation' (*PGL* 9.c–e). **πλείων . . . εὐεργέτηι:** the expression of thanks to God makes a more pious substitute for the conventional good wishes to the addressee.

49 Anonymous, *P.Bon.* 5, cols III.3–13 and IV.3–13. One of a collection of thirteen bilingual model letters preserved on a papyrus of the fourth or fifth century A.D. found at Oxyrhynchus or in the Fayum, and now in Bologna. This one comes from a set of three entitled 'συνβουλευτικαὶ περὶ ἐλαχίστων καταλελειμμένων / [de minimi]s legatis suasor[i]ae', offering consolation on being undeservedly neglected in a friend's will; other sets offer congratulations on the receipt of a more satisfactory legacy, and on manumission from slavery (the latter an interesting indication of the social milieu for which these models were intended). See also Introduction, 37–8, 42–3.

The Greek and Latin texts are set out in short lines in parallel columns, matched phrase for phrase, so as to make it clear which words render which. The Latin text but not the Greek has word-division, and is sporadically punctuated with points between both whole words and the elements of compounds; the Greek text is bare of breathings and accents.

As with any bilingual document of this kind, several questions arise: which of the two is the base text, from which the other is translated (or were both prepared simultaneously, whether from a base text in a third language or not); and was the completed document intended primarily for Greek-speakers, Latin-speakers, or those whose main language was neither (i.e., in this case, demotic (Coptic)-speaking Egyptians: cf. the headnote to **5** above)? Both the Latin and the Greek are moderately respectable by fourth/fifth-century standards, at least in vocabulary, but both are occasionally awkward syntactically, and both show apparent neologisms, seemingly formed specifically for the translation, which seems to rule out the possibility that one of the two versions on its own constituted the starting-point. General considerations would suggest that such a text is most likely to have been intended either for Greek-speakers who needed access to the official language of Imperial administration, or for demotic (Coptic) speakers needing access to both; the existence of signs of awkwardness in both the Greek and the Latin nudges the scales towards the latter. In any case, the presence of word-division and punctuation in the Latin but not the Greek text suggests that Latin is envisaged as the less familiar language of the two, and so in greater need of aids to the reader.

Bibliography. Vogliano and Castiglioni (1948), Montevecchi (1953) 18–28.

1 Licinnium / Λικίννιον: because this is a model letter, both the initial greeting and the final salutation are left to be supplied by the user; cf. n. on **76**.51 below.   **amicum tibi:**   although elsewhere in the document, the phrase *amico tuo* appears, the pronoun *tibi* is presumably chosen in preference to *tuum* here in order to match the Greek version's use of pronoun (σου) rather than possessive (σόν); but this in turn involves an unidiomatic conflation of the behaviour of *amicus* as n. and as adj.   **3 obitum:**   sc. *esse. obitus est* for *obiit* is late Latin usage (H–S §162 (ε), p. 291); but the desire for parallelism with the Greek acc. + part. constr. after ἔμαθον seems to have had some influence.   **4–5 ἐμνημονευκότα ... γεγονέναι:**   periphrasis for

ἐμνημονευκέναι, cf. **46** above; chosen to match the Lat. *memorem...fuisse*.
5 ὑπεικίας = ὑπεικείας, a word apparently otherwise unknown to Greek
lexicography, but intelligible as a coinage to match *obsequium*, standing to
the verb ὑπείκω ('defer') as *obsequium* does to *obsequor*. The addressee of the
letter has shown due 'deference' (presumably that of a client for his patron),
and might legitimately have expected something in return; for the idea of
reciprocity in play here, and for the use of wills to return previously unpaid
debts of favour, see Lendon (1997) 63–4, 68–70.   **6 quidem** (cf. 10):
the standard Latin equivalent for μέν, *OLD* 3.   **7 set** (cf. 11): standard
'vulgar' Latin substitution of t for d; cf. headnote to **5** above.   **8 for-
titer/εὐσταθῶς:**   not precisely equivalent semantically, but apparently
felt as equivalently clichéd accompaniments to the verb 'endure' in their
respective languages.   **9–11** The final consoling thought sounds appropriately high-minded and resigned ('Man proposes, the Fates dispose'), but
manages not to fit the situation: the problem arises precisely not from Fate
but from a human decision about what to bequeath to whom.   **9 sup-
premorum/ἐσχάτων:**   presumably neuter, 'last things' = 'possessions
at death'. It is the Greek phrase rather than the Latin that sounds the more
natural (as well as allowing the echo with διατάσσουσιν, which the Latin
tabulas...ordinant cannot match). *suppremorum* is spelled with a single p elsewhere in the same document; such inconsistency over single/double consonants ('gemination'/'simplification') is again standard in 'vulgar' Latin:
Lindsay (1894) 113–18.

A VII PRIVATE LETTERS: APOLOGETICS

A letter may be a convenient way of responding to reproaches and accusations, actual or anticipated, real or imagined. The response may be intended
solely for the first recipient, or may be meant to speak through him/her to
a wider audience. This brief section contains two pieces of self-justification
from notorious villains. The first is from a historical character, and is preserved embedded in a larger account of his career by another hand; the
second is a fictitious piece, in which the anonymous author writes expressly
to create/sustain the enjoyably evil character of his correspondent. Both,
that is to say, are wholly or partly enmeshed in games of presentation
played by others than their ostensible senders. In both, moreover, there
is an element of irony, in that the correspondent's true character emerges
in unintended ways, either from his evasions, or from the strength of his

conviction in his own rightness; cf. **72** below. For a more saintly exercise in exculpation, see also **69**.

50 L Sergius Catilina (Sallust, *Catilina* 35). The arch-conspirator Catiline, on the verge of the hasty departure from Rome into which the actions of the consul Cicero have cornered him, writes to a supposed sympathizer. Though he does not confess as much, indeed deliberately attempts to conceal it, he is on his way to join a rebel 'army' in Etruria. For the background, see Scullard (1982) 109–114. Catiline combines self-exculpation with a request for help for the wife he is leaving behind, and it is the latter (together with hopefully flattering references to the addressee's loyal friendship) that frames the letter. Although we have this letter because it is built into Sallust's account of the Catilinarian conspiracy, the number of unSallustian turns of phrase it contains (McGushin (1977) 196, Ramsey (1984) 159) has been held to argue for its authenticity.

1 Q. Catulo: a senior figure, consul in 78 and now leader of the *optimates* in the Senate. C.'s trust in him was misplaced: on receiving the letter, he read its contents to the Senate (Sal. *Cat.* 34.3).   **re cognita:** a carefully indirect ref. to Catulus' support when C. was accused (and acquitted) of illicit sexual relations with a Vestal Virgin (Sal. *Cat.* 15, with Ramsey (1984) 100); *cognita* is nom., agreeing with *fides*.   **2 defensionem:** a formal defence to one's critics, as opposed to *satisfactio*, a personal apology or explanation to a friend.   **in nouo consilio** is again carefully vague: C. refers to his intention to join the rebel army in open revolt, but his words *could* be taken to imply just that he has decided to go into self-imposed exile.   **de culpa:** the use of the prepositional phrase in place of the objective gen. is probably colloquial (as well as being the formula for the development of the gen. in Romance languages): Palmer (1954) 166.   **me dius fidius:** sc. *iuuet*, 'so help me the god of good faith'; *OLD fidius*.   **3 fructu . . . priuatus:** in his defeat in the consular elections for 62 B.C.   **statum dignitatis:** *dignitas* is the honour (perceived worth) that is both acknowledged in and reinforced by the holding of high office; it can be inherited from ancestors and augmented by the individual's own efforts, or (as in this case) damaged by the failure to win further positions of power and/or court-cases; see in general Lendon (1997).   **publicam . . . suscepi:** for this claim by C. (which our uniformly hostile sources present as self-serving), cf. Cic. *Muren.* 50, Plut. *Cic.*

14.1.   **meis nominibus** (abl. of description) is a technical term with *aes alienum* (as is *alienis nominibus* below), indicating the name against which the debt is registered in the lender's accounts.   **possessionibus:** *OLD possessio* 3.   **Orestillae:** Aurelia Orestilla, C.'s second wife, unflatteringly described by Sal. in *Cat*. 15.2.   **non dignos homines:** principally the *nouus homo* Cicero, who defeated him in the consular elections. **honore honestatos:** the two words, a pair in derivation (the so called *figura etymologica*) as well as in alliteration, perhaps seek to convey C.'s indignation. The use of alliterative *figura etymologica* is particularly characteristic of archaic Latin.   **4 hoc nomine** = *hac/qua de causa*; *OLD nomen* 25. **5 plura ... parari:** the suggestion that the writer has more to say, but cannot or does not want to write it now, is an epistolary *topos* (cf. (e.g.) **39** above); here it is used to add urgency to the request that follows.   **6 commendo ... fidei:** echoing *fides* and *commendationi* in the opening sentence.   **defendas:** jussive subj., colloquial for the imper.; the use of the subj. is perhaps helped by the proximity of verbs implying request and entreaty (*commendo*, *trado*, and the *rogo* implicit in *rogatus*), which could have introduced it as subj. of indirect command.   **haueto:** archaic fut. imper. as if from a verb *aueo*, used in place of the standard epistolary *uale*.

51 Phalaris, *Ep*. 66. The tyrant writes to justify his use of the notorious hollow bronze bull to execute not only its maker, Perilaos, but also other criminals and plotters against him. Ignoring any possible complaint about the cruelty of this mode of execution, P. insists that his use of it, given his own position, is only rational. For Phalaris, see also **13, 14, 25, 38, 60** and **70**, and Introduction, 28–9.

Τηλεκλείδηι: T., who is not otherwise mentioned in P.'s correspondence, seems to be envisaged as someone not belonging to the tyrant's inner circle, but voicing his criticisms (officious and interfering or entirely justified, according to one's viewpoint) from a position of greater detachment. The name is otherwise known to history only as that of a poet of Old Comedy.   **1 ἰδίαι τινί:** the tone is one of contemptuous mock bewilderment.   **γνώμηι:** LSJ II.5.   **τὸν δημιουργὸν τοῦ ταύρου Περίλαον:** for the manufacture of the hollow bronze bull by Perilaos (Perillus), his presentation of it to P. as a device to punish his enemies, and his own death as its first victim, see *Ep*. 122 and Lucian 1 (*Phalaris* 1). **τῶι τρόπωι τῆς αὐτῆς αἰκίας:** an awkward phrase, which in the light of τὸν αὐτὸν τρόπον τῆς ἐξετάσεως below it might be better to emend to τῶι αὐτῶι τρόπωι τῆς αἰκίας.   ἄμυνα can mean either 'vengeance' or 'self-defence'; the latter seems more appropriate here, particularly in the light of what P. goes on to say.   **2 ὅτι τοῦ μέλλειν κτλ:** assuming that διαφθείρεσθαι is passive and ἄλλους τινάς is subj. to it and μέλλειν, this seems intended to make P. sound evasive, presenting executions he himself has ordered as the automatic consequence of Perilaos' actions rather than his own. The alternative would be to take διαφθ. as middle, αὐτόν = Περίλαον (understood) as subj. to it and μέλλειν, and ἄλλους τινάς as obj.   **βιαζομένους** might be either middle (of people who, perversely 'force their way' (LSJ II.3) to imprisonment and execution by the tyrant), or passive (of those who 'are forced' by circumstances). Either way, the point is that P. himself is doubly blameless: he neither invented the bull nor compelled those people to commit crimes.   **ἀρξάμενοι ... ποιήσασθε:** the switch to the plural broadens the defence, from one just to T.'s criticisms to one addressed to all P.'s critics; but the very admission that T. is not alone is revealing.   **ὕπερ ἁπάντων ... ἀνθρωπίνης φύσεως** is another attempt to transfer the stigma: the real criminal against humanity is not P. but Perilaos; P. himself claims to have acted on behalf of civilized values in this first use of the bull, just as he claims full justification in all subsequent uses too.   **3 ὅσους ... οὐδὲ ὅσων:** P. distinguishes two categories of victims (after Perilaos): criminals guilty of offences against others, and personal enemies plotting to assassinate him. Any competent judge, he maintains, must concede that both entirely deserved their fates. **οὐ ... προσηκόντως:** the challenge to the consistency of his critics' attitudes adds a defiant note.   **ἐκσπόνδων** seems to be used metaphorically, of hostile or disloyal action in general, rather than literally of the breaking of formal treaties.   **ἤπου ... εἴην:** also defiant – those who think otherwise must themselves be mad.   **τοὺς ὑπὲρ ἄλλων ... εὖ ποιῶσι:** includes Perilaos as well as those guilty of ἀλλότρια ἀδικήματα. **δύσκλειαν ... ἀναδεχόμενος:** P. here admits both that his reputation is black and that he treats others badly as a means to securing his own position.   **πέπαυσο δὴ κτλ:** contemptuous and dismissive; T. (picked out again by the return to the 2nd sg.) is an irritant, stupidly bothering himself to no good purpose. The final phrase thus echoes the sneering tone of the letter's opening, and reinforces the characterization of its supposed author (cf. e.g. *Epp.* 4, 21, 53).

A VIII PRIVATE LETTERS: LITERARY MATTERS

Quite apart from constituting a literary form in themselves, letters are implicated with the business of literature in many different ways. They can be the vehicle for literary-critical and literary-theoretical discussion (whether of letter-writing itself or of other kinds of composition), and tools for the commissioning, emendation, copying and redistribution of literary works. In the form of the prefatory epistle, they also provide a useful device for framing and dedication. Many of these functions can be seen as specific types of more general epistolary tasks: asking for something to be sent (which may be a book); accompanying a gift (which may be a work in the recipient's honour); asking for or giving advice and instruction (which can be of a literary kind); asking for a favour (which can be the composition of a literary work). The following section aims at demonstrating something of this variety of literary ramifications, in both pagan and Christian circles, in the period between the first and the fourth centuries A.D.

52 C. Plinius Secundus, *Ep*. 9.2. Responding to a friend's encouragement to write more often, and to be more like Cicero, Pliny replies by insisting on the difference between his and Cicero's situation, and on his determination not to write merely 'literary' letters. A conventional epistolary motif ('I'm sorry I don't write more often') is thus used as the catalyst for reflection on more theoretical issues: Cicero's canonical status as Latin letter-writer, Pliny's epistolographic ambitions and his sense of his own disadvantaged position in Latin literary history.

Sabino: probably one Statius Sabinus, a military man from Firmum. **1 plurimas ... flagitas:**   for complaints about frequency/volume of correspondence, cf. (e.g.) **10**. 29ff. and **33** above, and for the question of short measure, **6** and **54**.   **frigidis:**   *OLD frigidus* 8c.   **auo-cant:**   *OLD auoco* 5b.   **2 M. Tulli ... exemplum:**   the collections now known as the *Ad familiares, Ad Q. fratrem* and *Ad M. Brutum* seem to have been in general circulation in the Augustan period (Shackleton Bailey (1977) 23–4), the letters *Ad Atticum* not until the time of Nero (Shackleton Bailey (1965) 59–64). That the letters as a set had achieved the status of classics well before Pliny's time is indicated by references in Seneca's *Epistles* (esp. 21.4) and Quintilian's *Institutio* (esp. 10.1.107). See also Introduction, 13–14, and **54** and **75** below.   **3 quam angustis terminis:**   P. is thinking mainly of the comparative triviality of the daily business he has to conduct, already referred to in *frigidis negotiis*. Both the contrast between Cicero's talent and that of later writers, and that between his freedom of movement and the restrictions placed on the moderns, are close to things said by Maternus in the concluding sections of Tacitus' *Dialogus de oratoribus* (36–41), written not long before this letter (and perhaps in answer to a discussion of the decline of oratory since Cicero by P.'s own teacher Quintilian).

scholasticas: the *schola* in question is that of the *rhetor* (rather than that of the philosopher, as the medievally conditioned use of 'scholastic' and 'schoolman' in English might suggest); 'schooling' in the élite culture of the Roman Empire was *par excellence* education in the arts of speaking (and, more generally, of cultivated literary expression).   **umbraticas** (cf. *umbratilis* and *OLD umbra* 5): the contrast is between the cloistered, indoor life of the man of words, and the 'outdoor' life of the man of action (like Sabinus); cf. e.g. Virg. *Geo.* 4.599–66. P.'s implicit insistence that he is in actual fact *not* writing over-composed, 'academic' letters is a shade disingenuous.

4 arma . . . soles: Sabinus' precise rank and posting are unknown, but *sudorem puluerem soles* (besides making a pointed contrast with *umbraticas*) suggest service in the East or N. Africa.   **5 habes** = 'there you have', 'I have given you'.   **iustam:** *OLD iustus* 5b.   **quam tamen . . . uelim:** the first of two inter-connected paradoxes, with which P. brings the letter to an elegant close, reflecting on the importance of letters in the maintenance of a friendship, and the proper etiquette for ensuring that they fulfil this function effectively. In quite an economical and characterful way, P. catches his own feeling of unease (for all that he has a respectable excuse), his grateful affection for S. precisely for being hard on him, and thus also his sense of how good a friend he believes S. to be.   **probari:** *OLD probo* 6b.

53 M. Cornelius Fronto, M. Aurelius Antoninus, *Ad M. Caes*. 3.

7–8. An exchange of letters between Fronto and the future emperor Marcus Aurelius, when the latter held the rank of Caesar and was completing his literary education; at the time of writing F. was about forty-five and A. eighteen or nineteen. A. asks for help with an exercise in composition, and F. responds with a mixture of courtly flattery and professorial didacticism. For F.'s epistolary style, see the note to **9** above. In his reply here, he is as much concerned to discuss literary elegance as to embody it; stylistic and rhythmical effects are accordingly less prominent (though e.g. the asyndeton in *classium . . . procellarum* and the careful variation of word-order in *aeque undis* *alluitur . . . mare aeque prospectat* stand out). Also noteworthy is F.'s use of Greek, taking its cue from A.'s letter, but as it were over-trumping it with a display of mastery of the appropriate technical terminology.

1 quom . . . recreas: on its own, an elegant (and friendly) variation on the standard wish for the addressee's health so often found at the start of a letter (cf. esp. **2** above); in the larger context of F.'s and A.'s correspondence, however, it becomes clear that exchanging news and expressions of concern about their own and each other's health was an important part of their relationship (and one which prompts unsympathetic modern critics to level charges of hypochondria, cf. **9** above and **54** below). *quom* is archaic spelling for *cum* (in line with the contemporary fashion for archaizing diction; cf. *multimodis* below, *veitae* and *quinctus* in **54**); *sit* is 'generic' subjunctive (Woodcock §§155–7).   **libenter** = (*sic*)*ut tibi libet*.   **sentio:**   *OLD* 6–7.   **2 a septima:**   sc. *hora*, i.e. during siesta. For ancient time-reckoning, see n. on **42**.1 above.   **in lectulo:**   a common place for writing and reading, in a world without desks.   **εἰκόνας:**   εἰκών (Lat. *imago*) is not exactly equivalent to the modern term 'image' or 'simile'; it means rather a vivid or 'imagistic' description, to be used for the purposes of comparison: see McCall (1969) 243–51, and n. on *ornet . . . deturpet . . . efficiat* below. F. has given A. ten such descriptions and set him to work out an application for each. F.'s keenness on εἰκόνες as an element in literary composition can be seen also in *Ad M. Caes.* 2.3, 4.12.2, *Ad Ant. Imp.* 1.2.5.   **minus** = *haud* (*OLD* 4).   **est autem quod:**   *quod* (not directly translatable) introduces a quotation of the instruction given by F. and converts it into a noun-clause (cf. *OLD quod* 2), 'it's the "there's a lake . . . " one'. *autem* here has roughly the same sense as *enim* (H–S 490f.).   **ἔνθενδ᾽ κτλ:**   'that is the source from which I (am trying to) create my image'.   **Aenaria:** mod. Ischia. F.'s example (as his own off-handedness about the precise location in his answer shows) is fictitious; there is no lake, let alone an islanded one, on Ischia.   **domina mea:**   Domitia Lucilla.

1 tui patris: Antoninus Pius.   **mari . . . mari . . . mare . . . maris:** the repetition is probably to be taken as a colloquial touch, matching the off-handedness of the thought, rather than as a piece of mock-legal formality.   **quod** is the indefinite adjective.   **igitur** (here and in the next sentence) is resumptive (= Greek δ᾽οὖν): *OLD igitur* 5. **tutum . . . tutatur:**   if the text is sound, the sentence structure here pictures the thought, with the rest of the clause safely enclosed between

the etymologically related adj. and verb (but *totum* has been suggested, precisely to *avoid* the repetition). On any reading, there is a notable alliteration of *t* and *s*.   **multimodis:**   an archaism, attributed by Cic. *Orat.* 153 to Naevius and Ennius, also found in Plautus, Terence and Lucretius.   **gratias ages:**   F. clearly has in mind formal, public expressions of thanks, such as might occur in a speech before the Senate; whether he has in mind specifically the *gratiarum actio* of an incoming consul (which might fix this exchange of letters to late 139, just before A. took up office as consul for 140) is open to debate; cf. Pliny, *Paneg.* 1; Kennedy (1972) 429, 543.   **scio . . . nouisti:**   stylistic variation, without any difference in shade of meaning.   **amem te:**   apparently subj. of wish, in place of the more usual (and colloquial) *amabo (te)*: *OLD amo* 10b.   **scitae** refers to the (hoped-for) ingenuity of the images (*OLD scitus* 3b), **concinnae** to the elegance with which they are expressed.
2 ei rei . . . ut . . . quid is an unexpected combination; *ei rei . . . quam* or *alicui rei ut eam* would have been smoother. Perhaps an attempt at informal diction?   **ornet . . . deturpet . . . efficiat:**   although   F.   seems deliberately to be avoiding technical terminology, this list of functions corresponds roughly to those given in other surviving discussions of the topic: cf. *Ad Herennium* 4.59 (*ornandi . . . probandi . . . apertius dicendi . . . ante oculos ponendi*); and, for the trio *aequiparet . . . deminuat . . . ampliet*, Cic. *Topica* 11 on *comparatio* (*maiorum . . . parium . . . minorum*).   **ut, si pingeres:** the comparison between writer and painter is particularly suitable to a discussion of εἰκόνες, but by no means confined to it: cf. e.g. Cic. *Orat.* 65, Quint. 10.6.2 (and for the still more venerable comparison of painter with poet, Simonides *apud* Plut. *Glor. Ath.* 3.346f. (etc.), *Ad Her.* 4.39, Hor. *AP* 361).   **τὰ ὁμογενῆ . . . τὰ στοιχεῖα:**   for his list of the distinguishing features on which the comparison between topic and image may rest, F. on his own admission borrows from standard rhetorical teaching on the 'bases of argument', the features of a situation from which a persuasive argument can be developed: cf. e.g. Ar. *Rhet.* 2.23–4, Cic. *Top.* 7–8, Quint. 5.10. The missing item in the list, following ὀνόματα, ought for the sake of a conventional pair with συμβεβηκότα to be some word or phrase relating to οὐσία, 'essential nature'. The Latin equivalents of these terms would be *genus, species, totum, partes, propria, differentia, contraria, consequentia et insequentia, uocabula, essentiae, accidentia, elementa*. Linking an image to its topic is an intellectual exercise, just like working out a logically coherent argument: comparison (or contrast) of A with B may rest on their shared

membership of the same genus or species, their whole body or some part of it, some property distinctive of one (or both), the mark that makes one (or both) what it is (they are) within its (their) genus, the possession by one of a property that has an opposite, the implications or accompaniments of a property one possesses, the implications of their names, their essential or 'accidental' properties, or the answers to the 'elementary' questions about them (when? what? how large? like what? etc.).   **Θεοδώρου:** Theodorus of Gadara, tutor to the future emperor Tiberius, often quoted by Quintilian; Kennedy (1972) 340–2.   **locos ἐπιχειρημάτων** combines the Greek and the Latin versions of the technical name, *loci argumentorum* and τόποι ἐπιχειρημάτων.   **ἕν τι τῶν συμβεβηκότων κτλ:** 'I chose one of the accidental attributes, the similarity in security and benefit.'   **uias ac semitas** refers to what F. previously called *rationem qua . . . quaeras*; the image of the road (to which F. is perhaps helped by the fact that the Greek for *ratio* in this context would be μέθοδος, 'route towards') is continued in *Aenariam peruenias*, as F. elegantly returns to his pupil's original plea to round off his discussion.   **4 τὴν δὲ ὅλην κτλ:** 'the whole technique of image-making'.   **alias diligentius et subtilius . . . capita:** i.e. F. has respected the conventional ban on including over-technical matter in a letter (Demetr. *Eloc.* [**73** below] 228, 232); in *alias*, moreover, there is a gentle echo of the equally conventional closing contrast between the second-rate written contact represented by the letter and a face-to-face meeting envisaged for the future (cf. **39**, etc.). **capita:**   *OLD caput* 17.

54 M. Aurelius Antoninus, M. Cornelius Fronto, *Ad Ant. Imp.* 2.4–5 (= 3.7–8 van den Hout). Another exchange between Fronto and M. Aurelius, not certainly datable, but apparently rather later than no. **53**, as A. seems no longer to be under F.'s active tuition, and is more engaged with official business. He is, however, still concerned to develop his Latin style. The main interest of the exchange lies in what F. has to say about Cicero as letter-writer.

salubritas . . . de tua quoque bona ualetudine: another mannered variant (cf. **53**) on the conventional assertion of the writer's own health and enquiry after his correspondent's.   **ueitae togatae:** the life of official business and formal occasions; *ueitae* is an archaic spelling of *uitae*.   **paululum . . . porgere:**   for apologetic or defensive references to the shortness of letters, cf. **6** and **52** above; *porgere* is a syncopated form of *porrigere*. **aliqua parte:** abl. of point of time; *contingit* is used absolutely (*OLD contingo* 8b). **dimidiatas:** lit. 'halved', here referring more loosely to the excerption of parts of whole letters.

quinctus: archaic spelling of *quintus*. Asked for news of his health, F. is not shy of giving it; and the very start of a letter is the proper place. **elegantius aut uerbo notabili dictum:** elegant composition (in its literal sense of the juxtaposition of word with word) and the use of select vocabulary – the two components of good classicizing style (Greek σύνθεσις and ἐκλογὴ ὀνομάτων). F.'s personal anthology from Cic.'s letters thus selected for style as well as literary, philosophical and political content. **duos ... unum:** i.e. two rolls of excerpts from the letters to M. Brutus the tyrannicide (which originally ran to nine books in all) and one of excerpts from the letters to Axius (two books or more). The Senator Q. Axius is mentioned frequently in the letters to Atticus (1.12 (=12 SB).1, etc.) and is a participant in Book 3 of Varro's *De Re Rustica*. **rei:** partitive gen. with *quid*, 'something of substance'. **Ciceronis epistulas:** F. (like Pliny in **52**) admires Cic.'s epistolary style, but – though acknowledging his pre-eminent status – is more critical of his oratory, which he faults for insufficient care over vocabulary: cf. *Ad. M. Caes* 4.3.3, *Ad Ant. Imp.* 3.1.1, *Ad Ver.* 2.1.14, *Ad Amic.* 1.14.2, *Bell. Parth.* 10.

55 Basileios, *Ep.* 135. A letter from St Basil (Introduction, 19; cf. **31**, **40–1**, **68**), offering some constructive criticism of two books sent to him by their author, a fellow churchman. Discussion of the right style for a Christian writer, and of the right way to use dialogue form, leads B. into an instructive analysis of Plato's distinctive approach, which a lesser writer should think twice before taking as a model.

Διοδώρωι (*ODC*³ s.v.): the future bishop of Tarsus (378), an influential teacher and a pillar of orthodoxy; at the time of writing he was a refugee, driven out of Antioch by his Arian opponents. **πρεσβυτέρωι:** by this time (contrast the use of the word by the author of **39**) a formal rank in the Church hierarchy, subordinate to Bishop. **1 ἐνέτυχον:** LSJ ἐντυγχάνω III (cf. Lat. *incido*, as used in **58** below); opening a book to read it is like running into a person. **τιμιότητός σου:** the same idiom as in **40** (τὴν σὴν σεμνοπρέπειαν) and **41** (τὴν τελειότητά

σου) above.   ἀργῶς... καὶ ἀσθενῶς: because of B.'s ill health, referred to also at the end of the letter.   λοιπόν: adverbial; in later
Greek usage = 'henceforward', 'in my (your, his,...) turn', 'moreover', 'finally' – i.e. some particular determination of the basic sense
'for the rest'.   πυκνόν: LSJ πυκνός ii, rather than v ('sagacious,
shrewd'). The series of commendatory terms that begins here (continuing with εὐκρινῶς, ἁπλοῦν, ἀκατάσκευον) makes a clear and conventional
literary-critical contrast with those attached to the other book – πολυτελεστέραι, ποικίλοις, χάρισι κεκομψευμένον, διασπῶσι, ὑποχαυνοῦσι.
ἀντιθέσεις = lit. 'counter-(pro)positions', ἀπαντήσεις = lit. 'meetings',
'encounterings'; both technical terms of argumentation from Aristotle onwards.   ὑπεναντίων: Arian heretics, whom both D. and B. were active in combating.   διαβολαὶ... καὶ συστάσεις: use of dialogue form
has allowed D. to let his opponents speak for themselves. συστάσεις (LSJ
b.i) refers to the 'close combat' or 'cut-and-thrust' of dialogue; ὑπεναντίων
is subj. not obj. gen.   γλυκύτητας... διαλεκτικάς: as the more elaborate and decorative, but also more informal kind, dialogue is reckoned
more receptive to charming effects than the austerer treatise or oration: cf.
Hermogenes, *Id.* 2.10, 387.5–12 Rabe (Platonic style); 2.4, 330.1–339.13
Rabe (γλυκύτης); [Aristides], *Rhet.* 2.6 (γλυκύτης).   ὑποχαυνοῦσιν:
lit. 'make somewhat flabby/flaccid/puffy'; χαῦνος/χαυνόω (designating
the opposite of both τόνος and πυκνότης) can characterize either moral
or (as here) stylistic imperfection; cf. Arist. *NE* 1107b23, [Longin.] *Sublim.*
4.3.   σου ἡ ἀγχίνοια: almost an honorific title, like τῆς τιμιότητός
σου above, 'Your Sagacity'.   ἔξωθεν: i.e. outside the Christian broth-
erhood; a regular way of referring to pagan classical writers and thinkers.
Ἀριστοτέλης καὶ Θεόφραστος: the dialogues of Aristotle (e.g. *Symposium*, *Eudemus*, *Protrepticus*, *On philosophy*) and Theophrastus (*Callisthenes*,
?*Megaricus*, ?*Megacles*) now survive (if at all) only in fragments, but were
widely read and admired in antiquity: see Cic. *De Or.* 1.49, *Or.* 19.62, Quint.
10.1.83. Something of the difference in approach to dialogue between
them and Plato, of which B. speaks here, can still be caught by comparing
Plato's dialogues with Cicero's, which follow a more Aristotelian formula.
Πλατωνικῶν χαρίτων: for B.'s assessment of Plato, as combining charm
with power in his compositions, cf. esp. Dion. Hal. *Demosth.* 5–7 (= *Ep.
Pomp.* 2), Hermogenes *Id.* 2.10, 387.5–12 Rabe.   παρακωμωιδεῖ τὰ
πρόσωπα: Thrasymachus in *Resp.* 1, Hippias in *Hippias* and *Protagoras*
and Protagoras in *Protagoras*. For a modern view of Plato's presentation and

use of minor characters, see Coventry (1990); of B.'s own brief analyses, the third (of the character of Plato's Protagoras) is perhaps more dubious than the other two, and in general the reduction of all such portrayals to simple satire is a large over-simplification. The phrase παρακωμωιδεῖ τὰ πρόσωπα ushers in a whole series of theatrical metaphors (cf. ἐπεισ-αγέι, ἐπεισκυκλεῖ ('wheels on using the *eccyclema*'), ὑποθέσεσιν), depicting Plato in his dialogues as playwright/stage-manager; the family relation-ship between dialogue and drama (cf. **73**.226) makes this an appropriate choice of imagery.   **ἀόριστα:**   lit. 'indefinite', 'undefined' – interlocu-tors whose characters are not fixed in advanced by the literary or historical record.   **ἐν τοῖς Νόμοις:**   sc. by taking as his speakers the otherwise un-known Cleinias and Megillus and the anonymous 'Athenian stranger'.

2 ὑποθήκας . . . ὠφελίμων λόγων: lit. 'advice consisting in (defining gen.) beneficial words'.   **ὑποβαλλώμεθα:**   LSJ ii.1.   **ἐπιβάλλει:** LSJ ii.7.   **ἀπαντῶσι:**   lit. 'arrive at', 'get to': LSJ ii.4.   **ἵνα δειχθῆι:**   B.'s protestation of the friendly and constructive aims of his criticism may or may not be sincere; equally, it is unclear whether D. either expected or wanted such a detailed response when he sent his two latest compositions.   **οὐκ ἀποκνήσει γράφων:**   D. was in-deed to prove a prolific author, though much of his work is now lost. **ὑποθέσεις:**   here 'pretexts' (LSJ i.4) or 'subject matter' (ii.1), rather than 'plot'.   **πραγμάτων:**   B.'s official business as Bishop of Caesarea. **ἀναγνώστου:**   lit. 'reader', it being an important part of the secretary's duties to read out his employer's mail, and other documents, to him. **τῶν εἰς τάχος γραφόντων:**   as opposed to a calligrapher (cf. *Ep.* 134 fin.); it is not clear whether the use of a regular system of shorthand (*OCD*[3] s.v. 'tachygraphy'), as opposed to sporadic abbreviation and a general lack of concern for appearance, is in question.   **τὰ ἐπίφθονα Καππαδοκῶν:** on the face of it, more like a conventional grumble about local shortages than hard evidence of economic decline. B. may however be making a covert reference to the recent division of the province in two by the Em-peror Valens, which had robbed him, to his great annoyance, of half his see (Jones (1971) 182–5).

56 Theon, *P.Mil.Vog.* 11. A papyrus letter (305 x 140 mm), perhaps found in Oxyrhynchus, written to accompany a consignment of philosophical books; a postscript identifies the place of writing (but of the letter or the copies of the books?) as Alexandria. Apart from the postscript, which is in cursive characters, the rest of the letter is in elegant capitals; as with the other papyrus letters in this collection, there are no accents, breathings or word-breaks; mute iota is written adscript not (as often) omitted. For the content, and apparent social context, compare esp. **35** above.

Bibliography. A. Vogliano, *Papiri dell'Università degli Studi di Milano* I (1937; repr. 1966) 17–20; *Corpus dei Papiri Filosofici* (*CPF*) I (Florence 1989) I.1*, 110–14 (A. Linguiti).

εὖ πράττειν: a rare form of salutation in papyrus letters. Its use in fourth/third-century B.C. philosophers' letters (all of Plato's except the third, Strato of Lampsacus in Diog. Laert. 5.60, Epicurus in Diog. Laert. 10.14; cf. 'Dionysius' in *Ep. Socrat.* 34) suggests that it is deliberately chosen here to lend a high tone; an occurrence in a letter of condolence (*P.Ross.Georg.* 3.2) points the same way (although there seems to be no such special point in *P.Oxy.* 822 and *PSI* 1445); see Introduction, 35.   **πᾶσαν εἰσφέρομαι σπουδήν:** εἰσφέρομαι + πᾶς/πολύς + n. is an idiom of the Hellenistic and Imperial periods, cf. LSJ εἰσφέρω II.4.   **κατασκευάζειν:** it is unclear whether T. is speaking of buying books, or having fresh copies made, or both.   **βυβλία:** the original spelling (βύβλος = 'papyrus'), replaced by βιβ- in the Hellenistic period, but common again in Imperial times (no doubt helped by the assimilation in sound between ι and υ).   **συντείνοντα:** LSJ II.2.   **καθήκειν:** Stoic technical terminology for moral duty, but not original to them (LSJ II.2) and by this period part of the philosophical *lingua franca*; cf. **46** above.   **οὐ τῆς τυχούσης . . . ὠφελεῖσθαι:** this suggests that T. is not a mere agent for H., but sees himself as someone committed to philosophical values on his own account; compare Aquila and Sarapion in **35** above.   **ἔρρωσο . . . αὐτός:** the formula is a common one (Exler 103–6), but much more often found at the beginning than at the end of a letter; ἐρρώμην is an 'epistolary' imperfect (Introduction, 36).   **ἄσπασαι οὓς προσήκει:** ἄσπασαι (or ἀσπάζου) is formulaic in this position (Exler 115), but οὓς προσήκει seems a somewhat cold and formal variant for a more specific object or objects: another deliberately 'philosophical' touch?   **ἐγράφη κτλ:** it is unclear whether this refers to the letter, or to the books it accompanies.   **Βοήθου κτλ:** the authors named are all celebrated Stoic philosophers: Boethus of Sidon (2nd century B.C.), Diogenes of Babylon (3rd–2nd century B.C.), Chrysippus of Soli (3rd century B.C., the 'second founder' of Stoicism), Antipater of Tarsus (2nd century B.C.) and Posidonius of Apamea (2nd–1st century B.C.). Of the titles given here, only the third and the last are attested in any other surviving source (and the third only in another papyrus, *P.Ross.Georg.* 1.22).   ἀσκήσεως: see n. on **35** above. ἀλυπίας: for this topic, see Max. Tyr. *Or.* 28, with Trapp (1997) 231–6. προτρέπεσθαι: more or less a technical term for moral exhortation, or exhortation to embrace philosophical values; this seems to be the work known otherwise as P.'s Προτρεπτικοί (sc. λόγοι), cf. frr. 1–3 Edelstein-Kidd.   φιλοσόφωι: see n. to **35** above.

57 Flavius Claudius Iulianus, *Ep.* 23 (= 9 = 107). A letter from the Emperor Julian (Introduction, 16; cf. **24, 67**) to the Prefect of Egypt, instructing him to institute a search for the library of a Christian bishop, recently lynched in a riot in Alexandria. J.'s letter of reproof to the Alexandrians for the murder is given as **67** below.

377d Ἐκδικίωι: Ekdikios Olympos (*PLRE* I 647–8, Olympus 3), Prefect of Egypt 362–3; perhaps the same E. as was a schoolfellow and friend of Libanios.   ἐπάρχωι: ἔπαρχος (LSJ 2) is the standard Greek equivalent of the Latin *praefectus*, in all its uses.   ἄλλοι μέν κτλ: an example of the rhetorical device known as the priamel, in which a personal preference is emphasized by being contrasted with the rejected preferences of others: cf. Sappho fr. 16.1–4 L–P, Pindar, *Ol.* 1.1–7, Hor. *Odes* 1.1.3–28, and in prose, Plato, *Lysis* 211 de, which J. may indeed be recalling here. J. contrasts his own lifelong passion for books with other, less intellectual upper-class pursuits: the breeding and racing of horses, keeping gamebirds and/or songbirds, and the the collecting and/or hunting of wild animals.   **378a** ἐκ παιδαρίου δεινὸς ἐντέτηκε πόθος: apparently a favourite phrase of J.'s, as he uses a variant also in *Or.* 4.130c, perhaps even a quotation. ἐντήκω is in any case idiomatic (esp. in the intrans. pf.) for ingrained feelings (LSJ II.3).   οἷς οὐκ ἀρκεῖ κτλ: another rather self-congratulatory hit at the materialism (and dishonesty) of J.'s competitors for the books.   ἰδιωτικήν: i.e. irrespective of our official relationship as Emperor and Prefect.   ὅπως ἀνευρεθῆι: the ὅπως-clause, explaining what the favour requested is, is not a final clause but an instance of an object clause following an implied or understood 'verb of effort' ('see to it that'), in which the subj. can sometimes stand for the fut. (Smyth §2214).   Γεωργίου: the Arian Bishop of Alexandria from 357, murdered in a riot on 24 Dec. 361: the story is to be found in

Sozomenos, *Hist. Eccl.* 4.10.8–12, 4.30.1–2 and 5.7; cf. Socrates, *HE* 2.28 and 3.2, Philostorgius, *HE* 7.2, Chadwick (1967) 136–45, 155 and Haas (1997) 280–95. **378b τῆς τῶν δυσσεβῶν Γαλιλαίων διδασκαλίας:** a characteristically tart and belittling ref. to Christianity, from the Emperor famous for his rearguard action against it; J. deliberately avoids styling Christianity a 'philosophy' or a form of piety, or mentioning its founder and namesake. **νοτάριος:** the Greek transliteration of the Latin *notarius*, lit. 'shorthand writer', 'stenographer'. **γέρως ἴστω τευξόμενος ἐλευθερίας:** word-order, morphology (γέρως, ἴστω) and construction (participle in indirect speech) are all consciously refined and carefully classicizing. **378c ἀμωσγέπως:** another learned, Atticizing touch, cf. Schmid II 76 (Aristides), III 100 (Aelian). **περὶ τὴν Καππαδοκίαν ὄντι:** during the six years (345–51) when J. was interned by the Emperor Constantius II at Macellum (near Caesarea) in Cappadocia, in the charge of Arian Christian tutors, and Georgios was in Caesarea; J. had not yet at that stage declared openly for paganism.

58 M. Valerius Martialis, *Epig.* 2, *praef.* A flippant dedicatory epistle from the beginning of Book 2 of Martial's *Epigrams*, in which M. imagines his addressee protesting that such an epistle is out of place, and accepts his strictures. Of the other thirteen books of the *Epigrams*, another four also have prose epistolary prefaces: Book 1 (to the reader), 8 (to Domitian), 9 (to Taranius) and 12 (to Priscus).

Deciano: a lawyer and fellow-countryman of M.'s, from Emerita in Spain, praised for his adherence to moderate Stoic principle in 1.8; cf. also 1.61.10, 1.24, 1.39 and 2.5. **cum:** *OLD* 14a. **praestamus:** *OLD* 9, cf. 11. **epistolam:** no example survives of an epistolary preface to a Greek or Latin play, though all of Terence's comedies and most of Plautus' have an extra-dramatic prologue; Quintilian 8.3.31 speaks of *praefationes* to tragedies by Pomponius Secundus and Seneca in which stylistic issues were discussed, and which may have been epistolary in form. The crucial contrast, as explained in *pro se loqui non licet*, is between literary forms in which the author's own 'voice' can be heard in the body of the work, and those (like drama and (sometimes) dialogue) in which it can not. **curione:** a further theatrical reference, either to the announcement of the play title by a crier before the performance, or perhaps to the prologue-speaker himself. **epigrammata ... faciunt:**

an interesting comment on both forms; letters and epigrams are alike in their limited length, and in the particular way they allow an author to speak directly to an addressee or addressees.   **in toga saltantis ... personam:**   the metaphor continues the theatrical reference. It is the epigrams that should be allowed to 'dance' exuberantly: a pompous, officious prose preface looks awkward beside them and blunts their effect. Both because of its weight and because of its symbolic association with formal civic business, the toga was grotesquely unsuited to any form of dancing, let alone before a mass audience. The phrase has a proverbial ring to it: Otto p. 274.   **uideris:**   fut. perf. indic. with imper. force (G–L §245).   **contra retiarium ferula:**   i.e. a grotesque mismatch, as of a gladiators' trainer with his staff (or even a schoolmaster with his cane?) against the *retiarius* with his net, trident and half-armour. As Decianus, in M.'s portrayal, becomes more heated in his protests, he shifts from placider theatrical to more violent gladiatorial imagery; the point is again the ridiculous and counter-productive discrepancy between the wit and pugnacity of epigram and the flat, ineffective pedantry of a prose epistle.   **reclamant:**   at the mismatch, like the (amphi)theatre crowd showing its disapproval at some aspect of the show (cf. Cic. *De or.* 3.196, *Or.* 173).   **me hercules:**   apparently more colloquial than *mehercule*, Cic. *Or.* 157.   **quid si scias:**   an epistolary joke, teasingly disregarding the proper chronology of writing, sending, reading and responding; M. is taking the recipient's reaction into account even before the letter has been finished, let alone read.   **debebunt tibi:**   the conclusion pokes gentle fun at both M. and D., and perhaps echoes the dedicatory epistle at the beginning of Ovid's *Amores*, announcing that the reader now has only three rather than the original five books to suffer through.   **incederint:**   cf. the Greek ἐντυγχάνω for 'open', 'read', as in **55** above. **primam paginam:**   the dedicatory epistle is felt not to be part of the main sequence of columns (*pagina*, *OLD* 1 a) on the book-roll, just as it also stands apart from the remaining contents in form; cf. the epistle to Book 9, said to stand *extra ordinem paginarum*.

59 Iulius Pollux, *Onomastikon* **1.1.** The rather more respectful (and self-important) epistle than Martial's **58**, from the first book of Iulius Pollux' *Onomastikon*, to the future Emperor Commodus. Each of the remaining nine books of the work also bears a prefatory letter to the same addressee. Commodus' subsequent record as ruler lends a certain irony to P.'s words.

Ἰούλιος Πολυδεύκης: a native of Naucratis in Egypt, famous as an orator as well as a scholar and teacher (Philostratus, *VS* 2.12, 592–3, Lucian, *Rhet. praec.* 24). Whether as a direct result of the flattery in the *Onomastikon* or not, he was appointed to the Imperial Chair of Rhetoric at Athens in or soon after 178.   Κομμόδωι: the son of Marcus Aurelius (cf. **9**, **53–4** above), born in 161, made Caesar (imperial heir) in 168, co-Emperor from 177, sole Emperor 180–92. At the time of writing he will have been of just the age to be finishing his literary education and (in theory) receptive to works like P.'s.   ὦ παῖ πατρὸς ἀγαθοῦ: grandiose diction, with a touch of tragic tone: cf. e.g. Soph. *Philoct.* 96 and 242.   κατ' ἴσον: a relatively rare and apparently unclassical variation for the more usual ἐξ ἴσου.   τὸ δ' ἐν τῆι χρείαι τῆς φωνῆς: a rhetor's (or grammarian's) definition of σοφία, cf. e.g. Quint. 2.20, but one which could also call for support on the Stoic acceptance of articulate utterance as a mode of *logos*, rationality, cf. L–S §§53T–U.   μάθημα: lit 'lesson', 'thing (to be) learned'.   ἔν γέ τι: P. modestly admits (as he is bound to) that good vocabulary is not the *sole* constituent of eloquence.   ὀνομαστικόν: sc. βιβλίον, lit. 'naming-book', differing from a λεξικόν in its thematic rather than alphabetical arrangement. The work as we now have it is not the full original text but an epitome, with additions by later readers; for a brief description, see *OCD*[3] s.v. 'Pollux'.   πεφιλοτίμηται: impersonal passive.   ἐπελθῆι: LSJ 1.3; P.'s words are both a promise that the work will not be too pedantically systematic (just as it forswears any ambition to be comprehensive), and an assertion of his own expertly knowledgeable control over its contents.

60 Phalaris, *Ep.* 78. The tyrant Phalaris (Introduction, 28–9) in benign mood (compare and contrast **11–12**, **23**, **38**, **51**, **84**) writes to the poet Stesichoros to commission a poem in honour of a friend's recently deceased wife (a function which has something in common with a letter of recommendation, cf. Section **IV** above). Subsequent letters (65, 79, 114) show that the commission was accepted and executed. P.'s request is clearly and persuasively urged (indeed, this may have been intended from the first as a model letter); the message begins with (*a*) an explanation of the circumstances of the request; and moves on to (*b*) a statement of the worthiness of both the friend and his wife; (*c*) the countering of a possible objection; (*d*) an exhortation to the recipient to live up to his past reputation; (*e*) encouragement to grant the request for the sake of the intermediary who is transmitting it; and (*f*) a conclusion that assumes consent and moves on confidently to the next stage in the transaction.

Στησιχόρωι: a frequent presence in P.'s correspondence, not only as poet but also as democratic political activist, and the father of a family of poetically gifted daughters: see Russell (1988) 97–9. **1 Νικοκλῆς** is not known to the historical record; the *name* may be borrowed from the orations of Demosthenes. In any case, it bears out Russell's observation (*ibid.* 104) that the names in P.'s correspondence 'are mostly rather grand, as befits the almost epic ethos', as do those of his brother, his wife and her father. **ἐπιφάνειαν**: LSJ ii.2. **τῶν... δυναμένων**: partitive gen. after ἔστι, a stylishly classicizing touch, cf. Aristides in Philostratus, *VS* ii.583. **μέγα... πένθος**: the interlaced word-order and alliteration of 'p' are deliberately high style, as is the metaphorical use of περιτέθειται (pf. mid.). **ἀδελφιδῆν... καὶ γυναῖκα**: a perfectly legitimate union in Classical and Hellenistic Greek culture; Roman law seems to have allowed marriage between uncle and brother's daughter, but not uncle and sister's child (Hallett (1984) 159–63, 196, 307–8). **πόθοις**: the plural is odd, and possibly modelled (mistakenly) on Plato's use of πόθοι to mean *instances* or *kinds* of longing (*Phileb.* 48a, *Laws* 633d, 870a). The picture given here of friendly relations between P. and S. is rather at variance with that to be found in the rest of the correspondence. **Κλεόνικον**: the brother's name is made up of the same elements as Nikokles', but in reverse order; both share the κλέος-component with the recently deceased wife. **ἠξίου ὅπως**: post-classical usage, cf. LSJ ἀξιόω ii.2. **ἔπαινον ἐν ποιήσει**: i.e. a *threnos* (lament). S. (as opposed to the later Simonides) is not known to literary history for this kind of poetry, as the composer of the letter goes on implicitly to concede in the next sentence but one. **ἀνωτάτω**: LSJ ἄνω c.ii. **2 πεφύλαξαι... ἀνθρώπους** defers to the known facts of literary history: to judge by surviving fragments and testimonia, all S.'s surviving poetry indeed took the form of grand ('Homeric') mythological narrative, about the heroes of the distant past. **ὠνίαν**: like (notoriously) that of Simonides: see Testimonia 22–3 Campbell. **φιλότης**: this use of the abstract n. as a vocative was reckoned as an Atticism (Schmid iv 642); cf. LSJ φιλότης *ad fin.* **ἀποστραφῆις**: aor. pass., lit 'turn yourself away from', governing a direct obj. acc. **3 λοιπόν**: LSJ 4–5. **νένευκας** 'have become inclined' (as a result of the letter so far), rather than 'have assented': LSJ 4. Assuming assent can be an effective means of persuading the still

hesitant.   **Κλεαρίστην γράφε κτλ:**   P. proceeds to give a brief résumé
of the dead woman's life, such as might appear on a funerary inscription, as
the basis for S.'s poem. He (or rather the author of the letter) works with a
pleasantly businesslike (but not necessarily unrealistic) idea of how poems
are created, with the inspiration of the Muses (ἐπιπνευσθείσης ... θεῶν)
supposed to intervene to convert the bare framework of fact into great poetry.   **ἐπιπνευσθείσης, κατέχηι:**   standard vocabulary for the ideas
of divine inspiration and possession, esp. of poets: LSJ ἐπιπνέω III, ἐπίπ-
νοια; κατέχω II.10, κάτοχος II.2.   **καί σου ... ἐπεσταλμένηι:**   the
grandiloquent closing wish (so to speak, a hugely inflated ἔρρωσο) seems to
owe something to the closing conventions of hymnic and epinician poetry,
which can similarly involve not only celebration of present success but also
anticipation of future achievements, both on the part of the poet and on the
part of his patron: cf. e.g. Pind. *Ol.* 1.115–16, *Isth.* 5.62–3, Theoc. 16.98–109.
σου τὴν ἱερὰν καὶ ὑμνόπολον κεφαλήν: again, high style and classicizing (LSJ 2), perhaps looking back to the most famous classical use of this
synecdoche, in Plato's *Phaedrus* 234d5–6 (cf. 264a8), esp. because in both
places it is closely associated with the topic of inspiration.   **τῆι νῦν:**
the poem is acknowledged in *Epp.* 65, 79 and 114 as satisfactorily completed,
but is of course fictitious.   **ἐπεσταλμένηι:**   it is perhaps a deliberately
knowing touch to end a letter with the verb ἐπιστέλλω in its *non*-epistolary
sense.

B PUBLIC LIFE AND OFFICIAL
CORRESPONDENCE

'Sometimes we write to kings and cities' (Demetrius, *De elocutione* [**73**
below] 234). The eleven letters in this section illustrate the operation of the
letter as a medium of public communication and administration, whether
in the kingdoms of the Hellenistic monarchs, the Roman Empire, the
early Christian church, or the imagined world of an archaic Greek tyrant;
although their geographical background ranges from Egypt and North
Africa (**61**, **65**, **67**) to Sicily (**70**), the centre of gravity is Asia Minor (**62–4**,
66, **68**), where the administrative problems under discussion extend from
the Hellenistic to the Roman Imperial period. They illustrate how the functions of official correspondence both overlap with those of private letters
(e.g. in recommending, exhorting, defending, and requesting favours) and

contain elements and emphases of their own; it is also interesting to see
how related purposes can be found in both a Hellenistic monarch's letter
and a Christian bishop's (**62**, **68**). In style, they are as a group by and
large more formal and solemn than their private counterparts (cf. again
Demetrius in **73**.234). It is intriguing to observe how differences in status
between writer and addressee(s) are negotiated in these letters. In general, a
courteous tone predominates: inferiors write respectfully to their superiors,
and superiors – in line with Julius Victor's *si inferiori, ne superba* (**75** below) –
write politely to their inferiors; the one clear exception, significantly, comes
in a (fictitious) letter from the ferocious tyrant Phalaris. This courtesy is
particularly striking in the case of letters from rulers to cities (**62**, **64**,
67), where the tone seems conditioned not solely by the sense of the letter as
an essentially friendly form (Introduction, 40–1), but also by a more general
ideology of royal and imperial benevolence (cf. e.g. Ma (1999) 182–94). See
also Introduction, 4–5, 7–10, 15, 42.

61 Amenneus, *P.Grenf.* ii.14 (b). One of a set of four letters of the
Ptolemaic period recovered from the foot end of an Oxyrhynchus mummy
case, three of which are either by or to one Asklepiades, who seems to have
been a middle-ranking official in the service of the *dioiketes*, the Finance
Minister, in Alexandria. In this one (dimensions not reported) a minor
official writes to report on local preparations for a visit by the *dioiketes*: we
may contrast the humble preoccupations at stake here (as in **65**) with the
grander issues and the power-play of the other letters in this section. Like the
other papyrus letters in this collection, it is written without word-division,
punctuation, accents or breathings; and with mute final iota adscript. One
hand writes the letter itself and its one-word address, another the record of
its date of receipt and contents.

Bibliography. Grenfell and Hunt (1897) 26–9.

'Αμεννεύς: an Egyptian name ('Amon has come'), contrasting with the
Greek names borne by the two senior officials.   ἀρχισωματοφύλακος:
an honorific court title, rather than a strict designation of function.
διοικητοῦ: it is not clear whether there was only one holder of this
rank at a time, or several; either way, Chrysippos ranks as a V.I.P.
λευκομετώπους are presumably birds, given what follows. The birds
listed (415 in all), together with the fifty pack-animals also mentioned,

give an idea of the size of the Minister's entourage.   ὄρνιθας: used both of domestic fowl and wildfowl, to cover all those not worth itemizing by species.   περιστριδεῖς: phonetic misspelling of περιστεριδεῖς, omitting an unstressed short syllable.   τὰς .[....]ς: the missing word is presumably something like 'saddles' or 'harness'.   ὁδοποίαι: the local community was responsible for ensuring that important visitors were not delayed by bad road-surfaces.   ἔτους κβ′: the regnal year of the current monarch; since the handwriting of the letter seems to put it into the second half of the 3rd century, the ref. is probably to Year 22 of Ptolemy III Euergetes I, i.e. 224 B.C.   Χοίαχ: co-ordinated with Nov. 27 – Dec. 26 in the Roman period, but not so exactly fixable earlier on. ξενίων: a loose gen. of connection (Smyth §1361).

62 Attalos III of Pergamum, *Inschr. Perg.* 248. A letter from King Attalos, informing the people of Cyzicus of the honours conferred on a fellow-citizen and (by implication) exhorting them to match these with benefactions of their own. The conferring of honours and privileges in this way was an important aspect of public life in both the Hellenistic and Imperial periods, serving both to maintain the identity and separateness of an élite governing class, and to facilitate its control by a monarch or emperor. The letter survives in an inscribed copy, set up in Pergamum, along with copies of two other related letters and a decree commanding their incorporation into the city's laws. The remains of the inscription, now in Berlin, make up a block 84 cm high, 44–48.5 cm wide, and 7.8–8.5 cm thick, with an average height of 8 mm for the characters and 3 mm between lines. Like letters on papyri, inscribed letters are innocent of punctuation, word-break, accents and breathings; mute final iota is written adscript rather than omitted, as on many papyri and on later inscriptions (e.g. **63–4**).

Structure, style and orthography. In keeping with a familiar tendency in administrative and legal documents, the body of the letter consists of just two sentences: one huge one, with an untidy series of subordinate clauses, to introduce the honorand and summarize his career; and a second much shorter one stating the purpose of the present communication. The style is a mixture of cumbersome officialese (especially obtrusive in the long sentence) and attempts at something more elegant (the litotes οὐκ... ἀγνοεῖν, the politely unassertive εἴ γε, and the tricolon καλοκαγαθίαν ... εὐσέβειαν ... εὔνοιαν καὶ πίστιν). In orthography, *nu* at word-end is usually written as *gamma* before palatal mutes (κ [χ, γ]) and *mu* before labial mutes (φ, φ [β]), as it would be in mid-word, but with some inconsistency (τὴν πρὸς αὐτόν, κρίναντες). There is one uncorrected miscarving, of προστήσησθαι for προστήσεσθαι.

Bibliography. Welles (1934) 264–73.

Ἄτταλος: Attalos III, the last independent king of Pergamum (born. *c.* 170 B.C.), who reigned 138–133 and bequeathed his kingdom to Rome. Κυζικηνῶν: Cyzicus (on the Propontis) was an independent city-state with a history of good relations with Pergamum. τῆι βουλῆι καὶ τῶι δήμωι: the standard formula for a city in its formal, political identity, specifying its two sovereign legislative bodies. Ἀθήναιος ... μου: grammatically part of the ὅτι-clause introduced by ἀγνοεῖν, but put at the head of the sentence for clarity and emphasis, to establish immediately the subject of the letter. The sentence as a whole consists of (i) a main clause, Ἀθήναιος ... ἀγνοεῖν, and (ii) a subordinate clause, εἴ γε ... βασιλείας; (ii) is itself composed of (*a*) a principal clause, εἴ γε ... ἐγέννησεν, with its own subordinate participle and relative clause, and (*b*) a dependent relative clause, divided into two long sub-clauses (τὸ μὲν πρῶτον ..., ὕστερον δέ ...), each again with its own dependent participles. In meaning, the contents of the subordinate clauses are just as important as those of the main clauses. καθηγεμόνος: a cult-title specific to Pergamum, where this Dionysus was particularly favoured by the royal family; see Allen (1983) 148–9, Hansen (1971) 409–10. συντρόφου: an alumnus of the corps of royal pages, 'brought up with' the King. ὅτι μέν: prefatory μέν, indicating additional and/or contrasting points to come, with no answering δέ (Denniston 369–84); it looks forward both to the review of Athenaios' career, and to the royal decision announced at the end of the letter. πατρός: Eumenes II (reigned 197–158). Ἄτταλος ὁ θεῖος: Attalos II (reigned 158–138). Σαβαζίου: a Phrygian god, identified sometimes with Zeus, sometimes with Dionysus, and specially favoured at Pergamum; for what is known of his cult, see *OCD*[3] s.v. μεταλλαξάντος: euphemistic. καλοκαγαθίαν ... εὐσέβειαν ... εὔνοιαν καὶ πίστιν: a careful spread of compliments to A.'s right dealing with men and gods in general, and specifically with the Attalid house. καὶ τῆς ... ἠξιώσαμεν αὐτόν: strictly speaking an anacoluthon, as we are still in the relative clause introduced by ὧι (= Athenaios, the same referent as for αὐτόν), but the length of the sentence makes the irregularity not only unobjectionable but positively desirable. **μυστηρίων:** the cult of Dionysus Kathegemon was one of those open to initiates only. **διασαφεῖται:** the reference seems to be to official diaries, *ephemerides* (*OCD*³ s.v.), in which events of the reign were recorded. **ὅπως εἰδῆτε:** A.'s purpose in writing was of course not simply to give information; the citizens of Cyzicus will have known what was expected of them. **ὡς ἔχομεν φιλοστοργίας:** LSJ ἔχω B.II.b. **δ':** the regnal year. **Δίου:** the first month of the Macedonian year. **Μένης:** the messenger entrusted with the delivery of the original letter from Pergamum to Cyzicus.

63 Mithridates of Pontus, *SIG*³ 741 III (= 73 Welles). A letter from the King to a local governor, commanding the offering of a reward for the apprehension of three of his pro-Roman enemies, dead or alive. It survives on an inscription from Nysa, set up not by Mithridates or his governor, but by the friends or family of the main victim, Chairemon, reclaiming his memory after his death and after the restoration of Roman power in the area; measuring 90 × 58 × 22 cm, this inscription also contains the text of a second wanted notice from M., a letter of praise for Chairemon from the Roman proconsul C. Cassius, and a dedication from the city of Nysa. M.'s letter is thus quoted somewhat against its author's original intentions.

Structure, style and orthography. After the greeting, the letter consists of just one clearly and simply structured sentence, divided between a justificatory ἐπεί-clause, and a main clause issuing the order and specifying the contents of the notice (the same structure is common in civic decrees); both the subordinate and the main clause are subdivided into two. The spelling κχ for χ in ἐκχθρότατα, ἐκχθίστοις (a kind of doubling of the consonant) may reflect a shift in the pronunciation of *chi* from plosive to fricative (Horrocks (1997) 112–13); mute final iota is omitted.

Bibliography. Welles (1934) 294–9.

Μιθριδάτης: Mithridates VI Eupator Dionysus, King of Pontus 120–63 B.C., who conducted a long-successful resistance to the growth of Roman power. At the time of writing of this letter, his armies were completing their victorious sweep through Asia Minor in the First Mithridatic War: see Scullard (1982) 74–9. **Λεωνίππωι:** probably at this stage governor of Caria; later a garrison commander in Sinope, executed for

an attempt to betray the city to the Romans.   **σατράπηι:** the use
of the Persian term for a provincial governor (στρατηγός is the normal
Hellenistic Greek word) underlines M.'s claim to be a successor of the
great oriental monarchs (as indeed does his own name, formed from that
of the god Mithra).   **Χαιρήμων:** not known apart from this inscription, but see the n. below on his sons.   **πράγματα:** LSJ III.2; the
same usage as Lat. *res publica(e)*.   **πολεμίοις:** the Romans; Cassius'
letter, mentioned in the headnote above, records a gift of 60,000 modii
of barley from Chairemon to the army.   **παρουσίαν:** the same word
as is used for the governor's visit in **61** above, but rather more threatening in this context.   **Πυθόδωρον καὶ Πυθίωνα:** one or other of
these (perhaps more likely the latter) produced a son, Pythodoros, who
was to become a friend and supporter of Pompey and son-in-law of Mark
Antony.   **ἐξέθετο . . . πέφευγεν:** further details emerge from the other
letter of M.'s preserved on the inscription. The sons were sent to Rhodes,
which M. never captured; C. himself took refuge in the temple of Artemis
at Ephesus, where he may have died in the massacre of refugees recorded
by Appian in *Mithridat.* 23.   **ποιῆσαι:** infin. for imper.   **κήρυγμα
ποιῆσαι ὅπως . . . λάβηι:**   ὅπως + subj. is regularly used in later Greek
(as seen also on papyri and in the NT) in place of the infin. after verbs
of requesting and commanding: Mayser II 1.251–2, Funk (1961) §392 =
Rehkopf (1976) §392.4.4.c.   **τάλαντα τεσσαράκοντα:** a very substantial sum; the difference between the two rewards shows (ominously)
what importance M. attaches to capturing his enemies alive.

64 C. Octavius Caesar Imperator, Doc. 12 Reynolds. A letter from
the triumvir Octavian (the future Emperor Augustus) to the people of
Ephesus, requesting the return of a statue looted from Aphrodisias during
the fighting between the triumviral forces and those of Caesar's assassins.
O. writes in order to maintain his prestige as a patron of the city (and of
deserving Greek communities in general), which will in turn reinforce his
position and influence at Rome, vis-à-vis that of his fellow triumvirs and
competitors for power. The letter survives in a copy inscribed in the early
third century A.D. on one of the walls of the theatre of Aphrodisias, in a
kind of public archive of documents relating to the city's history; this part
of the inscription covers a surface-area of 95.5 x 65.5 cm, about 1.5 metres
above ground level, with characters about 2 cm high.

Style, orthography and epigraphy. The style is formal and utilitarian, with no particular attempt at elegance. Long *iota* is spelled ei, reflecting the coalescence of the two sounds in the Hellenistic period (Horrocks (1997) 67, 102ff.). Punctuation, word-break, accents and breathings are, as usual, absent, with the exception of a blank space after στρατεύματος at the end of the salutation, and an arabesque after ἐπιλαμβάνωνται (to mark the boundary between this document and the next one along on the wall); mute iota is omitted. There is a corrected miscarving of ἐπιβοήθειαν for ἐπιβοηθεῖν. Both occurrences of the word Ἀφροδεισιέων and one of the two of Ἀφροδείτηι have been erased; this is due to the efforts of Christians in the 6th to 7th centuries A.D. to efface their city's link with the pagan goddess of sexual love (it was eventually renamed Stauropolis, 'City of the Cross').

Bibliography. Reynolds (1982) 33–41, 101–6, with Plate x.

Αὐτοκράτωρ = *Imperator*, a title which Octavian assumed in late 39 or early 38 B.C. **θεοῦ Ἰουλίου υἱός** = *diui Iulii filius*; O.'s connection with Julius Caesar is particularly pertinent to this communication, as it accounts for his concern for Aphrodisias and a statue belonging to Aphrodite (Venus being the divine patron and ancestor of the Julii). The contrast between O.'s elaborate self-identification in the salutation with the more economical formula used by Attalus and Mithridates brings out the Roman taste for grandiose nomenclature in public contexts; compare also Julian's style in **67** below, and the comments of 'Libanius' in **76**.51.   **ἄρχουσι βουλῆι δήμωι:** see note on **62** τῆι βουλῆι καὶ τῶι δήμωι.   **εἰ ἔρρωσθε ... καὶ αὐτός:** formulaic, in both Greek and Latin (cf. n. on **2** above); the addition of μετὰ τοῦ στρατεύματος (which to the modern ear is apt to sound either quaint or menacing) is also standard, not only for Octavian (cf. e.g. Doc. 6 Reynolds) but more generally (Cic. *Ad fam.* 5.2(= 95 SB), 5.7(= 100 SB).1).   **Πλαρασέων καὶ Ἀφροδεισιέων:** Plarasa and Aphrodisias were two settlements that had combined themselves administratively into a single polis.   **τῶι πολέμωι τῶι κατὰ Λαβιῆνον:** the war in which the Caesarian forces, under Q. Labienus, the son of Caesar's lieutenant T. Labienus, overran a substantial part of Asia Minor, before being defeated by Mark Antony's general P. Ventidius in 39 B.C.: Scullard (1982) 171–2.   **συνάρχοντι:** i.e. fellow triumvir.   **ἐντολάς** = Lat. *mandata*, not necessarily implying any superiority of issuer over recipient (though O. would surely not object to the inference that he was the more actively benevolent party in this business). εὔκαιρον ἐπιβοηθεῖν: the point seems to be that Ephesus, as the port at the end of the main road from Aphrodisias to the sea, was the natural place to try to recover looted property in transit.   σώματος: LSJ II.2.   Ἔρως ... ὅ: the rel. pr. is neut. not masc. because the statue is being thought of as an ἀνάθημα (cf. ἀνατεθείς).   τοῦ πατρός: Julius Caesar, who had evidently used his family connection with Venus to assume patronage of Aphrodisias, and sealed the relationship with a lavish dedication.   Ἀρτέμιδι: the patron goddess of Ephesus (Acts 19: 21–41, etc.).   καλῶς ποιήσετε: politely phrased (in what is something of a cliché of royal and imperial correspondence, cf. Welles (1934) 13.13, RDGE 66.37–8, SEG 9.8.1), but the expectation is clear.   οὐ χαρίεν: a touch of dry humour (but O.'s own (cf. Sueton. Aug. 46, 53) or that of a secretary?); χάρις is more Aphrodite's territory than Artemis'.   ἀνάγκη: as the city's patron.   πρόνοιαν: the benevolent forethought that is characteristic of both enlightened patrons/rulers and gods ('providence'). In applying the word to himself, O. is asserting his status and authority. οὕς ... εὐεργέτηκα: a record of past benefactions increases the pressure to continue at the same level. εὐεργετεῖν and εὐεργεσία are key words in the ideology (and reality) of relationships between cities and their leading citizens and rulers in the Hellenistic and Imperial periods: see Veyne (1990) 71–200, Ma (1999) 179–242. In O.'s use of this vocabulary here we see an example of the way Romans could insert themselves as the new ruling class into pre-existing structures created by Hellenistic kings and cities.   ἦν ... νομίζω: bland words, but again carrying a clear implication; cf. Attalos' οὐ πείθομαι ὑμᾶς ἀγνοεῖν in **62**.

65 The Strategos of the Panopolite Nome, *P. Beatty Panop.* 1.213–16.

A letter from the official in charge of the administrative district (nome, *nomos*) of Panopolis in Egypt, passing on orders from the provincial Governor to the local police. It survives as one item in a register of copies of the strategos' outgoing correspondence for the month of Thoth (= 29 Aug. – 27 Sept. by the Julian calendar), A.D. 298. The main text is written by a scribe and, as normal with papyrus letters, is devoid of word-break, punctuation, accents or breathings. Iota is substituted for ei (cf. headnote to **64** above), Ἑρμωνθιτῶν is mis-spelled as Ἑρμοντιθῶν (metathesis and shortening of an unstressed long syllable), and there are phonetic misspellings of oi for i in κινδύνωι (corrected) and of ai for e in ὑποστήσητε (uncorrected). The last word ('signed') is added in a hand that seems to be the strategos' own.

Bibliography. Skeat (1964) vii–xxv, xxxviii–xl, 26–7.

νυκτοστρατήγοις: in spite of appearances, the word is used of the night watch generically, not just its commanding officers.   **ἐπέθηκε:** LSJ A.VI.   **διασημότατος** = Lat. *(uir) perfectissimus*, the standard later Latin honorific epithet for an official of Athenodorus' rank.   **ἡγούμενος** = Lat. *praeses prouinciae* (LSJ ἡγέομαι II.3.b); Egypt had by this time been divided into two provinces, the Thebaid and Lower Egypt, each with its own internal sub-divisions.   **Ἑρμοντιθῶν:** Hermonthis was on the Nile, about 130 km. SE of Panopolis as the crow flies, but nearer 200 by river.   **φαβρίκος:** φαβρῖξ is a hellenization of the Lat. *fabrica*; the reference seems to be to a major (?military) workshop. The location of the workshop is unspecified, but clearly important to a reconstruction of the situation behind the letter. If it was in the provincial capital, and the provincial capital was Antinoopolis (a good 200 km north of Panopolis; cf. **35** above), then a comprehensible picture emerges: it is suspected that Nilos the smith is heading south, towards his home town, and the hope is to intercept him on the way.   **παρασταθῆναι:** LSJ C.I and II.   **ἐργαλίων** = ἐργαλείων.   **τὸ μεγαλῖον (μεγαλεῖον) αὐτοῦ:** see n. on τὴν σὴν σεμνοπρέπειαν in **40** above.   **ἡπίχθην** = ἠπείχθην (ἐπείγω).   **ἐπιστῖλαι** = ἐπιστεῖλαι, in the sense 'send instructions (by letter)'.   **ὅπως ... παραστήσητε:** see n. on **63** κήρυγμα ποιῆσαι ὅπως.   **ἵνα μὴ ... ὑποστήσηται:** i.e. you will be in trouble if you don't find him.   **Lιε″ καὶ Lιδ″ καὶ Lζ″:** the standard form of dating in the reign of the Emperor Diocletian – fifteen years since D.'s accession (284), fourteen since the elevation of his comrade Maximian to the rank of Caesar (285), seven since the establishment of the tetrarchy (292).   **Θώθ** = Aug. 29 – Sep. 27 by the Julian calendar.   **σεσημίωμαι** = σεσημείωμαι (σημειόω).

66 C. Plinius Secundus, M. Ulpius Traianus Augustus, Pliny, *Ep.* 10.33–4.
An exchange of letters from the period at the end of Pliny's life when he was the Emperor's special envoy (*legatus Augusti consulari potestate*), charged with sorting out the administration of the province of Bithynia-with-Pontus. A modest and apparently sensible suggestion is turned down because of an over-riding concern with public order. Pliny's style in these

more official and functional letters contrasts interestingly with the studied elegance of the rest of his published correspondence (as seen in **16**, **30** and **52** above). Trajan's firm and clearly reasoned answer shows the kind of detailed concern for the minutiae of local administration the Emperor was expected to show in his ever-pressing correspondence: cf. Aurelius in **54** above, and Millar (1977) 213–28.

10.33 1 circumirem: on official business.   **Nicomediae:** the provincial capital (mod. Ismit, in Turkey).   **Gerusian:** Greek acc. A *gerousia* was a kind of civic centre for (well-off) senior citizens (perhaps normally 60+), often organized around a gymnasium; see Jones (1940) 225, 353.   **Iseon:** also Greek acc.; the cult of Isis had been celebrated in this part of the world since Hellenistic times.   **2 uiolentia ... inertia:** ablatives.   **otiosos et immobiles:** the suspicion must be that class envy, as much as simple idleness, was responsible for this inactivity.   **sipo:** something like a stirrup-pump.   **3 collegium fabrorum:** a trade-guild or professional club composed of the manufacturers of fire-fighting equipment; such organizations are known to have been a standard feature of city life in the western half of the Empire, but on the evidence of this exchange of letters (and a complete blank in the inscriptional record) unknown in the East.

10.34 1 secundum exempla complurium: T. acknowledges what P. left unsaid, that his proposal follows a known pattern.   **prouinciam ... ciuitates ... uexatas:** the volatile nature of civic life in Bithynia, and the readiness of the population to indulge in partisan unrest, is best illustrated by the contemporary orations of Dio Chrysostom (Dio of Prusa, also in Bithynia): see esp. his *Orr.* 39, 40, 43, 45, 50. *ciuitates* (pl.) presumably refers to Nicomedia plus the province's second city, Nicaea (unless, as some critics suspect, *eas* is corrupt; an alternative reading would produce a reference to all the province's cities, as distinct from its country districts).   **hetaeriae:** a Latinization of the Greek ἑταιρίαι, the standard term for politically active special-interest 'clubs' of 'comrades' since the 5th century B.C.   **2 satius ... est:** this solution seems by far the less effective of the two, but from the Emperor's point of view limiting fire-damage takes second place to limiting threats to civic order.   **praediorum:** in context, tenement blocks, though *praedia* is a broad term covering all kinds of real estate.   **adcursu populi:** ancient civic life (like that of cities in medieval and early modern Europe) depended heavily on the readiness of citizens to respond co-operatively to a call for help from one of their fellows. For an example of the effectiveness of a cry of 'Fire!', see Apuleius, *Met.* 4.10.4.

67 Flavius Claudius Iulianus, *Ep.* 21 = 10 Bidez = 60 Weiss. The Emperor Julian's letter of reproach to the Alexandrians for the murder of the Arian Christian Bishop George of Cappadocia (for whom see **57** above) in December 361, illustrating again (cf. Trajan in **66**) the Emperor's constant concern for civic order. While vehemently rejecting the 'piety' G. stood for, J. argues that devotion to their own religious and other traditions ought to have prevented the people of Alexandria from acting as they did. At the same time, the amicable appeal to their better nature is backed by a clear threat of firmer sanctions if needed. Compared to Octavian's letter to the Ephesians (**64**), this is a much fuller and more rhetorical piece (e.g. in the opening rhetorical question, and the introduction of quasi-dialogues with the addressees); indeed, an interesting comparison is with *Or.* 32 of Dio Chrysostom (dating from the reign of Vespasian or Trajan), in which Dio too reproaches the Alexandrians for their notorious volatility and reminds them of their distinguished ancestry (see Trapp (1995) 167–75). In tone and purpose, for all that it is an official, public communication, the letter also has something in common with the letters of advice and instruction given in section **A V** above.

The letter survives not in MSS of the works of Julian, but as quoted in the *Ecclesiastical History* of the fifth-century writer Socrates (Scholasticus), 3.3; it is possible that what S. gives is not the full original text, but an edited version.

Αὐτοκράτωρ Καῖσαρ ... Σεβαστός: compare the naming formula in Octavian's letter; J.'s is longer, showing something of the inflation of titles that came with the Empire, but still restrained by the standards of inscribed Imperial letters even from the 2nd century A.D.: cf. e.g. Reynolds (1982) Docs. 15–25. Ἀλεξανδρέων: for the Alexandrians' reputation for disorderly behaviour, see Bowman (1990) 212–16, Trapp (forthcoming, b). 378c Ἀλέξανδρον ... Σάραπιν: the two principal sources of Alexandrian civic pride, their descent from the greatest of all Greek kings and conquerors, and their possession of one of the greatest of all the ancient world's sacred sites. For Sarapis and the temple at Alexandria, see Amm. Marc. 22.16, Bowman (1990) 175–9, Haas (1997) 146–8 and *OCD*[3] s.v. J. had a strong personal attachment of his own to the memory of Alexander (Athanassiadi (1992) 192–3), but his reference to Sarapis is made in deference to local pride rather than as an expression of his own opinions (which favoured Helios-Mithras instead).   **378d** τῆς οἰκουμένης: for this description of the Emperor's status, cf. Pollux' ref. to M. Aurelius in **59** above.   τὰ δεινὰ... μετοικίσας: a quotation from the second century B.C. philosopher and tragic poet Melanthius of Rhodes (*TrGF* 131.1), also used twice by Plutarch (*Mor.* 453e, 551a) and so probably a cliché that had long since floated free of its original context.   **379a** ἐκείνους: as often (e.g. also in lawcourt oratory) the demonstrative indicates the other party to a dispute.   μακαριώτατον: LSJ μακάριος 1.3. Κωνστάντιον: J.'s Arian Christian predecessor (and one-time rival) Constantius II, Emperor 337–61.   στρατηγός: Flavius Artemius (*PLRE* 1 Artemius 2), another Arian Christian given his military command in Egypt (*dux Aegypti*) by Constantius in 360; the incident in question is also recorded by Theodoret, *Hist. Eccl.* 3.18.1 J. subsequently had him tried and executed, at the Alexandrians' instigation (Amm. Marc. 22.11.2, but with confused chronology); later Christian sources portray him as a martyr.   **379b** ὁπλίτας: in educated classicizing Greek, the same word is used for 'legionaries' as for (e.g.) the Spartans at Thermopylae or the Athenians at Marathon.   εἰ: for this use of εἰ + subj./opt. to express the aim or motive of the action described in the main clause, see Smyth §2354; cf. also LSJ παραφυλάττω 2.   πολιτικώτερον: πολιτικός is a slippery word ('related/proper to the polis' can have many shades of meaning); here it is defined by the assimilation to μετριώτερον and the contrast with τυραννικώτερον.   **379c** ἐξόν: acc. absol. of the impersonal ἔξεστι.   δικαστῶν ψήφοις looks like a classicizing anachronism: had G. been tried, it would surely have been in a Roman-style court, by a judge (*iudex*), not by a jury in the style of fifth-century Athens.   οὕτω γὰρ... ὠμότητα: another studiedly elegant sentence, both in structure (the three participle clauses, especially the long final one, with its two-part dependent rel. cl.) and in phrasing (esp. the opening formula, with its arrangement of abstract nouns, 'the business would have been not X but Y', for which cf. e.g. Max. Tyr. 18.1, ὕβρις ἦν τὸ χρῆμα, οὐκ ἔρως).   ἐμμελής, ἀθώιους and ἀνίατα are all likewise choice items of vocabulary (see LSJ s.vv.).   **379d** ἧι... ἐπέστειλα: this letter does not survive.   **380a** φυλάττει καθαράς: this sentence, which has clearly been mistransmitted in some way, has been much worked over by editors;

perhaps the best solution is to assume that φυλάττει καθαράς is a gloss that has displaced the rarer and more difficult word originally written by J., which it was intended to explain.   **380b** νόμοι γάρ κτλ: a little set-piece sermon on the rule of law, of a fairly conventional kind: cf. e.g. Plato, *Crito* 50a–c, 'Zaleucus' *ap.* Stob. *Flor.* 44.20–1, Max. Tyr. 16.3 and 37.2.   πλήν = δέ (LSJ III.3).   ἀλλά...γοῦν 'but even so', Denniston 458–9 (cf. 442).   θεῖον: J.'s mother's brother, *PLRE* Iulianus 12, who had been Praefectus Aegypti some twenty years earlier; another convert from Christianity to paganism, and the recipient of several surviving letters from Julian and Libanius, he is praised and commemorated by Julian in *Misopogon* 365c.   **380c** τὸ...ἀκαταφρόνητον...τὸ ἀπηνέστερον: these abstract nouns formed from the adj. plus the neuter article, with dependent genitives attached, are another classicizing touch, imitated in particular from Thucydides (cf. e.g. Rusten (1989) 22–3).   μὴ...διακαθᾶραι: the use of the infin. without ὥστε to express consequence ('final-consecutive infin.') is again a classicizing touch: Schmid I 97 and IV 81–2 (cf. K–G II §473.7).   κάθαπερ νόσημα: the use of medical imagery to describe political disorder and rulers' actions goes back to Plato (e.g. *Grg.* 518e ff., *Resp.* 372e ff.).   **380d** εἴπερ ἐστέ...Ἕλληνες: with this challenge to the Alexandrians to live up to their ancestry, cf. the (more sarcastic) appeal in Dio 30.63 ff.   προτεθήτω: it is not clear whether J. means in inscribed or in a less-permanent form, on wood or papyrus.

68 Basileios, *Ep.* 102. A letter from St Basil to the people of Satala, informing them of the appointment of a new Bishop, and requesting a warm welcome for him. B. was at this time under orders from the Emperor Valens to make appointments to a number of vacant sees outside his normal jurisdiction (cf. *Ep.* 99); in this letter he goes out of his way to stress his neglect of his own and his appointee's personal interests, so as to emphasize the magnitude of the favour being done to Satala. Here and in **69** following, we see Christian bishops exercising the kinds of function once reserved for kings, emperors and provincial governors.

The style of the letter is more formal and less obviously graceful than B.'s private correspondence (contrast **40–1, 55** above), but still shows concern for elegance of expression, as e.g. in the careful balance of clauses in the opening sentence and the long (and complex) third (οὕτω... δεομένη), the tricolon with anaphora of λήθην further on, and the restrained but still

pointed use of imagery. In function, the letter has something in common
with the letters of recommendation given in section **A IV** and (though more
approximately) with **62** above.

Σαταλεῦσι: Satala was a garrison town in Armenia Minor, the province
adjoining B.'s home territory of Cappadocia, something over 500 km from
Caesarea. B. addresses himself to the whole citizen body, not just its ecclesiastical leaders.   ἐνώπιον Κυρίου: the prepositional use of ἐνώπιον is Hellenistic and later, and largely confined to non-literary texts
(cf. LSJ ii).   κατὰ τὸ γεγραμμένον: Zach. 2:8.   τὸν ἄνδρα:
one Poemenius, also mentioned in *Ep.* 103 (where B. comments punningly
on the appropriateness of his name, ποιμένα ἄξιον . . . τοῦ ὀνόματος), and
the addressee of *Ep.* 122.   εἰς οἰκειότητος λόγον: LSJ λόγος 1.4 *ad
fin.*   λαός: the word once used in Homeric Greek to designate the
mass of the army has now become (among other usages) the standard
word for a Christian congregation: *PGL* 5.   προστασίαν . . . ζημιωθείς:
as a verb of removing/depriving, ζημιόω takes two accusatives, one of
which remains when the verb is put into the passive (Smyth §§1628, 1632).
σαλευούσης: LSJ ii.2.   θλίψιν: the metaphorical use (LSJ 3) is
post-classical and non- literary.   ἑνὸς ἐγενόμην: LSJ γίγνομαι ii.3.a.
λοιπόν: see n. on **55** above.   ἐξηρτημένου: the somewhat faded
metaphor is reinvigorated by the comparison with a baby, which literally
'depends' from its mother's breast.   Νικίαν: not otherwise known.
τιμιότητι: see n. on **40** τὴν σὴν σεμνοπρέπειαν.

69 Aurelius Augustinus, *Ep.* 65. A letter from Augustine to an ecclesiastical superior, explaining and defending his actions in removing a priest
from his office. A. insists that he has done the right thing, but seems nervous
that his judgement may be challenged, or misrepresented (giving this letter
something in common with the two items in section **A VII** above).

Domino . . . salutem: compare the similarly formal and grandiloquent
salutation in **43**, also to a fellow clergyman, but one of the same rank,
and cf. n. on **76**.51 below.   **Xanthippo** (or Sanctippo)**:**   Bishop
of Thagura and Primate of Numidia, known also from *Ep.* 59 and
the acts of the Council of Africa; *seni* seems to be the standard term
of respect for a clergyman of this rank, rather than simply meaning 'elderly'.   **1 dignationem . . . prudentiae:**   see n. on **40** τὴν
σὴν σεμνοπρέπειαν.   **Abundantium:**   known only from this letter.
fundo: a district or (small) centre of habitation, rather than an estate,

as in classical Lat.   **presbyterum:**   cf. n. on **39** ὁ πρεσβύτερος.
ambularet: biblical phrasing, cf. L–S II and n. on **39** περιπατοῦντας.   **conuersationis:**   *OLD* 3, 'habitual behaviour', not 'conversation'.   **diuino ... commendato:**   abl. absol. (or 'ablative of circumstance'), but *commendato* is a neuter n. ('loan, deposit') not the part. of
commendo.   **natalis domini:**   celebrated on 25 Dec. in the Western
church from the first half of the 4th century onwards; the fast day was the day
before; cf. *ODC*³ s.vv. 'Christmas', 'Fasts and fasting', 'Vigil'.   **perrecturus:**   from *pergo*.   **nam** in later Latin, like *enim*, tends to lose its explanatory force and to become more like an alternative to either *et* or *sed* (i.e.
to become like Gk δέ).   **haereticorum:**   the Donatists (whose heart-
land was Numidia); cf. n. on **43**.   **circumlatrantium** (used also by
Lactantius *Inst.* 2.8.50 of pagan philosophers) expresses both the perceived
viciousness of the individuals described, and the writer's contempt for them.
ne ... subreperet: above all (presumably) in the form of false represen-
tations from Abundantius himself.   **2 qui ... Aprilis:**   it is this detail
that fixes the chronology of the letter and the events it details. The year
has to be 402; Augustine's hearing must have taken place at the very end
of December 401, just after Abundantius' second offence; and the letter
will have been written some time between January and April.   **concilium:**   the meeting of the ecclesiastical Council of Africa which took
place on 13 Sept. 401 (Munier (1974) 203–4).   **et si ... audiat** gives
the content of A.'s explanation to Abundantius, but as direct statement,
not as indirect speech, because the statement remains applicable (and it
is as important for Xanthippus to be reminded of it as for Abundantius).
nos autem ... :   from here on A. becomes more noticeably defensive.
Apparently aware that he has not followed precisely the prescribed form
(though the details of the argument are hazy), he insists that there was
no realistic alternative, and repeats the grounds for his decision.   **sex
episcopis ... terminare:**   as the text stands, *episcopis* must be taken
as instrumental abl.; some manuscripts, however, read *terminari* (passive),
which together with the easy emendation *quia* ⟨*a*⟩ might give a better
clause.   **concilio:**   the first Council of Africa, which met some time
between 345 and 348 (Munier (1974) 8).   **plebem:**   cf. the use of λαός
in Christian Greek (e.g. by Basil in **68** above).

70 Phalaris, *Ep.* **84.** The tyrant Phalaris (**11–12**, **25**, **38**, **51**) writes to
reproach the people of Messene (Messina) for appropriating a set of offerings he had sent for dedication in the temple(s) of their city. Once more

(cf. esp. **51**) the reader is treated to the spectacle of the cruel tyrant claiming the moral high ground over his critics: he may be a hated imperialist but it is they who are truly corrupt, in their dealings both with gods and with men. The question of the tyrant's offerings, and their acceptability is also taken up in Lucian's two declamation pieces *Phalaris* I and II, with the extra twist that there the proposed dedication is the notorious bronze bull itself. As a ruler's communication with a city, P.'s letter has something in common with both **64** (misappropriated dedications) and **67** (reproof for misbehaviour).

Μεσσηνίοις: an anachronism on the part of the author: in P.'s day this Sicilian city was called Zancle, and was only renamed 'Messene' (subsequently Doricized to 'Messana') in the 5th century, after an influx of immigrants from Messinia in the Peloponnese. This was one of the pieces of evidence used by Richard Bentley ((1697) 145–69) to prove that the *Epistles of Phalaris* were not really a work of the 6th century B.C.　**1 θεοῖς:** the ref. is carefully vague, as the author probably did not know which the principal divinities of sixth-century Zancle/Messana were.　**Δελφικούς:** another not wholly successful attempt at learned colour; the author has wrongly assumed that 'Delphic' can indicate a type of tripod, whereas in classical usage it designates only the (unique) tripod at Delphi on which the Pythia sits.　**σωτηρίας:** from illness, thanks to the doctor Polyclitus, as emerges from *Ep.* 21, also to the people of Messana.　**ὅπερ...
δεδράκατε:** the Messenians' action is modelled in the Athenians' seizure of offerings from Dionysius I to Olympia and Delphi (Diod. Sic. 16. 57. 2ff.).
2 μυσαρόν: 'polluted' or 'polluting', i.e. unclean in a religious sense: cf. Eurip. *Or.* 1624 with Willink's n. for the word and *OCD*[3] s.v. 'pollution' for the concept. With clever sarcasm, P. rejects the suggestion that his offerings to the gods are unacceptable to them because of his cruelty.　**3 τοὺς δὲ
πολιτευομένους κτλ:** we are to understand that P. has in the past had (so far unsuccessful) dealings with unscrupulous Messenians willing to betray their city to him for money or favour; this gives P. another opportunity to taunt his addressees with self-serving inconsistency in their actions.
4 διπλῆν παρέμφασιν: because 'saying farewell' to something can carry the negative overtone 'and good riddance', as e.g. in Demosth. 19.248, Lucian *Paras.* 32 (and cf. the parallel phrase χαίρειν λέγειν); for a similarly dismissive flourish at letter-end ('Heraclitus' to his useless doctors), cf. *Ep. Heracl.* 6.

C EMBEDDED LETTERS

Two examples have already been given of letters embedded in some larger context: **17**, from a novel (Petronius' *Satyrica*), and **50**, from a historical narrative (Sallust's *Catiline*). In both cases, the letters in question were quoted as discrete and uninterrupted wholes. In the two items that now follow, from contexts in comic drama and forensic oratory, what is presented is not so much a transcription as a dramatic reading, interrupted by comments and asides by the reader and/or his audience. All four pieces together provide only the briefest and most partial of introductions to the topic of embedded letters and their literary and rhetorical uses, which is a far larger one than can be illustrated by brief excerpts in an anthology such as this. Much depends, for instance, in drama and (especially) the novel on the relationship of the letter and its contents with the surrounding narrative context, which can only properly be explored in an unexcerpted text. For more extensive discussion, see Rosenmeyer (2001), esp. chs 2–4 and 6–7; also Introduction, 33–4.

71 Phoenicium (Plautus, *Pseudolus* 23–77). A letter from the slave-girl Phoenicium to her young Athenian lover Calidorus, read out by Calidorus' family slave, Pseudolus, as part of the opening, expository dialogue of the play. C. has been carrying the letter around for several days, distraught, but unable to confide in anyone (9–11); it is his decision at last to share his secret that launches the action, and it is his chosen confidant, the clever slave, who will be responsible for resolving it. Both setting (Hellenistic Athens) and predicament (frustrated young lovers, the threat of the sale of the girl to a rich rival) are standard for Greco-Roman New Comedy. Pseudolus' joking comments as he reads make effective (but as it turns out, not too hard-hearted) fun of the desperation and anguish of both the sender and the recipient of the letter; this refusal to share their view of things in turn serves as an advance reassurance to the audience that all will turn out well in the end. It is also notable that the letter's author, Phoenicium, is otherwise a mute character; only here is she allowed to speak (ventriloquized by an old male slave, for a male hearer, just as the character herself is the creation of a male playwright for a predominantly male audience).

23–30 Expected to start reading the letter, Ps. instead begins with a teasing complaint about the bad handwriting (potentially accompanied in performance with a good deal of comic business with the prop letter).

It is a mark of the scene as a whole (as of many literary developments of the letter, perhaps especially in drama) that it should make as much play with the physical form of the message as with its contents.   **24 scandit:** instead of being neatly spaced and on the line (as a man's would be?).   **tuo** = 'your usual, characteristic'.   **25 pol** = lit. 'by Pollux'. **Sibulla:** one of the class of supernaturally prophetic females thought to inhabit various locations around the Mediterranean world (though it is not wholly clear whether Ps./Plautus has 'a' or 'the' Sibyl in mind). **legerit:** pf. subj., for an unreal conditional and an action presented as completed.   **26 interpretari:** i.e. unusual powers are needed to guess what is in such an illegible message.   **27 qur** = *cur*.   **litteris:** dat. after *inclementer dicis*, as if after *maledicis*.   **29 opsecro** = *obsecro*. **herc(u)le** = lit. 'by Hercules'.   **quas:** the facetious question seems to follow on more smoothly from C.'s preceding remark if this is taken as a relative, with its antecedent *manibus* (picking up C.'s *manu*) attracted into the rel. cl., and some word/phrase for 'do you mean?' (e.g. *dicis*) understood.   **30 gallina scripsit:** comparing the straggly script to the results of a hen's scratching (a comparison which perhaps works better for Latin than for Greek cursive, as suggested by Roland Mayer). English cannot speak of untidy writing as 'hen's feet', but French has *pieds/pattes de mouche*, German *Krähenfüsse*, and Flemish (hitting the jackpot) *haenepvoten*. **31 immo enim:** *immo* rejects the suggestion that Ps. isn't going to read the letter and ought to give it back, *enim* (with no causal/explanatory force) strengthens the rejection.   **32–4 aduortito animum:** lit. 'turn your mind this way'; the sequence of jokes that follows depends on taking the phrase in a naively concrete sense (aided by the erotic commonplace that lover's hearts are 'not their own').   **35–40** Ps.' second false start. His teasing suggestion that he can 'see' the letter's author, which C. of course takes literally, plays on the epistolary commonplace of the letter as its writer's substitute embodiment (cf. e.g. **16** above, **73**.227 below). **36 eccam** = *ecce eam*; the accusative pronoun is governed by *ecce*, as if the latter were a transitive verb, e.g. *uide*.   **porrectam:** in the string of letters making up her name (the first word of the message); there is a sexual *double entendre* in this word and *cubat* following.   **37 quantumst** = *quantum est* (sc. *eorum/earum*), 'as much as there is of them'. Uninterrupted, C. would have continued with *perdant* or *perduint*, 'blast'. **41–4** In this verse transposition of what within the dramatic situation would be a prose letter, the standard opening formula (*X*(nom.) *Y*(dat.)

suo s.d.) is elaborated by (*a*) the explanatory label *amatori*, (*b*) the immediate reference within the salutation itself to the writing materials and the letter's role as a go-between; (*c*) the substitution of *impertit* for *dicit*; and (*d*) the punning continuation (*salus* = both 'health' and 'safety/rescue') in *salutem . . . expetit*. Compare above all Ovid's versification of letter form in **10** above, and contrast the straightforward epistolary conclusion in l. 73.   **41 Phoenicium:** neut., as often with female names in comedy. **43 abs** = *ab*.   **46 remittam:** the subj. can be taken as either final or deliberative.   **47–8** Ps.' advice perhaps recalls the proverbially bad bargain struck by Diomedes in *Iliad* 6.234–6, exchanging gold armour for bronze.   **lignean** = *lignea-ne*.   **ueis** = *uis*.   **sis** = *si uis* = 'please'.   **49 faxo:** *fac-so*, from *facio*; perhaps originally an aorist subj., but operating as either future, as here, or future perfect; in *faxo scies* the two verbs are in parataxis (later Lat. would subordinate the latter, *faciam ut scias*).   **50 usus . . . siet:** like the simple verb *utor*, *usus est* governs the abl. of the item needed; *subito* is adv. (*quam subito* being a vivid alternative for *quam cito*), *mi* = *mihi*, *siet* = *sit*, and *argento . . . inuento* is an example of the '*ab urbe condita*' construction ('I need the finding of money'). **51 Macedonio:** a touch of particularizing colour, helping to anchor the play to its setting in the Greek past; Macedonian soldiers were a familiar, and unpopular, feature of life in Hellenistic Athens, especially in the decades around 300 B.C.   **52 minis uiginti:** abl. of price, and more Greek colour, as the *mina* (mna) was not a Roman currency unit. The price is apparently on the low side for a girl in comedy: 20 minas is what the pimp Sannio claims to have paid for Bacchis in Ter. *Adelph.* 191; Planesium in Plaut. *Curc.*, Philematium in *Most.*, Palaestra in *Rud.* and the *citharistria* in Ter. *Phorm.* all go for 30, and Lucris in *Pers.* for 60.   **54 unae:** *OLD unus* 7.   **55 symbolum** = Greek σύμβολον, *sumbolon*, a token requiring to be 'put together' with its pair in order to do its job of identification/authorization; here the match is to be between two separate impressions from the same signet ring. There is a kind of symmetry in the situation sketched here between the soldier's sculpted portrait in wax, threatening the girl's removal abroad, and her own written 'portrait' in the wax of her letter, pleading for her rescue.   **59 proxuma Dionysia:** the chronology of the play requires *proxuma* to be understood as *proxuma dies*, and *Dionysia* as acc., 'governed by' *proxuma dies*, as *Kalendas* is in the phrase *pridie Kalendas Ianuarias*; *Dionysia* is another touch of Greek (Athenian) colour.   **61 ted** = *te*.   **sine pellegam:** another parataxis, of imper. and jussive subj.   **62 fabularier** (infin.) plays on the epistolary cliché of correspondence as conversation (cf. **10** above and **73**. 223 below). **63 dulce amarumque:** an erotic cliché going back to Sappho (fr. 130 L–P; cf. Theognis 1353); for its take-up in Hellenistic Greek, cf. Meleager 61 G–P, Posidippus 2 G–P, and in Latin poetry, Cat. 68.18.   **64–73** The remainder of the letter seeks to spur C. into action by dwelling on the lover's pleasures he stands to lose; his own conviction that all is already lost makes this a torment, but at the same time Ps.'s recitation of the letter (with its renewed opportunity for comic delivery and gestures) creates ironic distance both from it and from the situation as a whole. **65 suauisauiatio:** a comic invention, but not unique to this passage (unless, as has been suggested, this line is interpolated from *Bacchides* 116). **67 morsiunculae:** another comic invention (*morsio* (*mordere*) + *-ncula*); the first of a sequence of diminutives, indicating the speaker's warm feelings for the items listed, not small size.   **67ᵃ** A line known only from a damaged manuscript; the missing word must have been something like *obseruatiunculae*.   **orgiorum** 'secret rites' rather than 'orgies' in the modern sense (although in context the reference is roughly the same). **68 horridularum:** dimin. of *horridus*, which applies to any surface roughened or raised in peaks.   **69 harunc** = *harum-ce*.   **70** The combination of tricolon and double alliteration both underlines the seriousness of the threat (in the context of the rhetoric of Ph.'s letter) and provides the kind of playful heightening of language proper to comedy.   **71 quae:** indefinite adj.   **test . . . tibist** = *te est . . . tibi est*.   **73 quid:** adverbial.   **75 pumiceos:** for pumice as something proverbially dry, cf. Cat. 1.2 (*arida . . . pumice*) with Ellis's note.   **77 genu'** (= *genus*) **nostrum:** could be either 'my kind' (i.e. hard-headed types or scheming slaves, or both), or 'my family'.   **siccoculum:** perhaps a medical term, like its Greek cognate ξηροφθαλμία; the joke would then be that Ps. is passing off his lack of sympathy as something beyond his control ('it runs in the family' or 'an occupational disease', depending on how *genus* is understood).

72 Timarchides (Cicero, *Verrines* 2.3.154–7). A letter of advice from one associate of Gaius Verres, the disgraced ex-governor of Sicily, to another. It is quoted by Cicero in the course of the prosecution of Verres (70 B.C.) with which he made his name at Rome, as evidence of the depth of the corruption of Verres' administration, and accompanied by a sarcastic commentary. This, then, is a letter being read (or misread, by selection and tendentious interpretation) for a strikingly different purpose to that entertained by its original author; the reading also gives an unflattering twist to the commonplace that a letter embodies its writer's character (cf. n. on **71**.35–40, and **73**.227 below): compare the use made of the epistolary self-portraits of Catiline and Phalaris (**50**, **51**) in their respective contexts.

The passage comes from the part of Cicero's prosecution of Verres which was never actually delivered in court, because the accused had already admitted defeat and gone into exile. The topic of the speech as a whole is Verres' destruction of Sicilian grain-production in pursuit of his own enrichment; in sections 12–163 Cicero focuses on the abuses in levying the 10 per cent tax (tithe) on agricultural produce over which he presided.

154 Timarchides: a very minor member of V.'s staff (whence C.'s sarcasm about his pretensions), unflatteringly characterized in *Verr.* 2.2.134–6. **accensis:** lit. someone 'added to the list', a 'supernumerary'. **decumanum:** the *decima/decuma* was the one-tenth tax on agricultural produce, administration of which was delegated by the governor to contractors (tax farmers) called *decimani/decumani*. **Aproni:** Q. Apronius, the chief *decumanus*, described in the same kind of unflattering detail as Timarchides in *Verr.* 2.3.22–3. **decessisset:** at the end of 71 B.C. **Recita. EPISTVLA TIMARCHIDI:** a court official is asked to read out the whole letter; in what follows, C. repeats and comments on excerpts rather than going through the full text sentence by sentence. The main thrust of the letter (at least in C.'s version) is that Apronius should carry on confidently as before, in spite of the recent change of governor, from Verres to L. Caecilius Metellus. **Timarchides ... dicit:** it is not clear whether the omission of the addressee's name from the salutation is a deliberate security measure on T.'s part, or the result of editorializing by C. **L. Papirius:** L. Papirius Potamo, previously mentioned in 2.3.137. **praetoris:** V. had been *praetor urbanus* in 74, and governed Sicily (73–1) as propraetor with consular status. **155 ad illum:** i.e. to T. himself (in which case C. will uncharitably be interpreting what may have been (relatively) disinterested advice as covert scrounging). **L. Volteio:** known only from this passage. **cohorte:** *OLD* 5. **in uestram ... peruenerat:** what A. did of his own accord under Verres, he needs no one else's advice to do again under Metellus; T. is thus satirized not only for unscrupulousness but also for an inflated idea of his own influence.   **in fuga** (cf. *fugitiuo* below) may be metaphorical rather than literal: T. is 'on the run' because his former patron is off the scene and he has not (yet) re-established his position.   **patrono suo praecipit:** the accusation that T. is enjoining V. to use bribery (in connection with his present court-case) does not arise directly from the letter, but is slipped in by C. by association.   **postulante:** *OLD* 3.   **156 Sacerdote:** C. Sacerdos, V.'s immediate predecessor as governor of Sicily, in 74. **Peducaeo:** Sextus Peducaeus, governor in 75.   **hoc ipso Metello:** L. Caecilius Metellus, the current governor.   **ludibundus:** C.'s emphatic repetition of the word in the comments that follow insinuates that T.'s use of it is sadly typical of the attitudes of V.'s staff.   **coniectura domestica:** the sarcasm again hits at the whole staff, and its head, not just at T.   **ludibundi . . . ludorum:** the etymological echo again implicates V. as well as T., and conveys outrage at and contempt for both.   **quis istuc . . . uolunt:** the question and answer reinforce the charge of naïve pretentiousness against T., and bring us back to C.'s underlying insistence, that the real blame attaches to the man who allowed such misgovernment to flourish.   **Sextio:** V.'s *proximus lictor*, the one who walked closest to him in official processions and served as his executioner (cf. 2.5.113 and 119).

D EPISTOLARY THEORY

This concluding section contains some representative examples of ancient epistolary theory, ranging in date from the 2nd or 1st century B.C. to late antiquity. On the question of what makes a good letter, the texts collected here are broadly in agreement, though each has its own particular emphases and details. Stylistically, letters should be relatively plain, avoiding grandeur and complexity, in favour of something closer to everyday conversational tone; but at the same time, they should be composed with some concern for style and form. They should be relatively brief; and they should in appropriate ways reflect the purposes of the communication in hand, and the status of the parties to it. These are neither very surprising nor very exciting stipulations, and conform closely to the kinds of idea and intuition the letter-writers collected in this anthology have been seen acting on and articulating over and over again. Much of the interest lies instead in the ways in which the theoretical treatments qualify the agreed doctrines and try to relate them to other literary and critical issues, in their efforts to suggest a canon of classic epistolography, and in the choices they make of points for special attention. For further discussion of ancient epistolary theory, see Introduction, 42–6. A much fuller collection of relevant texts, with a brief but helpful introduction and somewhat erratic translations, is given by Malherbe (1988).

73 Demetrios, *De elocutione* 223–35. This is the earliest surviving theoretical discussion of letter-writing (though it evidently draws on at least some earlier material, now lost to us); it may date from as early as the 2nd century B.C. The treatise as a whole covers sentence structure (at the level of clause and period), and the correct employment of the four styles (grand, elegant, plain and forceful) by reference to which it is claimed that all literary composition can be categorized. Letters fit into this framework as an example of a mixed style, combining the plain and the elegant; as suits the overall direction and purpose of the treatise, the emphasis is more on the appreciation of letters as good writing than on practical composition. D. combines positive criteria for good letter-writing with the establishment of a series of boundary-lines between the letter and other literary forms. The good letter is said to steer clear of stylistic features (and subject-matter) more at home in epideictic oratory, drama, judicial oratory, and philosophical writing; it has some common ground with dialogue, but here too care must be taken to keep some distinction between the two. Another notable feature is the status D. accords to Aristotle, as a classic of epistolography and source of illustrative examples. This too conforms to a more general trend of the treatise, which shows a notable interest in Peripatetic authors and theories. See further Innes (1995) 311–40.

223 χαρακτήρ: D.'s word for 'style', whether at the level of his four major categories or (as here) at that of a literary kind falling under them (cf. n. on **76**.1 below). **ἰσχνότητος:** the distinctive quality of the 'plain' style, discussed in the preceding pages (190–222). **ʼΑρτέμων:** mentioned as an editor of Ar.'s letters also by the late-antique commentators Olympiodorus and Elias, but perhaps not otherwise attested (because not identical with any of the other Artemons known from antiquity). If the *De eloc.* does indeed date from the 2nd century B.C., then Artemon himself might belong to the early part of that century, or even to the end of the third. **ʼΑριστοτέλους ... ἐπιστολάς:** references and fragments are collected by Rose (1886) 411–21 (frr. 651–70) and Plezia (1977) 7–33.

ἀναγράψας: LSJ ii; the word denotes 'writing something up' so as to make it *publicly* available.   διάλογον ... διαλόγου: the description of a letter as one side of a dialogue reflects the same perception as is expressed elsewhere by characterizing the letter as a substitute for one side of a conversation (cf. n. to **10**. 29–30 above), but from the point of view of someone interested in placing and legislating for the letter as a *literary* kind.   **224** ὑποκατασκευάσθαι: κατασκευάζω (LSJ 1.10) denotes *some* degree of stylistic elaboration; the prefix ὑπο- specifies a *modest* degree.   δῶρον πέμπεται: the idea of the letter as a kind of gift coheres with the widespread sense of a close connection between letters and friendship (231 below); but both ideas are clearly more appropriate to some sorts of letter than to others.   **225** Ἀντίπατρον: a major political figure; besides being a close friend of Ar.'s, he was at different times Philip of Macedon's representative in Athens and Alexander's viceroy in Europe during his eastern campaigns. The catalogue of Ar.'s writings in Diog. Laert. 5.27 records four letters to him.   εἰ δέ ... φθόνος: Ar. fr 665 Rose = F8 Plezia. The identity of the aged exile is not known.   ἐπιδεικνυμένωι: it is the pretentiousness of the thought (the image of death as a 'return' from 'exile') rather than the style or the argumentative structure that makes this statement 'unconversational'.   **226** καὶ λύσεις: this paragraph continues with D.'s modifications to the idea of a kinship between letter and dialogue. His sense that short sentences and abrupt changes of direction are inappropriately 'histrionic' for a letter reflects stylistic ideals shared by some but not all the writers represented in this volume (contrast Cicero's practice, for example). Where D. sees the risk of obscurity and the crossing of a generic boundary better respected, others would see a positively desirable conversational liveliness: see Seneca's and Julius Victor's remarks on conversational style in **74** and **75** below.   ἐν τῶι Εὐθύδημωι: Plato, *Euthyd.* 271a, from the very beginning of the dialogue; only two lines are omitted between the two quotations.   ὑποκρίτηι: the rationale of D.'s worry becomes still clearer here: letters resemble dialogue, and dialogue is related to drama; letter-writing must be kept separate from drama, so the connection with dialogue must be carefully qualified too.   **227** τὸ ἠθικόν ... εἰκόνα ... τῆς ἑαυτοῦ ψυχῆς: a central perception about letters, with large implications both for the care to be taken in writing a letter, and for the interest to be had in reading them. See further Introduction, 39–40.   **228** συνεστάλθω: LSJ 1.2 and 3. D. here associates two requirements that are often made or acknowledged separately. For both of them (brevity and modest stylistic level) compare Julius Victor and 'Libanius' in **75** and **76** below.   **τοῦ Πλάτωνος πολλαί:** P.'s letters as we have them begin with εὖ πράττειν not χαίρειν (cf. nn. on **46** εὐψυχεῖν and **56** εὖ πράττειν above), but the general point – that they are long, and pieces of philosophical teaching or argument rather than everyday letters – does indeed apply to over half of them.   **ἡ Θουκυδίδου:** probably a ref. to a work now lost, rather than to Nicias' letter to Athens in 7.11–15.   **229 λελύσθω . . . περιοδεύειν:** the distinction is between a greater and lesser degree of patterning in sentence-structure, giving a greater or lesser impression of formality and making greater or lesser demands on the reader's/hearer's attentiveness. D. has given his definition of the period in §§10–31, and treats it again as a feature of the grand and forceful styles in 45–7 and 241–52. Just as the letter should avoid stylistic features more appropriate to the stage and to epideictic oratory, so it should also avoid those more at home in the lawcourts.   **φιλικόν:** an important point, given the perception of the letter as essentially a friendly form (cf. 224, 231–2); using periodic style in letters is 'unfriendly' because it implies (or makes) a distanced, formal relationship like that between orator and audience instead of the closer intimacy proper to the letter.   **τὸ γάρ . . . λεγόμενον:** more literally 'as they say (the thing that is said) following the proverb "(call) a fig a fig"'. The fuller version of the proverb (*Corp. Paroem. Gr.* II 654.95b Leutsch-Schneidewin) is τὰ σῦκα σῦκα, τὴν σκάφην σκάφην λέγει/ὀνομάζει, '(he) calls figs figs and a tub a tub'.   **230 τοῦτο . . . ἐπιστολικόν:** Ar. fr. 670 Rose = T4(b), F16 Plezia, from an unspecified source.   **231 εἰ γάρ τις . . . γράφει:** perhaps a hit at the letters of Epicurus.   **φιλοφρόνησις . . . ἁπλοῖς:** a repetition of the essential positive points about the letter, both of which rule out the use of the form to present technical philosophical or argumentative matter.   **232 παροιμίαι:** proverbs are regularly recommended by the theorists as particularly suitable for inclusion in letters (cf. Julius Victor and 'Libanius' in **75** and **76** below), but are not particularly frequent in practice. As the following sentence perhaps suggests, the theorists are anxious to find a kind of 'adornment' that can be advanced as special to the letter as opposed to the 'higher' forms of communication with which rhetorical theory for the most part deals.   **γνωμολογῶν καὶ προτρεπόμενος:** D. here comes close to ruling out the use of the letter as a vehicle for moral philosophy, which is striking given the popularity of this application.   **λαλοῦντι . . . ⟨ἀπὸ⟩ μηχανῆς:** another version

of D.'s central antithesis between informal, friendly diction and more pretentious, distancing modes of communication (here the words of a god,
speaking in high style from the stage-crane in the tragic theatre).   **233**
Ἀριστοτέλης: fr. 656 Rose = τ4(c), F17 Plezia. Ar.'s use of something like
a piece of formal argumentation is ruled acceptable in this case because
it deals with gratefulness, which is appropriate to the friendly atmosphere
of the letter, and does so in a witty rather than a stiffly argumentative
manner (because punning on the fact that χάρις ('charm') can mean both
'gratitude' and 'a Grace').   **234 πόλεσιν . . . καὶ βασιλεῦσιν:**   cf. Section **B** above. Although this is presented as a new point, two of the three
quotations already made from Aristotle seem to be from letters to rulers
or public figures of some kind.   **μικρὸν ἐξηρμέναι:**   a cautious mod-
ification to D.'s basic insistence that the letter should be simple in style,
but one that he is careful to limit as tightly as he can.   **στοχαστέον:**
rhetorical teaching standardly insisted on the need to take account of the
varied characters and emotions of different audiences (e.g. Plato, *Phdr* 271 d
ff., Alcidamas, *On written speeches* 22–3, Ar. *Rhet* 2.1, *Rhet. Alex.* 29), but here
the emphasis is on *status* rather than character as the factor prompting an
altered style.   **αἱ Ἀριστοτέλους πρὸς Ἀλέξανδρον:**   the catalogue
in Diog. Laert. 5.27 (cf. n. on **225** above) mentions four such; they seem
to have contained moral and political advice, and may have included the
works alternatively known as *On Colonies* and *On Kingship*: see Plezia (1977)
τ10–15, F4–6.   **πρὸς τοὺς Δίωνος οἰκείους Πλάτωνος:**   *Ep.* 7; cf. the
similar comment about P.'s non-epistolary letters in **228**.

74 Seneca, *Ep.* 75.1–4. The opening paragraphs of Seneca's *Ep.* 75
(cf. **33–4** above), included here as a reminder (cf. **33** above) of how usefully
the idea of the letter as essentially a friendly and conversational form can
converge with a particular style of moral philosophy. Seneca explains that,
to be true to his ideals as a philosophical adviser/instructor, his letters must
be unelaborate and 'natural' in style, so as to complement the sincerity
with which he puts his thoughts into words. He thus implicitly disagrees
with Demetrius' insistence (**73**.232) that the letter is not an apt vehicle for
anything more philosophical than proverbial wisdom.

1 putide: *OLD putidus* 3b.   **2 ostendere quam loqui:**   i.e. in S.'s
view, the best philosophical and argumentative writing is the kind that draws
least attention to itself; the unrealizable dream is of language that could

convey thoughts directly, as if in a totally transparent medium.   **etiam si disputarem . . . :**   an argument *a fortiori*: if even in potentially vehement debate S. avoids showy gesture and stylistic elaboration, all the more will he do so in quiet, instructive conversation, and its written equivalent, the philosophical letter.   **oratoribus:**   as in Demetrius' discussion (**73**.225, 229), formal oratory serves as a point of contrast to define what the letter should not be.   **3 multum . . . non oportet:**   a different emphasis from the other three texts in this section: for the philosopher as opposed to the rhetor or the literary critic, care over style is ultimately dispensable (contrast e.g. Julius Victor in **75** below *ad fin*, 'Libanius' in **76**.1).

75 C. Iulius Victor, *Ars rhetorica* 27. A discussion of letter-writing from the end of the wide-ranging handbook of C. Iulius Victor (*RE* Iulius 532), an otherwise unknown rhetorician of (probably) the fourth century A.D.; it and the treatment of conversation (*de sermonibus*) that immediately precedes it form a kind of appendix to the main treatise. It is plausibly conjectured that Victor draws on the work of a predecessor, the third-century rhetor Julius Titianus, known from Sidonius Apollinaris (*Ep.* 1.1.2) as a disciple of Fronto (cf. **9** and **53–4** above) and the author of a set of *Letters of Famous Women* in Ciceronian style (Giomini and Celentano (1980) xxii–xxiii, Radermacher in *RE* s.v. Iulius 532). Although as keen as the other treatises in this section to encourage attention to style and generic propriety in letter-writing, this is by some way the most practically oriented of them, dealing with such things as handwriting and scrupulousness in replying, as well as more purely stylistic matters.

Epistolis . . . sunt: the standard association of letters and informal conversation, cf. **73**.225, **74**.1, **76**.2.   **negotiales . . . familiares:**   an obvious sounding classification, but in fact not easy to parallel exactly. Of the other works collected here, Demetrius (234) distinguishes letters to private individuals and letters to cities and rulers; and 'Libanius' displays his forty-one kinds without reference to either the public/private or the business/friendship distinction. Elsewhere, Cicero sometimes distinguishes public from private (*Pro Flacco* 37), sometimes between letters conveying factual information and letters communicating a mood (*Ad fam.* 2.4(48 SB).1 f.).   **conpendii opera:**   lit. 'with the application of conciseness'.   **una . . . exceptione etc.:**   the stipulation parallels Demetrius' (228) and 'Libanius'' (46–7) insistence that the letter, though

carefully composed, should not be over-elaborate or too grand in style.
breuitas: the insistence on limited length is also matched by Demetrius
(228) and 'Libanius' (48–9), but is presented somewhat more bluntly here.
quod Cato ait: this dictum (of the elder Cato, 234–149 B.C.) is known
only from this text. The wording is notably witty, with both *circumferatur*
and *ambitio* echoing the Greek term for a complex sentence, *periodos* (lit.
'circuit'), and comparing the 'ambitious' sentence and its author to an
eager candidate for election going the rounds as he canvasses.   **unum
'te' ... frequentissimum est:**   a difficult statement, which on the face
of it might mean either 'there is often just one "te"' or '"te" is often used
on its own'. The former seems marginally the better sense in itself, and
to make a truer statement about Cicero's epistolary style: see Tyrrell and
Purser on *Att.* 5.6 (= 99 SB).2 and Shackleton Bailey on *Att.* 1.5 (1 SB).5.
intelligentia: clearly used below to mean 'sense, meaning' (i.e. how
a given word or sentence 'is to be understood') rather than 'intelligence,
understanding', so presumably to be taken in the same sense here too.
epistolis Tullianis: for Cicero's status as a canonical letter-writer, and
for the prominence of the now lost letters to Axius, see **52** and **54** above
(Pliny and Fronto).   **lucem:**   with this demand for clarity in letter-
writing, and for the proper balance of clarity with brevity, cf. 'Libanius' in
76.48–9 below.   **notas ... secretiores:**   for the topic of coded and
concealed communication, see Aeneas Tacticus, *Poliorcetica* 31 (4th century B.C.), with the commentaries of Hunter (1927) 203–18 and Whitehead
(1990) 183–93. For Caesar's and Augustus' use of code in their letters,
see Suet. *Div. Iul.* 56.6 (with Gell. *NA* 17.9.1) and *Div. Aug.* 88; some of
Caesar's coded correspondence was with Cicero (Suet. *loc. cit.*), but Cicero's
own use of code, alleged here, is hard to document elsewhere (*Att.* 13.32
(= 305 SB).3 is a reference to abbreviations, not code).   **potes enim:**
a sensible point, not made by any other treatise, which faintly echoes one of
Plato's worries about writing, expressed in *Phdr.* 275de.   **absentium:**
cf. the formal definition of the letter in **76**.2 below.   **putidior:**   cf.
74.1 above.   **amputatae breuitati:**   in the manner of Sallust or
Tacitus; this stipulation echoes Julius' earlier insistence that brevity should
not extend to the omission of vital words, thus enclosing the treatment
of clarity in a kind of ring-composition.   **dilatione ... obruenda:**
these words expand on the prohibition on elaborate, periodic style already contained in Cato's dictum; compare the strictures of Demetrius
in **73**.229 above.   **epistola:**   the treatment of the social etiquette of

letter-writing that follows is not matched in any of the other surviving treatises, and gives this one its distinctively practical flavour. The ideals of conduct implied in it, with their stress on a dignified considerateness, have much in common with those expressed in Cicero's *De officiis* 1.20–151 (the discussion of justice, liberality, magnanimity and seemliness).   **si inferiori, ne superba:** as illustrated by the letters from kings and emperors in Section **B** above (esp. **62**, **64**, **67**).   **neque indocto indiligenter:** the point (parallelled in *si inferiori, ne superba* and *nec minus familiari non amice*) is that good form should be maintained even when no close personal friendship is in question: the gentleman makes an effort, and does not stand on the letter of his entitlement, even when the other party doesn't fully deserve such treatment, or isn't in a position fully to appreciate it.   **paucis consolare:** advice respected in only some of the items in Section **A VI** above.   **posse euenire ... tristiore:** for the thought that circumstances may change even as a letter is in transit, cf. Ovid in **45**.15–22 above.   **epistolae minime:** the sense of the letter as essentially a friendly form (cf. Demetrius in **73**.231–2 above) seems to be in play here; the dat. *epistolae* depends on *oportet* (cf. H–S 198d).   **praefationes:** compare and contrast 'Libanius' in **76**.51 below.   **obseruabant ueteres:** the practice extended even to Emperors, see Millar (1977) 214–15.   **karissimis:** although grammarians debated its legitimacy (Quint. 1.7.10), Latin usage sometimes allowed *k* in place of *c* at the beginning of a word (cf. *Kalendae, Kaeso, Karthago*); the spelling *karus* is also found on inscriptions.   **commendatitias:** as in Section **A IV** above.   **graece:** as most prominently in the letters of Cicero, Fronto and Aurelius above.   **prouerbio:** cf. **73**.232, **76**.50.   **uersiculo ... uersus:** as in (e.g.) **28** and **67** (cf. **24**) above; but, as **28** shows, what is here treated as a purely stylistic device (to reinforce an effect of elegant informality) can on occasion be used in a more purposeful, even manipulative way. Christian writers (e.g. **41**, **42**, **43**) use quotations from scripture as well, or instead.   **ad epistolas:** *OLD ad* 42a ('For, at, in (an employment or function)').

76 'Libanios', *De forma epistolari* **1–4, 46–51.** This late-antique text (dating from some time after the middle of the 5th century A.D.) survives in two not widely differing versions, one attributed to Libanius (314–*c.* 393; see Introduction, 16–17 and **47** above) and the other to the Neoplatonist philosopher and scholar Proclus (410/12–485). Both a work of literary taxonomy and a practical guide to letter-writing, it provides both definitions and specimens/models for the forty-one categories of letter it distinguishes.

1 ἐπιστολικὸς χαρακτήρ: the same phrase as is used by Demetrius (**73**.223), but not in quite the same sense ('form' or 'type' – LSJ II.4 – rather than 'style' – LSJ II.5).   **μὴ ἁπλῶς. . . καὶ τέχνηι:**   like Demetrius and Julius Victor (but unlike Seneca), 'Libanius' is emphatic that careful attention to style is needed in letter-writing, even if (46ff.) the style to be aimed at is not itself an elaborate one.   **2 ἐπιστολή. . . παρόντα:** the definition, which follows a familiar formula of ultimately Stoic origin (compare the pseudo-Platonic *Definitions*, with L–S §32 (190–5), esp. 32H = Cic. *TD* 4.53), is noticeably more reflective than what is to be found in the other treatises in this section: the association of the letter with conversation and conversational style is commonplace (**73**.225, 231; **74**.1; **75** init.), but the explicit, formal stipulation of the conditions that the letter is essentially a utilitarian form and that the two parties to the communication are assumed to be physically separate, is not shared with the other three (though the latter is mentioned in passing by Julius Victor).   **3 φερομένων:** either 'spoken of (as letters)' or '(letters) in circulation': LSJ φέρω A.VIII.1.
4 προσηγορίαι. . . αἵδε: the list of categories that follows classifies the forty-one types of letter supposedly distinguishable partly by function (advice, blame, request, etc.) and partly by mode (mockery, coded, etc.), with the emphasis principally on the former. Even given the definitions and examples that follow (not printed here), it is open to question how real some of the distinctions drawn are (e.g. between μεμπτική, ὀνειδιστική and ἐπιτιμητική), at least for the purposes of practical letter-writing. Even as a way of categorizing letters in published collections, or in collections of models, it seems awkward to categorize on the assumption that any letter has a single dominant purpose that dictates its style and tone in their entirety. Yet this kind of taxonomy does seem to be reflected in later-antique and Byzantine letter-collections.   **μετριαστική** could in theory mean either 'emollient' or 'jesting' (LSJ μετριάζω 1.1 and 5); the definition following (§40) tips the balance in favour of the former by adding καὶ ταπεινοφρονοῦμεν, 'and are humble' (although in one branch of the MS tradition the text is altered in a way that suggests the latter possibility instead); unfortunately the model letter, which might have settled things decisively, is missing.   **μικτή:**   the category to which most ordinary letters would seem to belong, even thought here included only as an

afterthought.   **46 ἀττικίζειν μὲν μετρίως**...: 'Libanius'' requirement for the restrained application of stylistic graces in letter-writing is in
the same spirit as Demetrius' and Julius Victor's prescriptions, but differs
in the directness with which he uses the (Aristotelian) ideas of excess, deficiency and the happy medium to express it.   **ἀττικίζειν:** i.e. write in
the style of the classic Attic authors of the 5th and 4th centuries B.C., following both their syntax and their preferences in vocabulary. On Atticism, see
Swain (1996) 17–64 and Horrocks (1997) 79–86.   **47 οἱ παλαιοί:** i.e.
the authors and critics acknowledged as the classics, setting the standards
of correct writing for the present day too. The fact that they are here taken
to include the third-century Philostratus is another indication of the late
date of this treatise.   **Φιλόστρατος ὁ Λήμνιος:** a relative and pupil
of the Philostratus who wrote the *Lives of the Sophists* and the *Life of Apollonius*.
The quotation comes from his *Epistle on Letter-Writing*, addressed to the
sophist Aspasius (*VS* 2.33, 627–8), of which a longer extract is preserved
with the Philostratean *Epistles* (*Flavii Philostrati Opera*, ed. C.L. Kayser
(1871) II 257.32–258.28).   **δεῖ γάρ... μέσην τινά:** a paraphrase
rather than a direct quotation of Ph.'s words (II 258.8 ff. Kayser).   **48**
σαφηνείαι ... συντομίαι ... ἀρχαϊσμῶι: a more careful quotation (II
258.21–3), but still not exact. Ph.'s list of desirable qualities, here endorsed
by 'Libanios', again falls squarely into the common ground of epistolary
theory, since clarity is the distinctive virtue of the plain style, and archaizing
is a particular way of taking stylistic pains.   **49 τοξότας:** the imagery
of targets and archery to express the notion of achieving a virtuous
mean between two undesirable extremes follows Aristotle, *NE* 1094a23–4,
1106b28–33 and 1138b21–5.   **ἐπιστάλσεων:** 'missives', 'dispatches'
rather than (as LSJ) 'orders'.   **50 μέγεθος:** 'Libanius'' approach to
the requirement for brevity is more relaxed than Demetrius' (**73**.228)
and Julius Victor's.   **χάρις ἱστορίων:** the emphasis on graceful-
ness/charm chimes with Demetrius' classification of the letter (χάρις being
the distinctive virtue of the elegant style, in which the letter partly shares,
73.235).   **παλαιῶν συγγραμμάτων:** cf. on οἱ παλαιοί in 47 above.
παροιμίων: as also recommended by Demetrius, cf. n. on **73**.232.
φιλοσόφων ... προσενεκτέον: a disagreement with Demetrius (**73**.232),
but more in line with Julius Victor; 'Libanius' does not however have in
mind the kind of philosophical use of the letter seen in Epicurus or Seneca,
only the use of philosophical reflections as incidental decoration.   **51**
πρὸ τοῦ κατ᾽ ἐπίσταλσιν χαρακτῆρος: i.e. in the opening salutation,

which is not seen as part of any given letter-type, because common to them all; the prepositional phrase κατ' ἐπίσταλσιν (cf. ἐπιστάλσεων in 49 above) here operates like an adjective, equivalent to ἐπιστολιμαίου. **μὴ ληρεῖν... ὀνόμασι χρῆσθαι:** the prohibition is itself evidence that such a tendency was operative in contemporary letter-writing, however much this author might disapprove. Other items in this collection provide only mild examples (**39, 41, 43, 69**); compare also (e.g.) *P.Oxy.* 3862–4. Elaborate salutations seem particularly characteristic of Christian letters, which perhaps gives an extra edge to this classicizing author's criticism. **κολακεία... καὶ δυσγένεια:** the underlying thought is that servility in the salutation is inconsistent with the sense of the letter as a communication between friends (κολακεία, flattery, is a standard anti-type to true friendship in ancient ethical thinking).   **ὁ δεῖνα τῶι δεῖνι χαίρειν:** the standard formula, predominating in surviving private papyrus letters (Exler 23–36).

ABBREVIATIONS

Arndt–Gingrich	Arndt, W. F. and Gingrich, F. W. (1957). *A Greek–English lexicon of the New Testament.* 4th ed. Cambridge.
BGU	Seckel, E., Schubart, W. et al. (1895–). *Aegyptische Urkunden aus den staatlichen Museen zu Berlin, griechische Urkunden (Berliner griechische Urkunden).* Berlin.
CLA	Bruckner, A. and Marichal, R. (1967). *Chartae latinae antiquiores* IV. Olten.
CPL	Cavenaile, R. (1958). *Corpus papyrorum Latinarum.* Wiesbaden.
Denniston	Denniston, J. D. (1954). *The Greek particles.* 2nd ed. Oxford.
D–K	Diels, H. (1951–2). *Die Fragmente der Vorsokratiker.* 6th ed., rev. W. Kranz. 3 vols. Berlin.
Exler	Exler, F. X. J. (1923). *The form of the ancient Greek letter.* Washington.
FGrHist	Jacoby, F. (ed.). (1922–). *Die Fragmente der griechischen Historiker.* Berlin and Leiden.
G–L	Gildersleeve, B. L. and Lodge, G. (1913). *Latin grammar.* 3rd ed. London.
Goodwin	Goodwin, W. W. (1894). *A Greek grammar.* 2nd ed. London.
Halm	Halm, K. (ed.). (1863). *Rhetores Latini minores.* Leipzig.
H–S	Hofman, J. B. (1972). *Lateinische Syntax und Stylistik.* Rev. A. Szantyr (*Handbuch der Altertumswissenschaft* II.2.2.). Munich.
Inschr. Perg.	Fränkel, M. (1890–5). *Die Inschriften von Pergamon.* 2 vols. Berlin.

Jannaris	Jannaris, A. N. (1897). *An historical Greek grammar*. London.
K–G	Kühner, R. (1898–1904). *Ausführliche Grammatik der griechischen Sprache, zweiter Teil: Satzlehre* 3rd ed., rev. B. Gerth. 2 vols. Hanover.
LIMC	*Lexikon iconographicum mythologiae classicae*. (1981–97). Zurich.
L–P	Lobel, E. and Page, D. L. (1955). *Poetarum Lesbiorum fragmenta*. Oxford.
LS	Lewis, C. T. and Short, C. (1879). *A Latin dictionary*. Oxford.
L–S	Long, A. A. and Sedley, D. N. (1987). *The Hellenistic philosophers*. 2 vols. Cambridge.
LSJ	Liddell, H. G., Scott, R., Jones, H. S. and McKenzie, R. (1968). *A Greek–English lexicon*. 9th ed. with Supplement. Oxford.
Mayser	Mayser, E. (1906–34). *Grammatik der griechischen Papyri aus der Ptolemäerzeit mit Einschluss der gleichzeitigen Ostraka und in der Ägypten verfassten Inschriften*. Leipzig. 2nd. ed. (Vol. 1.2–3) Berlin–Leipzig 1938; (Vol. 1.1, rev. H. Schmoll) Berlin 1970.
M–S	Meisterhans, K. (1900). *Grammatik der attischen Inschriften*. 3rd ed., rev. E. Schwyzer, Berlin.
N–H	Nisbet, R. E. M. and Hubbard, M. A. *A commentary on Horace: Odes. Book I* (1972). *Book II*. (1978). London.
OCD[3]	Hornblower, S. and Spawforth, A. J. S. (1996). *The Oxford classical dictionary*. 3rd ed. Oxford.
O.Claud.	Bingen, J. et al. (1992). *Mons Claudianus: ostraca graeca et latina* I. Cairo.

*ODC*³	Cross, F. L. (1997). *The Oxford dictionary of the Christian church*. 3rd ed., rev. E. A. Livingstone. Oxford.
OLD	Glare, P. G. W. (1968–82). *The Oxford Latin dictionary*. Oxford.
Otto	Otto, A. (1890). *Die Sprichwörter und sprichwörtlichen Redensarten der Römer*. Leipzig.
PGL	Lampe, G. W. H. (1961). *A patristic Greek lexicon*. Oxford.
PIR	Groag, E., Stein, A. and Petersen, L. (1933–). *Prosopographia imperii romani saec. I.II.III.* 5 vols. Berlin.
PLRE	Martindale, J. R., Jones, A. H. M. and Morris, J. (1971–92). *The prosopography of the later Roman empire*. 4 vols. Cambridge.
PMG	Page, D. L. (1962). *Poetae melici Graeci*. Oxford.
P.Beatty Panop.	Skeat, T. C. (1964). *Papyri from Panopolis in the Chester Beatty Library, Dublin*. Dublin.
P.Bon.	Montevecchi, O. (1953–). *Papyri Bononienses (P.Bon.)*. Milan.
P.Cair.Zen.	Edgar, C. C., Guéraud, O. and Jouguet, P. (1925–40). *Catalogue général des antiquités égyptiennes du Musée du Caire; Zenon papyri*. 5 vols. Cairo.
P.Col.Zen.	Westermann, W. L. et al. (1934–40). *Zenon papyri: business papers of the third century B.C. dealing with Palestine and Egypt*. New York.
P.Goodspeed	Goodspeed, E. J. (1902). *Papyri from Karanis in the Chicago Museum*. Chicago.
P.Grenf.	Grenfell, B. P. and Hunt, A. S. (1897). *New classical fragments and other Greek and Latin papyri*. Oxford.
P. Mich.	Edgar, C. C. et al. (1931–). *Papyri in the University of Michigan collection*. Ann Arbor.

P.Oxy.   Grenfell, B. P. et al. (1898–). *The Oxyrhynchus papyri*. London.
P.Petr.   Mahaffy, J. P. and Smyly, J. G. (1891–1905). *The Flinders Petrie papyri*. 3 vols. Dublin.
P.Ross.Georg. Zereteli, G. et al. (1925–35). *Papyri russischer und georgischer Sammlungen*. Tiflis.
PSI   Vitelli, G., Norsa, M. et al. (1912–). *Papiri greci e latini*. Florence.
RAC   *Reallexikon für Antike und Christentum*. (1941–). Leipzig and Stuttgart.
RDGE   Sherk, R. K. (1969). *Roman documents from the Greek east*. Baltimore.
SB   Shackleton Bailey: see Bibliography s.v.
Schmid   Schmid, W. (1887–97). *Der Atticismus in seinen Hauptvertretern*. 4 vols. Stuttgart.
SEG   *Supplementum epigraphicum graecum*. (1923–). Leiden.
SIG   Dittenberger, W. (1915–24). *Sylloge inscriptionum graecarum*. 2nd ed., rev. F. H. von Gärtringen. 4 vols. Leipzig.
Smyth   Weir Smyth, H. (1956). *Greek grammar*. 2nd ed., rev. G. Messing. Cambridge, Mass.
SVF   von Arnin, H. (1903–24). *Stoicorum veterum fragmenta*. Leipzig.
TrGF   Snell, B., Kannicht, R. and Radt, S. (1971–). *Tragicorum Graecorum fragmenta*. Göttingen.
Woodcock   Woodcock, E. C. (1959). *A new Latin syntax*. London.

BIBLIOGRAPHY

Adams, J. N. (1977). *The vulgar Latin of the letters of Claudius Terentianus (P.Mich. VIII, 467–72)*. Manchester.

Adams, J. N. (1982). *The Latin sexual vocabulary*. London.

Allen, R. (1983). *The Attalid kingdom*. Oxford.

Allen, W., Jr et al. (1978). 'Horace's first book of *Epistles* as letters'. *CJ* 68: 119–33.

Allen, W. S. (1974). *Vox Graeca*. 2nd ed. Cambridge.

Alston, R. (1995). *Soldier and society in Roman Egypt*. London.

Altman, J. G. (1982). *Epistolarity. Approaches to a form*. Columbus, OH.

Anderson, G. (1986). *Philostratus*. London.

Anderson, G. (1993). *The second sophistic*. London.

Arnott, W. G. (1973). 'Imitation, variation, exploitation: a study in Aristaenetus'. *GRBS* 14: 197–211.

Arnott, W. G. (1982). 'Pastiche, pleasantry, prudish eroticism: the Letters of "Aristaenetus"'. *YCS* 27: 291–320.

Athanassiadi, P. (1992). *Julian: an intellectual biography*. London (= rev. ed. of Ead. *Julian and hellenism*, Oxford, 1981).

Bagnall, R. S. (1993). *Egypt in late antiquity*. Princeton.

Barb, A. A. (1963). 'The survival of magic arts', in Momigliano, A. (ed.), *The conflict between paganism and Christianity in the fourth century*. Oxford, 100–25.

Barker, E. P. (1932) tr., *Seneca's letters to Lucilius*. Oxford.

Baxter, J. H. (1930). *Saint Augustine. Select letters*. London and New York (Loeb).

Benner, A. R and Fobes, F. H. (1949). *Alciphron, Aelian, Philostratus. The letters*. Cambridge, Mass. and London (Loeb).

Bentley, R. (1697). *A Dissertation upon the Epistles of Phalaris, Themistocles, Socrates, Euripides and the Fables of Aesop*. Appended to Wotton, W., *Reflections upon ancient and modern learning*. 2nd ed. London.

Bentley, R. (1699). *A Dissertation upon the Epistles of Phalaris. With an answer to the objections of the Honourable Charles Boyle, Esquire*. London.

Bessières, M. (1923). *La Tradition manuscrite de la correspondance de S. Basile*. Oxford.

Bianchetti, S. (1987). *Falaride e Pseudofalaride: Storia e leggenda*. Florence.

Bidez, J. (1960) ed., *L'Empereur Julien: Oeuvres complètes*. 2nd ed. Paris (Budé).

Bidez, J. and Cumont, F. (1922) eds., *Imperatoris Caesaris Flauii Claudii Iuliani Epistulae, Leges, Poematia, Fragmenta uaria*. Paris and London.

Birley, A. (1966). *Marcus Aurelius*. London.

Boardman, J. (1980). *The Greeks overseas. Their early colonies and trade*. Rev. ed. London.

Bonner, S. F. (1977). *Education in Ancient Rome*. Berkeley and Los Angeles.

Bouffartigue, J. (1992). *L'Empereur Julien et la culture de son temps*. Paris.

Bowersock, G. (1978). *Julian the Apostate*. London.

Bowie, E. L. (1970/74). 'The Greeks and their past in the second sophistic'. *Past and Present* 46: 3–41. Rev. in Finley, M. I. (ed.) *Studies in ancient society*: 166–209. London.

Bowman, A. K. (1983). *The Roman writing tablets from Vindolanda*. London.

Bowman, A. K. (1990). *Egypt after the Pharaohs*. Rev. ed. Oxford.

Bowman, A. K. (1994). *Life and letters on the Roman frontier: Vindolanda and its people*. London.

Bowman, A. K. and Thomas, J. D. (1983). *Vindolanda: the Latin writing-tablets* (*Britannia* Monograph 4). London.

Bowman, A. K. and Thomas, J. D. (1994). *The Vindolanda writing tablets: tabulae Vindolandenses II*. London.

Bowman, A. K. and Thomas, J. D. (1996). 'New writing-tablets from Vindolanda'. *Britannia* 27: 299–328.

Branham, R. B. and Goulet-Cazé, M.-O. (1996). *The Cynics: The Cynic movement in antiquity and its legacy*. Berkeley and London.

Bravo, B. (1974). 'Une lettre sur plomb de Berezan'. *Dialogues d'histoire ancienne* 1: 111–87.

Bremer, J. M. (1981). 'Greek hymns', in Versnel, H. S. (ed.), *Faith, hope and worship*. Leiden, 193–215.

Brown, P. (1967). *Augustine of Hippo*. London.

Browning, R. (1975). *The Emperor Julian*. London.

Browning, R. (1983). *Medieval and modern Greek*. Cambridge.

Bruckner, A. and Marichal, R. (1967) eds., *Chartae latinae antiquiores* IV. Olten.

Brunt, P. A. (1971). *Italian manpower*. Oxford.

Buck, C. D. (1955). *The Greek dialects: grammar, selected inscriptions, glossary*. Chicago.

Bülow-Jacobsen, A. and McCarren, V. P. (1985) 'P.Haun. 14, P.Mich. 679, and P.Haun. 15 – a re-edition'. *ZPE* 58: 71–9.

Burkert, W. (1985). *Greek religion*. Oxford.

Casson, L. (1994). *Travel in the ancient world*. 2nd ed. Baltimore and London.

Chadwick, H. (1967). *The early Church*. Harmondsworth.

Chadwick, J. (1973). 'The Berezan lead letter'. *PCPhS* n.s. 19: 35–7.

Champlin, E. (1980). *Fronto and Antonine Rome*. Cambridge, Mass.

Chapa, J. (1998). *Letters of condolence on Greek papyri* (*Papyrologica Florentina* 29). Florence.

Chilton, C. W. (1971). *Diogenes of Oenoanda. The fragments*. Oxford.

Clay, D. (1983). *Lucretius and Epicurus*. Ithaca and London.

Coleman, R. G. (1974). 'The artful moralist: a study of Seneca's epistolary style'. *CQ* n.s. 24: 276–89.

Costa, C. D. N. (1988) ed., *Seneca. 17 letters*. Warminster.

Costa, C. D. N. (2001) ed., *Greek fictional letters*. Oxford.

Cotton, H. (1984). 'Greek and Latin epistolary formulae: some light on Cicero's letter writing'. *AJP* 105: 409–25.

Cotton, H. (1985). '*Mirificum genus commendationis*: Cicero and the Latin letter of recommendation'. *AJP* 106: 328–34.

Courtney, E. (2001). *A companion to Petronius*. Oxford.

Courtonne, Y. (1957–66) ed., *S. Basile. Lettres*. 3 vols. Paris (Budé).

Coventry, L. (1990). 'The role of the interlocutor in Plato's dialogues', in Pelling, C. B. R. (ed.) *Characterization and individuality in Greek literature*. Oxford, 174–96.

Cribiore, R. (2001). 'Windows on a woman's world: some letters from Roman Egypt', in Lardinois, A. and McClure, L. (eds.), *Making silence speak: women's voices in Greek literature and society*. Princeton, 223–39.

Crönert, W. (1910). 'Die beiden ältesten griechischen Briefe'. *RhM* 65: 157–60.

Cugusi, P. (1970–9) ed., *Epistolographi Latini minores*. Turin.

Cugusi, P. (1983). *Evoluzione e forme dell'epistolografia latina nella tarda repubblica e nei primi due secoli dell'impero, con cenni sull'epistolografia preciceroniana*. Rome.

Cugusi, P. (1989). 'L'epistolografia. Modelli e tipologie', in Cavallo, G. et al. (eds.), *Lo spazio letterario di Roma antica. II La circolazione del testo*. Rome, 379–419.

Cugusi, P. (1992). *Corpus epistularum latinarum papyris tabulis ostracis servatarum* (*CEL*). Florence.

Cunningham, J. G. (1872–5) tr., *Letters of Saint Augustine, Bishop of Hippo*. (= Dods, M. ed., *The works of Aurelius Augustine, Bishop of Hippo*, VI and XIII.) 2 vols. Edinburgh.

Curtius, E. R. (1953). *European literature and the Latin middle ages*. Tr. W. Trask. London.

Daniélou, J. (1973). *Gospel message and Hellenistic culture*. Tr. J. A. Baker. London.

Davies, R. (1989). *Service in the Roman army*. Edinburgh.

Davis, R. W. (1973). 'The enlistment of Claudius Terentianus'. *BASP* 10: 21–5.

Davisson, M. H. (1985). '*Tristia* 5.13 and Ovid's use of epistolary form and context'. *CJ* 80: 238–46.

Deferrari, R. J. (1926–34) ed., *St Basil. The letters*. 4 vols. London and New York (Loeb).

Deissmann G. A. (1927). *Light from the ancient East*. Tr. L. Strachan. London.

Dickinson, R. J. (1973). 'The *Tristia*: poetry in exile', in Binns, J. W. (ed.) *Ovid*. London, 154–90.

Dilke, O. A. W. (1973). 'Horace and the verse letter', in Costa, C. D. N. (ed.) *Horace*. London and Boston, 94–112.

Dineen, L. (1929). *Titles of address in Christian Greek epistolography* (Catholic University of America, Patristic Studies 18). Washington (repr. Chicago 1980).

Divjak, J. (1981) ed., *Epistolae ex duobus codicibus nuper in lucem prolatae* (Corpus Scriptorum Ecclesiasticorum Latinorum 88). Vienna.

Doenges, N. A. (1981). *The letters of Themistocles*. New York.

Doty, W. G. (1973). *Letters in primitive Christianity*. Philadelphia.

Dover, K. J. (1997). *The evolution of Greek prose style*. Oxford.

Dudley, D. R. (1937). *A history of Cynicism*. London.

Düring, I. (1951) ed. and tr., *Chion of Heraclea. A novel in letters*. Gothenburg (repr. New York, 1979).

Easterling, P. E. and Knox, B. M. W. (1985) eds., *The Cambridge history of classical literature* I. *Greek Literature*. Cambridge.

Eidinow, J. S. C. (1995). 'Horace's Epistle to Torquatus (*Ep.* 1.5)'. *CQ* 45: 191–9.

Eno, R. B. (1989) tr., *Saint Augustine. Letters, vol. 6*. Washington (cf. Parsons (1951–6)).

Evans, H. B. (1983). *Publica carmina: Ovid's books from exile*. Lincoln, Nebraska.

Ferguson, J. (1970). *Socrates. A source book*. London.

Förster, R. (1921–2). *Libanii opera X–XI*. Leipzig (Teubner).

Fremantle, W. H. (1893) tr., *The principal works of St Jerome* (= Schaff, P. and Wace, H., eds., *A select library of Nicene and post-Nicene Fathers, 6: Jerome, Letters and select works*). Oxford (repr. Peabody, Mass., 1995).

Funk, R. W. (1961) = Blass, F. and Debrunner, A., *A Greek grammar of the New Testament and other early Christian literature*. Tr. and rev. R. W. Funk. Cambridge and Chicago.

Gager, J. G. (1992). *Curse tablets and binding spells from the ancient world*. New York and Oxford.

Gallay, P. (1964–7) ed., *S. Grégoire de Nazianze. Lettres*. 2 vols. Paris (Budé).

Gallay, P. (1969) ed., *Gregor von Nazianz. Briefe* (GCS 53). Berlin.

Gera, D. L. (1995). 'Lucian's choice: *Somnium* 6–16', in Innes, D. et al. (eds.) *Ethics and rhetoric*. Oxford, 237–50.

Giannantoni, G. (1990) ed. and comm., *Socratis et Socraticorum reliquiae*. 4 vols. Naples.

Giomini, R. and Celentano, M. S. (1980) eds., *C. Iulii Victoris Ars rhetorica*. Leipzig (Teubner).

Gösswein, H. U. (1975). *Die Briefe des Euripides*. Meisenheim am Glan.

Goldbacher, A. (1895–1923) ed., *S. Aureli Augustini Hipponiensis episcopi epistulae* (Corpus Scriptorum Ecclesiasticorum Latinorum 34, 44, 57–8). 5 vols. Prague, Vienna, Hamburg.

Goldstein, J. A. (1968). *The letters of Demosthenes*. New York.

Graf, F. (1997). *Magic in the ancient world*. Tr. F. Philip. Cambridge, Mass. and London.

Grandgent, C. H. (1907). *An introduction to vulgar Latin*. Boston.

Grenfell, B. P. and Hunt, A. S. (1897). *The Oxyrhynchus papyri* I. London.

Griffin, M. T. (1974). '*Imago vitae suae*', in Costa, C. D. N. (ed.), *Seneca*. London, 1–38.

Griffin, M. T. (1992). *Seneca, a philosopher in politics*. Rev. ed. Oxford.

Griffin, M. T. (1995). 'Philosophical badinage in Cicero's letters to his friends', in Powell, J. G. F., ed., *Cicero the philosopher: twelve papers*. Oxford, 325–46.

Guignet, M. (1911). *Les Procédés épistolaires de S. Grégoire de Nazianze comparés à ceux de ses contemporains*. Paris.

Gulley, N. (1972). 'The authenticity of the Platonic Epistles', in *Pseudepigrapha I* (Fondation Hardt, Entretiens 18). Vandoeuvres–Geneva, 11–22.

Haas, C. (1997). *Alexandria in late antiquity*. Baltimore and London.

Hadot, I. (1969). *Seneca und die griechisch-römisch Tradition der Seelenleitung*. Berlin.

Hadot, I. (1986). 'The spiritual guide', in Armstrong, A. H. (ed.), *Classical Mediterranean spirituality*. London, 436–55.

Hallett, J. (1984). *Fathers and daughters in Roman society*. Princeton.

Hansen, E. V. (1971). *The Attalids of Pergamum*. Ithaca.

Harris, W. V. (1989). *Ancient literacy*. Cambridge, Mass. and London.

Hercher, R. (1873) ed., *Epistolographi graeci*. Paris.

Hilberg, I. (1996) ed., *Sancti Eusebii Hieronymi epistulae* (Corpus Scriptorum Ecclesiasticorum Latinorum LIV–LVI). 2nd ed. (ed. 1, 1910–18) 4 vols. Vienna.

Hinz, V. (2001). *Nunc Phalaris doctum protulit ecce caput. Antike Phalarislegende und Nachleben der Phalarisbriefe* (Beiträge zur Altertumskunde 148). Munich and Leipzig.

Holford-Strevens, L. (1988). *Aulus Gellius*. London.

Holloway, R. R. (1991). *The archaeology of ancient Sicily*. London.

Holzberg, N. (1994). *Die griechische Briefroman: Gattungstypologie und textanalyse*. Tübingen.

Holzberg, N. (1996). 'Novel-like works of extended prose fiction II. E. Letters: Chion', in Schmeling, G. (ed.), *The novel in the ancient world*. Leiden–New York–Cologne, 645–53.

Horrocks, G. C. (1997). *Greek. A history of the language and its speakers*. London.

Hunt, A. S. and Edgar, C. C. (1932) ed. and tr., *Select papyri I: non-literary (private affairs)*. London and Cambridge, Mass. (Loeb).

Hunt, A. S. and Edgar, C. C. (1934) ed. and tr., *Select papyri II: non-literary (public documents)*. London and Cambridge, Mass. (Loeb).

Hunter, L. W. (1927). *Aeneas on siegecraft*. Oxford.

Hutchinson, G. O. (1998). *Cicero's correspondence. A literary study*. Oxford.

Innes, D. C. (1995) = *Aristotle, Poetics* (tr. S. Halliwell); *Longinus, On the Sublime* (tr. W. Hamilton Fyfe, rev. D. A. Russell); *Demetrius, On style* (ed. and tr. D. C. Innes). Cambridge, Mass. and London (Loeb).

Jocelyn, H. (1973). 'Homo sum: humani nil a me alienum puto'. *Antichthon* 7: 14–46.

Jones, A. H. M. (1940). *The Greek city*. Oxford.

Jones, A. H. M. (1971). *The cities of the eastern Roman provinces*. 2nd ed. Oxford.

Jones, C. P. (1971). *Plutarch and Rome*. Oxford.

Jones, R. M. (1926). 'Posidonius and the flight of the mind through the universe'. *CPh* 21: 97–113.

Jordan, W. (1990). *Ancient concepts of philosophy*. London.

Kassel, R. (1958). *Untersuchungen zur griechischen und römischen Konsolationsliteratur*. Munich.

Kelly, J. N. D. (1975). *Jerome*. London.

Kennedy, G. A. (1972). *The art of rhetoric in the Roman world*. Princeton.

Kennedy, G. A. (1983). *Greek rhetoric under Christian emperors*. Princeton.

Kennedy, G. A. (1989) ed., *The Cambridge history of literary criticism I. Classical criticism*. Cambridge.

Kenney, E. J. (1996) ed., *Ovid. Heroides XVI–XXI*. Cambridge.

Kenney, E. J. and Clausen, W. V. (1982) eds., *The Cambridge history of classical literature II. Latin literature*. Cambridge.

Kermode, F. and Kermode, A. (1995) eds., *The Oxford book of letters*. Oxford.

Keyes, C. W. (1935). 'The Greek letter of introduction'. *AJP* 56:28–44.

Kilpatrick, R. S. (1986). *The poetry of friendship: Horace, Epistles I*. Edmonton.

Kindstrand, J. F. (1981). *Anacharsis. The legend and the apophthegmata*. Uppsala.

Knox, P. E. (1995) ed., *Ovid, Heroides. Select epistles*. Cambridge.

Koskenniemi, H. (1956). *Studien zur Idee und Phraseologie des griechischen Briefes bis 400 n.Chr.* Helsinki.

Labourt, J. (1949–63) ed., *Saint Jérôme. Lettres*. 8 vols. Paris (Budé).

Le Bohec, Y. (1994). *The Roman imperial army*. London.

Lefkowitz, M. R. (1981). *The lives of the Greek poets*. London.

Lendon, J. E. (1997). *Empire of honour*. Oxford.

Levick, B. (2000). *The government of the Roman empire: a sourcebook*. 2nd ed. London.

Lewis, N. (1983). *Life in Egypt under Roman rule*. Oxford.

Lieu, J. (1986). *The second and third Epistles of John*. Edinburgh.

Lindsay, W. M. (1894). *The Latin language*. Oxford.

Long, A. A. (1986). *Hellenistic Philosophy*. 2nd ed. London.

Luck. G. (1967–77) ed., *P. Ovidius Naso. Tristia*. 2 vols. Heidelberg.

Ludolph, M. (1997). *Epistolographie und Selbstdarstellung. Untersuchungen zu den 'Paradebriefen' Plinius des Jüngeren*. Tübingen.

Ma, J. (1999). *Antiochos III and the cities of western Asia Minor*. Oxford.

McCall, M. H. (1969). *Ancient rhetorical theories of simile and comparison*. Cambridge, Mass.

McGushin, P. (1977). *C. Sallustius Crispus, Bellum Catilinae: a commentary*. Leiden.

MacMullen, R. (1966). *Enemies of the Roman order*. Cambridge, Mass.

Malherbe, A. J. (1977) ed., *The Cynic epistles*. Missoula.

Malherbe, A. J. (1988). *Ancient epistolary theorists* (SBL 19). Atlanta, GA.

Mayer, R. G. (1994) ed. and com., *Horace: Epistles I*. Cambridge.

Melville, A. D. and Kenney, E. J. (1992) tr. and comm., *Ovid. Sorrows of an exile (Tristia)*. Oxford.

Merkelbach, R. (1975). 'Nochmals die Bleitafel von Berezan'. *ZPE* 17: 161–2.

Millar, F. G. B. (1977). *The emperor in the Roman world*. London.

Miller, A. P. (1975). 'Notes on the Berezan lead letter'. *ZPE* 17: 157–60.

Milligan, G. (1910) ed., *Selections from the Greek papyri*. Cambridge.

Mitchell, J. F. (1968). 'Consolatory letters in Basil and Gregory Nazianzen'. *Hermes* 96: 299–318.

Mitchell, S. (1976). 'Requisitioned transport in the Roman empire: a new inscription from Pisidia'. *JRS*: 106–31.

Moles, J. L. (2000). 'The Cynics', in Rowe, C. J. and Schofield, M. (eds.), *The Cambridge history of Greek and Roman political thought*. Cambridge, 415–34.

Montevecchi, O. (1953) ed., *Papyri Bononienses (P. Bon.) I (1–50)*. Milan.

Montserrat, D. (1996). *Sex and society in Greco-Roman Egypt*. London.

Morrow, G. R. (1935). *Studies in the Platonic Epistles*. Urbana, Ill.

Mullett, M. (1997). *Theophylact of Ochrid. Reading the letters of a Byzantine archbishop*. Aldershot.

Munier, C. (1974) ed., *Concilia Africae a. 345–525* (Corpus Christianorum, Series Latina 149). Turnhout.

Murphy, J. J. (1974). *Rhetoric in the middle ages*. Berkeley.

Nehamas, A. (1998). *The art of living. Socratic reflections from Plato to Foucault*. Berkeley.

Norman, A. F. (1992). *Libanius. Autobiography and select letters*. 2 vols. Cambridge, Mass. and London (Loeb).

O'Brien, M. B. (1930). *Titles of address in Christian Latin epistolography* (Catholic University of America, Patristic Studies 21). Washington.

Oltramare, A. (1926). *Les Origines de la diatribe latine*. Geneva.

Onians, R. B. (1951). *The origins of European thought*. Cambridge.

Palmer, L. R. (1954). *The Latin Language*. London.

Parke, H. W. (1967). *The oracles of Zeus: Dodona, Olympia, Ammon*. Oxford.

Parker, R. C. T. (1996). *Athenian religion. A history*. Oxford.

Parsons, P. J. (1980). 'Background: the papyrus letter', in Veremans, J. and Decreus, F. (eds.), *Acta colloquii didactici classici octavi* (Didactica classica gandensia 20). Ghent, 3–19.

Parsons, W. (1951–6) tr., *Saint Augustine. Letters*. 5 vols. Washington (cf. Eno (1989)).

Penella, R. J. (1979). *The Letters of Apollonius of Tyana: A critical text with prolegomena, translation and commentary*. Leiden.

Penwill, J. L. (1978). 'The *Letters* of Themistocles; an epistolary novel?' *Antichthon* 12: 83–103.

Perpillou-Thomas, F. (1993). *Fêtes d'Egypte ptolémaïque et romaine d'après la documentation papyrologique grecque*. Louvain.

Pighi, G. B. (1964). *Lettere latine d'un soldato di Traiano (P.Mich. 467–472)*. Bologna.

Plezia, M. (1977) ed., *Aristotelis privatorum scriptorum fragmenta*. Leipzig (Teubner).

Pollard, J. (1977). *Birds in Greek life and myth*. London.

Preisigke, F. (1925). *Wörterbuch der griechischen Papyrusurkunden mit Einschluss der griechischen Inschriften Aufschriften Ostraka Mummienschilder usw. aus Ägypten*. Berlin (Suppl. F. Preisigke, E. Kiessling, Berlin 1925–31; E. Kiessling, Amsterdam 1969; H. Rupprecht, A. Jördens, Wiesbaden 1991).

Radice, E. (1975). 'The letters of Pliny', in Dorey, T. A. (ed.), *Empire and aftermath*. London, 119–43.

Radicke, J. (1997). 'Die Selbstdarstellung des Plinius in seinen Briefen'. *Hermes* 125: 447–69.

Ramsey, J. T. (1984) ed., *Sallust's Bellum Catilinae*. Chico, Calif.

Rawson, E. D. (1983). *Cicero: a portrait*. 2nd ed. Bristol.

Reed, J. T. (1997). 'The epistle', in Porter, S. E. (ed.), *Handbook of classical rhetoric in the Hellenistic period, 330 B.C–A.D. 400*. Leiden–New York–Cologne, 171–93.

Rehkopf, F. (1976) = Blass, F. and Debrunner, A., *Grammatik des neutestamentlichen Griechisch. Bearbeitet von Friedrich Rehkopf*. Göttingen.

Reuters, F. H. (1963). *Die Briefe des Anacharsis* (Schriften und Quellen der alten Welt 14). Berlin.

Reynolds, J. (1982). *Aphrodisias and Rome* (*JRS* Monographs, 1). London.

Reynolds, L. D. and Wilson, N. G. (1991). *Scribes and scholars*. 3rd ed. Oxford.

Riginos, A. S. (1976). *Platonica*. Leiden.

Rose, V. (1886) ed., *Aristotelis qui ferebantur librorum fragmenta*. Leipzig (Teubner).

Rosenmeyer, P. A. (1994). 'The epistolary novel', in Morgan, J. R and Stoneman, R. (eds.), *Greek fiction: the Greek novel in context*. London and New York, 146–65.

Rosenmeyer, P. A. (2001). *Ancient epistolary fictions. The letter in Greek literature*. Cambridge.

Rousseau, P. (1978). *Ascetics, authority and the Church in the age of Jerome and Cassian*. Oxford.

Rowlandson, J. L. (1998) ed., *Women and society in Greek and Roman Egypt. A sourcebook*. Cambridge.

Rudd, N. (1989) ed., *Horace, Epistles Book II and Epistle to the Pisones*. Cambridge.

Rudd, N. (1992). 'Strategies of vanity: Cicero *Ad familiares* 5.12 and Pliny's letters', in Woodman, A. J. and Powell, J. G. F. (eds.), *Author and audience in Latin literature*. Cambridge, 18–32.

Ruether, R. R. (1969). *Gregory of Nazianzus, rhetor and philosopher*. Oxford.

Rütten, T. (1992). *Demokrit – Lachender Philosoph und sanguinischer Melancholiker. Eine pseudohippokratische Geschichte*. Leiden–New York–Copenhagen–Cologne.

Russell, D. A. (1974). 'Letters to Lucilius', in Costa, C. D. N. (ed.), *Seneca*. London, 70–95.

Russell, D. A. (1983). *Greek declamation*. Cambridge.

Russell, D. A. (1988), 'The ass in the lion's skin: thoughts on the *Letters* of Phalaris'. *JHS* 108: 94–106

Russell, D. A. (1990). *An anthology of Latin prose*. Oxford.

Russell, D. A. (1992) ed., *Dio Chrysostom: Orations VII, XII, XXXVI*. Cambridge.

Russell, D. A. (1996) tr., *Libanius. Imaginary speeches*. London.

Russell, D. A. and Winterbottom, M. (1972) eds., *Ancient literary criticism*. Oxford.

Rusten, J. S. (1989) ed., *Thucydides. The Peloponnesian War, Book II*. Cambridge.

Rutherford, R. B. (1989). *The Meditations of Marcus Aurelius. A study*. Oxford.

Schneider, J. (1954). 'Brief'. *RAC* II. Stuttgart, 564–85.

Scourfield, J. H. D. (1993). *Consoling Heliodorus: a commentary on Jerome, Letter 60*. Oxford.

Scullard, H. H. (1981). *Festivals and ceremonies of the Roman republic*. London.

Scullard, H. H. (1982). *From the Gracchi to Nero*. 5th ed. London.

Sellar, W. C. and Yeatman, R. J. (1936). *Garden rubbish*. London.

Shackleton Bailey, D. R. (1965–70) ed., *Cicero's letters to Atticus*. Cambridge.

Shackleton Bailey, D. R. (1971). *Cicero*. London.

Shackleton Bailey, D. R. (1977) ed., *Cicero: Epistulae ad familiares*. Cambridge.

Shackleton Bailey, D. R. (1980a) ed., *Cicero: Epistulae ad Quintum fratrem et M. Brutum*. Cambridge.

Shackleton Bailey, D. R. (1980b) ed., *Cicero. Select letters*. Cambridge.

Sharples, R. W. (1996). *Stoics, Epicureans and Sceptics*. London.

Shelton, J.-A. (1990). 'Pliny the Younger and the ideal wife'. *CM* 41: 163–86.

Sherwin-White, A. N. (1966). *The letters of Pliny. A historical and social commentary*. Oxford.

Sherwin-White, A. N. (1969a) ed., *Fifty letters of Pliny*. 2nd ed. Oxford.

Sherwin-White, A. N. (1969b). 'Pliny. The man and his letters'. *GR* 16: 76–90.

Skeat, T. C. (1964). *Papyri from Panopolis in the Chester Beatty Library, Dublin.* Dublin.

Smalley, S. S. (1984). *1, 2, 3 John.* Waco, Texas.

Smith, M. F. (1992) ed., *Diogenes of Oenoanda. The Epicurean inscription.* Naples.

Smith, W. D. (1990) ed. and tr., *Hippocrates: Pseudepigraphic writings.* Leiden.

Städele, A. (1980). *Die Briefe des Pythagoras und der Pythagoreer* (Beiträge zur klassischen Philologie 115). Meisenheim am Glan.

Steen, H. A. (1938). 'Les clichés épistolaires dans les lettres sur papyrus grecques'. *Classica et Medievalia* 1: 119–76.

Steiner, D. T. (1994). *The tyrant's writ.* Princeton.

Stirewalt, M. L., Jr (1993). *Studies in ancient Greek epistolography.* Atlanta.

Stockton, D. (1969) ed., *Thirty-five letters of Cicero.* Oxford.

Stowers, S. K. (1986). *Letter writing in Greco-Roman antiquity.* Philadelphia, PA.

Summers, W. C. (1910) ed., *Select Letters of Seneca.* London.

Swain, S. C. R. (1996). *Hellenism and Empire.* Oxford.

Sykutris, J. (1931) 'Epistolographie'. *RE suppl.* 5: 185–220.

Sykutris, J. (1933). *Die Briefe des Sokrates und die Sokratiker.* Studien zur Geschichte und Kultur des Altertums 18. Paderborn.

Thomas, R. (1992). *Literacy and orality in ancient Greece.* Cambridge.

Thraede, K. (1970). *Grundzüge griechisch-römischer Brieftopik* (Zetemata 48). Munich.

Trapp, M. B. (1990). 'Plato's *Phaedrus* in second-century Greek literature', in Russell, D. A. (ed.), *Antonine Literature.* Oxford, 141–73.

Trapp, M. B. (1995). 'Sense of place in the *Orations* of Dio Chrysostom', in Innes, D. et al. (eds.) *Ethics and rhetoric.* Oxford, 163–75.

Trapp, M. B. (1997). *Maximus of Tyre. The philosophical orations.* Oxford.

Trapp, M. B. (forthcoming). 'Letters in/and biography', in Mossman, J. et al. (eds.), *Biographical limits.* London and Swansea.

Trapp, M. B. (forthcoming, b). 'Images of Alexandria in the writings of the Second Sophistic', in Hirst, A. (ed.), *Alexandria, real and imagined.* Aldershot.

Turner, E. G. (1971). *Greek manuscripts of the ancient world.* Oxford.

Turner, E. G. (1980). *Greek papyri. An introduction.* Rev. ed. Oxford.

Väänänen, V. (1981). *Introduction au latin vulgaire.* 3rd ed. Paris.

van den Hout, M. P. J. (1999). *A commentary on the letters of M. Cornelius Fronto.* Leiden.

van Groningen, B. A. (1963). *Short manual of Greek palaeography*. Leiden.

Veyne, P. (1990). *Bread and circuses: historical sociology and political pluralism.* Tr. B. Pearce. London.

Vinogradov, Y. G. (1971). 'Drevneisheye grecheskoye pismo s ostrova Berezan'. *Vestnik Drevnei Istorii* 118: 74–100.

Vogliano, A. and Castiglioni, L. (1948). 'Papiri bolognesi'. *Acme* 1: 199–216, 407–8.

Walbank, F. W. (1981). *The Hellenistic world*. London.

Watson, G. R. (1969). *The Roman soldier*. London.

Webster, G. (1985). *The Roman imperial army*. 3rd ed. London.

Weichert, V. (1910) ed., *Demetrii et Libanii quae feruntur 'Typoi epistolikoi' et 'Epistolimaioi characteres'*. Leipzig (Teubner).

Welles, C. B. (1934). *Royal correspondence in the Hellenistic period*. London.

Westermann, W. L. (1919). 'An Egyptian farmer', in *Classical Studies in honor of Charles Forster Smith* (University of Wisconsin Studies in Language and Literature 3). Madison, 171–90.

White, J. L. (1986). *Light from ancient letters*. Philadelphia, PA.

Whitehead, D. (1990) tr., *Aineias the tactician: how to survive under siege*. Oxford.

Wilhelm, A. (1904). 'Der älteste griechische Brief'. *JÖAI* 7: 94–105.

Willcock, M. M. (1995) ed., *Cicero, The letters of January to April 43 B.C.* Warminster.

Williams, G. (1968). *Tradition and originality in Roman poetry*. Oxford.

Williams, G. D. (1994). *Banished voices*. Cambridge.

Williams, W. (1990) ed., *Pliny. Correspondence with Trajan from Bithynia (Epistles X)*. Warminster.

Wilson, J. P. (1998). 'The "Illiterate trader"?' *BICS* 42: 29–53.

Witkowski, S. (1910) ed., *Epistulae privatae graecae*. 2nd ed. Leipzig (Teubner).

Woodhead, A. G. (1981). *The study of Greek inscriptions*. 2nd ed. Cambridge.

Wright, F. A. (1933) ed., *Select letters of Saint Jerome*. London and New York (Loeb).

Wright, W. C. (1923) ed., *The works of the Emperor Julian III*. London and New York (Loeb).

Youtie, H. C. and Winter, J. G. (1951). *Papyri and ostraka from Karanis*. Michigan Papyri VIII. Ann Arbor.

Zilliacus, H. (1949). *Untersuchungen zu den abstrakten Anredeformen und Höflichkeitstiteln im Greichischen*. Helsingfors.

INDEXES

1 TEXTS

2 GENERAL

In general, references are not
duplicated here from the Contents
page (v) and Index 1 above.

Cicerone
Plinio il Giovane